BEASTARS
Volume 3

D0595366

Story & Art by
Paru Itagaki

Plot Treatment...

Cherryton Academy is an integrated boarding school for a diverse group of carnivores and herbivores. Recently, Tem, an alpaca member of the Drama Club, was slain and devoured on campus. The murderer has yet to be identified, and everyone's nerves are on edge.

The Drama Club presents two performances of a show to welcome new students. In the lead role, Louis strives to represent the importance of peaceful coexistence between carnivores and herbivores, as well as increase his popularity and thereby further his campaign to become the school's next Beastar. But when Louis succumbs to a stress fracture in his leg, Bill takes his place for the second performance.

Bill has ambitions of his own. He would like to see carnivores become preeminent at Cherryton. However, he is so nervous before his performance that he dopes himself with rabbit blood. Furious at Bill for buying and consuming the blood of a rabbit, Legoshi attempts to punish him in front of the audience. The intense battle between the two large carnivores only ends when injured Louis limps onstage and puts a stop to it.

Now that the show has closed, Legoshi can't stop thinking about Haru. He longs to see her again...

BEASTARS

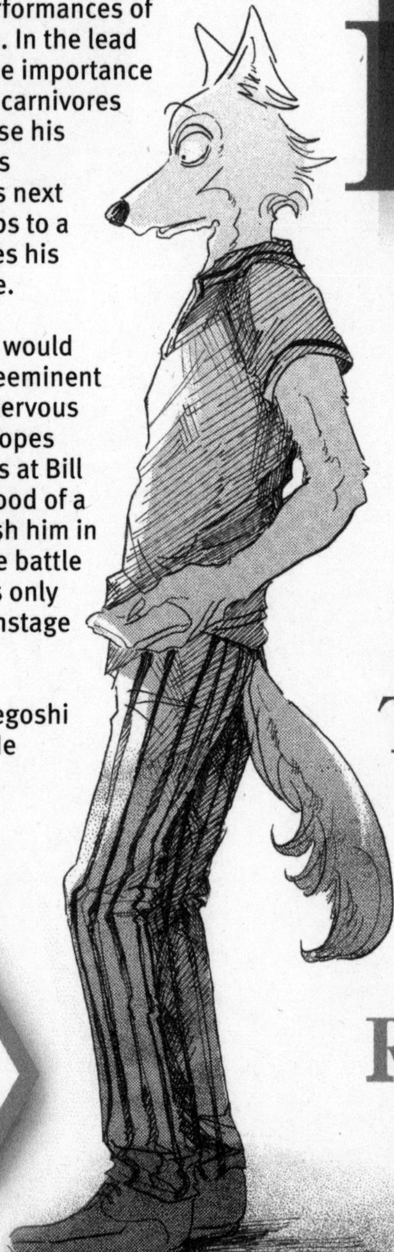

Legoshi

- ★Gray wolf ♂
- ★High school second-year
- ★Member of the Drama Club production crew
- ★Physically powerful yet emotionally sensitive
- ★Struggles with his identity as a carnivore

CAST OF CHARACTERS

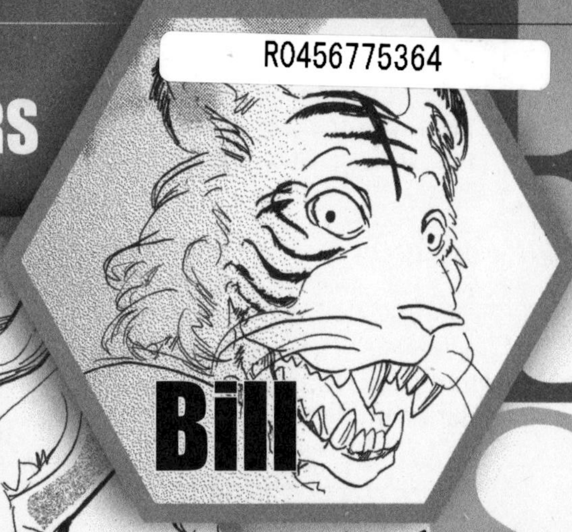
Bill

★Bengal tiger ♂
★High school second-year
★Member of the Drama Club actors pool

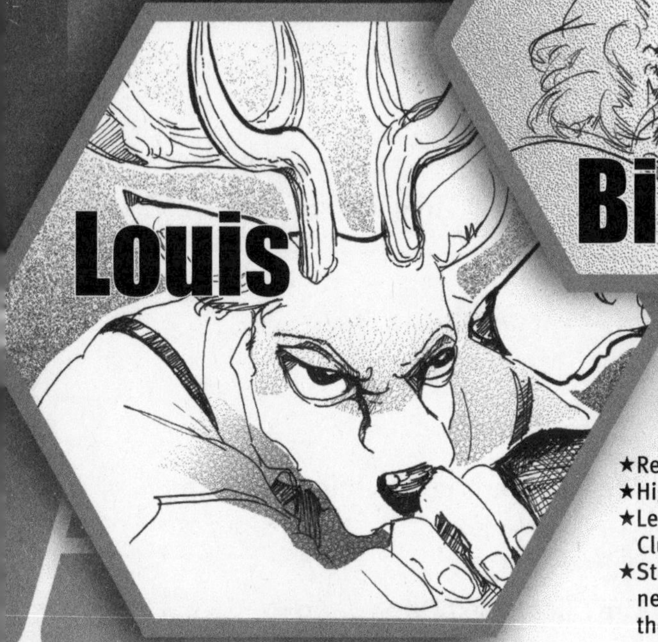
Louis

★Red deer ♂
★High school third-year
★Leader of the Drama Club actors pool
★Striving to become the next Beastar and rule the school

★Labrador retriever ♂
★High school second-year
★Legoshi's best friend

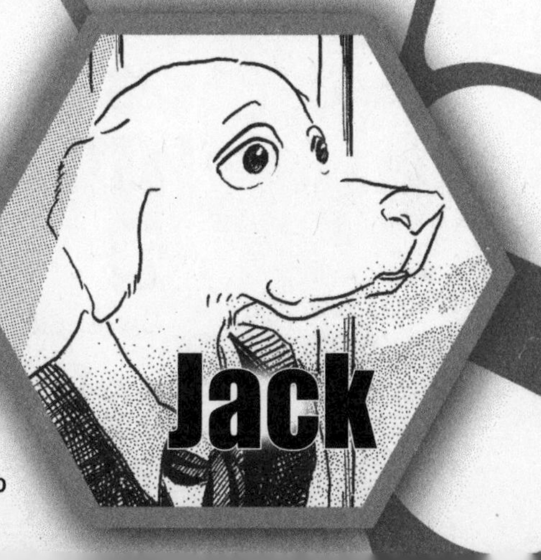
Jack

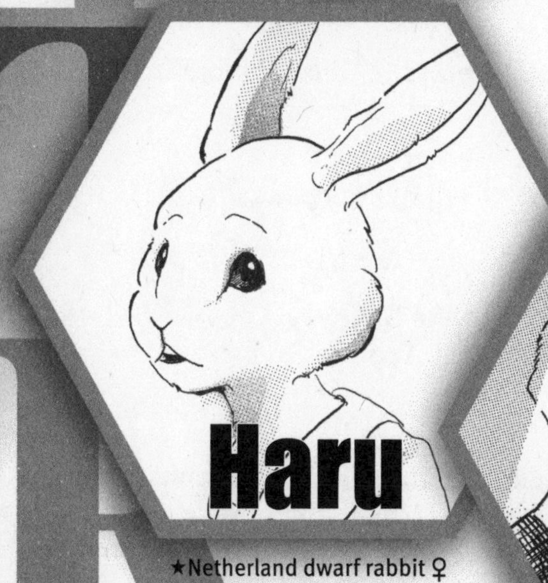
Haru

★Netherland dwarf rabbit ♀
★High school third-year
★Member of the Gardening Club

BEASTARS

Volume 3

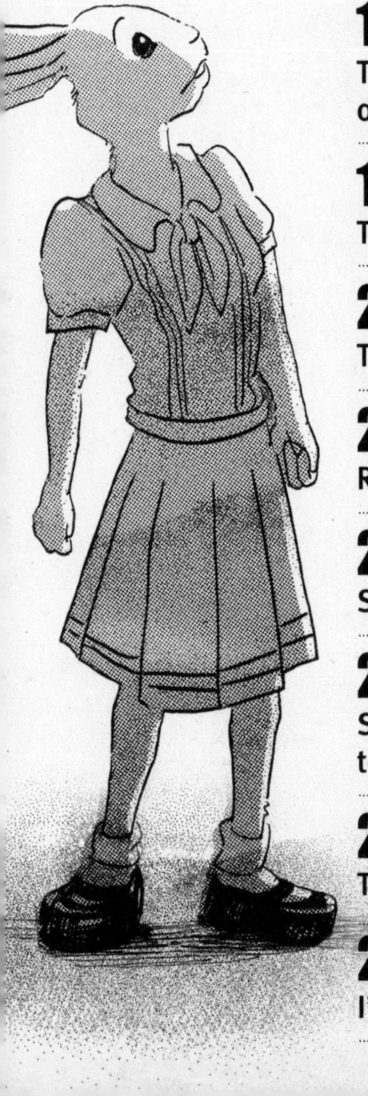

CONTENTS

Chapter 17: He Howls "No" like a Child

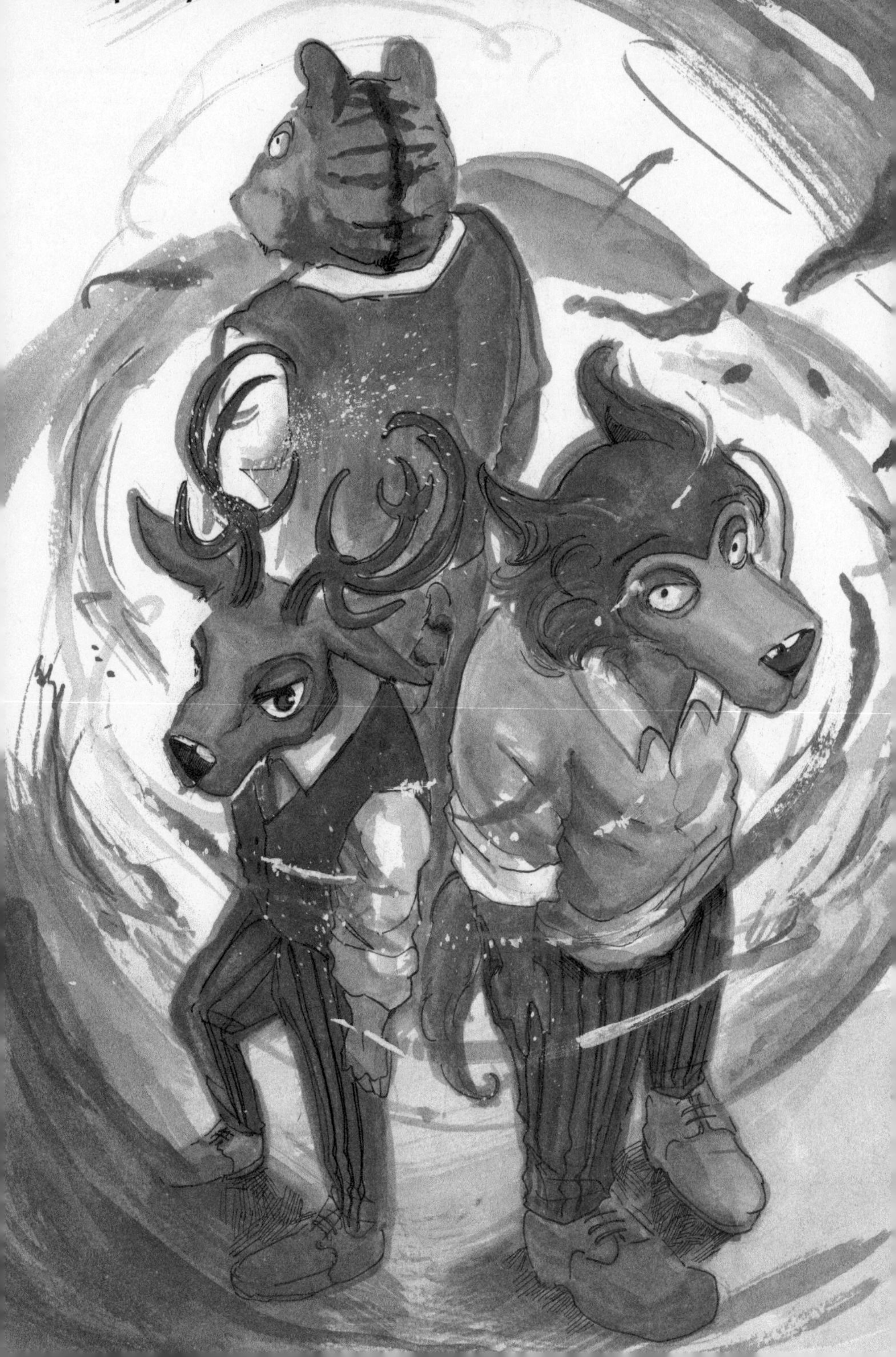

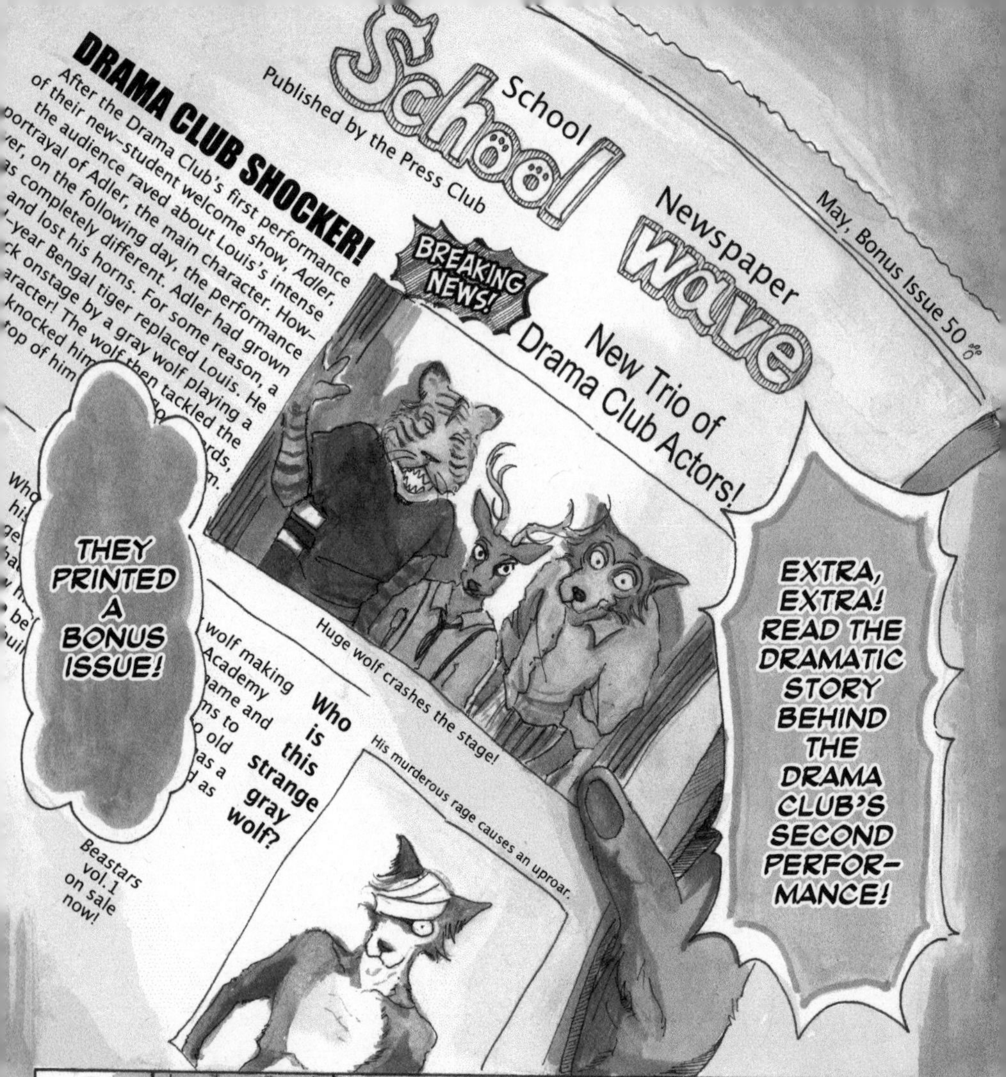
May, Bonus Issue 50
School
School wave
Newspaper
Published by the Press Club
BREAKING NEWS!
New Trio of Drama Club Actors!
DRAMA CLUB SHOCKER!
After the Drama Club's first performance
of their new-student welcome show, Adler,
the audience raved about Louis's intense
portrayal of Adler, the main character. How-
on the following day, the performance
completely different. Adler had grown
and lost his horns. For some reason, a
year Bengal tiger replaced Louis. He
onstage by a gray wolf playing a
Huge wolf crashes the stage!
His murderous rage causes an uproar.
Who is this strange gray wolf?
Beastars vol. 1 on sale now!
EXTRA, EXTRA! READ THE DRAMATIC STORY BEHIND THE DRAMA CLUB'S SECOND PERFORMANCE!
THEY PRINTED A BONUS ISSUE!

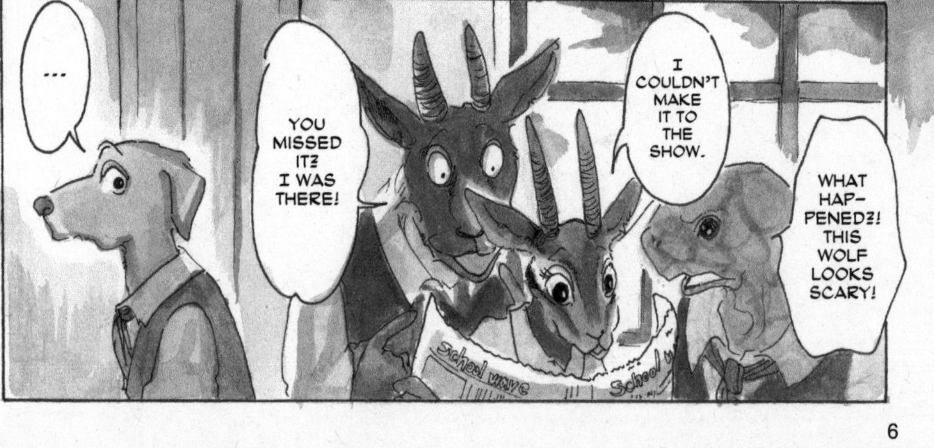
WHAT HAPPENED?! THIS WOLF LOOKS SCARY!
I COULDN'T MAKE IT TO THE SHOW.
YOU MISSED IT? I WAS THERE!
...
School wave

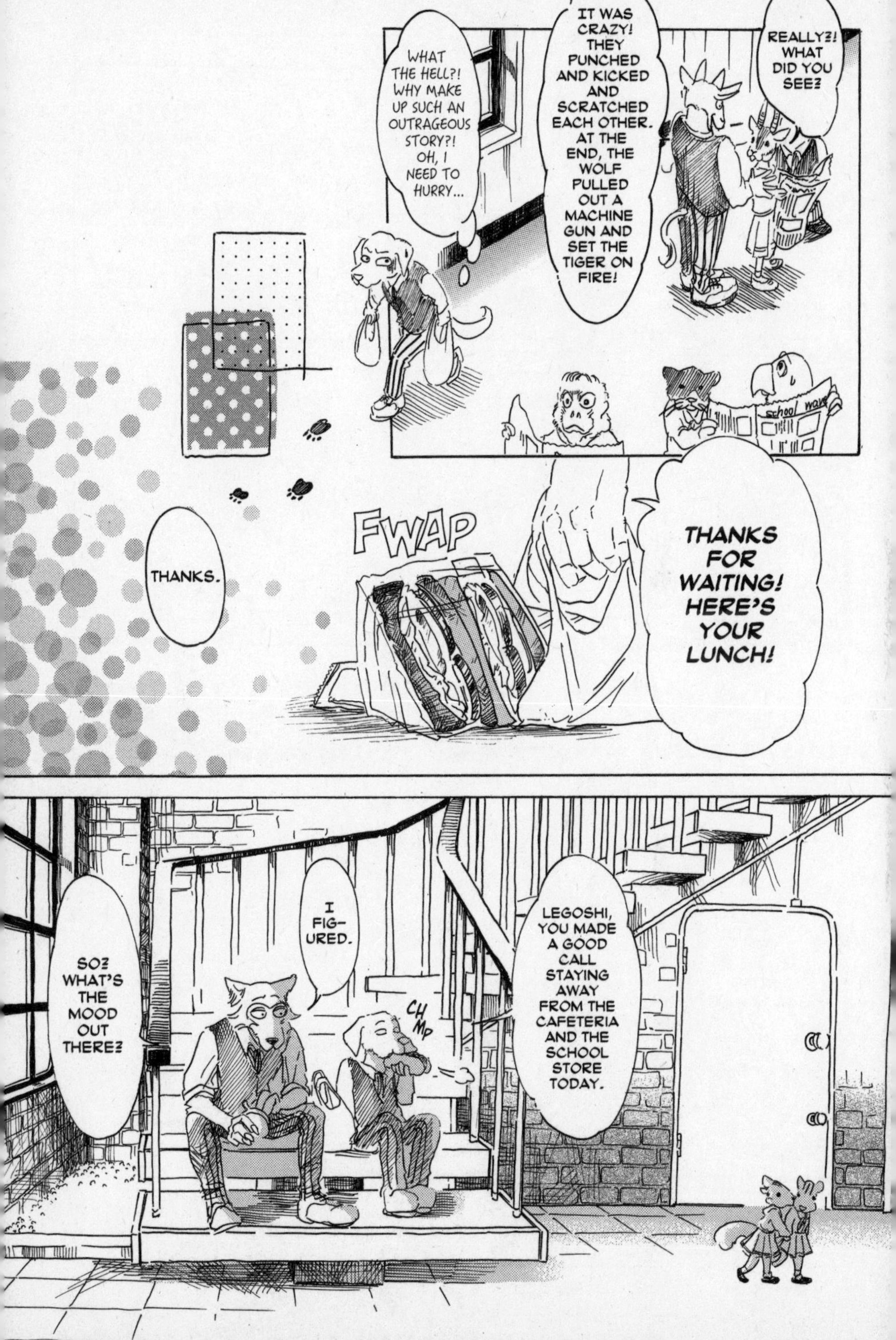
REALLY?! WHAT DID YOU SEE?
IT WAS CRAZY! THEY PUNCHED AND KICKED AND SCRATCHED EACH OTHER. AT THE END, THE WOLF PULLED OUT A MACHINE GUN AND SET THE TIGER ON FIRE!
WHAT THE HELL?! WHY MAKE UP SUCH AN OUTRAGEOUS STORY?! OH, I NEED TO HURRY...
SCHOOL WAVE
THANKS FOR WAITING! HERE'S YOUR LUNCH!
FWAP
THANKS.
LEGOSHI, YOU MADE A GOOD CALL STAYING AWAY FROM THE CAFETERIA AND THE SCHOOL STORE TODAY.
CHMP
I FIG-URED.
SO? WHAT'S THE MOOD OUT THERE?

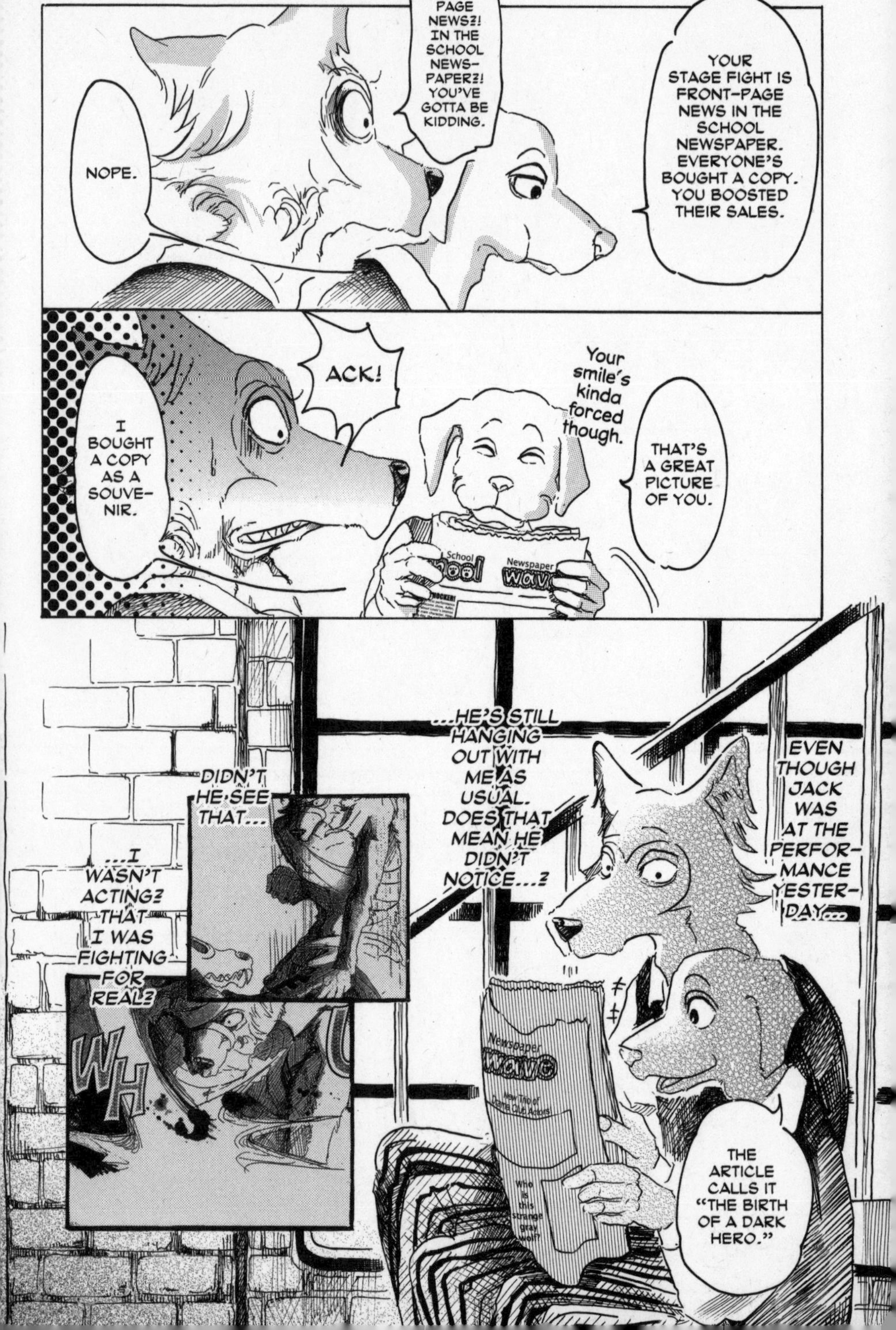
YOUR STAGE FIGHT IS FRONT-PAGE NEWS IN THE SCHOOL NEWSPAPER. EVERYONE'S BOUGHT A COPY. YOU BOOSTED THEIR SALES.
FRONT-PAGE NEWS?! IN THE SCHOOL NEWSPAPER?! YOU'VE GOTTA BE KIDDING.
NOPE.
THAT'S A GREAT PICTURE OF YOU.
Your smile's kinda forced though.
ACK!
I BOUGHT A COPY AS A SOUVENIR.
School
Newspaper
EVEN THOUGH JACK WAS AT THE PERFORMANCE YESTERDAY...
...HE'S STILL HANGING OUT WITH ME AS USUAL. DOES THAT MEAN HE DIDN'T NOTICE...?
DIDN'T HE SEE THAT...
...I WASN'T ACTING? THAT I WAS FIGHTING FOR REAL?
Newspaper
New Trio of Drama Club Actors
Who is this strange gray wolf?
THE ARTICLE CALLS IT "THE BIRTH OF A DARK HERO."

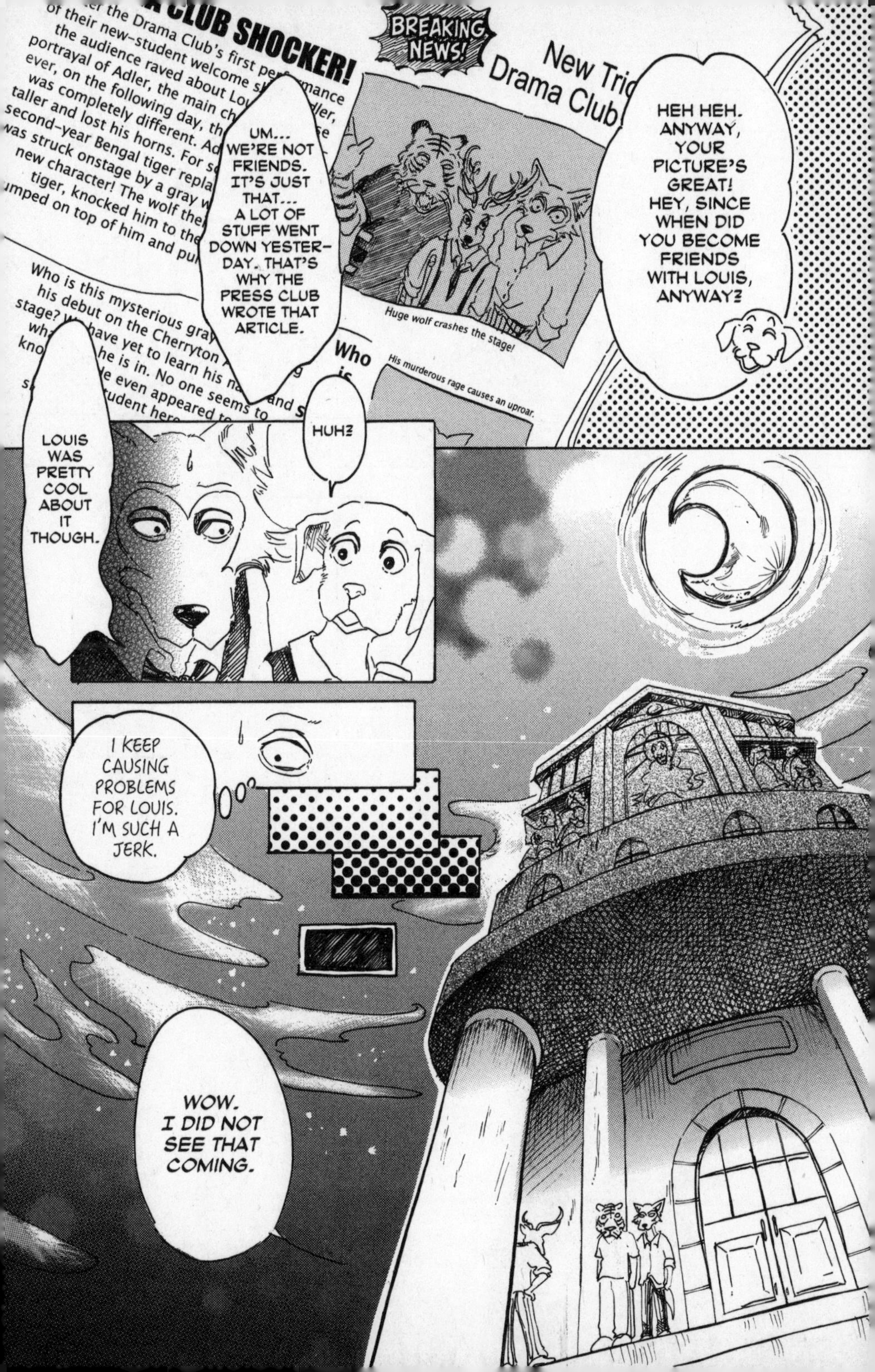
BREAKING NEWS!
CLUB SHOCKER!
New Tri
Drama Club
Huge wolf crashes the stage!
His murderous rage causes an uproar.
Who is this mysterious gray
HEH HEH. ANYWAY, YOUR PICTURE'S GREAT! HEY, SINCE WHEN DID YOU BECOME FRIENDS WITH LOUIS, ANYWAY?
UM... WE'RE NOT FRIENDS. IT'S JUST THAT... A LOT OF STUFF WENT DOWN YESTERDAY. THAT'S WHY THE PRESS CLUB WROTE THAT ARTICLE.
HUH?
LOUIS WAS PRETTY COOL ABOUT IT THOUGH.
I KEEP CAUSING PROBLEMS FOR LOUIS. I'M SUCH A JERK.
WOW. I DID NOT SEE THAT COMING.

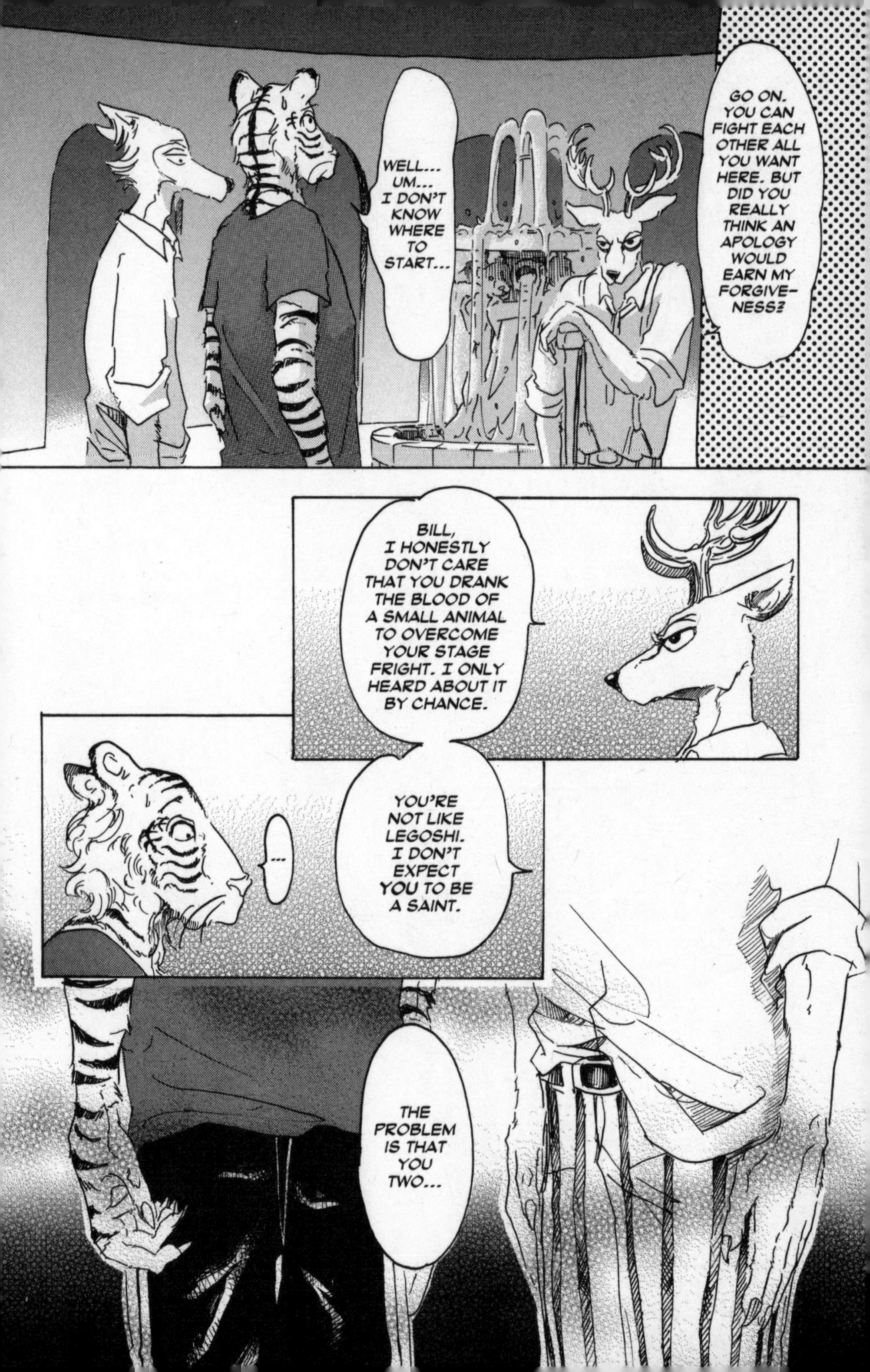
GO ON. YOU CAN FIGHT EACH OTHER ALL YOU WANT HERE. BUT DID YOU REALLY THINK AN APOLOGY WOULD EARN MY FORGIVE-NESS?
WELL... UM... I DON'T KNOW WHERE TO START...
BILL, I HONESTLY DON'T CARE THAT YOU DRANK THE BLOOD OF A SMALL ANIMAL TO OVERCOME YOUR STAGE FRIGHT. I ONLY HEARD ABOUT IT BY CHANCE.
YOU'RE NOT LIKE LEGOSHI. I DON'T EXPECT YOU TO BE A SAINT.
...
THE PROBLEM IS THAT YOU TWO...

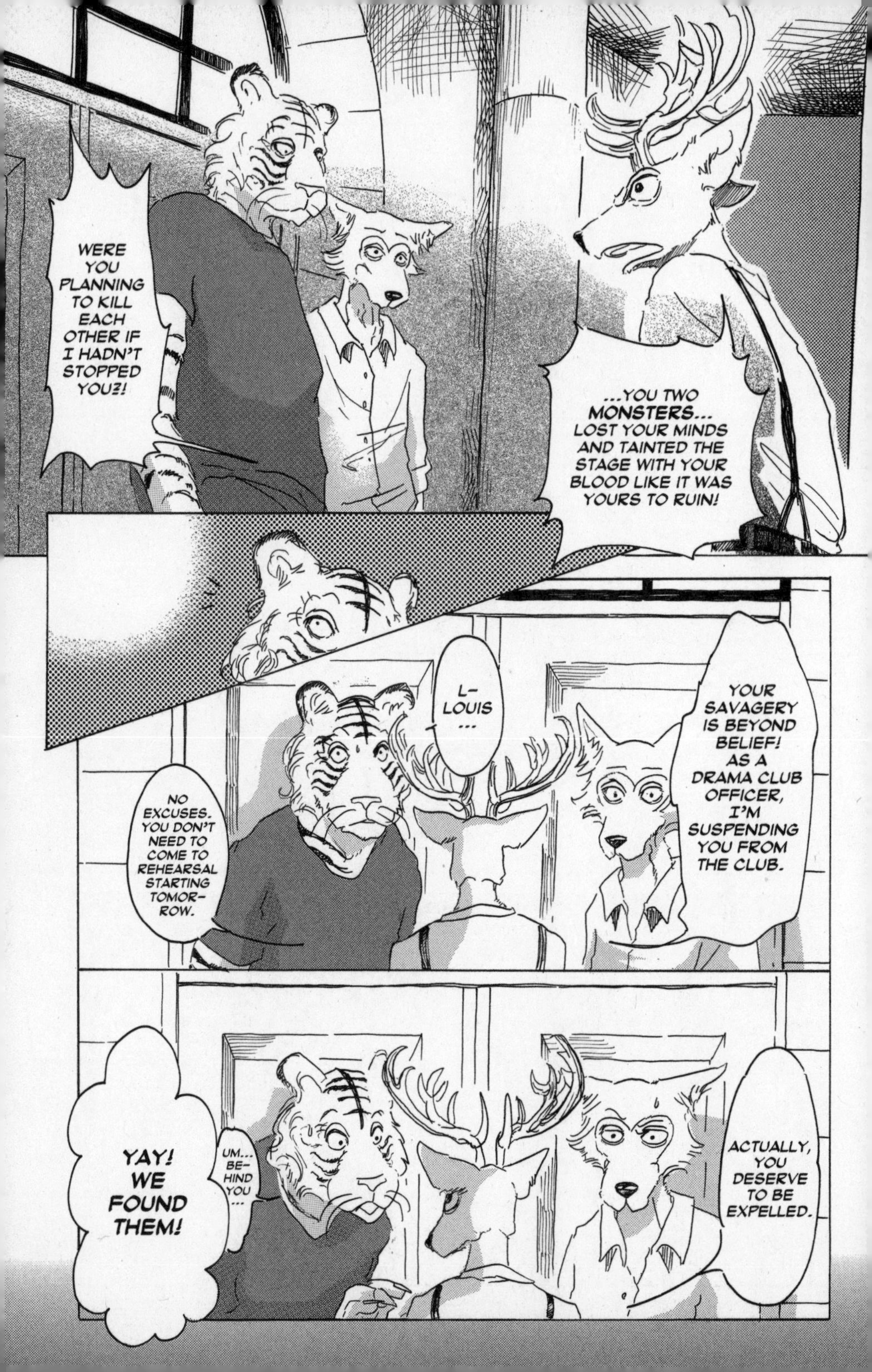
WERE YOU PLANNING TO KILL EACH OTHER IF I HADN'T STOPPED YOU?!
...YOU TWO **MONSTERS...** LOST YOUR MINDS AND TAINTED THE STAGE WITH YOUR BLOOD LIKE IT WAS YOURS TO RUIN!
YOUR SAVAGERY IS BEYOND BELIEF! AS A DRAMA CLUB OFFICER, I'M SUSPENDING YOU FROM THE CLUB.
L-LOUIS...
NO EXCUSES. YOU DON'T NEED TO COME TO REHEARSAL STARTING TOMOR-ROW.
ACTUALLY, YOU DESERVE TO BE EXPELLED.
UM... BE-HIND YOU...
YAY! WE FOUND THEM!

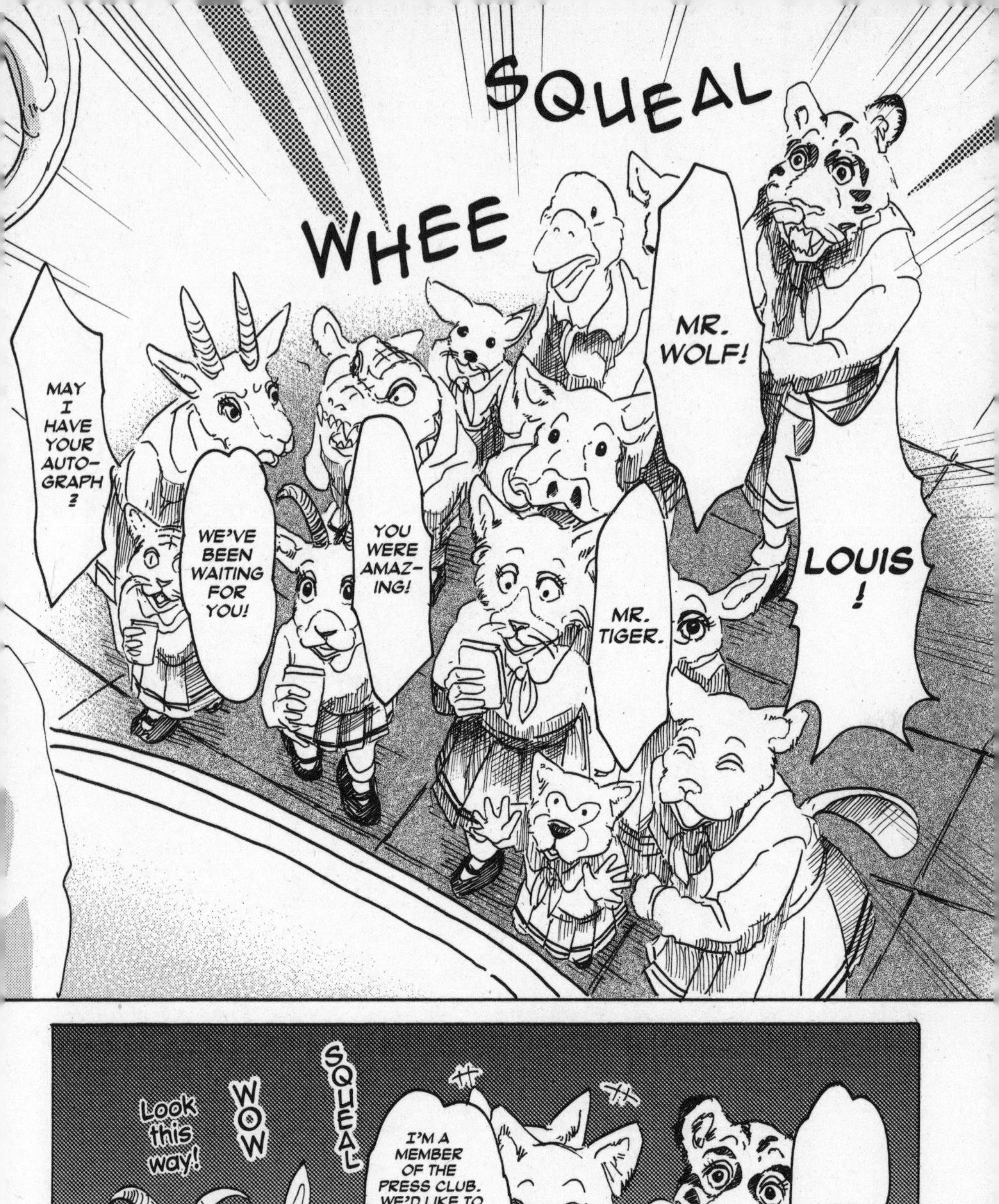
SQUEAL
WHEE
MR. WOLF!
LOUIS!
MR. TIGER.
YOU WERE AMAZ-ING!
WE'VE BEEN WAITING FOR YOU!
MAY I HAVE YOUR AUTO-GRAPH?

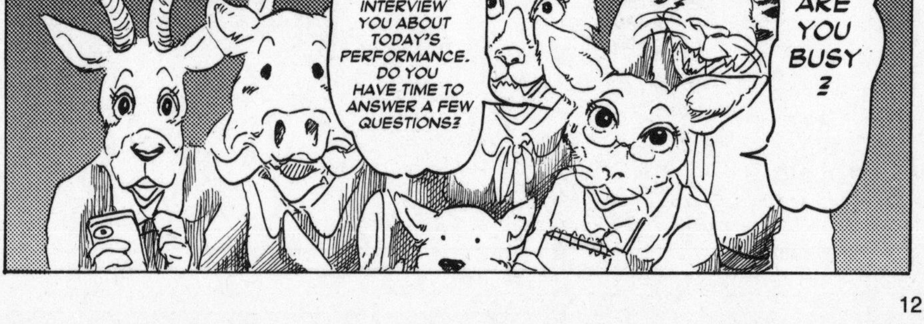
ARE YOU BUSY?
I'M A MEMBER OF THE PRESS CLUB. WE'D LIKE TO INTERVIEW YOU ABOUT TODAY'S PERFORMANCE. DO YOU HAVE TIME TO ANSWER A FEW QUESTIONS?
SQUEAL
WOW
Look this way!

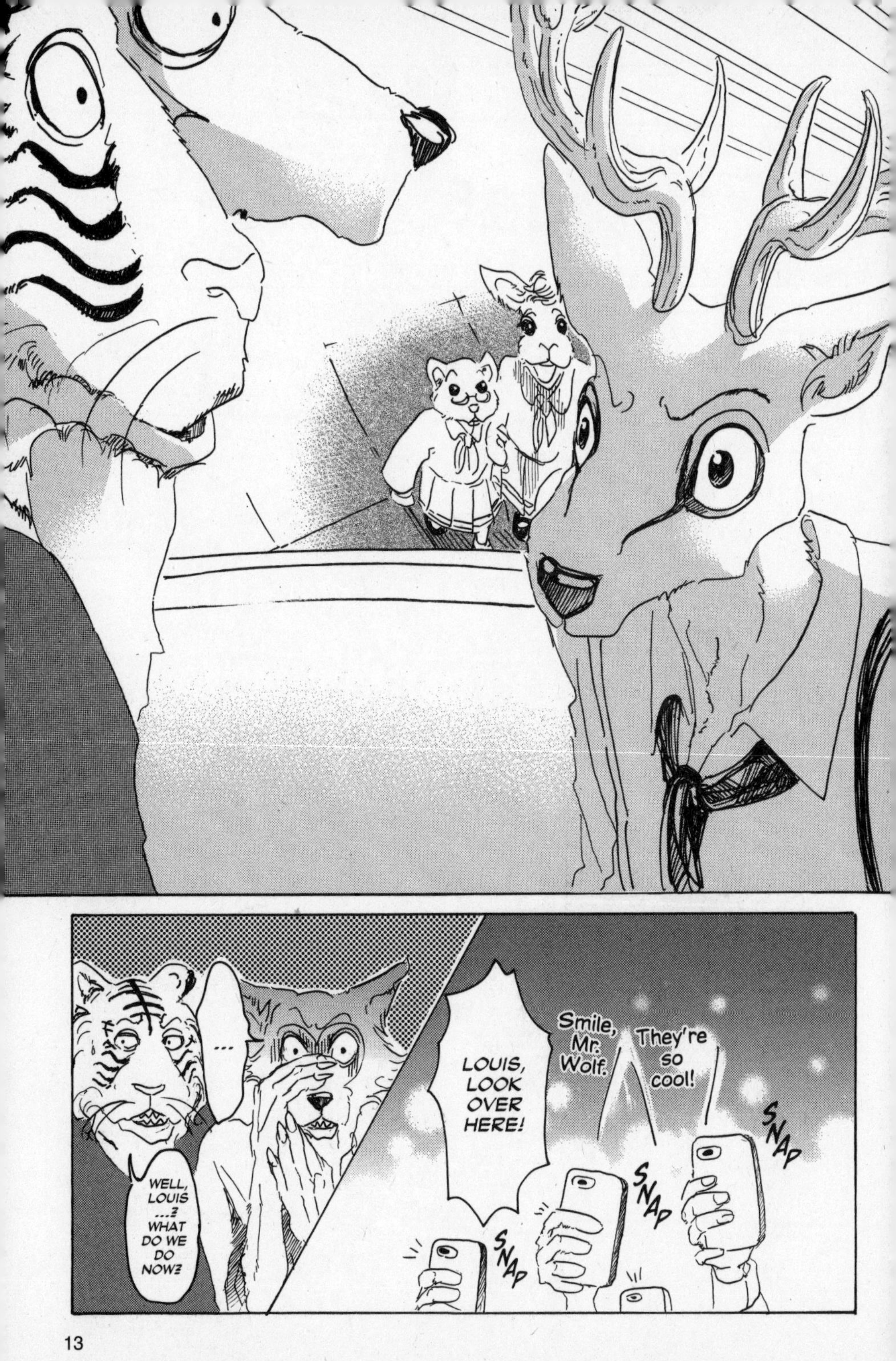
They're so cool!
Smile, Mr. Wolf.
LOUIS, LOOK OVER HERE!
SNAP
SNAP
SNAP
...
WELL, LOUIS ...? WHAT DO WE DO NOW?

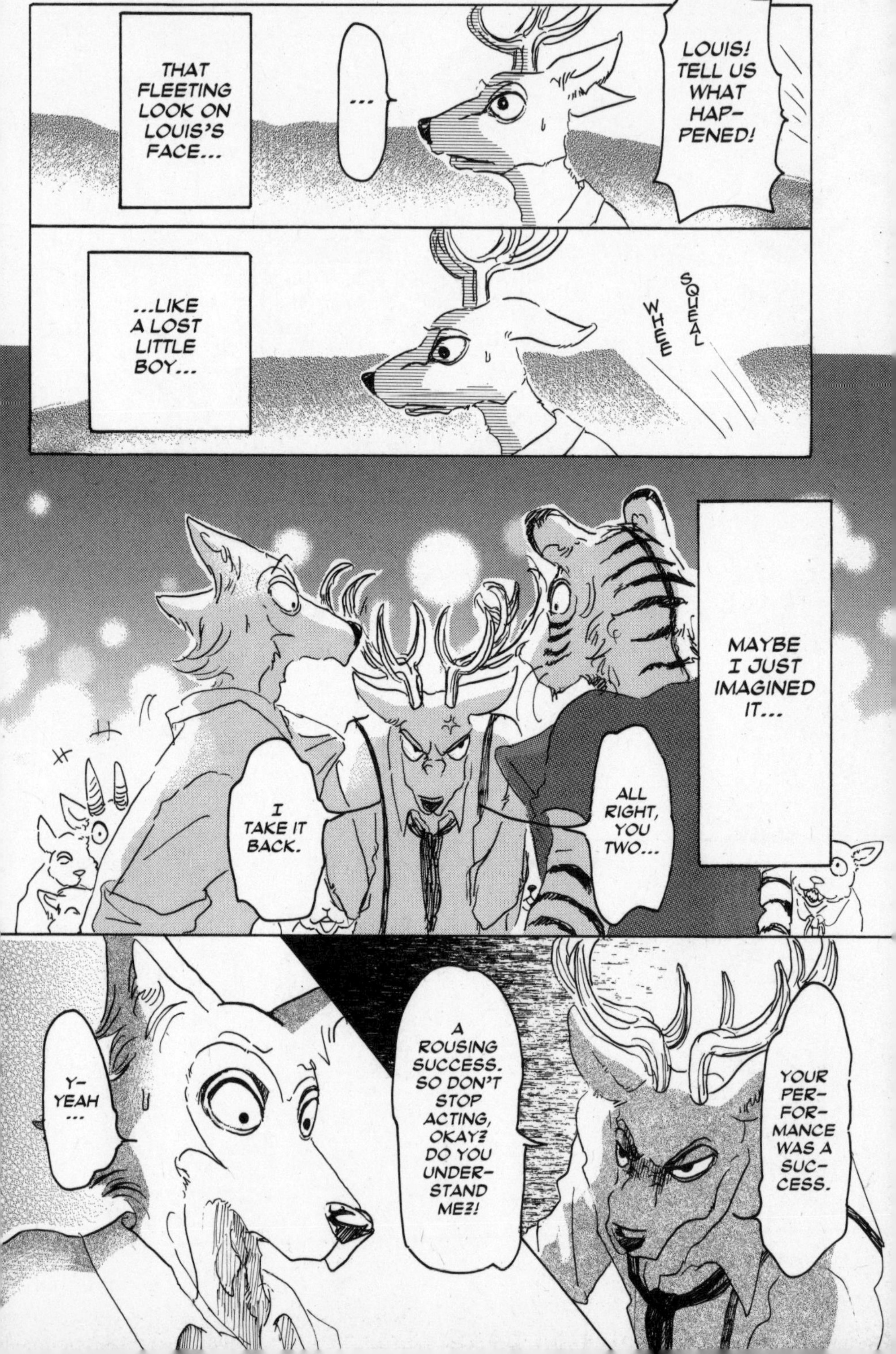
LOUIS! TELL US WHAT HAPPENED!
...
THAT FLEETING LOOK ON LOUIS'S FACE...
SQUEAL
WHEE
...LIKE A LOST LITTLE BOY...
MAYBE I JUST IMAGINED IT...
ALL RIGHT, YOU TWO...
I TAKE IT BACK.
YOUR PERFORMANCE WAS A SUCCESS.
A ROUSING SUCCESS. SO DON'T STOP ACTING, OKAY?! DO YOU UNDERSTAND ME?!
Y-YEAH...

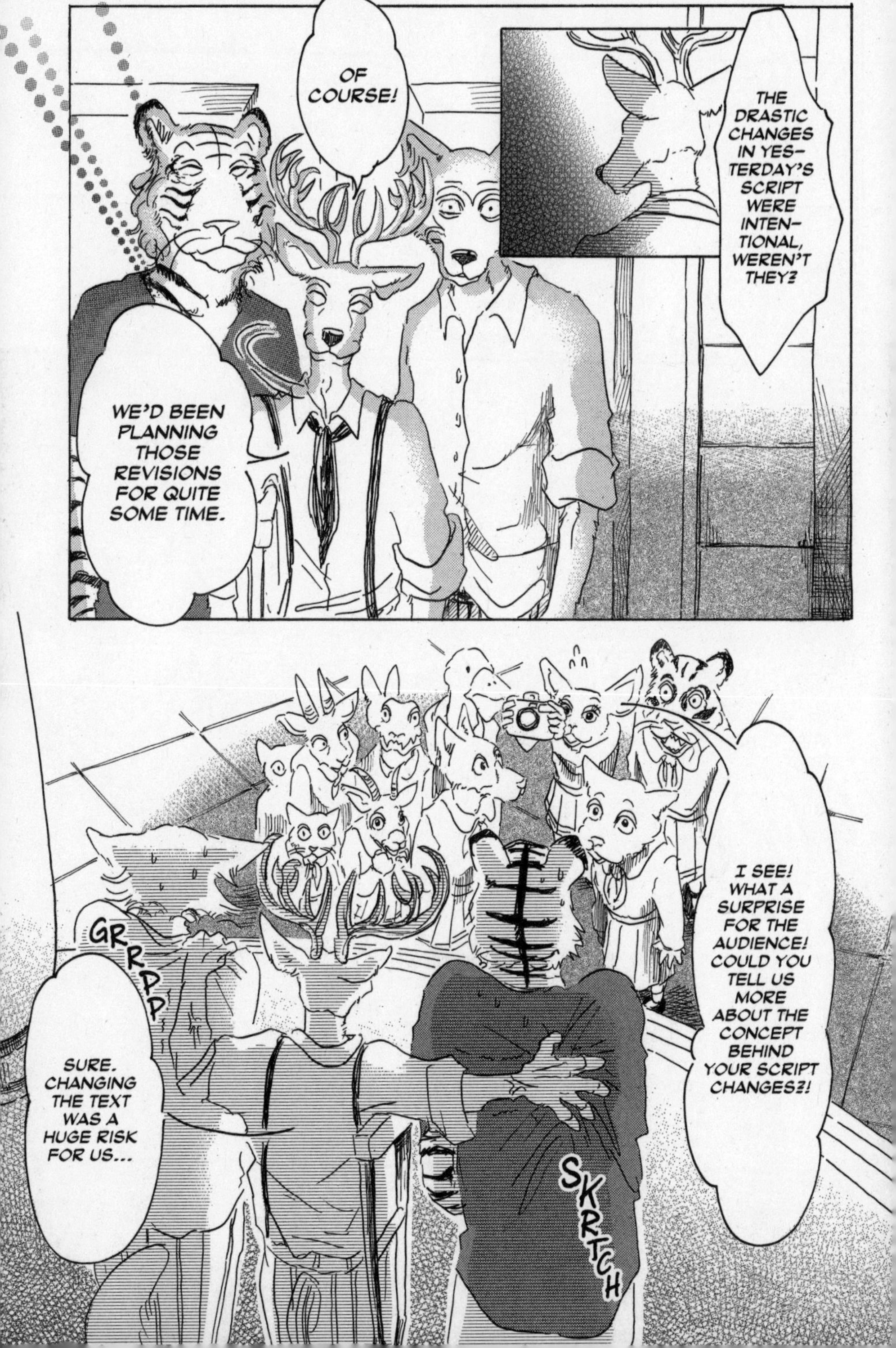
THE DRASTIC CHANGES IN YESTERDAY'S SCRIPT WERE INTENTIONAL, WEREN'T THEY?
OF COURSE!
WE'D BEEN PLANNING THOSE REVISIONS FOR QUITE SOME TIME.
I SEE! WHAT A SURPRISE FOR THE AUDIENCE! COULD YOU TELL US MORE ABOUT THE CONCEPT BEHIND YOUR SCRIPT CHANGES?!
GRRPP
SURE. CHANGING THE TEXT WAS A HUGE RISK FOR US...
SKRTCH

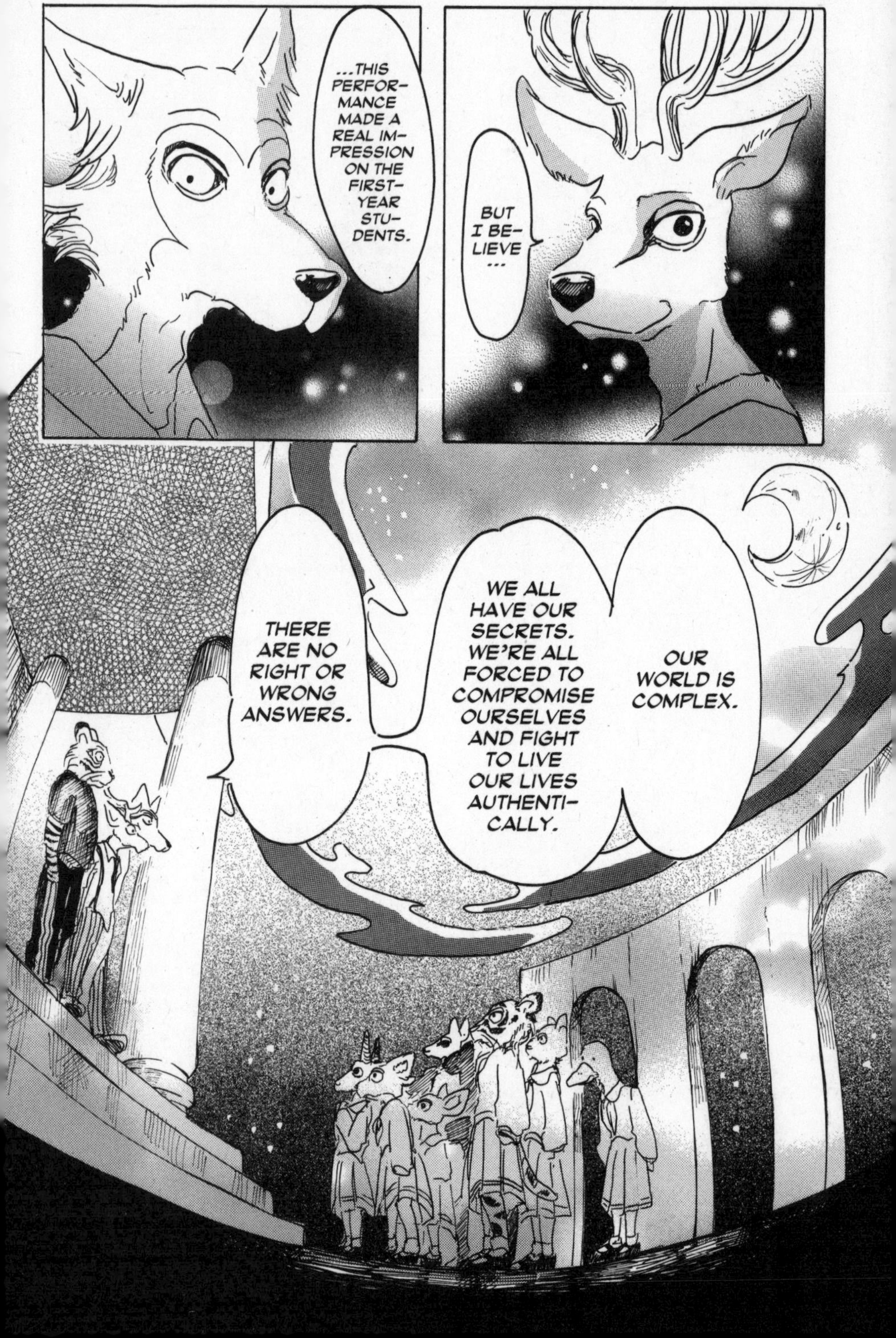
BUT I BE-LIEVE...
...THIS PERFOR-MANCE MADE A REAL IM-PRESSION ON THE FIRST-YEAR STU-DENTS.
OUR WORLD IS COMPLEX.
WE ALL HAVE OUR SECRETS. WE'RE ALL FORCED TO COMPROMISE OURSELVES AND FIGHT TO LIVE OUR LIVES AUTHENTI-CALLY.
THERE ARE NO RIGHT OR WRONG ANSWERS.

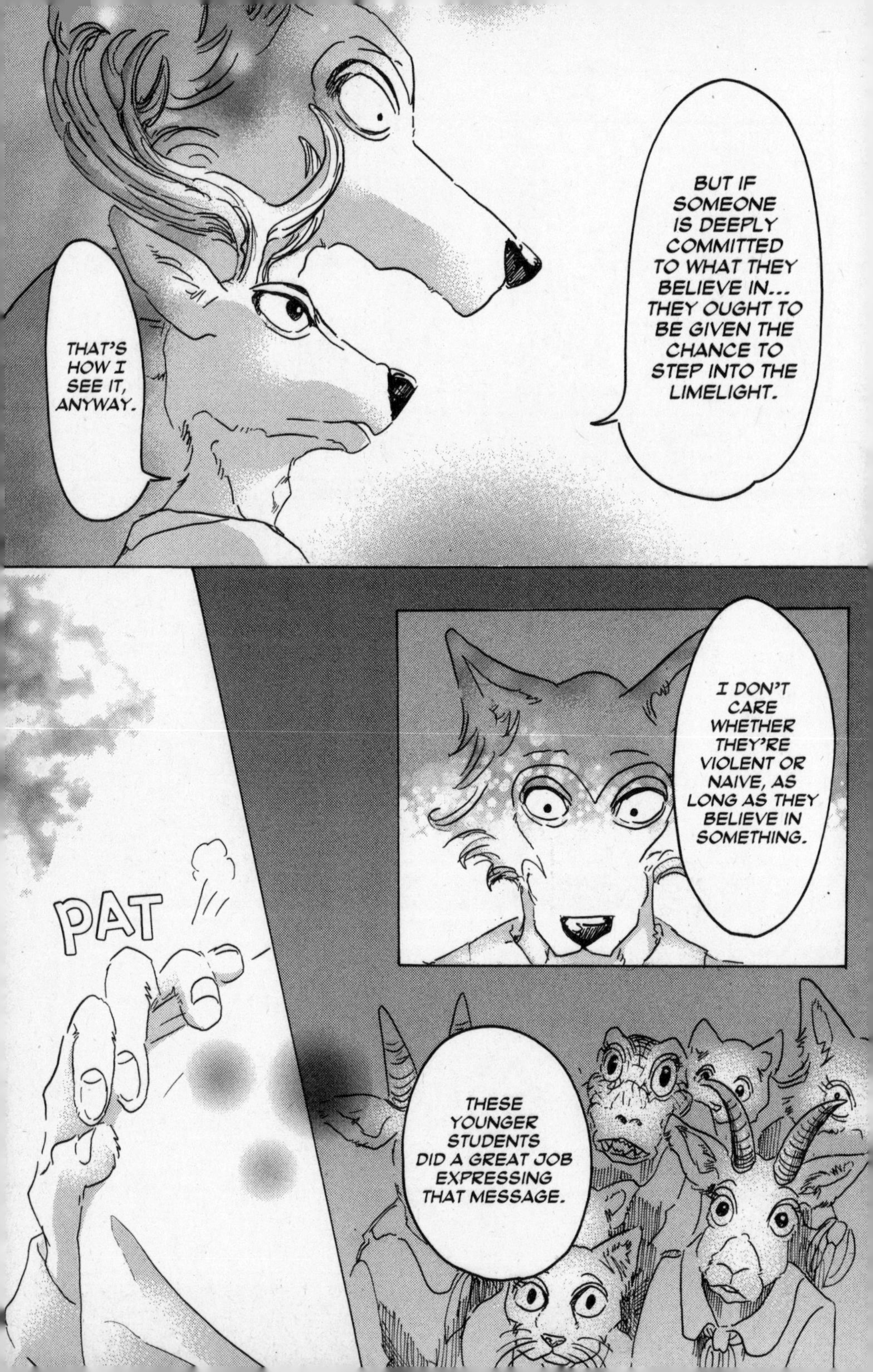
BUT IF SOMEONE IS DEEPLY COMMITTED TO WHAT THEY BELIEVE IN... THEY OUGHT TO BE GIVEN THE CHANCE TO STEP INTO THE LIMELIGHT.
THAT'S HOW I SEE IT, ANYWAY.
I DON'T CARE WHETHER THEY'RE VIOLENT OR NAIVE, AS LONG AS THEY BELIEVE IN SOMETHING.
THESE YOUNGER STUDENTS DID A GREAT JOB EXPRESSING THAT MESSAGE.
PAT

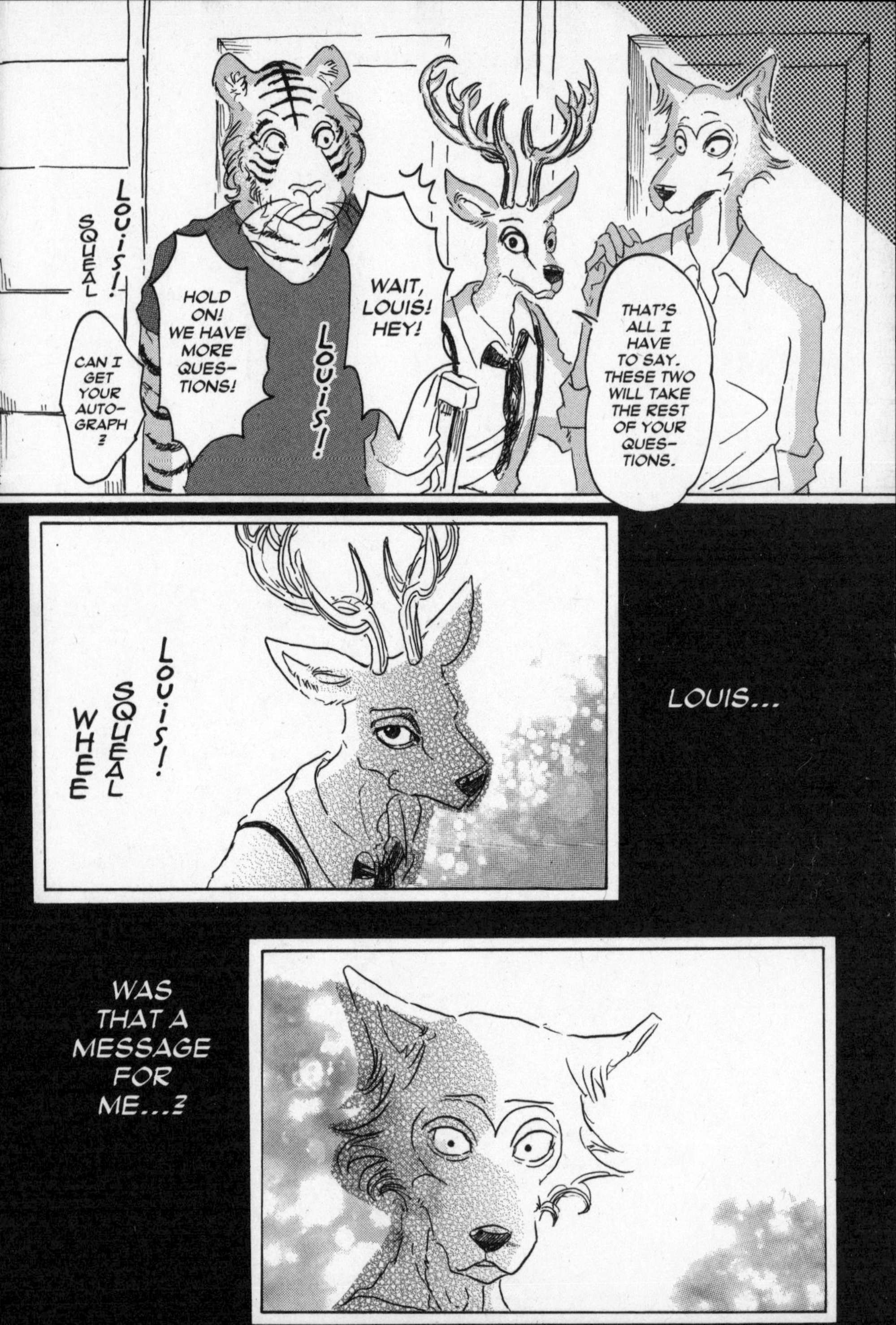
THAT'S ALL I HAVE TO SAY. THESE TWO WILL TAKE THE REST OF YOUR QUESTIONS.
WAIT, LOUIS! HEY!
LOUIS!
HOLD ON! WE HAVE MORE QUES- TIONS!
LOUIS!
SQUEAL
CAN I GET YOUR AUTO- GRAPH?
LOUIS...
LOUIS!
SQUEAL
WHEE
WAS THAT A MESSAGE FOR ME...?

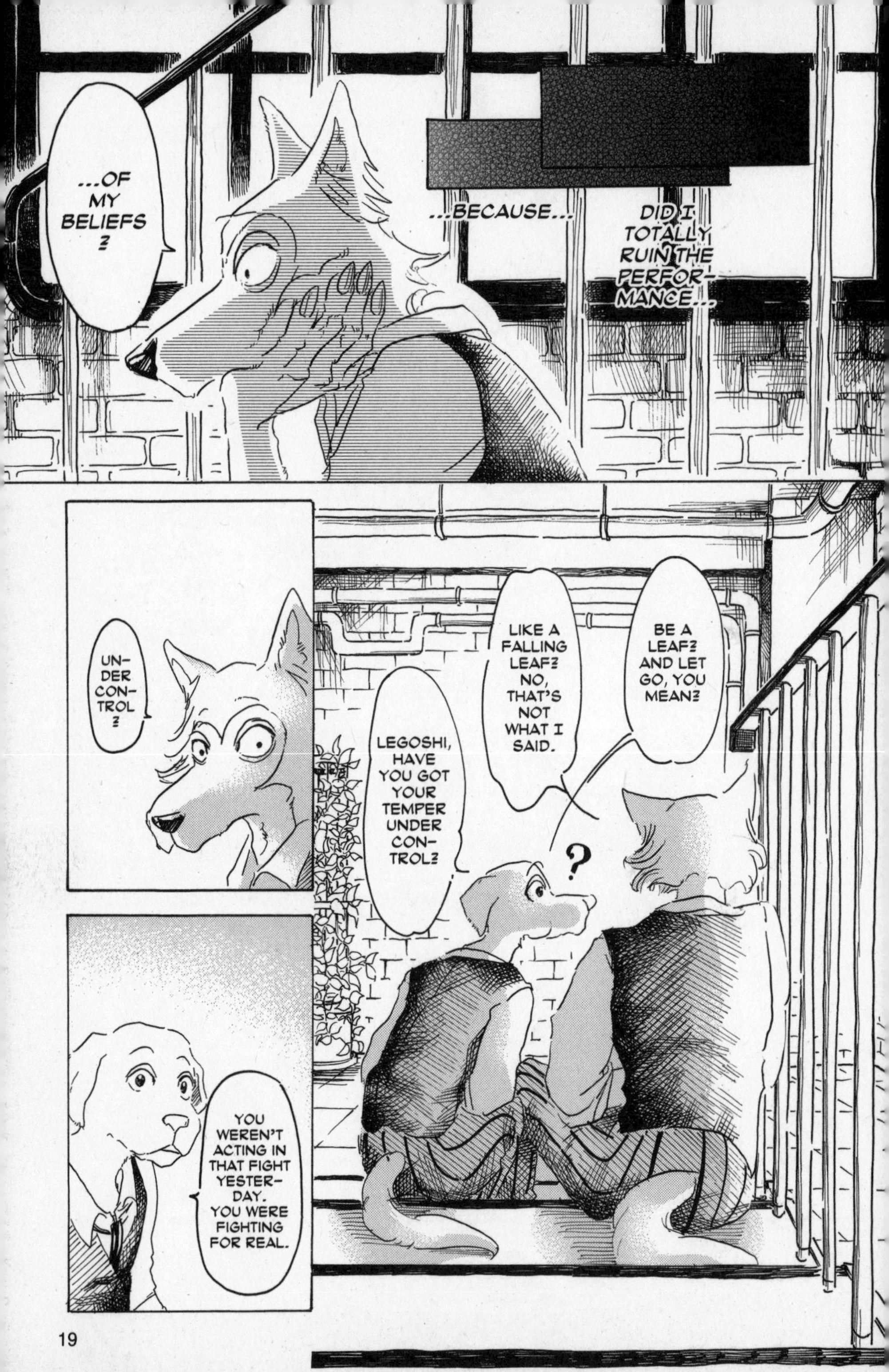
DID I TOTALLY RUIN THE PERFORMANCE...
...BECAUSE...
...OF MY BELIEFS?
BE A LEAF? AND LET GO, YOU MEAN?
LIKE A FALLING LEAF? NO, THAT'S NOT WHAT I SAID.
LEGOSHI, HAVE YOU GOT YOUR TEMPER UNDER CONTROL?
?
UNDER CONTROL?
YOU WEREN'T ACTING IN THAT FIGHT YESTERDAY. YOU WERE FIGHTING FOR REAL.

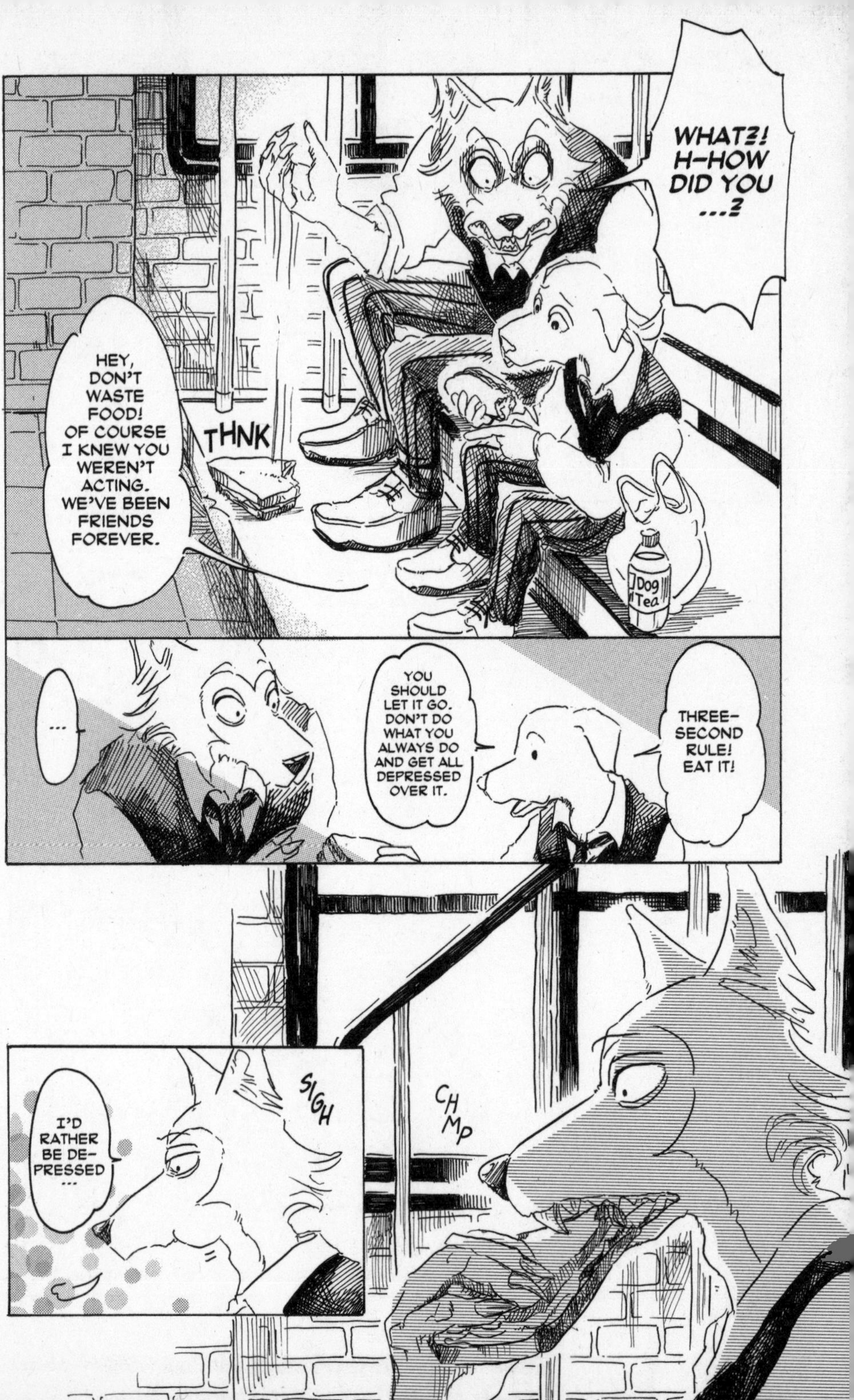
WHAT?! H-HOW DID YOU ...?
THNK
HEY, DON'T WASTE FOOD! OF COURSE I KNEW YOU WEREN'T ACTING. WE'VE BEEN FRIENDS FOREVER.
Dog Tea
THREE-SECOND RULE! EAT IT!
YOU SHOULD LET IT GO. DON'T DO WHAT YOU ALWAYS DO AND GET ALL DEPRESSED OVER IT.
...
CHMP
SIGH
I'D RATHER BE DE-PRESSED ...

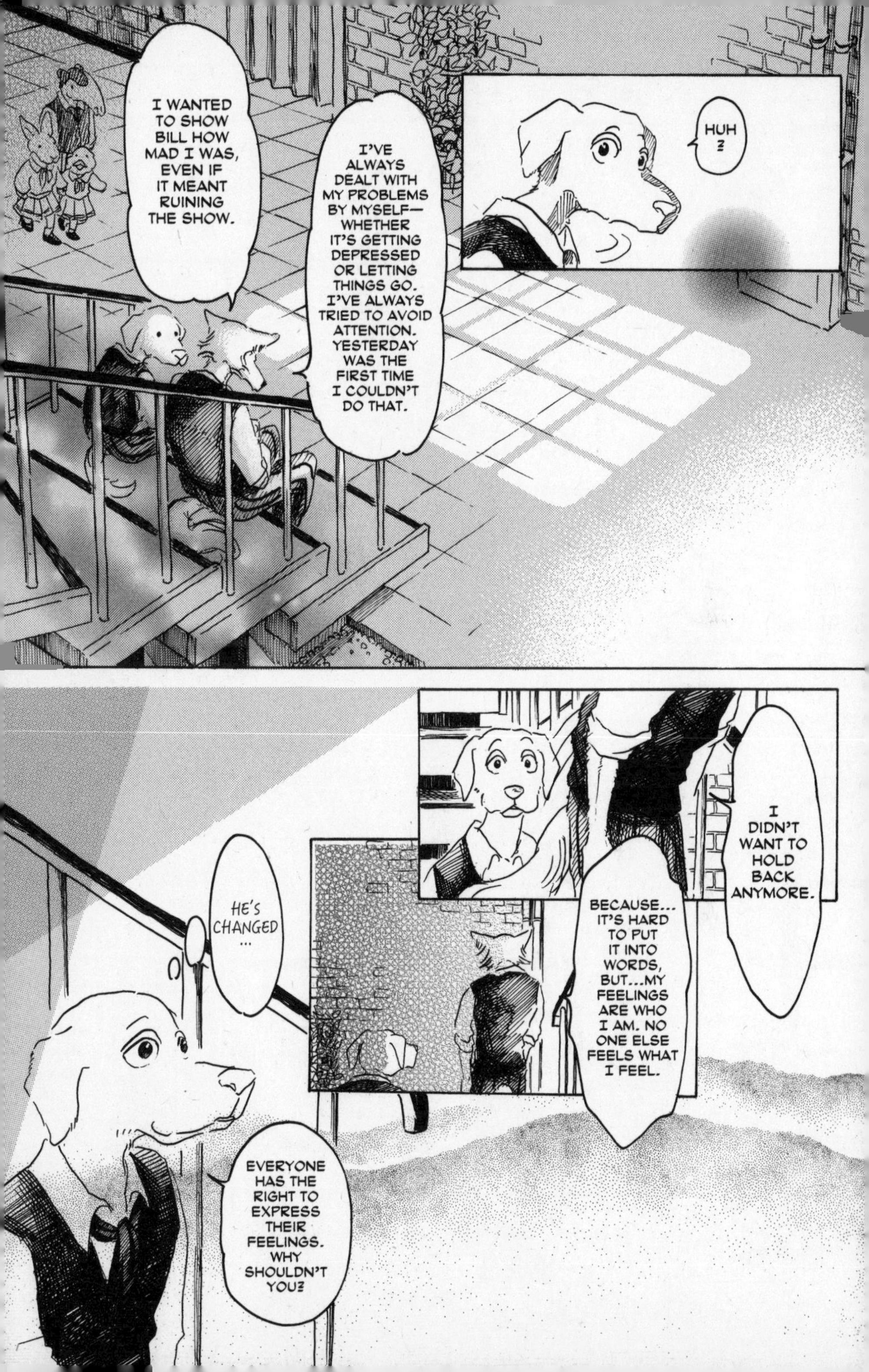
HUH?
I'VE ALWAYS DEALT WITH MY PROBLEMS BY MYSELF— WHETHER IT'S GETTING DEPRESSED OR LETTING THINGS GO. I'VE ALWAYS TRIED TO AVOID ATTENTION. YESTERDAY WAS THE FIRST TIME I COULDN'T DO THAT.
I WANTED TO SHOW BILL HOW MAD I WAS, EVEN IF IT MEANT RUINING THE SHOW.
I DIDN'T WANT TO HOLD BACK ANYMORE.
BECAUSE... IT'S HARD TO PUT IT INTO WORDS, BUT...MY FEELINGS ARE WHO I AM. NO ONE ELSE FEELS WHAT I FEEL.
HE'S CHANGED...
EVERYONE HAS THE RIGHT TO EXPRESS THEIR FEELINGS. WHY SHOULDN'T YOU?

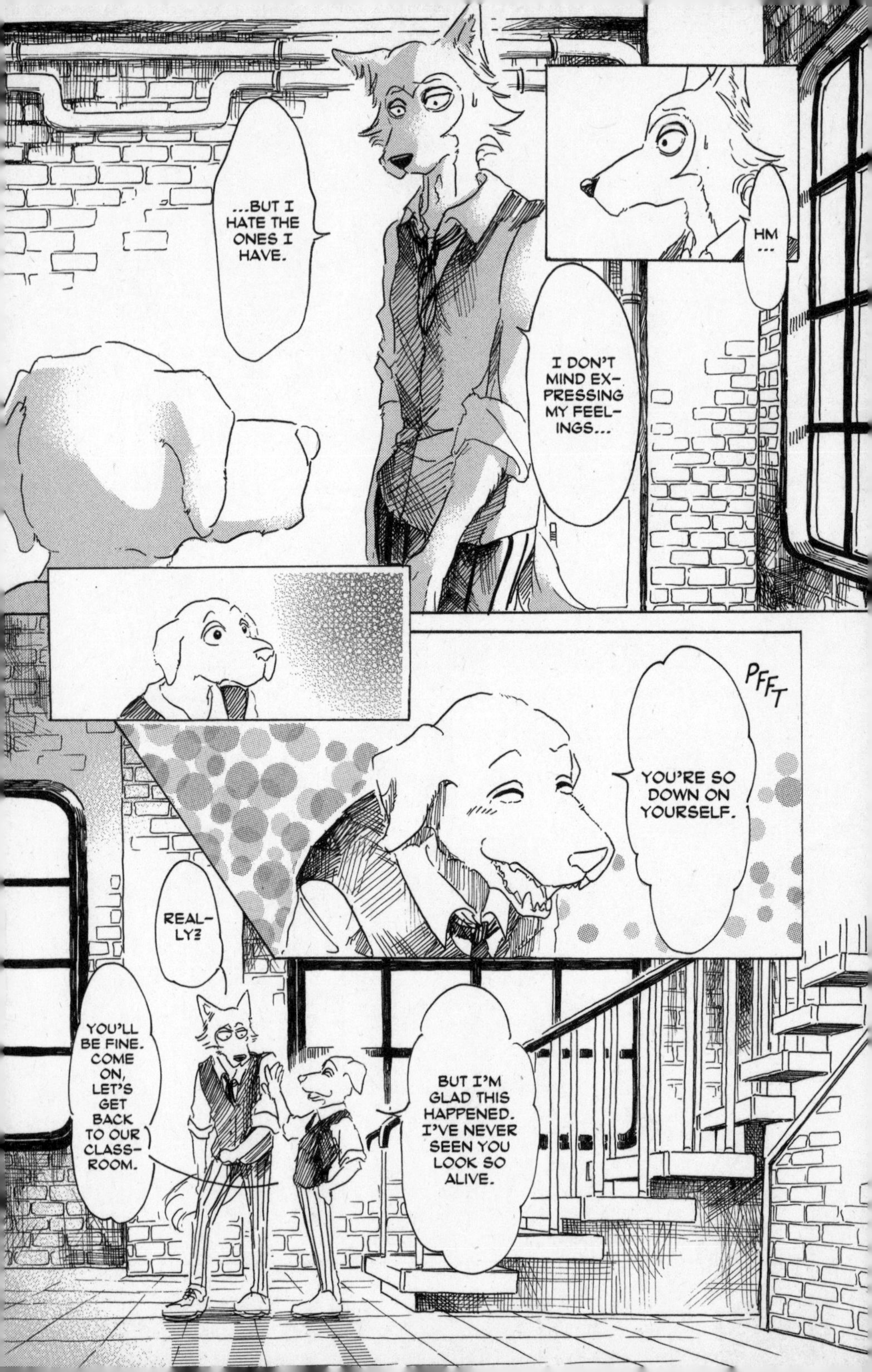
HM...
I DON'T MIND EXPRESSING MY FEELINGS...
...BUT I HATE THE ONES I HAVE.
PFFT
YOU'RE SO DOWN ON YOURSELF.
REALLY?
BUT I'M GLAD THIS HAPPENED. I'VE NEVER SEEN YOU LOOK SO ALIVE.
YOU'LL BE FINE. COME ON, LET'S GET BACK TO OUR CLASSROOM.

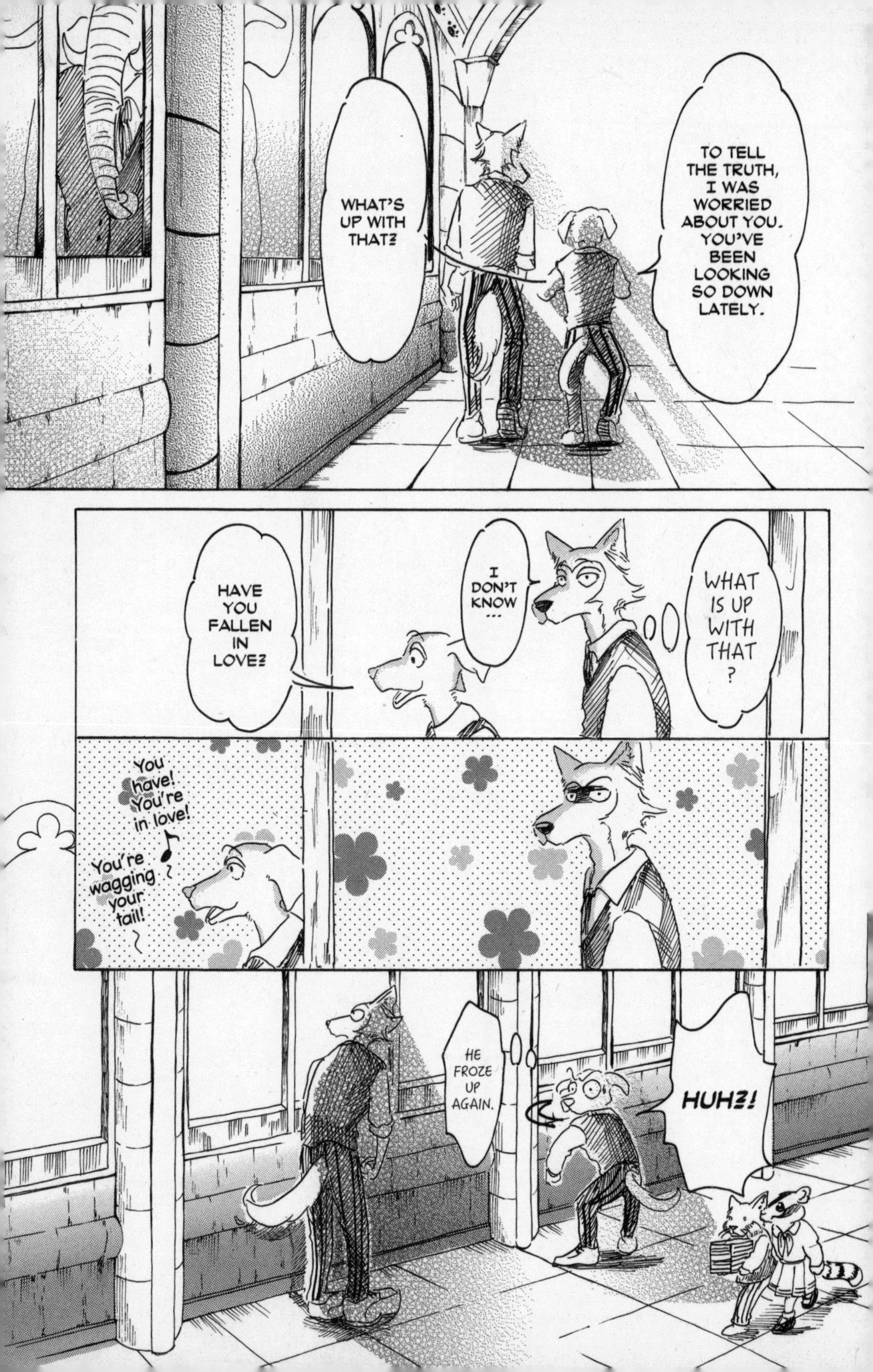
TO TELL THE TRUTH, I WAS WORRIED ABOUT YOU. YOU'VE BEEN LOOKING SO DOWN LATELY.
WHAT'S UP WITH THAT?
WHAT IS UP WITH THAT?
I DON'T KNOW...
HAVE YOU FALLEN IN LOVE?
You have! You're in love!
You're wagging your tail!
HUH?!
HE FROZE UP AGAIN.

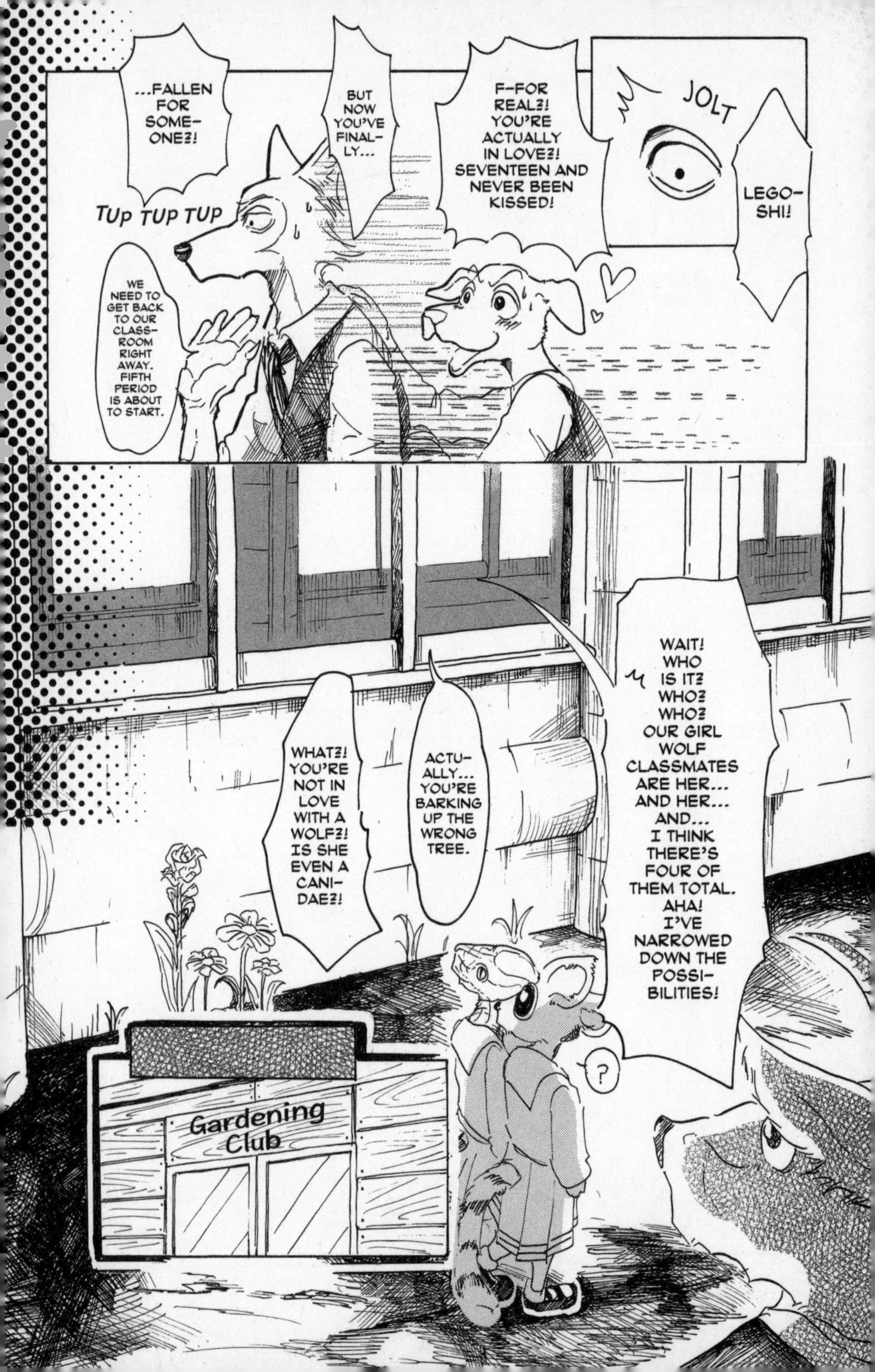
JOLT
LEGO-SHI!
F-FOR REAL?! YOU'RE ACTUALLY IN LOVE?! SEVENTEEN AND NEVER BEEN KISSED!
BUT NOW YOU'VE FINAL-LY...
...FALLEN FOR SOME-ONE?!
TUP TUP TUP
WE NEED TO GET BACK TO OUR CLASS-ROOM RIGHT AWAY. FIFTH PERIOD IS ABOUT TO START.
WAIT! WHO IS IT? WHO? WHO? OUR GIRL WOLF CLASSMATES ARE HER... AND HER... AND... I THINK THERE'S FOUR OF THEM TOTAL. AHA! I'VE NARROWED DOWN THE POSSI-BILITIES!
ACTU-ALLY... YOU'RE BARKING UP THE WRONG TREE.
WHAT?! YOU'RE NOT IN LOVE WITH A WOLF?! IS SHE EVEN A CANI-DAE?!
?
Gardening Club

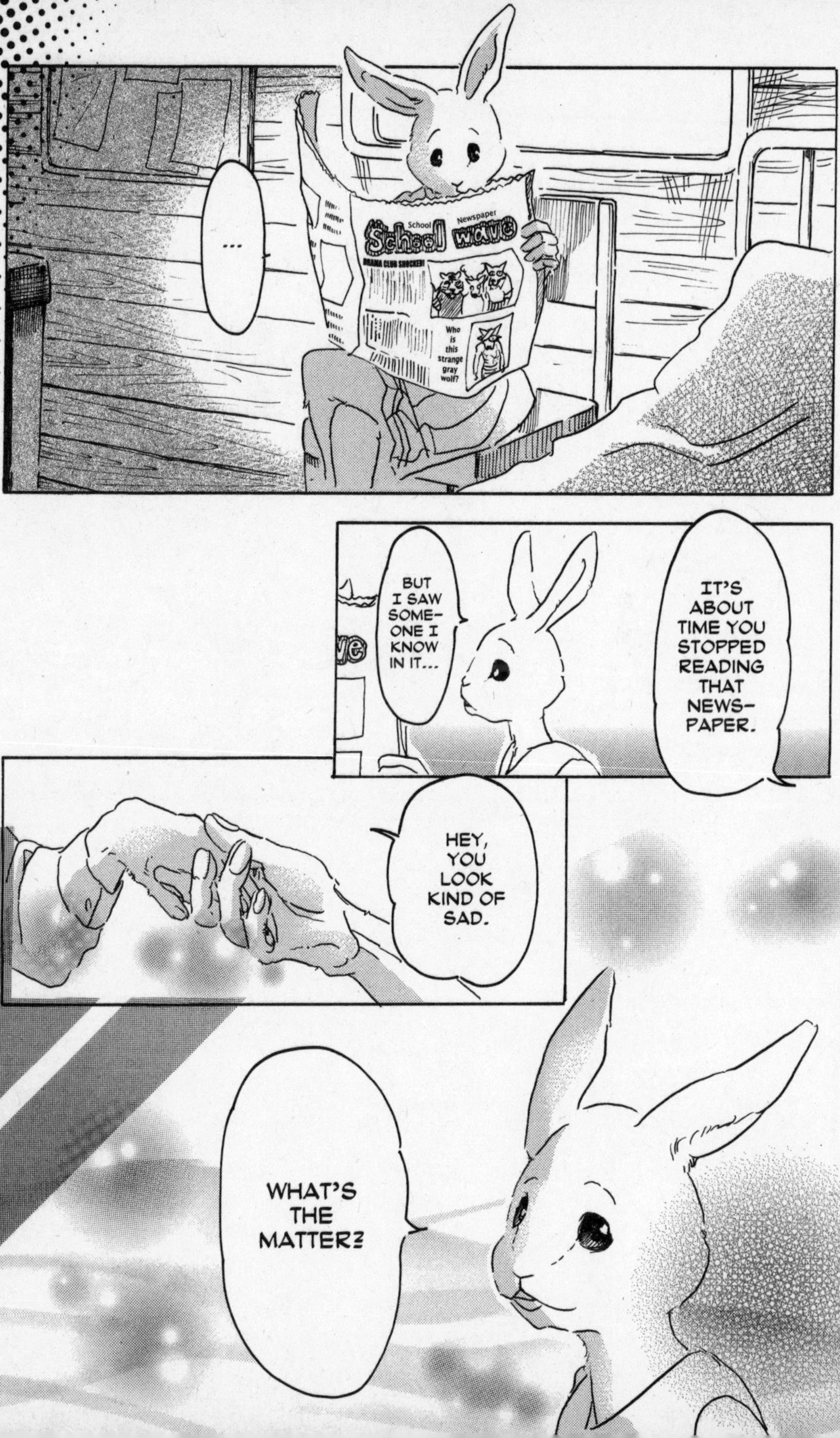
School Newspaper
School wave
DRAMA CLUB SHOCKER!
Who is this strange gray wolf?
...
IT'S ABOUT TIME YOU STOPPED READING THAT NEWSPAPER.
BUT I SAW SOMEONE I KNOW IN IT...
HEY, YOU LOOK KIND OF SAD.
WHAT'S THE MATTER?

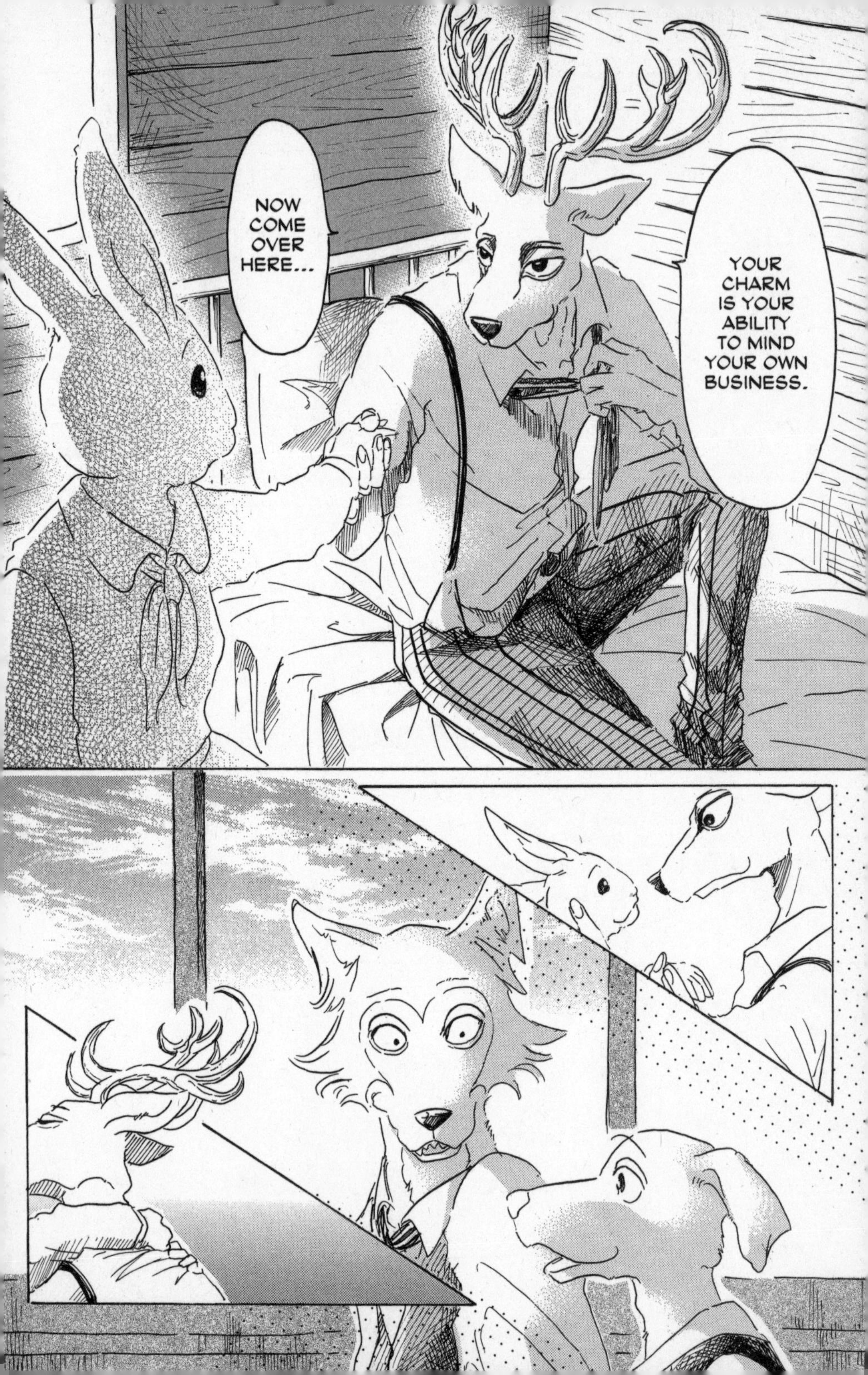
YOUR CHARM IS YOUR ABILITY TO MIND YOUR OWN BUSINESS.
NOW COME OVER HERE...

Chapter 18: The Beasts' Summer Festival of the Meteor

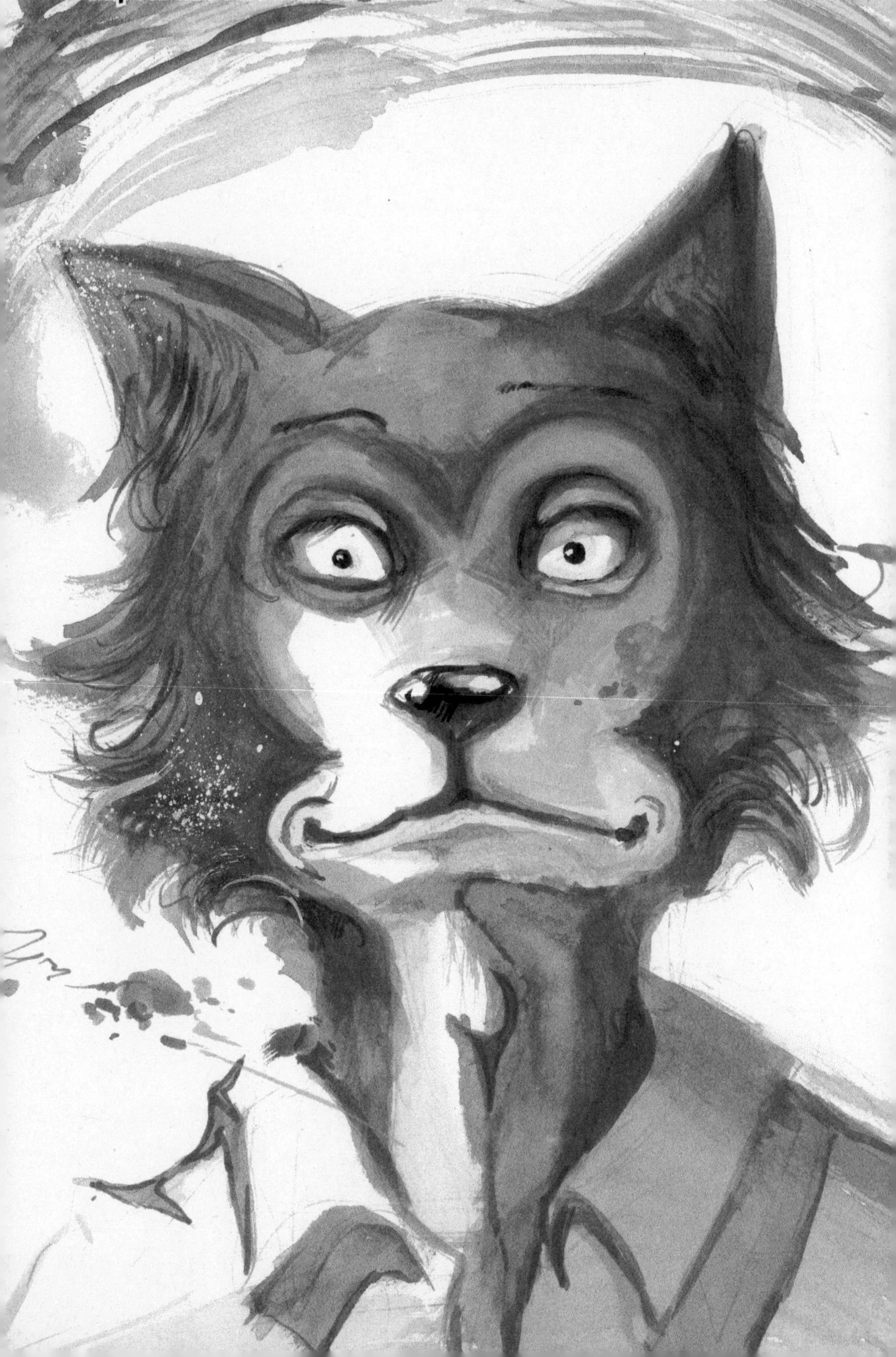

BEASTARS Vol. 3

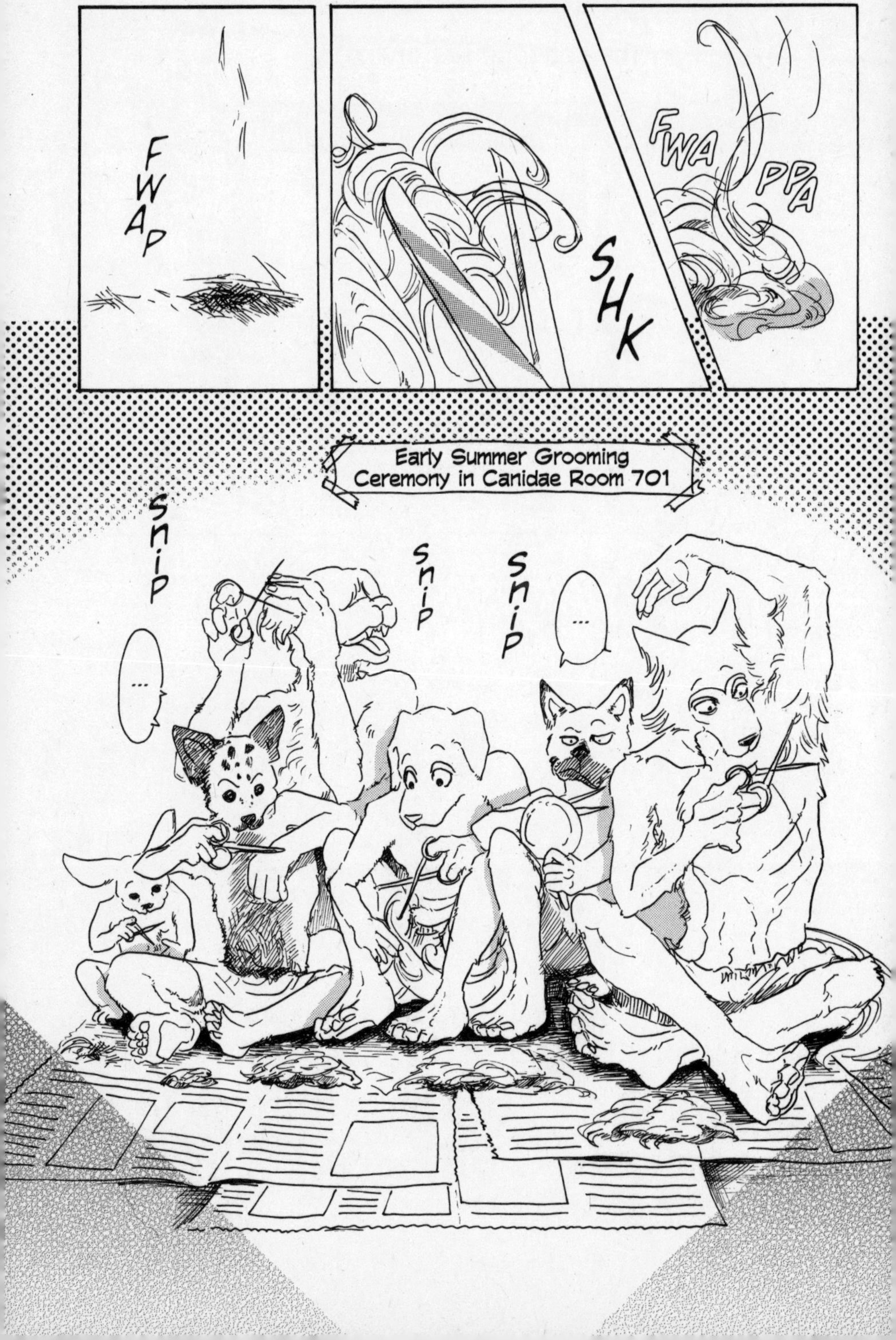
FWAPPA
SHK
FWAP
Early Summer Grooming Ceremony in Canidae Room 701
...
snip
snip
snip
...

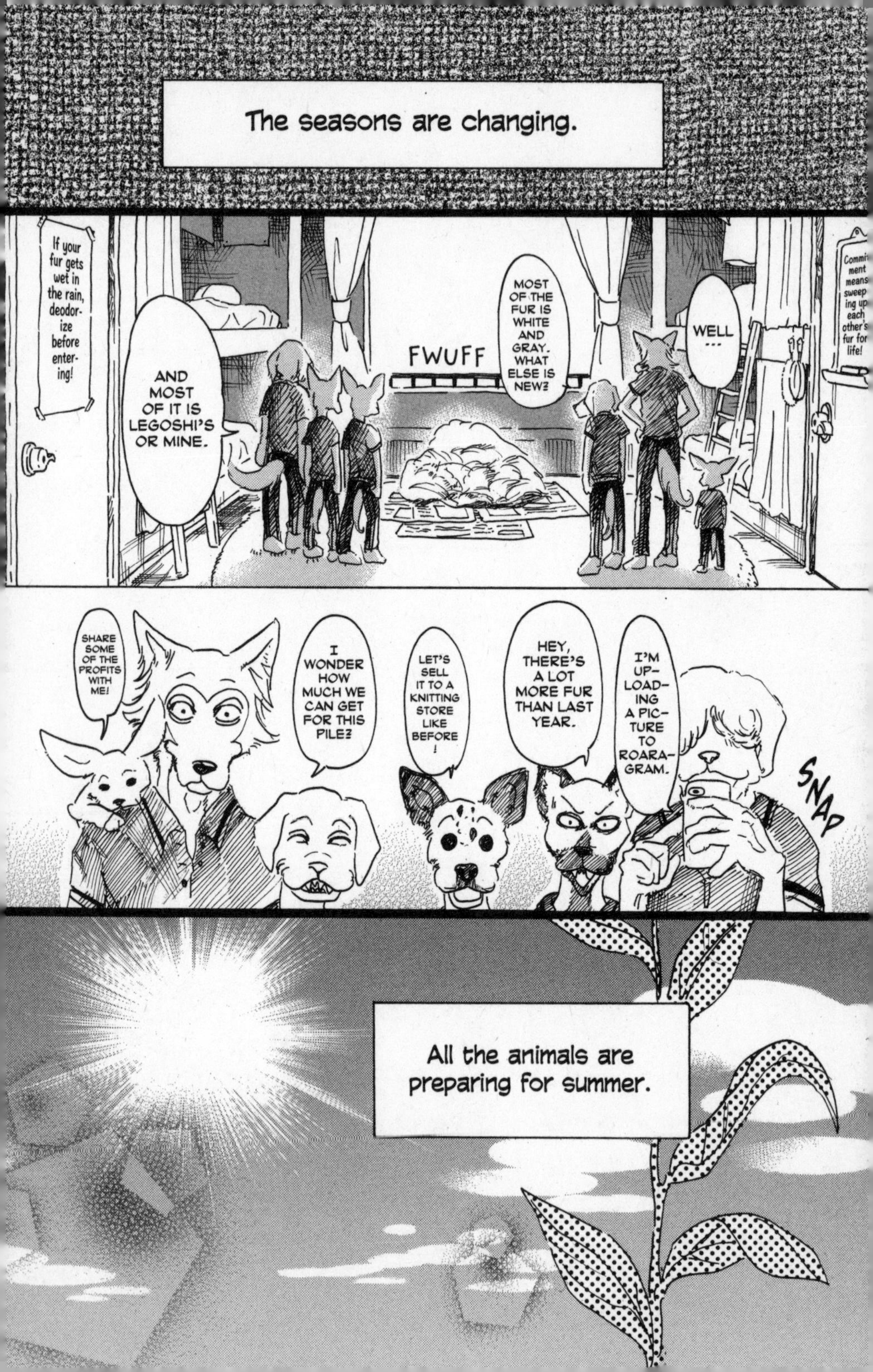
The seasons are changing.
Commi ment means sweeping up each other's fur for life!
WELL...
MOST OF THE FUR IS WHITE AND GRAY. WHAT ELSE IS NEW?
FWUFF
AND MOST OF IT IS LEGOSHI'S OR MINE.
If your fur gets wet in the rain, deodorize before entering!
SNAP
I'M UPLOADING A PICTURE TO ROARAGRAM.
HEY, THERE'S A LOT MORE FUR THAN LAST YEAR.
LET'S SELL IT TO A KNITTING STORE LIKE BEFORE!
I WONDER HOW MUCH WE CAN GET FOR THIS PILE?
SHARE SOME OF THE PROFITS WITH ME!
All the animals are preparing for summer.

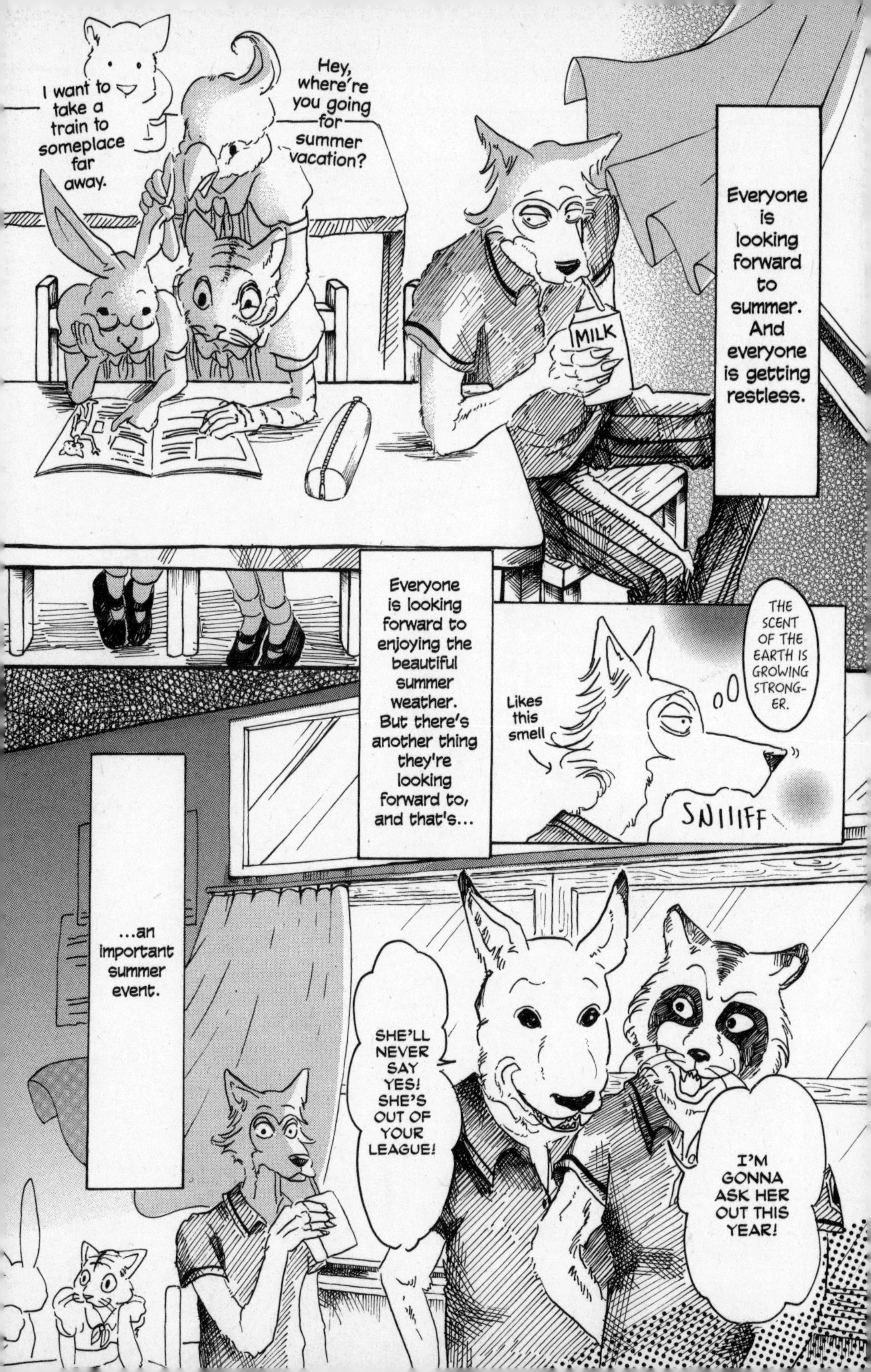
Everyone is looking forward to summer. And everyone is getting restless.
Hey, where're you going for summer vacation?
I want to take a train to someplace far away.
THE SCENT OF THE EARTH IS GROWING STRONG-ER.
Likes this smell
SNIIIFF
Everyone is looking forward to enjoying the beautiful summer weather. But there's another thing they're looking forward to, and that's...
I'M GONNA ASK HER OUT THIS YEAR!
SHE'LL NEVER SAY YES! SHE'S OUT OF YOUR LEAGUE!
...an important summer event.

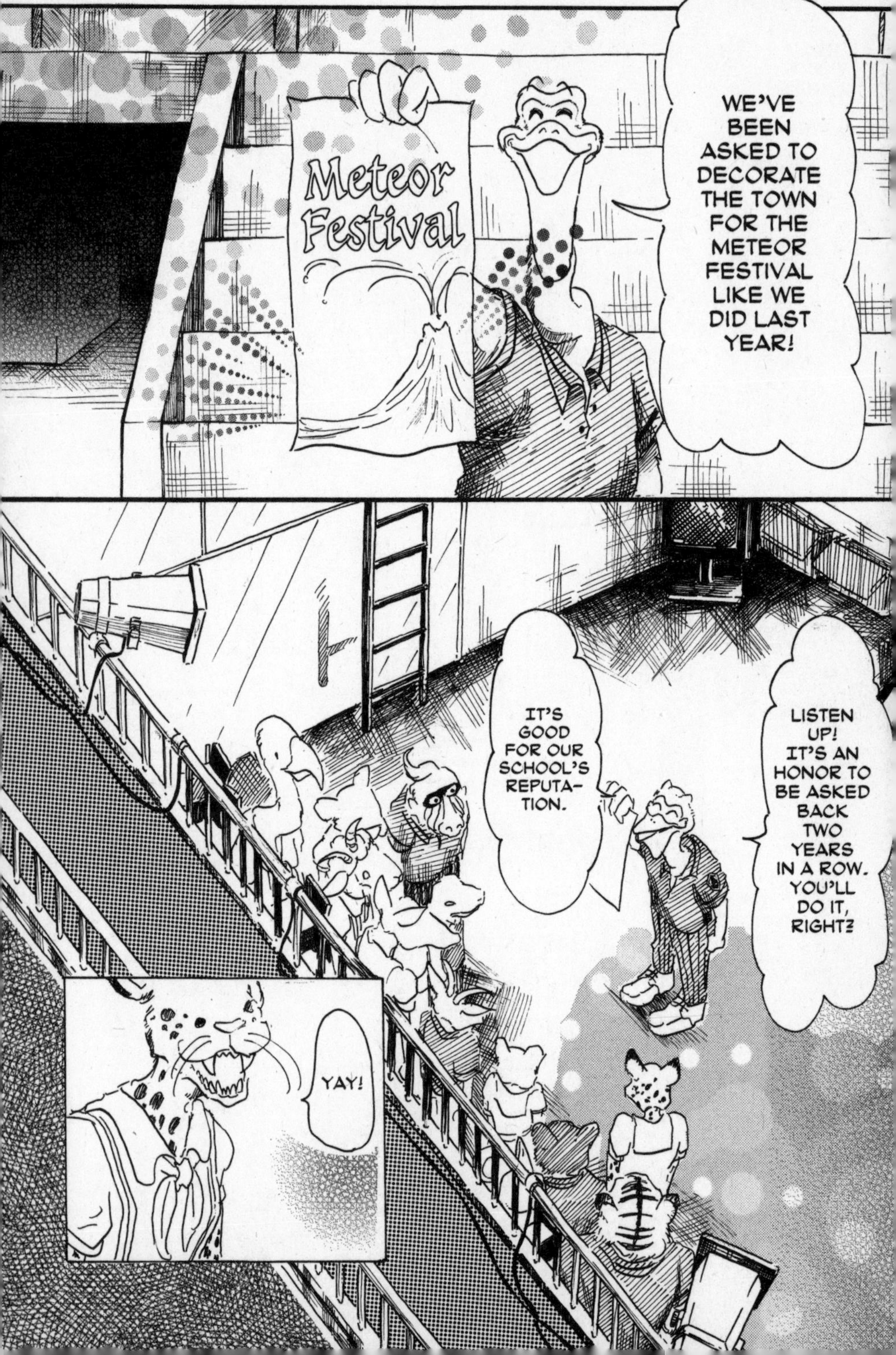
WE'VE BEEN ASKED TO DECORATE THE TOWN FOR THE METEOR FESTIVAL LIKE WE DID LAST YEAR!
Meteor Festival
LISTEN UP! IT'S AN HONOR TO BE ASKED BACK TWO YEARS IN A ROW. YOU'LL DO IT, RIGHT?
IT'S GOOD FOR OUR SCHOOL'S REPUTA-TION.
YAY!

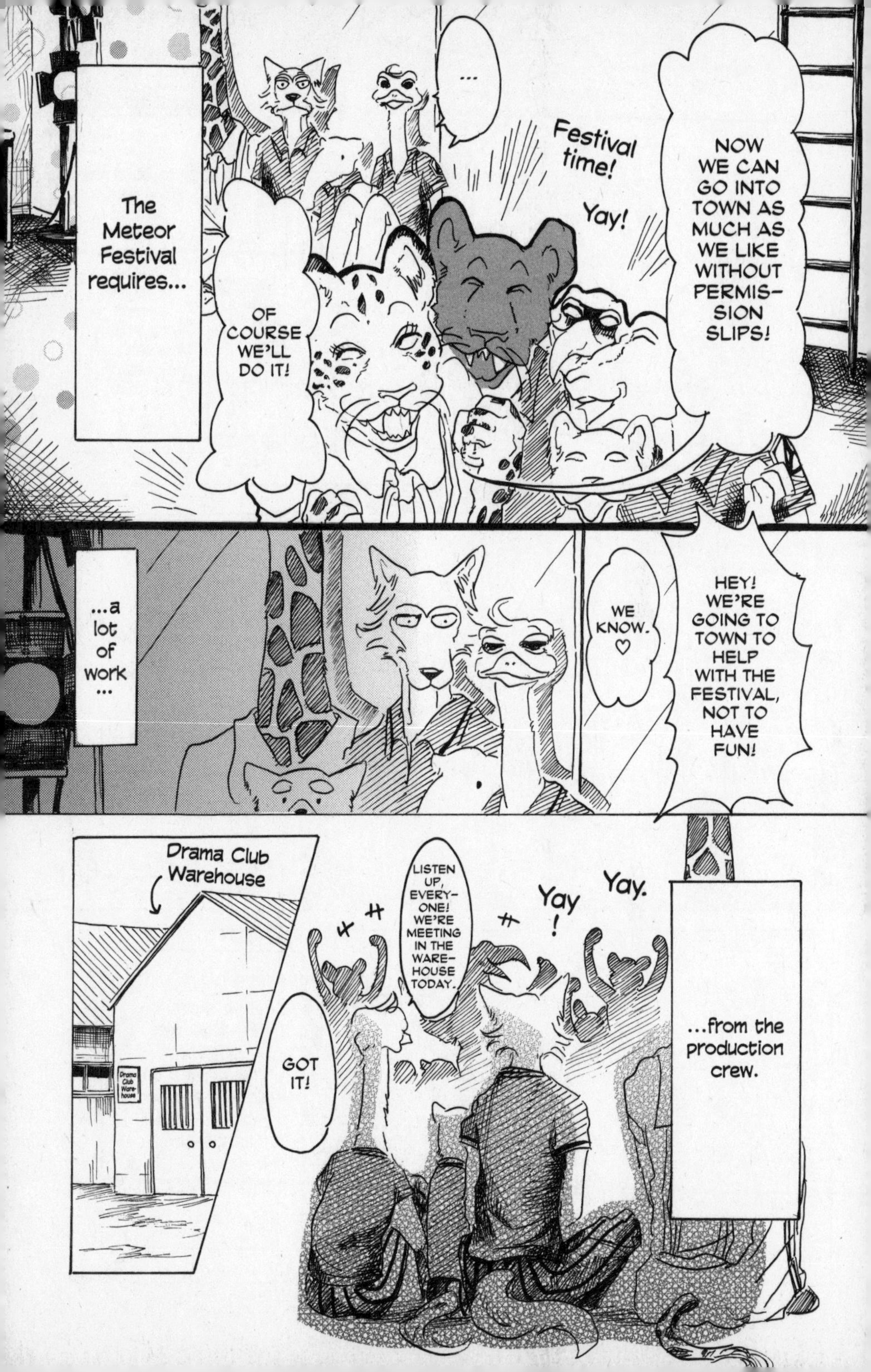

NOW WE CAN GO INTO TOWN AS MUCH AS WE LIKE WITHOUT PERMISSION SLIPS!
Festival time!
Yay!
...
OF COURSE WE'LL DO IT!
The Meteor Festival requires...
HEY! WE'RE GOING TO TOWN TO HELP WITH THE FESTIVAL, NOT TO HAVE FUN!
WE KNOW. ♡
...a lot of work...
...from the production crew.
Yay.
Yay!
LISTEN UP, EVERYONE! WE'RE MEETING IN THE WAREHOUSE TODAY.
GOT IT!
Drama Club Warehouse
Drama Club Warehouse

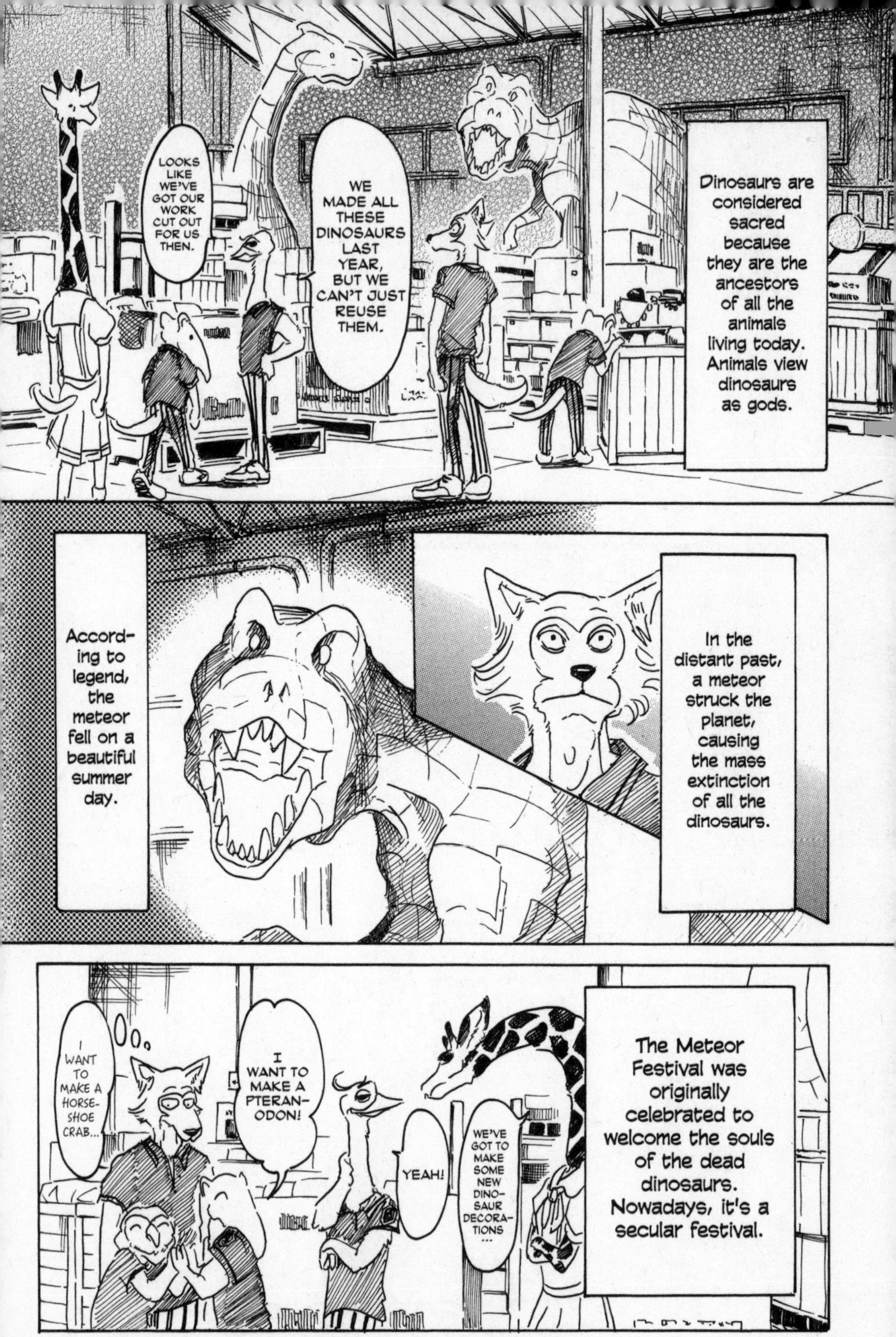
Dinosaurs are considered sacred because they are the ancestors of all the animals living today. Animals view dinosaurs as gods.
WE MADE ALL THESE DINOSAURS LAST YEAR, BUT WE CAN'T JUST REUSE THEM.
LOOKS LIKE WE'VE GOT OUR WORK CUT OUT FOR US THEN.
In the distant past, a meteor struck the planet, causing the mass extinction of all the dinosaurs.
According to legend, the meteor fell on a beautiful summer day.
The Meteor Festival was originally celebrated to welcome the souls of the dead dinosaurs. Nowadays, it's a secular festival.
WE'VE GOT TO MAKE SOME NEW DINOSAUR DECORATIONS...
YEAH!
I WANT TO MAKE A PTERANODON!
I WANT TO MAKE A HORSESHOE CRAB...

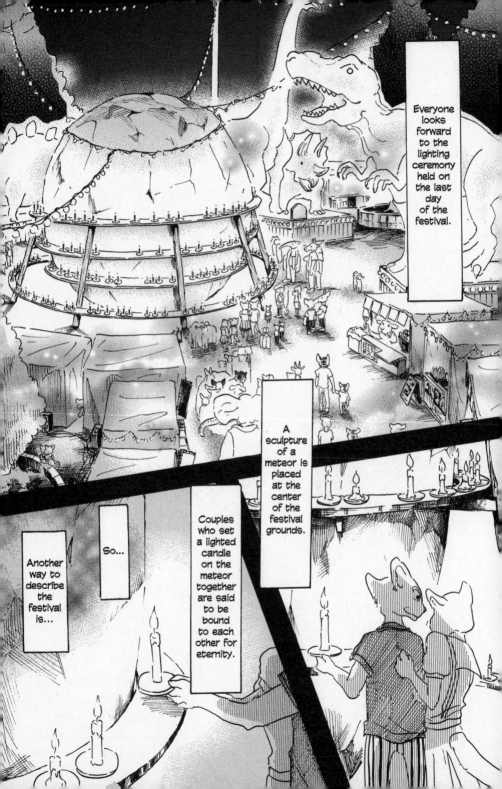

Everyone looks forward to the lighting ceremony held on the last day of the festival.

A sculpture of a meteor is placed at the center of the festival grounds.

Couples who set a lighted candle on the meteor together are said to be bound to each other for eternity.

So...

Another way to describe the festival is...

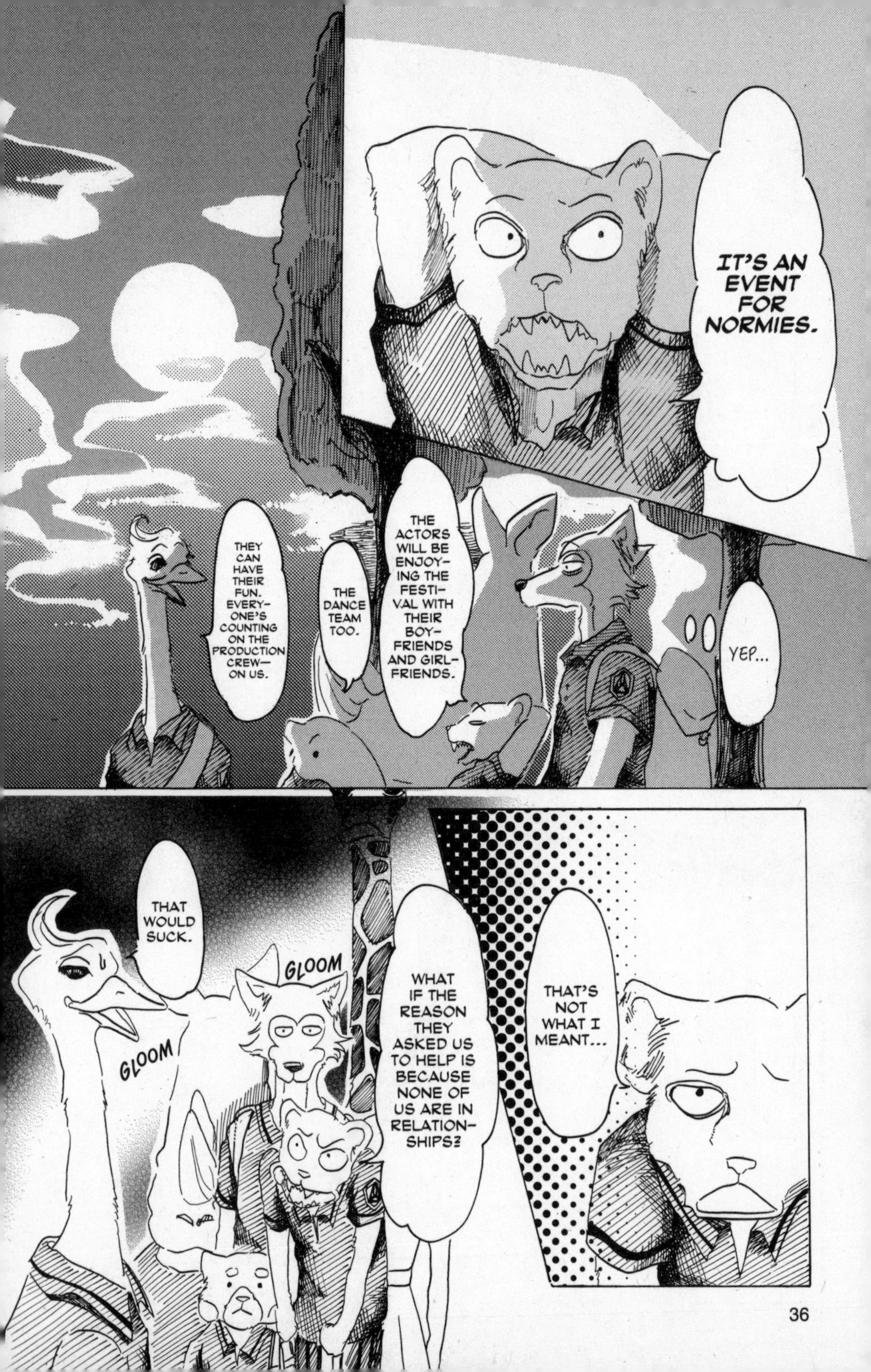
IT'S AN EVENT FOR NORMIES.
YEP...
THE ACTORS WILL BE ENJOYING THE FESTIVAL WITH THEIR BOYFRIENDS AND GIRLFRIENDS.
THE DANCE TEAM TOO.
THEY CAN HAVE THEIR FUN. EVERYONE'S COUNTING ON THE PRODUCTION CREW—ON US.
THAT'S NOT WHAT I MEANT...
WHAT IF THE REASON THEY ASKED US TO HELP IS BECAUSE NONE OF US ARE IN RELATIONSHIPS?
GLOOM
THAT WOULD SUCK.
GLOOM

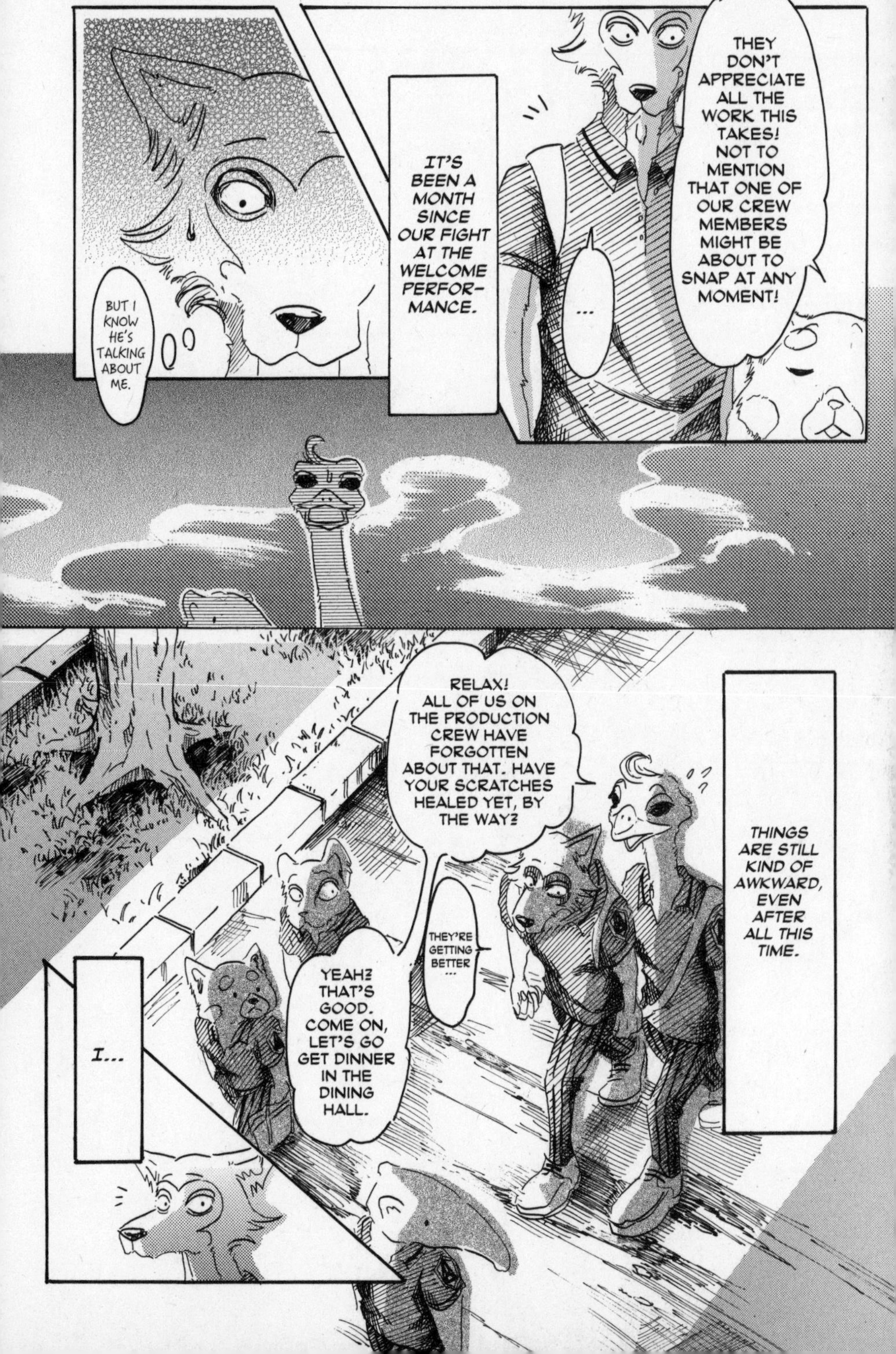
THEY DON'T APPRECIATE ALL THE WORK THIS TAKES! NOT TO MENTION THAT ONE OF OUR CREW MEMBERS MIGHT BE ABOUT TO SNAP AT ANY MOMENT!
IT'S BEEN A MONTH SINCE OUR FIGHT AT THE WELCOME PERFOR-MANCE.
...
BUT I KNOW HE'S TALKING ABOUT ME.
THINGS ARE STILL KIND OF AWKWARD, EVEN AFTER ALL THIS TIME.
RELAX! ALL OF US ON THE PRODUCTION CREW HAVE FORGOTTEN ABOUT THAT. HAVE YOUR SCRATCHES HEALED YET, BY THE WAY?
THEY'RE GETTING BETTER ...
YEAH? THAT'S GOOD. COME ON, LET'S GO GET DINNER IN THE DINING HALL.
I...

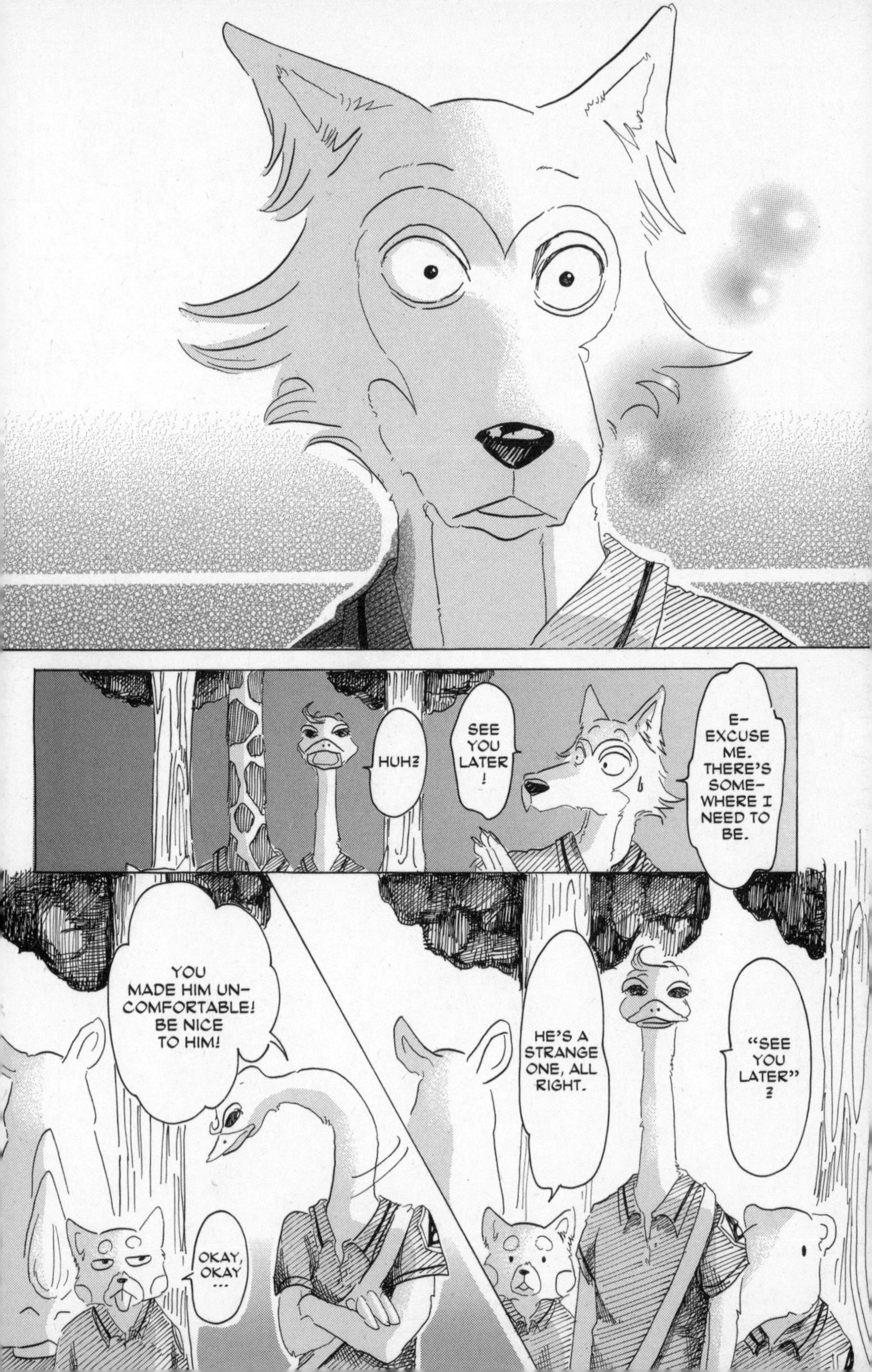
E-EXCUSE ME. THERE'S SOME-WHERE I NEED TO BE.
SEE YOU LATER!
HUH?
"SEE YOU LATER"?
HE'S A STRANGE ONE, ALL RIGHT.
YOU MADE HIM UN-COMFORTABLE! BE NICE TO HIM!
OKAY, OKAY...

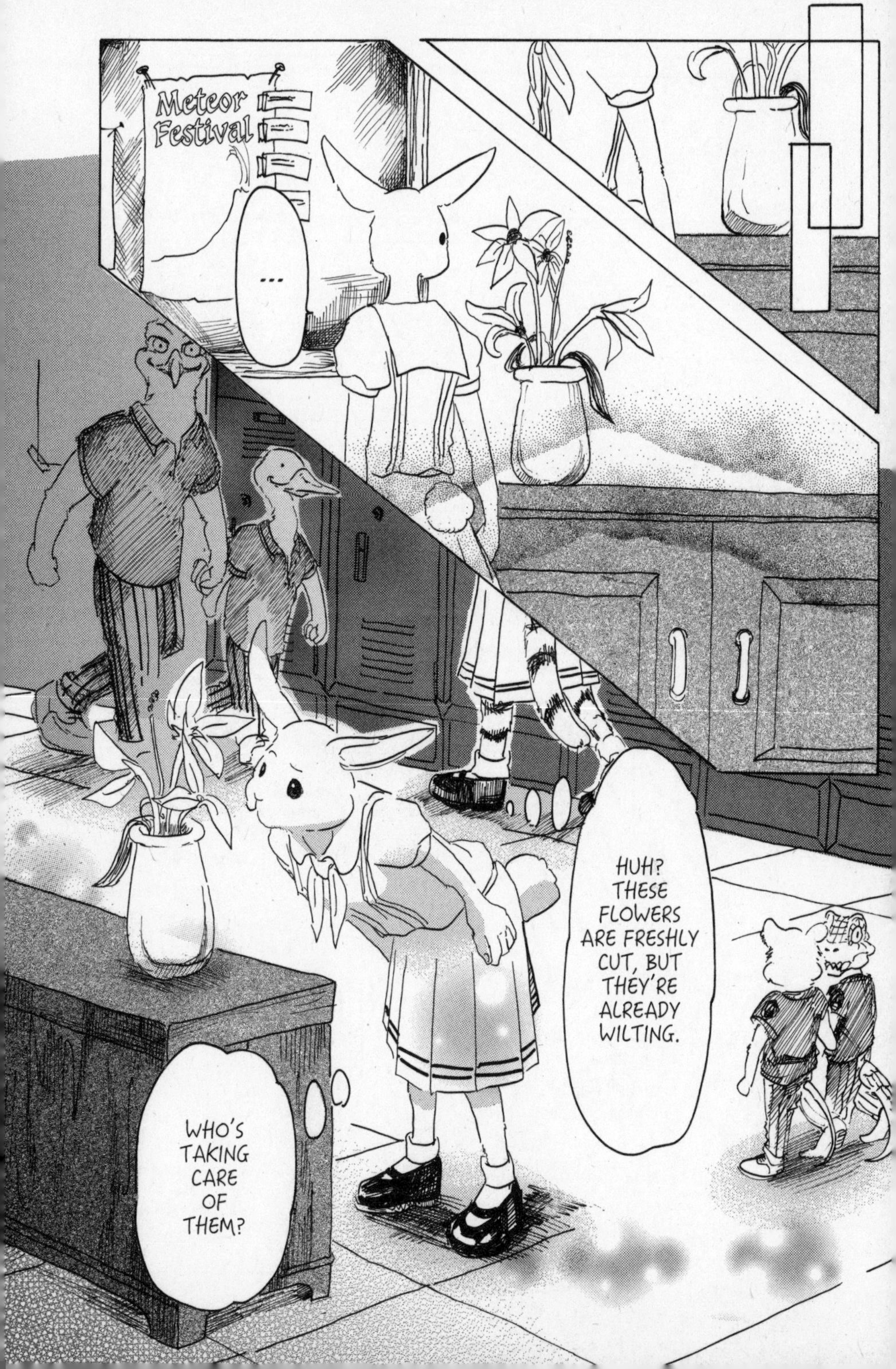
Meteor Festival
...
HUH? THESE FLOWERS ARE FRESHLY CUT, BUT THEY'RE ALREADY WILTING.
WHO'S TAKING CARE OF THEM?

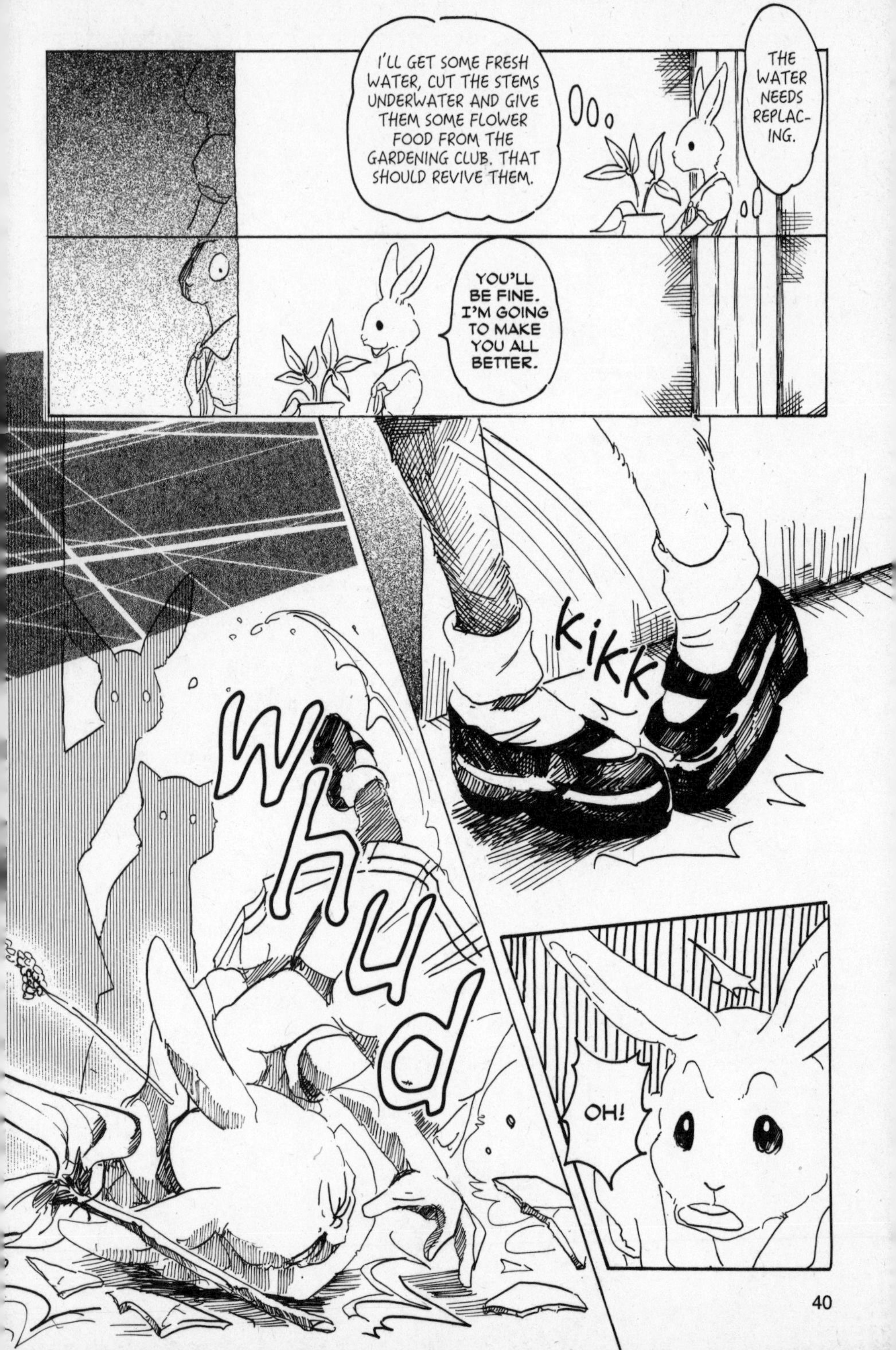
THE WATER NEEDS REPLACING.
I'LL GET SOME FRESH WATER, CUT THE STEMS UNDERWATER AND GIVE THEM SOME FLOWER FOOD FROM THE GARDENING CLUB. THAT SHOULD REVIVE THEM.
YOU'LL BE FINE. I'M GOING TO MAKE YOU ALL BETTER.
KIKK
WHUD
OH!

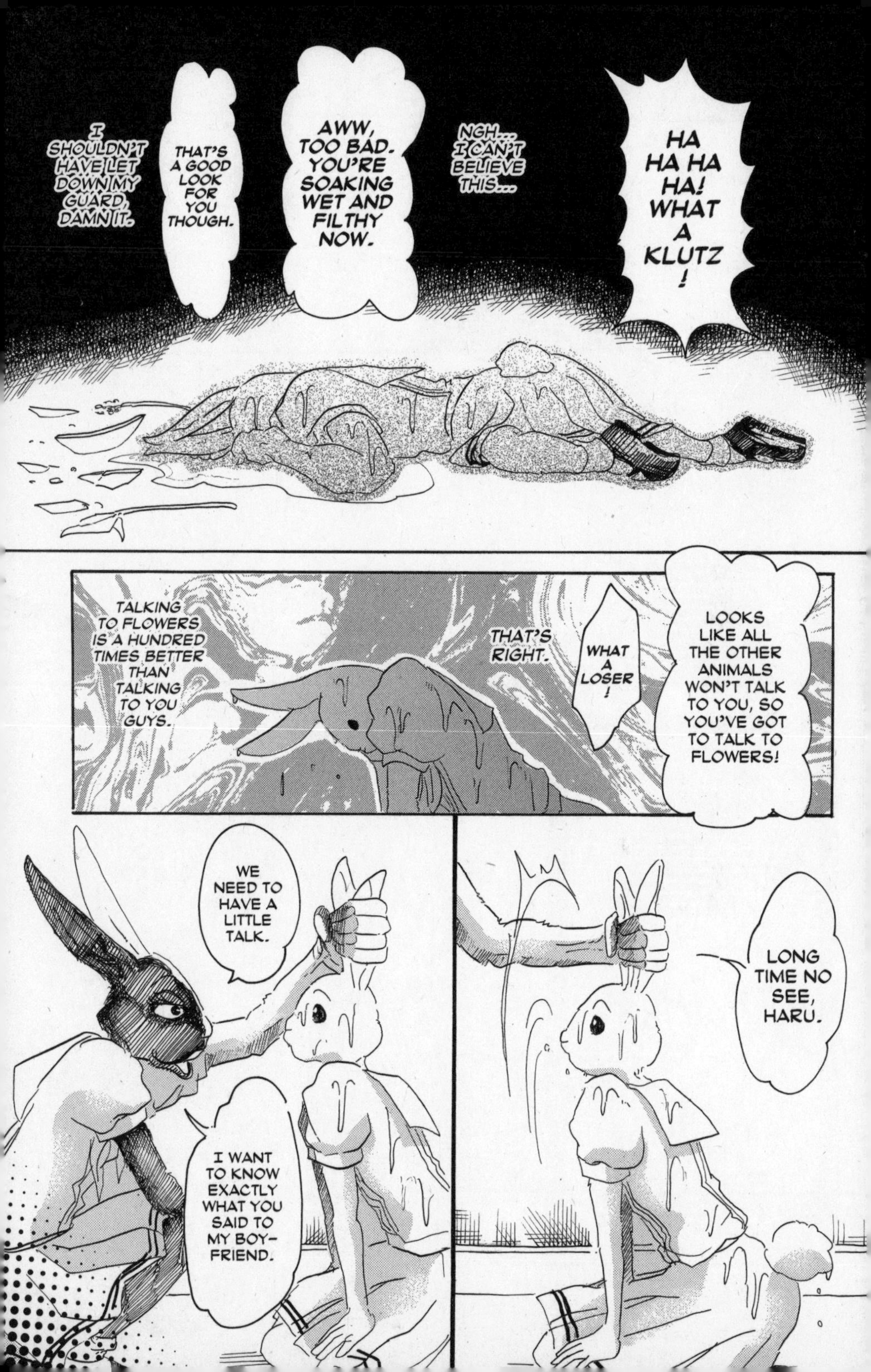
HA HA HA HA! WHAT A KLUTZ!
NGH... I CAN'T BELIEVE THIS...
AWW, TOO BAD. YOU'RE SOAKING WET AND FILTHY NOW.
THAT'S A GOOD LOOK FOR YOU THOUGH.
I SHOULDN'T HAVE LET DOWN MY GUARD, DAMN IT.
LOOKS LIKE ALL THE OTHER ANIMALS WON'T TALK TO YOU, SO YOU'VE GOT TO TALK TO FLOWERS!
WHAT A LOSER!
THAT'S RIGHT.
TALKING TO FLOWERS IS A HUNDRED TIMES BETTER THAN TALKING TO YOU GUYS.
LONG TIME NO SEE, HARU.
WE NEED TO HAVE A LITTLE TALK.
I WANT TO KNOW EXACTLY WHAT YOU SAID TO MY BOY-FRIEND.

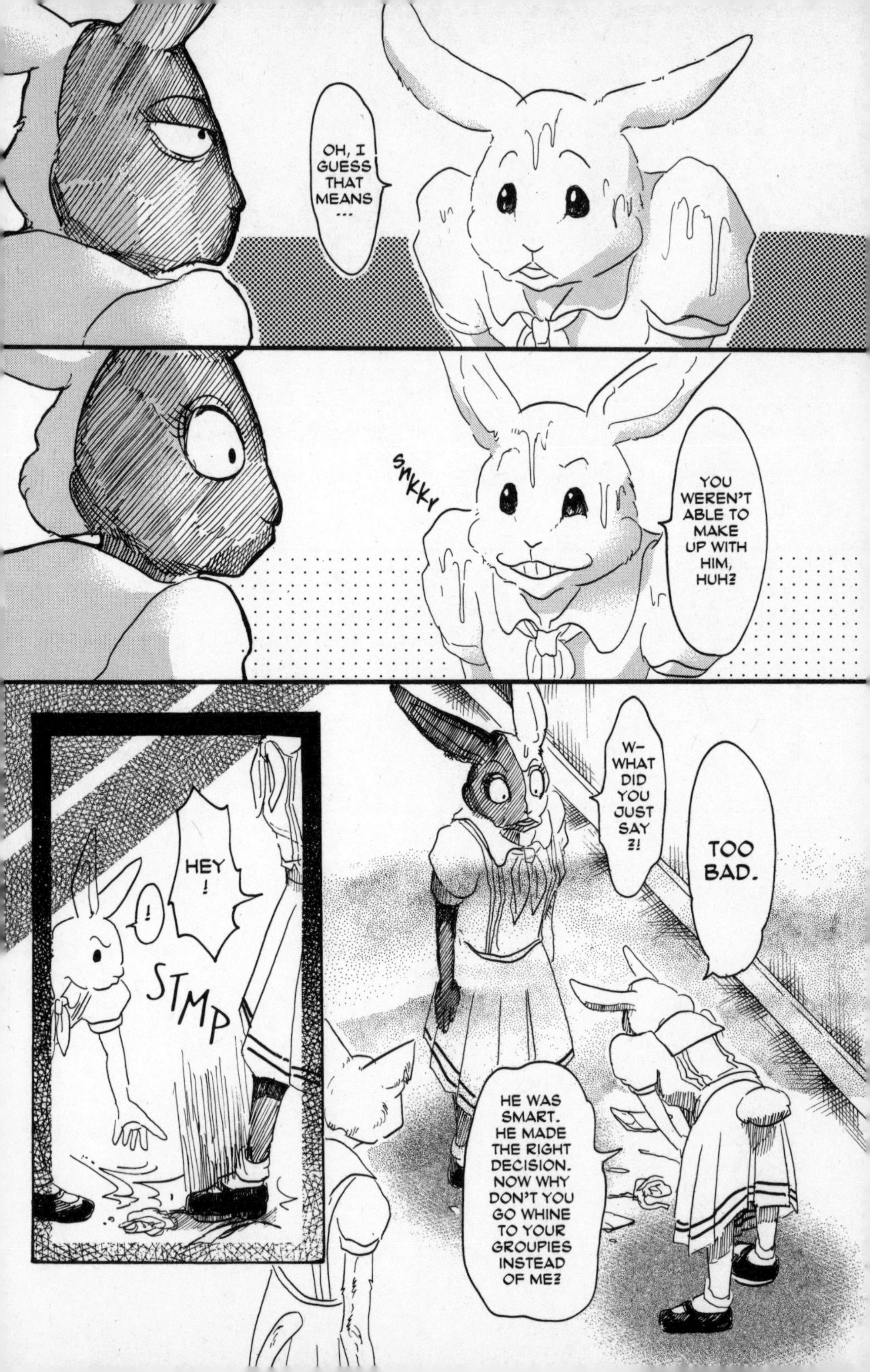
OH, I GUESS THAT MEANS ---
SNKKR
YOU WEREN'T ABLE TO MAKE UP WITH HIM, HUH?
TOO BAD.
W-WHAT DID YOU JUST SAY?!
HE WAS SMART. HE MADE THE RIGHT DECISION. NOW WHY DON'T YOU GO WHINE TO YOUR GROUPIES INSTEAD OF ME?
HEY!
!
STMP

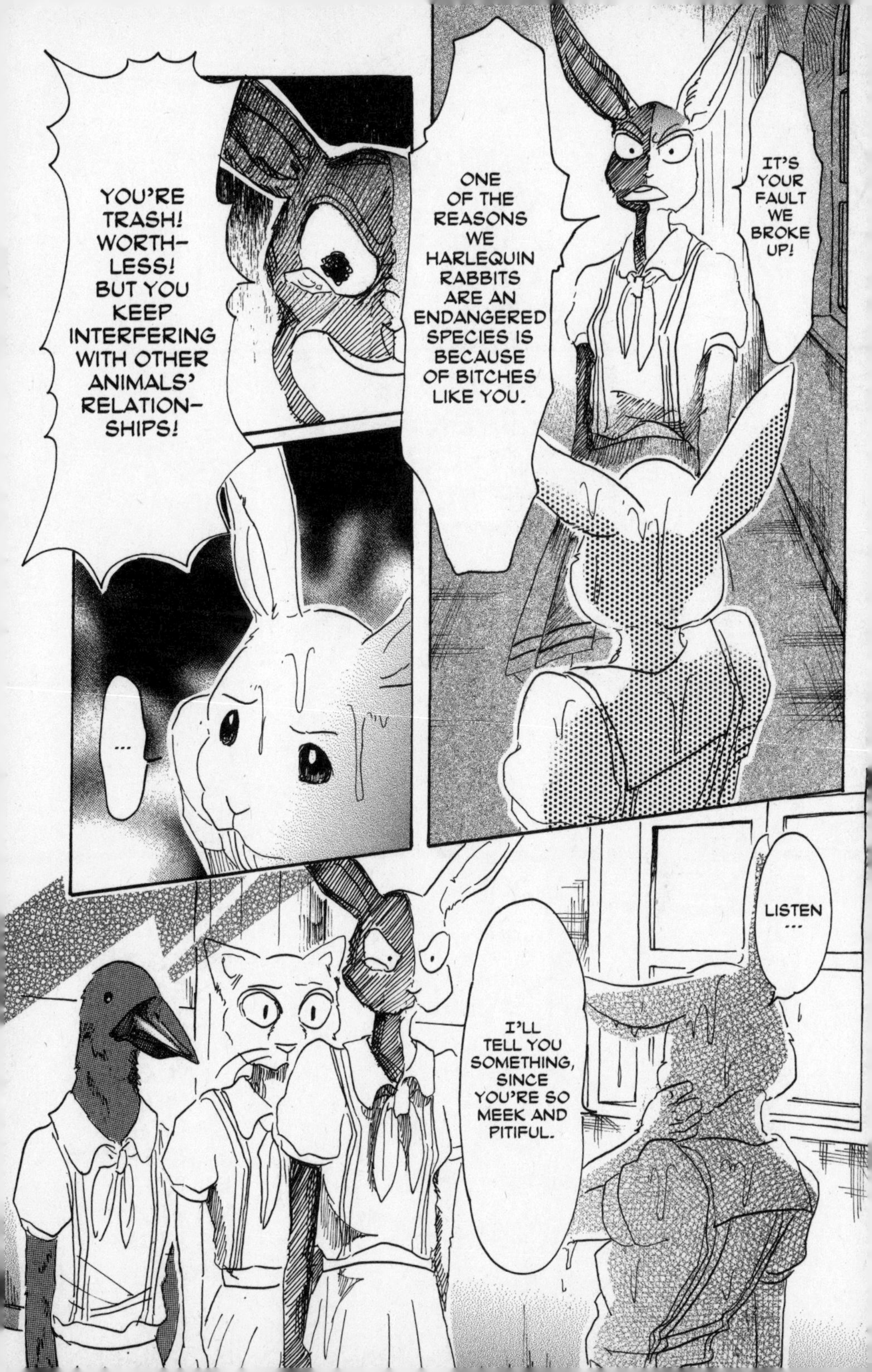
IT'S YOUR FAULT WE BROKE UP!
ONE OF THE REASONS WE HARLEQUIN RABBITS ARE AN ENDANGERED SPECIES IS BECAUSE OF BITCHES LIKE YOU.
YOU'RE TRASH! WORTH-LESS! BUT YOU KEEP INTERFERING WITH OTHER ANIMALS' RELATION-SHIPS!
...
LISTEN...
I'LL TELL YOU SOMETHING, SINCE YOU'RE SO MEEK AND PITIFUL.

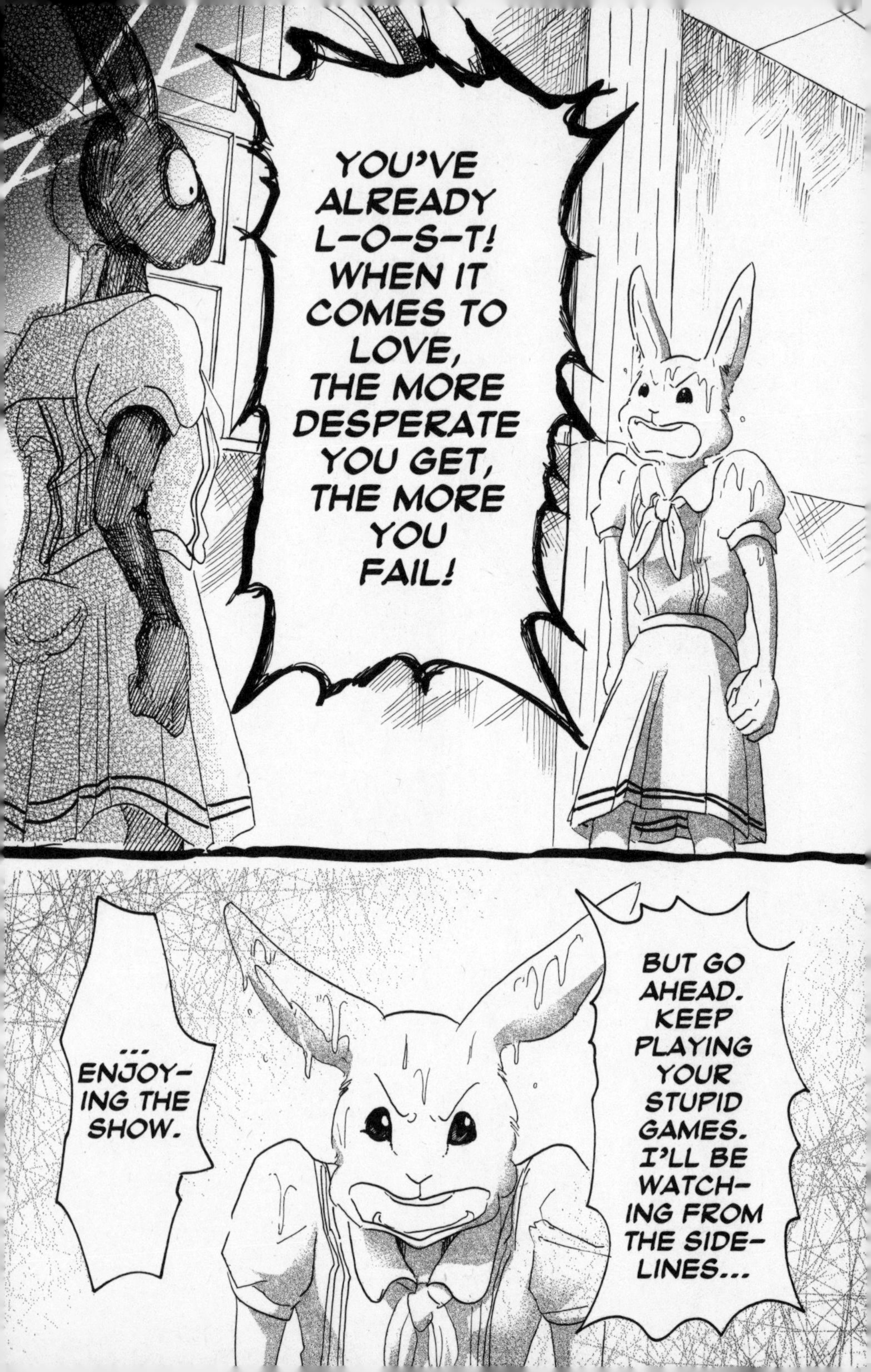
YOU'VE ALREADY L-O-S-T! WHEN IT COMES TO LOVE, THE MORE DESPERATE YOU GET, THE MORE YOU FAIL!
BUT GO AHEAD. KEEP PLAYING YOUR STUPID GAMES. I'LL BE WATCH-ING FROM THE SIDE-LINES...
...ENJOY-ING THE SHOW.

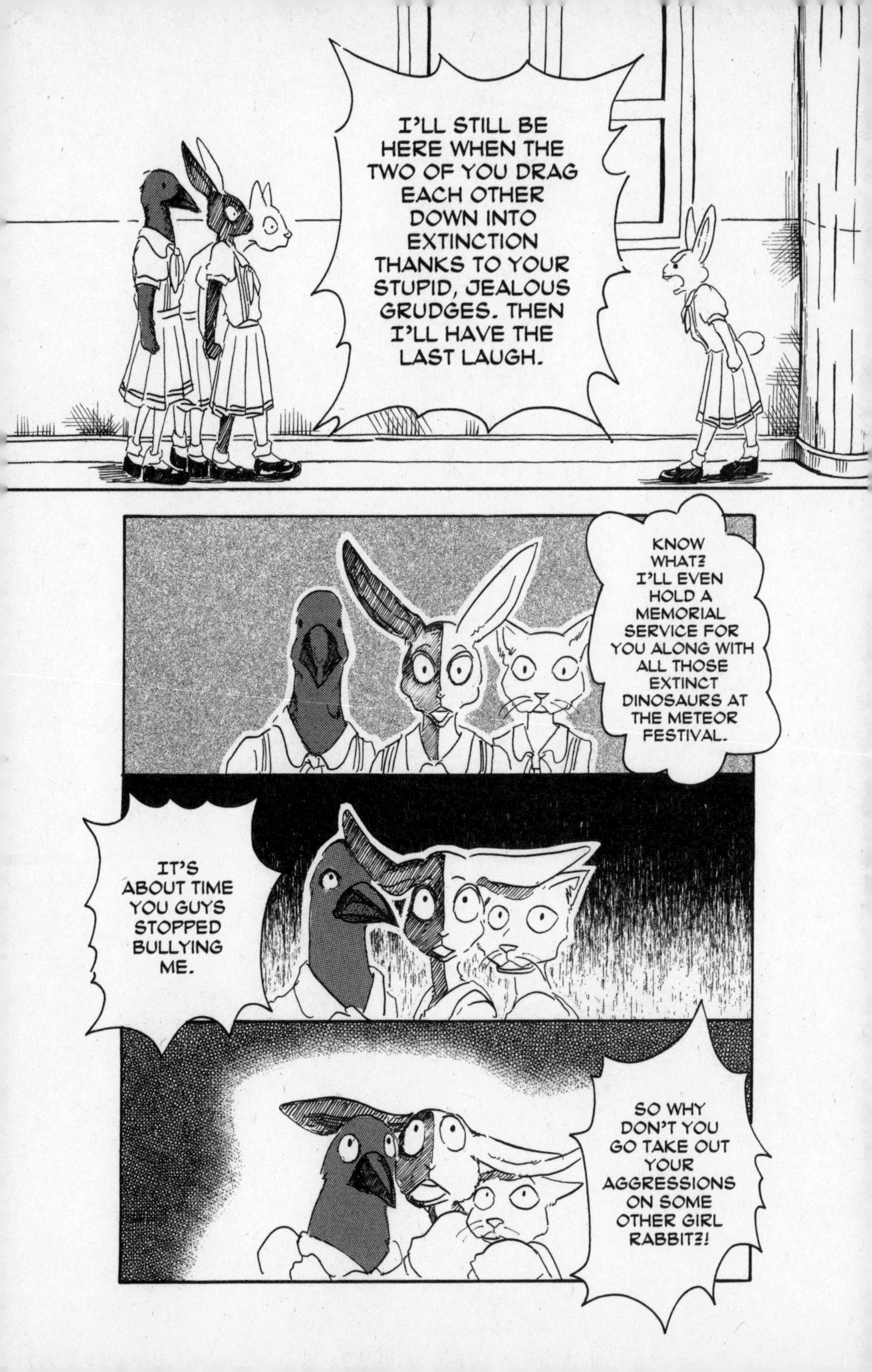
I'LL STILL BE HERE WHEN THE TWO OF YOU DRAG EACH OTHER DOWN INTO EXTINCTION THANKS TO YOUR STUPID, JEALOUS GRUDGES. THEN I'LL HAVE THE LAST LAUGH.
KNOW WHAT? I'LL EVEN HOLD A MEMORIAL SERVICE FOR YOU ALONG WITH ALL THOSE EXTINCT DINOSAURS AT THE METEOR FESTIVAL.
IT'S ABOUT TIME YOU GUYS STOPPED BULLYING ME.
SO WHY DON'T YOU GO TAKE OUT YOUR AGGRESSIONS ON SOME OTHER GIRL RABBIT?!

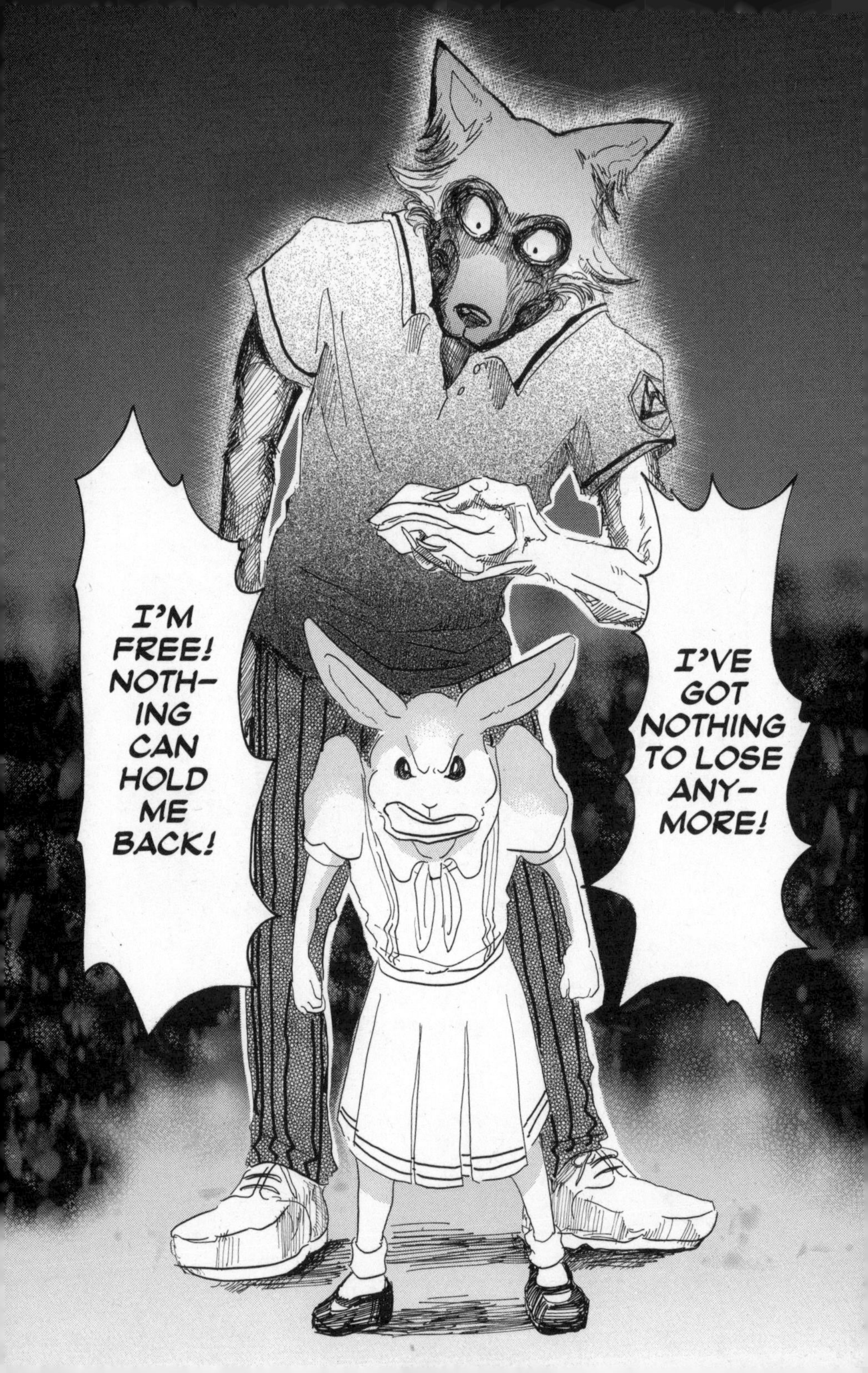
I'VE GOT NOTHING TO LOSE ANY-MORE!
I'M FREE! NOTH-ING CAN HOLD ME BACK!

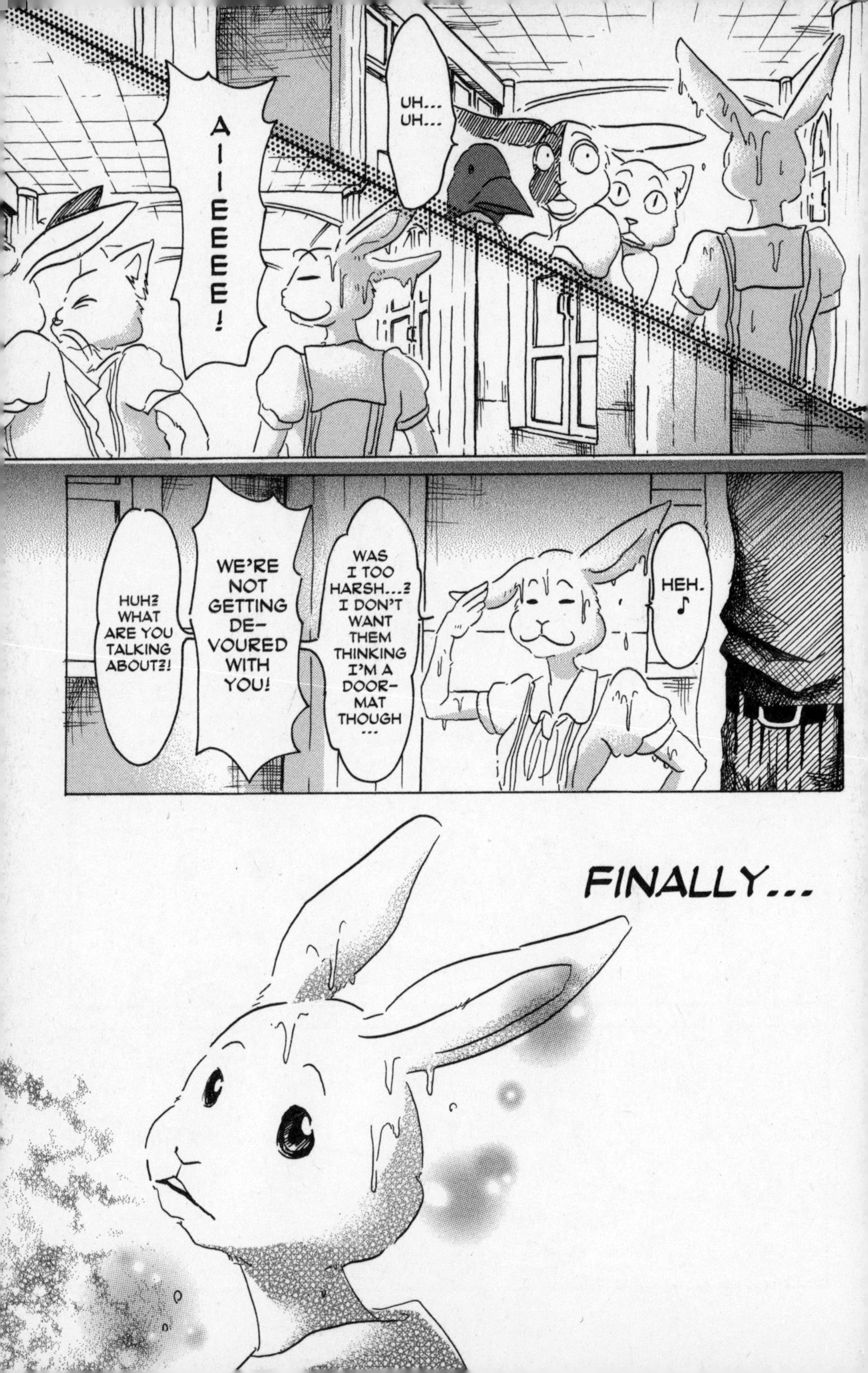
UH... UH...
AIIEEEE!
HEH. ♪
WAS I TOO HARSH...? I DON'T WANT THEM THINKING I'M A DOORMAT THOUGH...
WE'RE NOT GETTING DE-VOURED WITH YOU!
HUH? WHAT ARE YOU TALKING ABOUT?!
FINALLY...

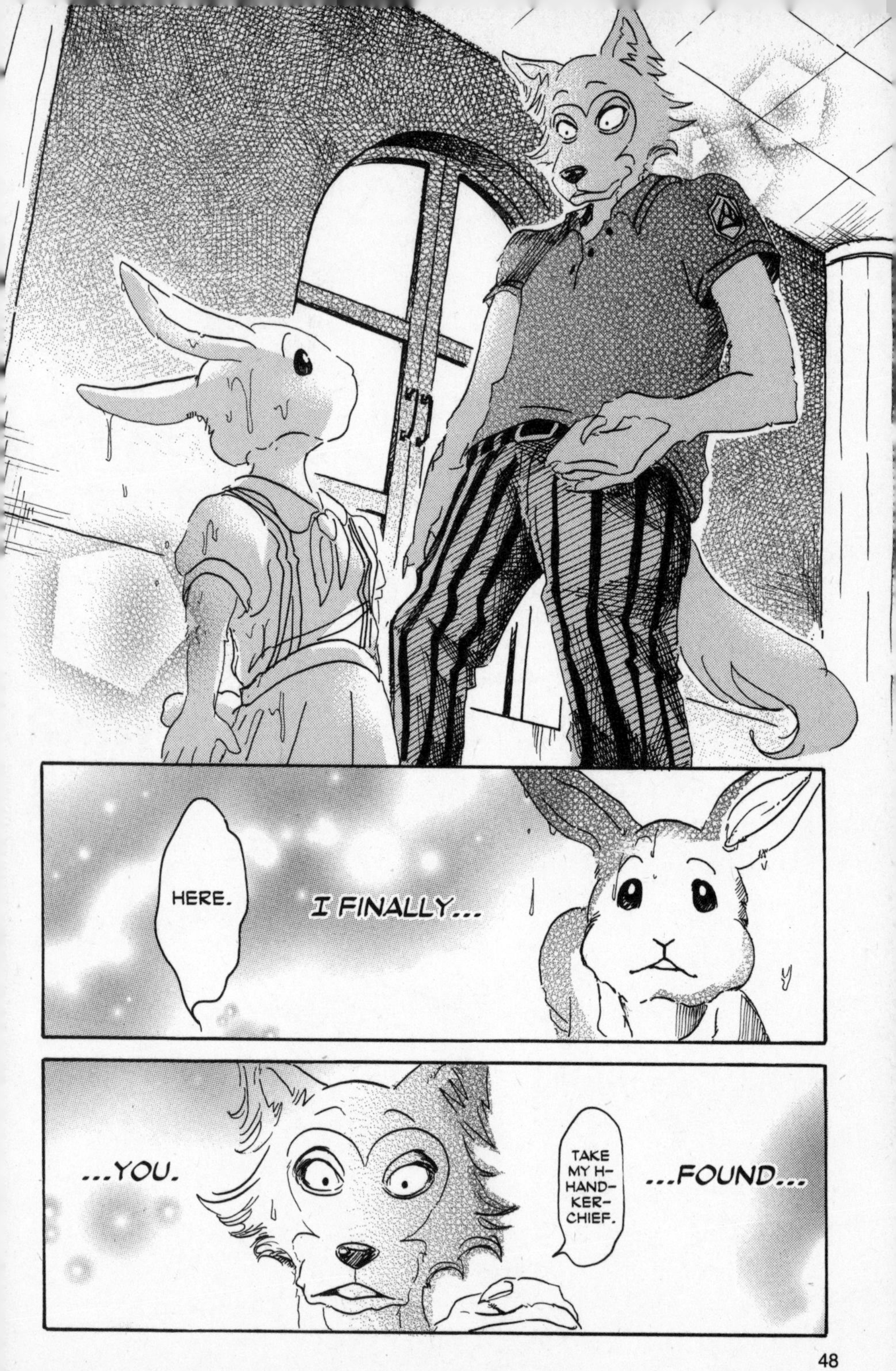
I FINALLY...
HERE.
...FOUND...
TAKE MY H-HAND-KER-CHIEF.
...YOU.

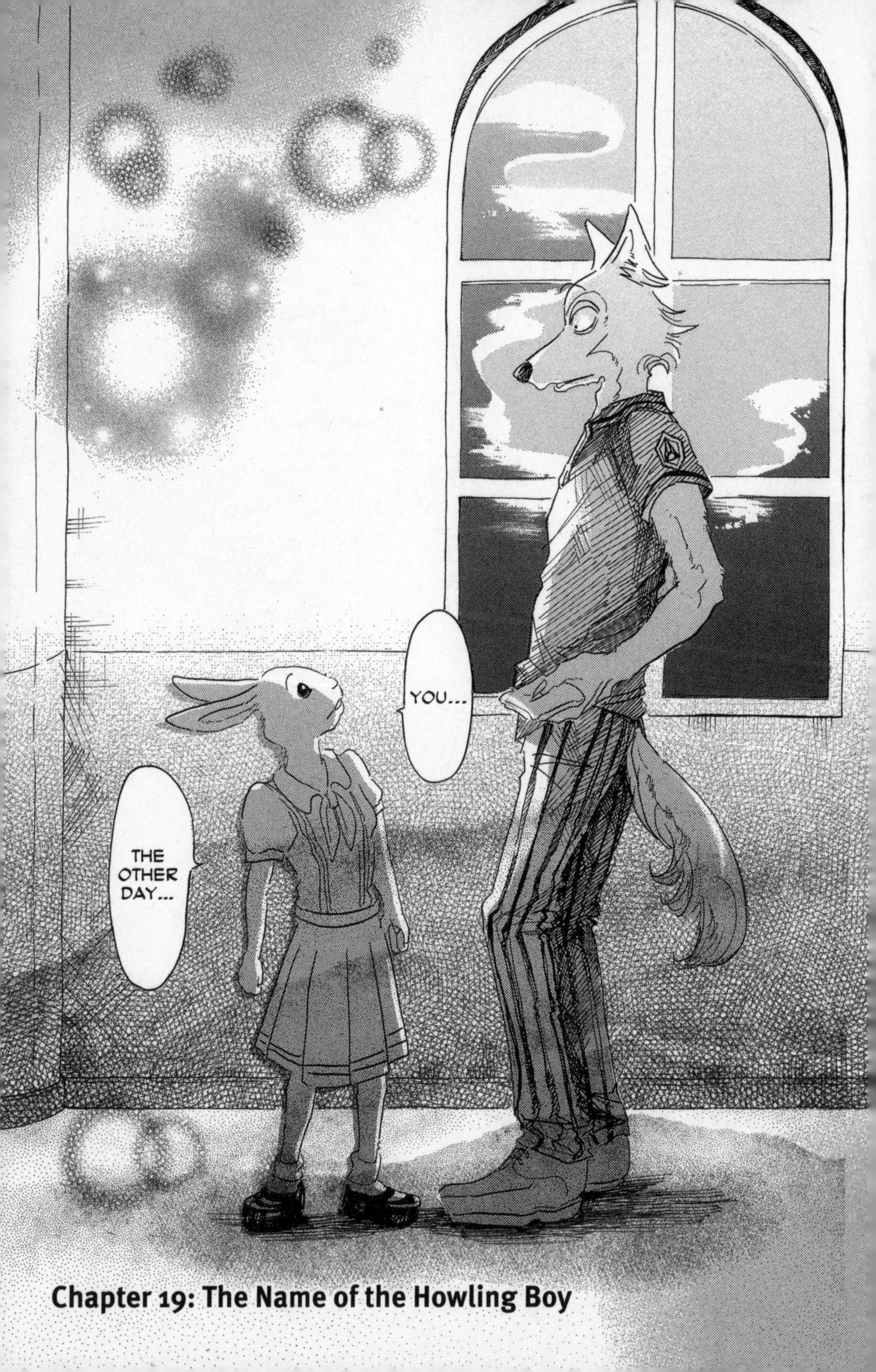
YOU...
THE OTHER DAY...

Chapter 19: The Name of the Howling Boy

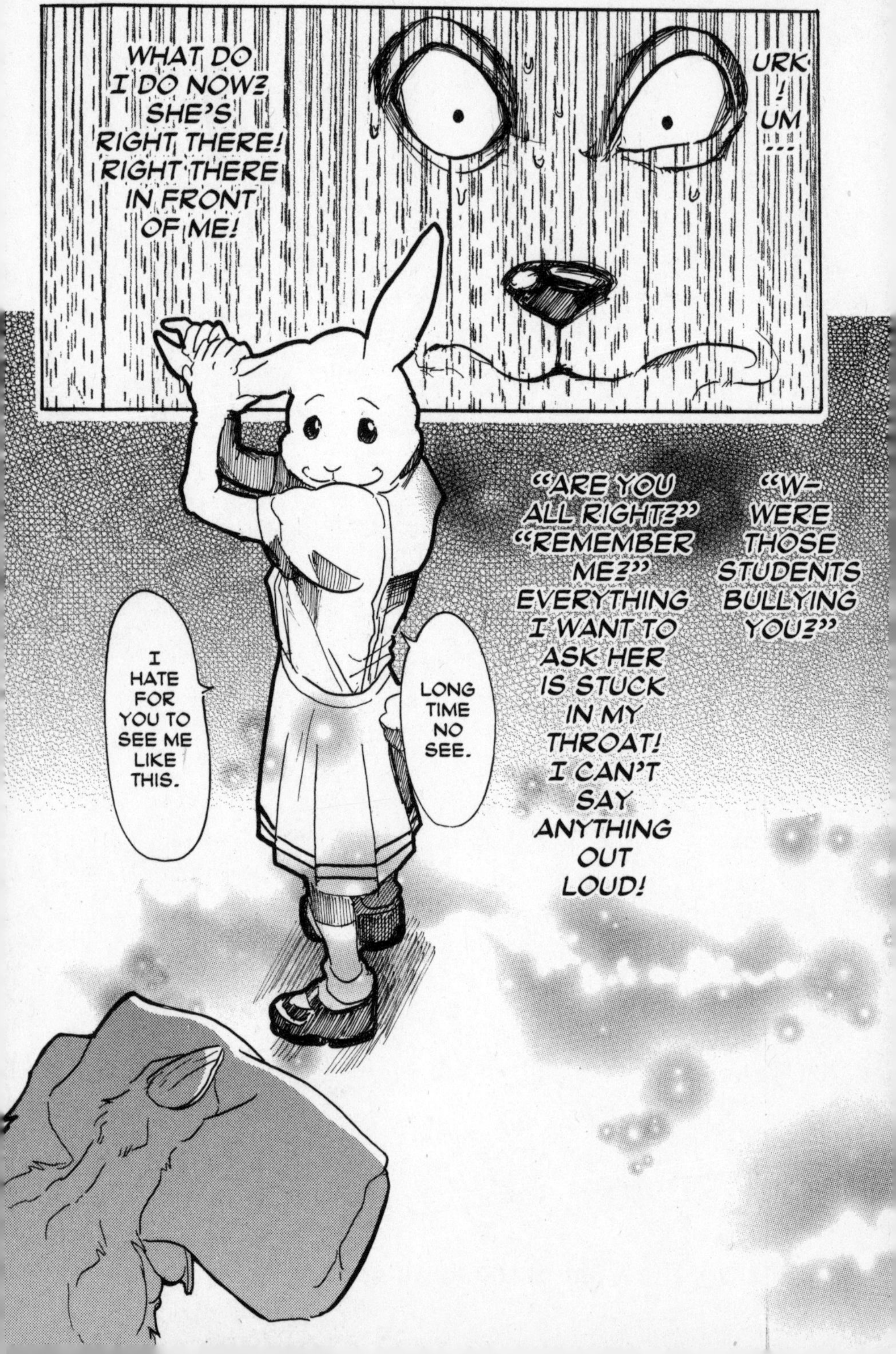
URK! UM...
WHAT DO I DO NOW? SHE'S RIGHT THERE! RIGHT THERE IN FRONT OF ME!
"W-WERE THOSE STUDENTS BULLYING YOU?"
"ARE YOU ALL RIGHT?" "REMEMBER ME?" EVERYTHING I WANT TO ASK HER IS STUCK IN MY THROAT! I CAN'T SAY ANYTHING OUT LOUD!
LONG TIME NO SEE.
I HATE FOR YOU TO SEE ME LIKE THIS.

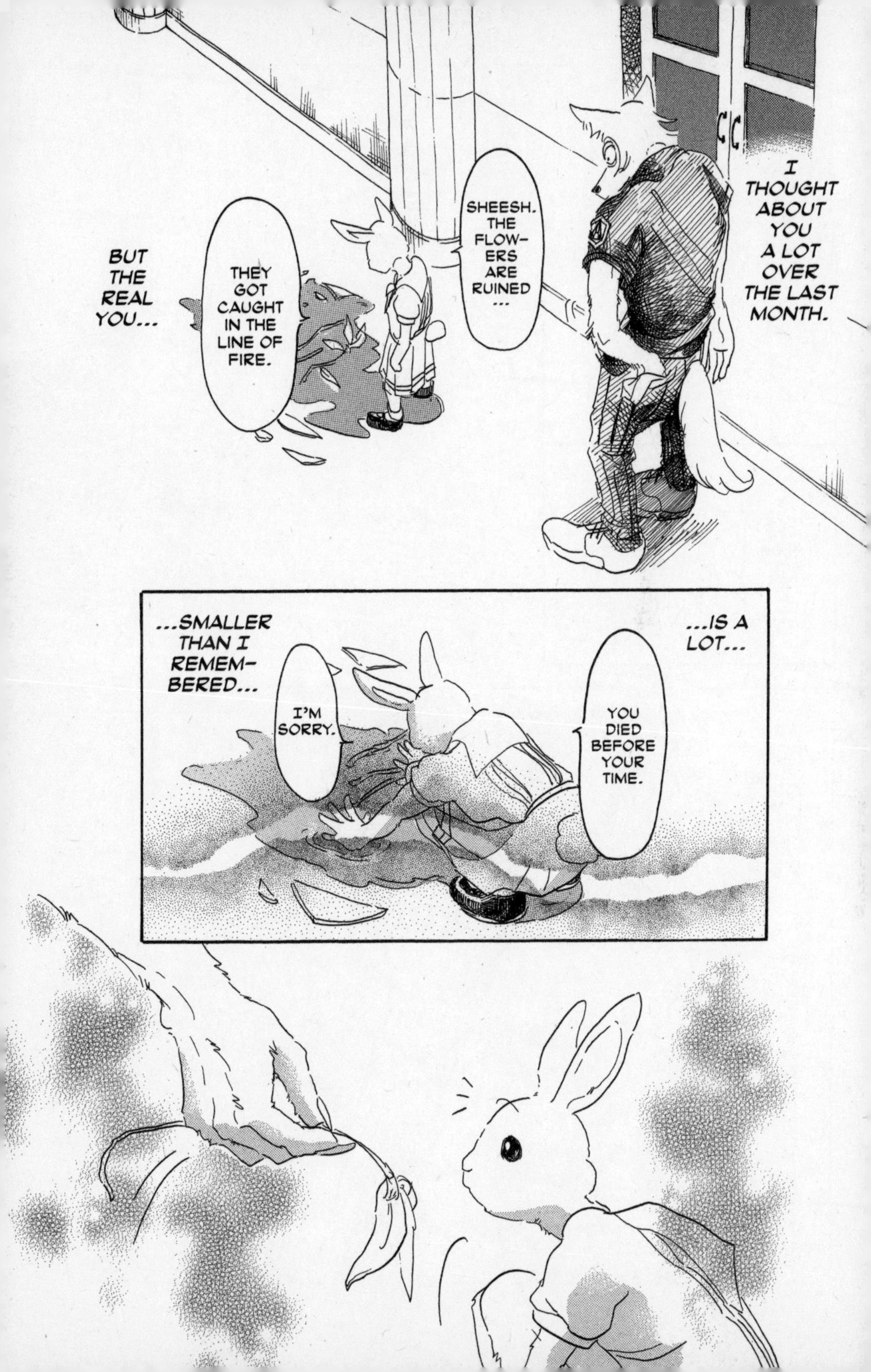
I THOUGHT ABOUT YOU A LOT OVER THE LAST MONTH.
SHEESH. THE FLOW-ERS ARE RUINED ...
THEY GOT CAUGHT IN THE LINE OF FIRE.
BUT THE REAL YOU...
...IS A LOT...
YOU DIED BEFORE YOUR TIME.
I'M SORRY.
...SMALLER THAN I REMEM-BERED...

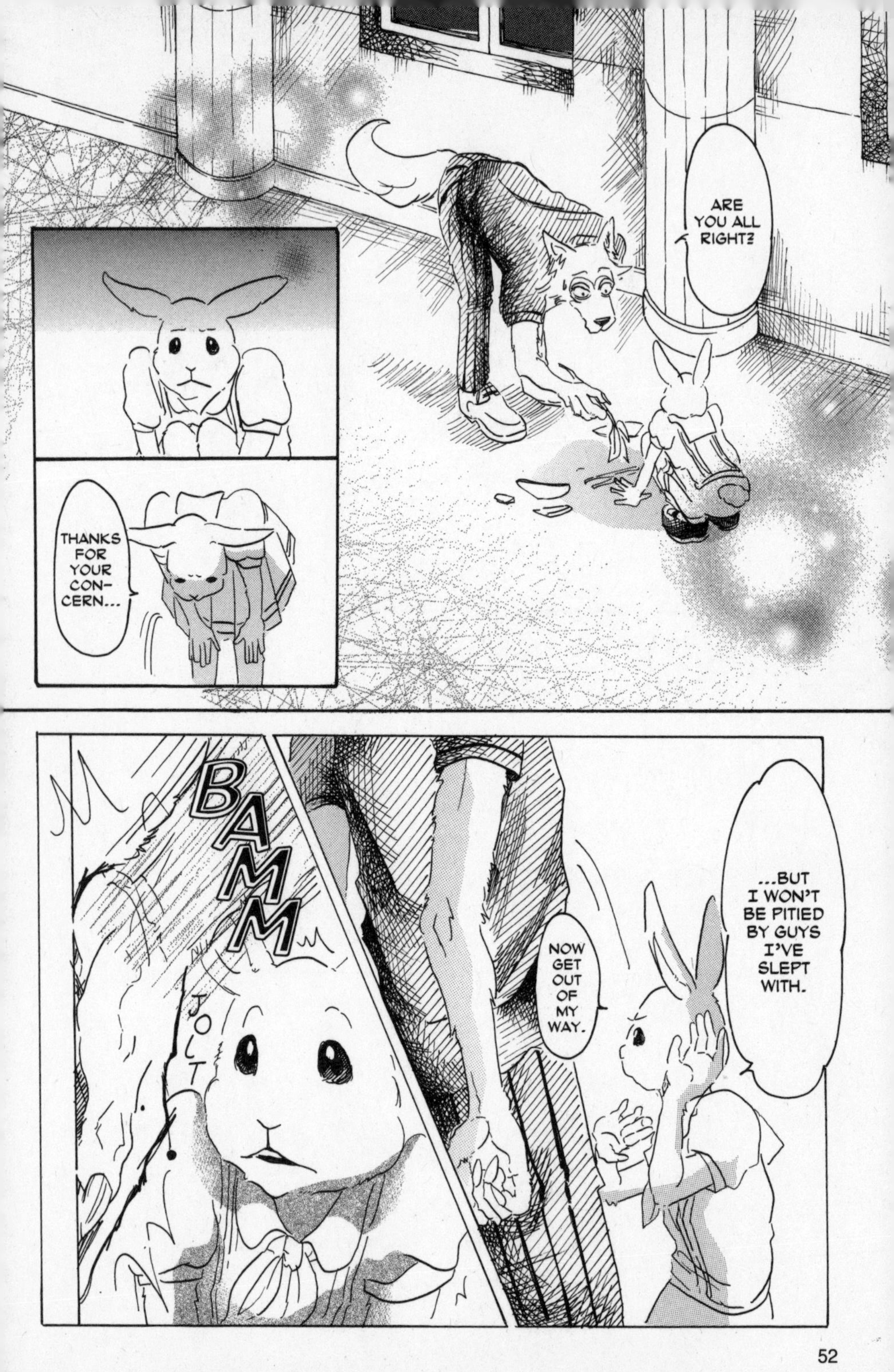
ARE YOU ALL RIGHT?
THANKS FOR YOUR CON-CERN...
...BUT I WON'T BE PITIED BY GUYS I'VE SLEPT WITH.
NOW GET OUT OF MY WAY.
BAMM
JOLT

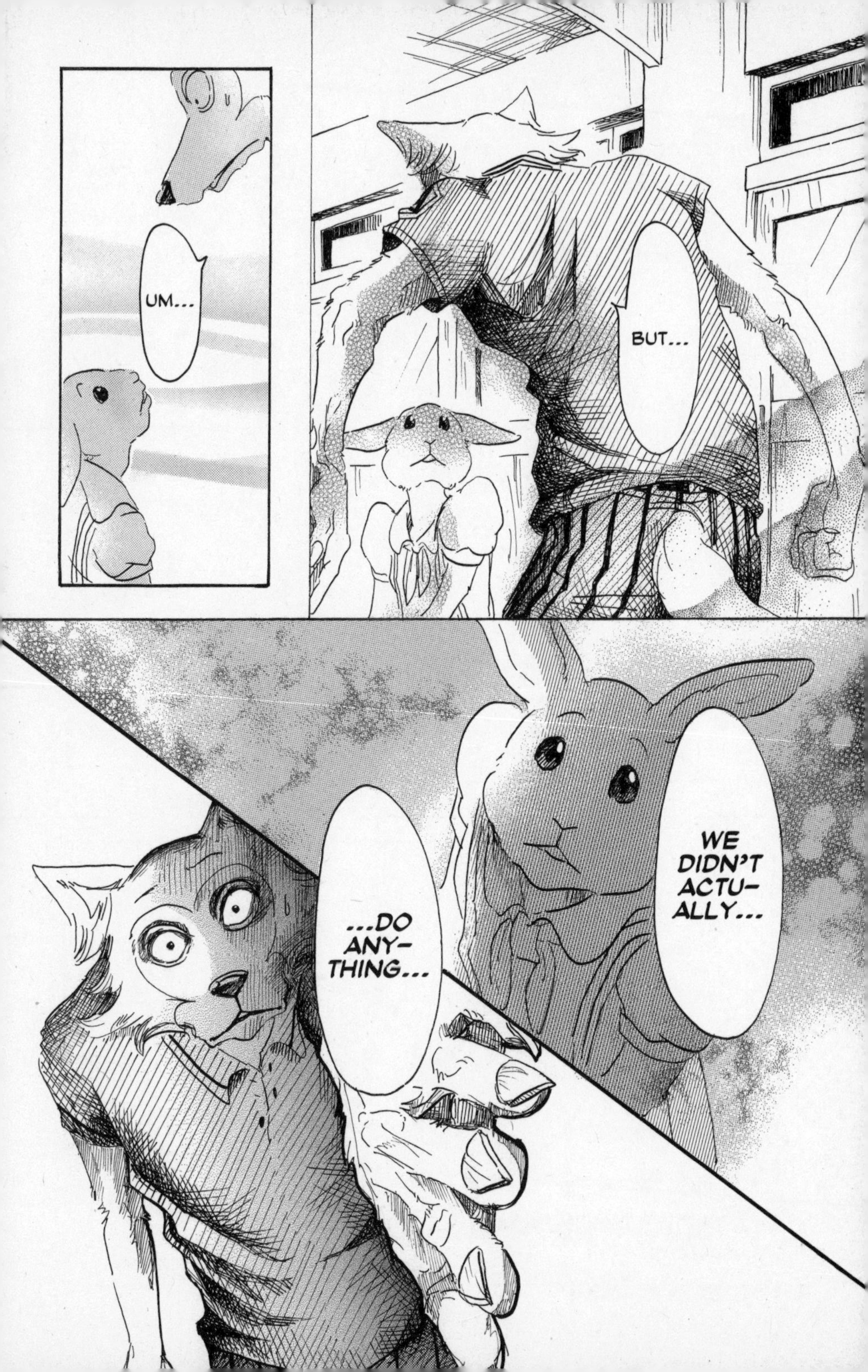
BUT...
UM...
WE DIDN'T ACTU-ALLY...
...DO ANY-THING...

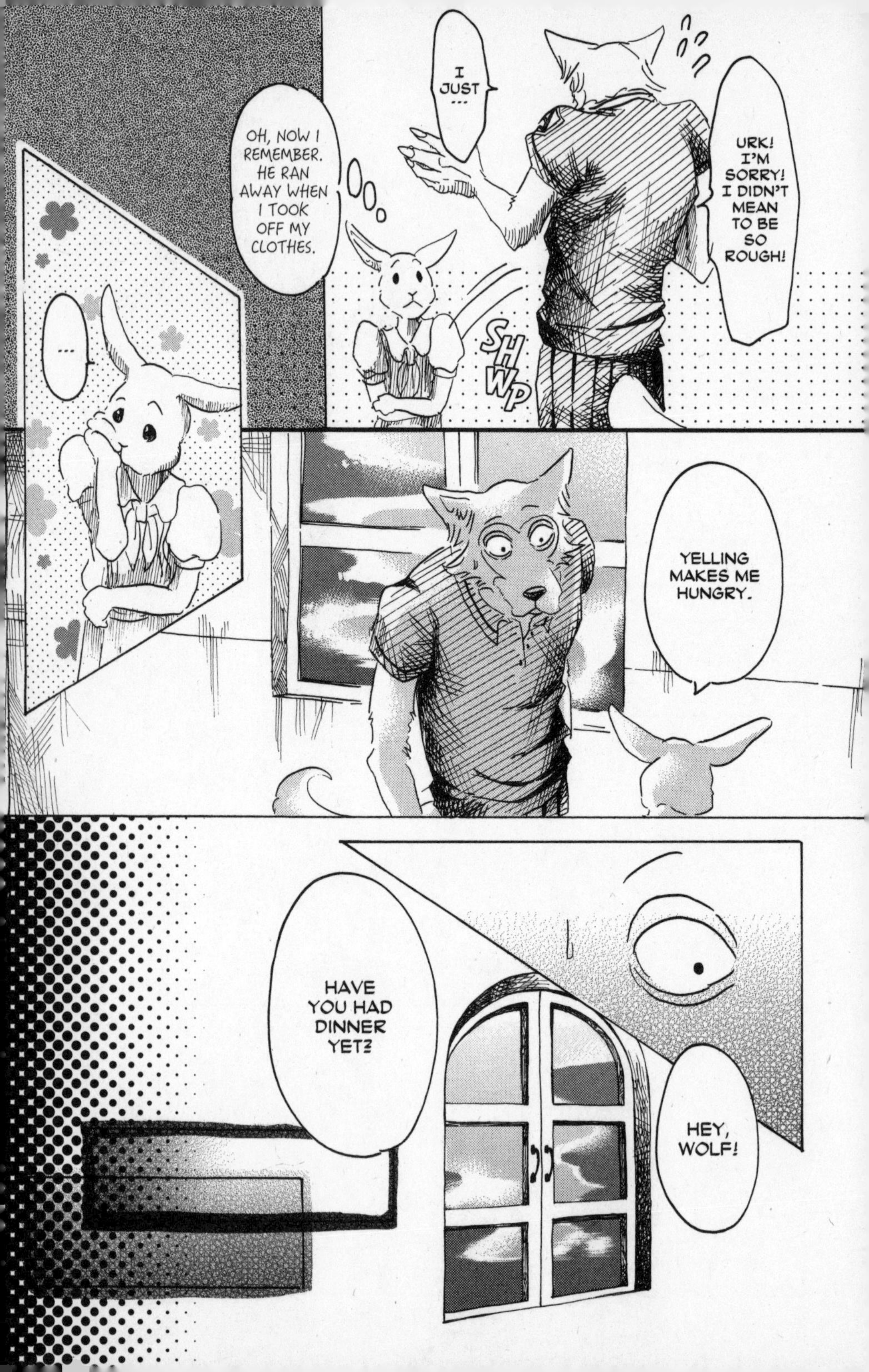
URK! I'M SORRY! I DIDN'T MEAN TO BE SO ROUGH!
I JUST ...
OH, NOW I REMEMBER. HE RAN AWAY WHEN I TOOK OFF MY CLOTHES.
SHWP
YELLING MAKES ME HUNGRY.
...
HEY, WOLF!
HAVE YOU HAD DINNER YET?

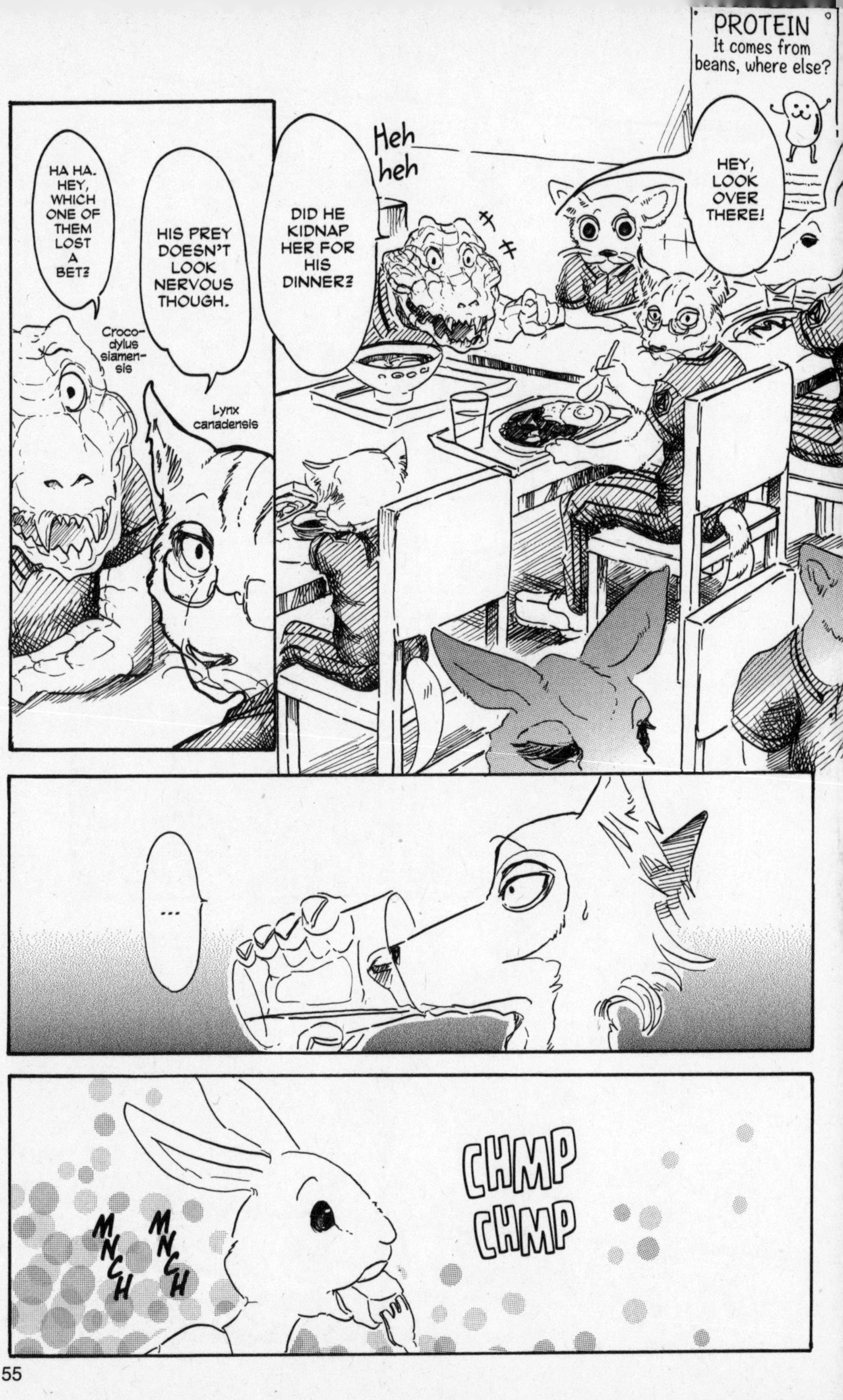

PROTEIN
It comes from beans, where else?
HEY, LOOK OVER THERE!
Heh heh
DID HE KIDNAP HER FOR HIS DINNER?
HIS PREY DOESN'T LOOK NERVOUS THOUGH.
HA HA. HEY, WHICH ONE OF THEM LOST A BET?
Crocodylus siamensis
Lynx canadensis
...
CHMP CHMP
MNCH MNCH

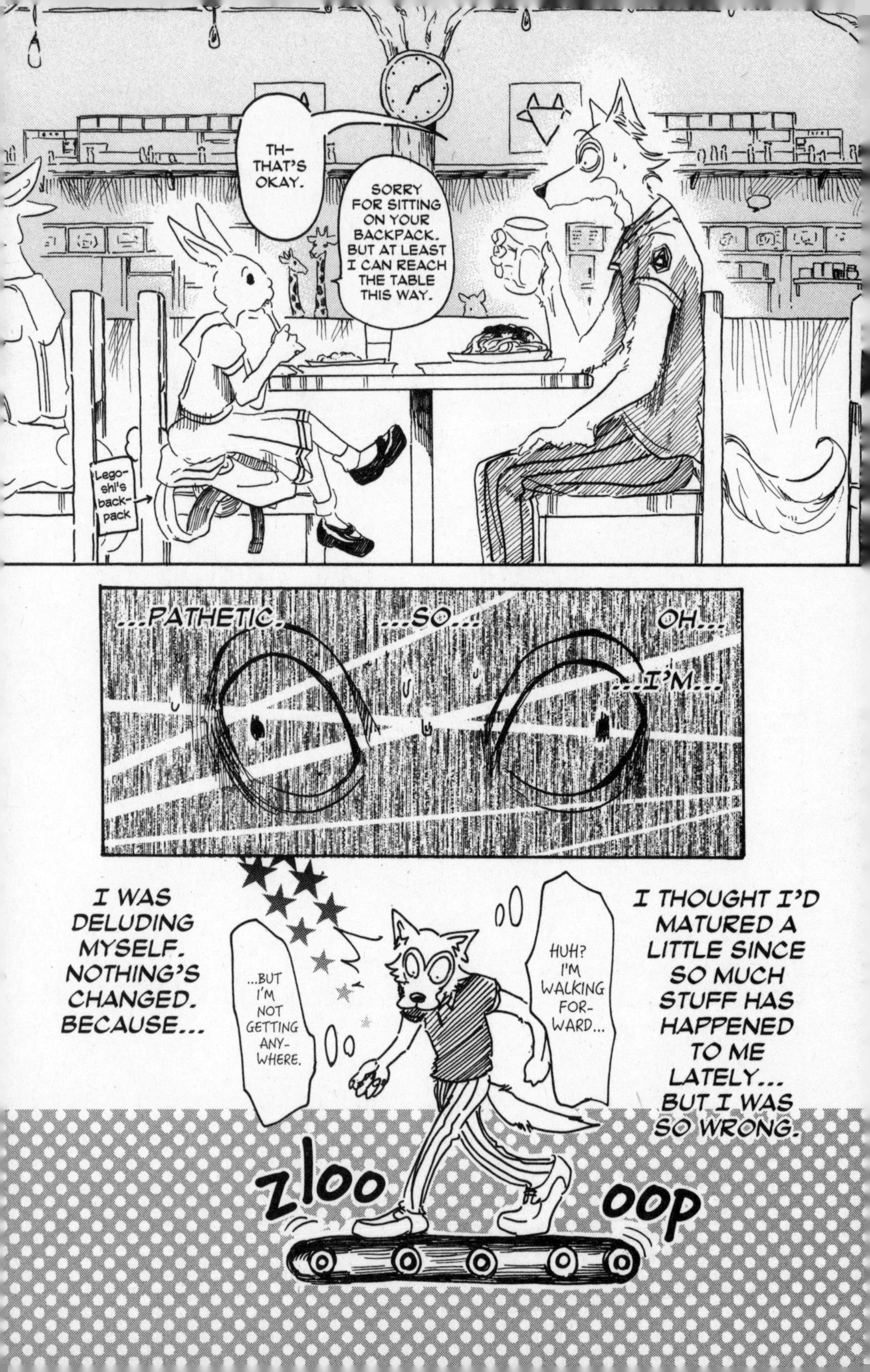
SORRY FOR SITTING ON YOUR BACKPACK. BUT AT LEAST I CAN REACH THE TABLE THIS WAY.
TH- THAT'S OKAY.
Lego-shi's back-pack
OH...
...I'M...
...SO...
...PATHETIC.
I THOUGHT I'D MATURED A LITTLE SINCE SO MUCH STUFF HAS HAPPENED TO ME LATELY... BUT I WAS SO WRONG.
HUH? I'M WALKING FOR-WARD...
...BUT I'M NOT GETTING ANY-WHERE.
I WAS DELUDING MYSELF. NOTHING'S CHANGED. BECAUSE...
ZLOO
OOP

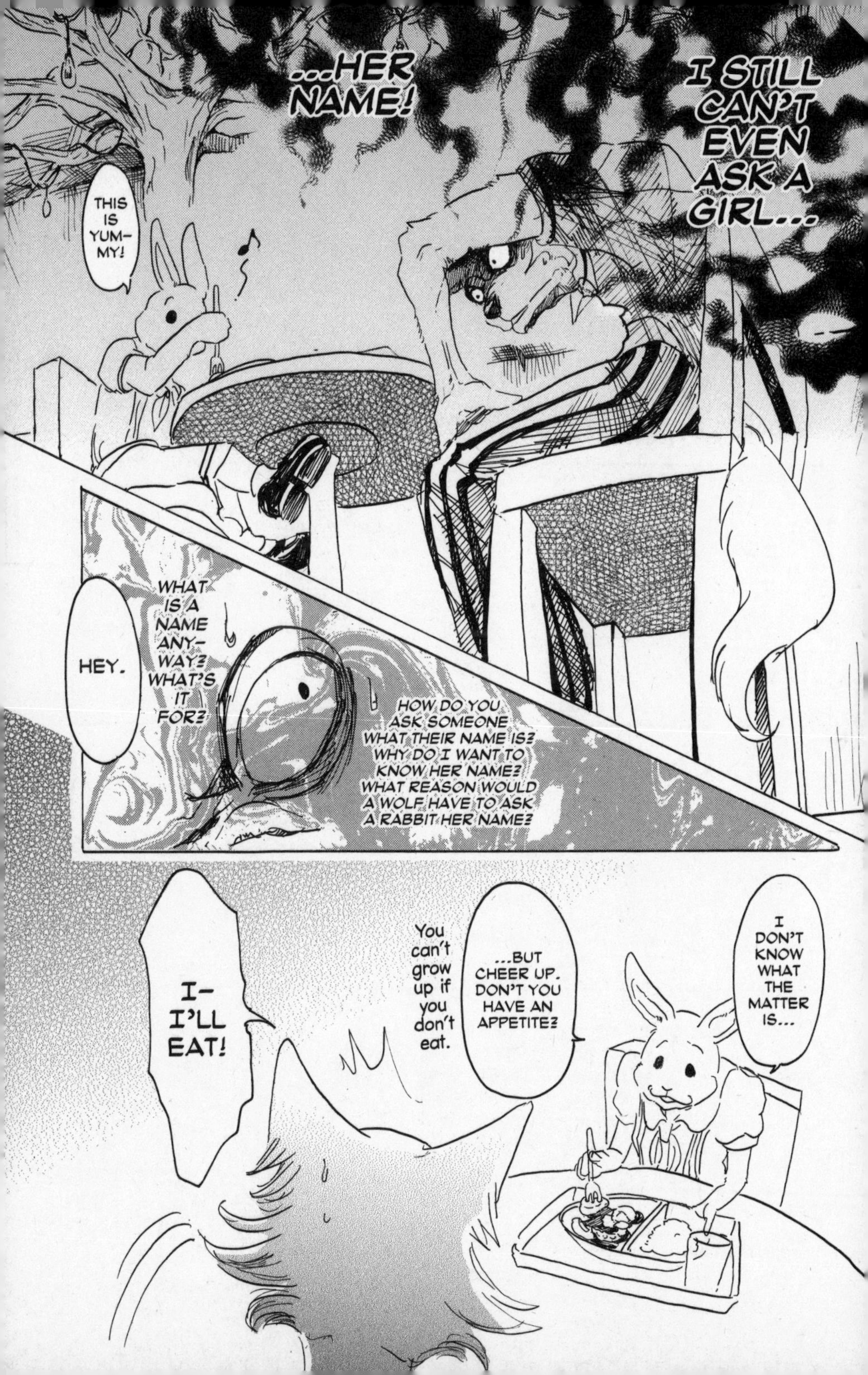
I STILL CAN'T EVEN ASK A GIRL...
...HER NAME!
THIS IS YUM-MY!
HOW DO YOU ASK SOMEONE WHAT THEIR NAME IS? WHY DO I WANT TO KNOW HER NAME? WHAT REASON WOULD A WOLF HAVE TO ASK A RABBIT HER NAME?
WHAT IS A NAME ANY-WAY? WHAT'S IT FOR?
HEY.
I DON'T KNOW WHAT THE MATTER IS...
...BUT CHEER UP. DON'T YOU HAVE AN APPETITE?
You can't grow up if you don't eat.
I- I'LL EAT!

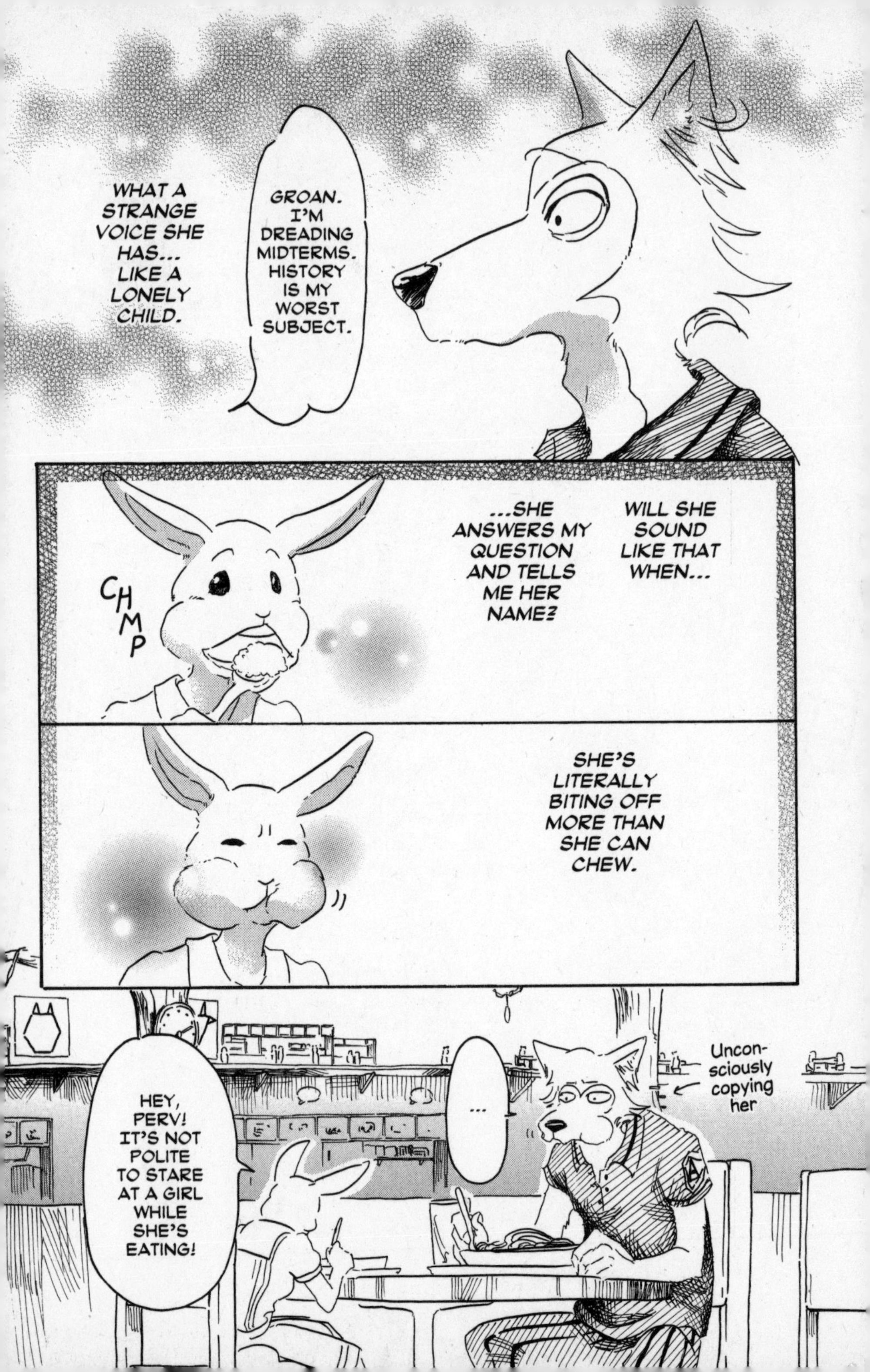

GROAN. I'M DREADING MIDTERMS. HISTORY IS MY WORST SUBJECT.
WHAT A STRANGE VOICE SHE HAS... LIKE A LONELY CHILD.
WILL SHE SOUND LIKE THAT WHEN...
...SHE ANSWERS MY QUESTION AND TELLS ME HER NAME?
CHMP
SHE'S LITERALLY BITING OFF MORE THAN SHE CAN CHEW.
Unconsciously copying her
...
HEY, PERV! IT'S NOT POLITE TO STARE AT A GIRL WHILE SHE'S EATING!

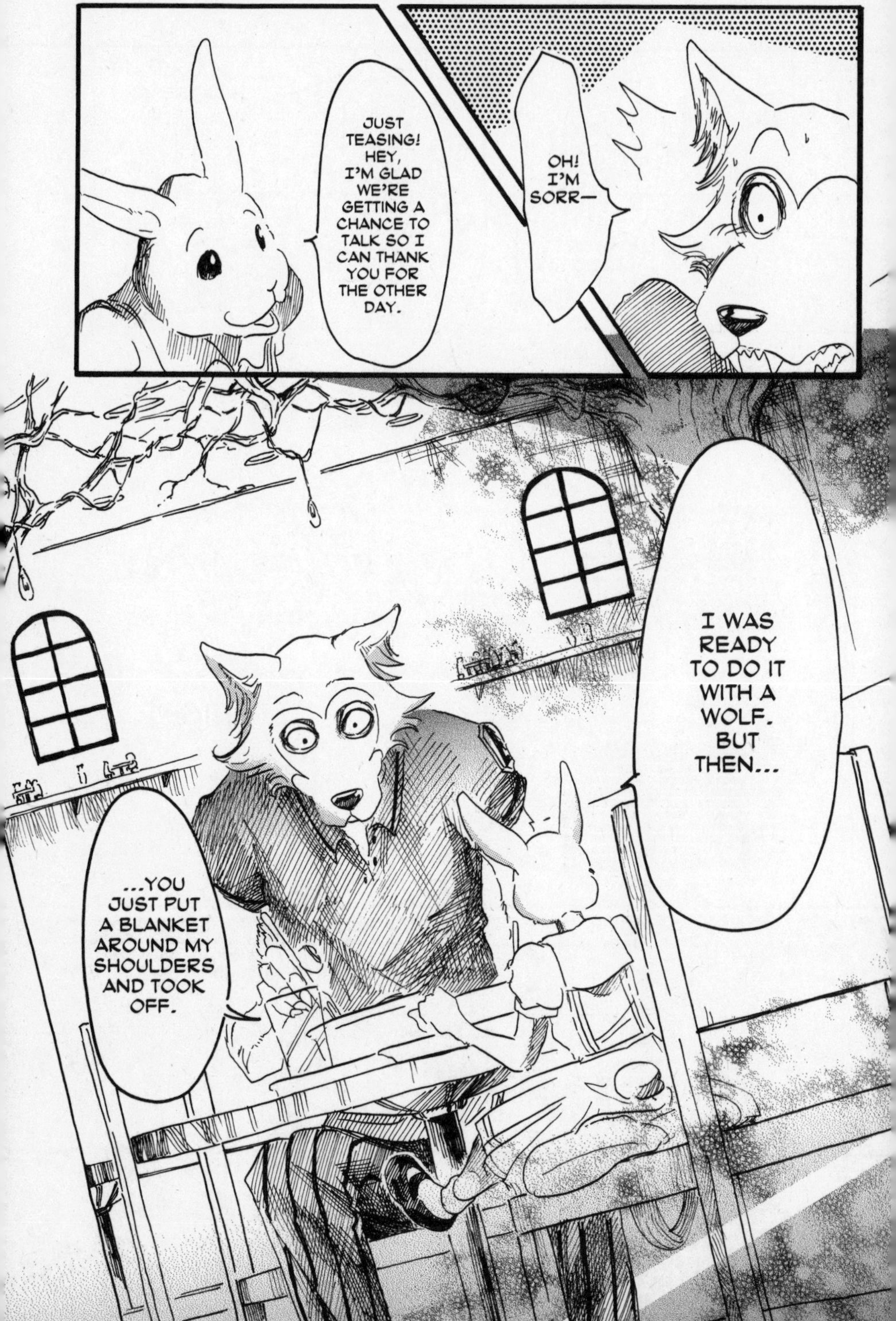
OH! I'M SORR—
JUST TEASING! HEY, I'M GLAD WE'RE GETTING A CHANCE TO TALK SO I CAN THANK YOU FOR THE OTHER DAY.
I WAS READY TO DO IT WITH A WOLF. BUT THEN...
...YOU JUST PUT A BLANKET AROUND MY SHOULDERS AND TOOK OFF.

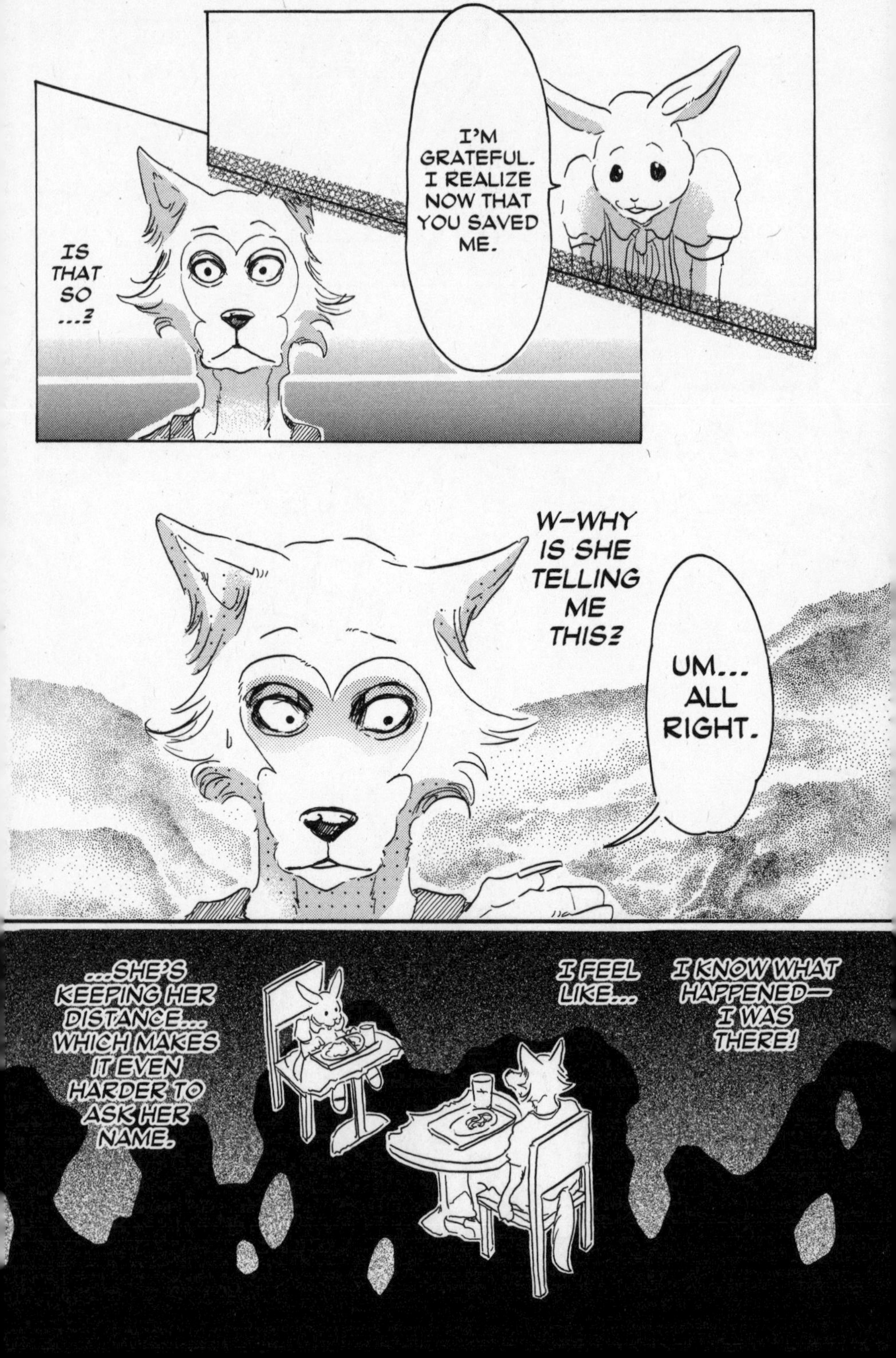
I'M GRATEFUL. I REALIZE NOW THAT YOU SAVED ME.
IS THAT SO...?
W-WHY IS SHE TELLING ME THIS?
UM... ALL RIGHT.
I KNOW WHAT HAPPENED— I WAS THERE!
I FEEL LIKE...
...SHE'S KEEPING HER DISTANCE... WHICH MAKES IT EVEN HARDER TO ASK HER NAME.

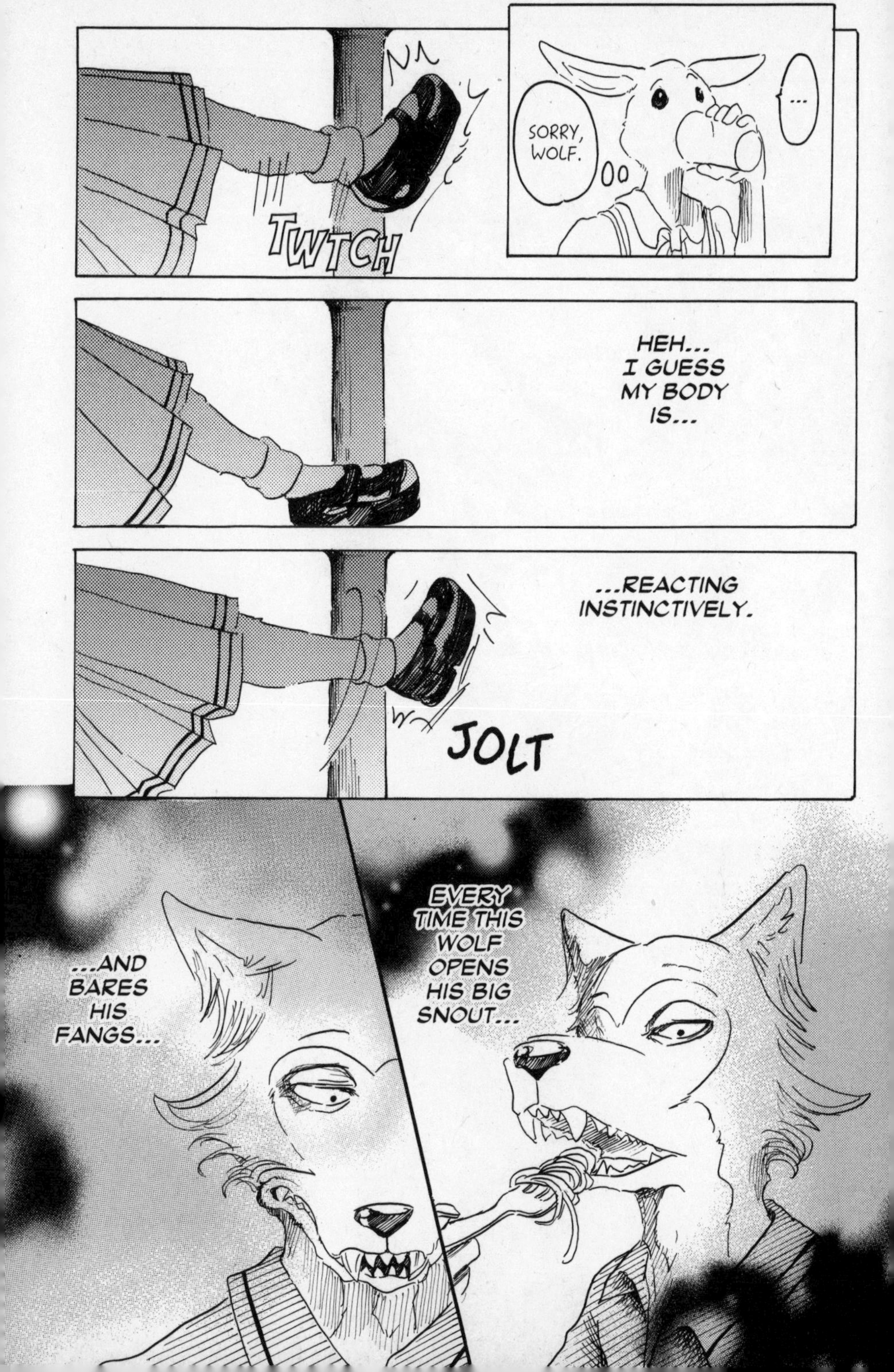
...
SORRY, WOLF.
TWTCH
HEH... I GUESS MY BODY IS...
...REACTING INSTINCTIVELY.
JOLT
EVERY TIME THIS WOLF OPENS HIS BIG SNOUT...
...AND BARES HIS FANGS...

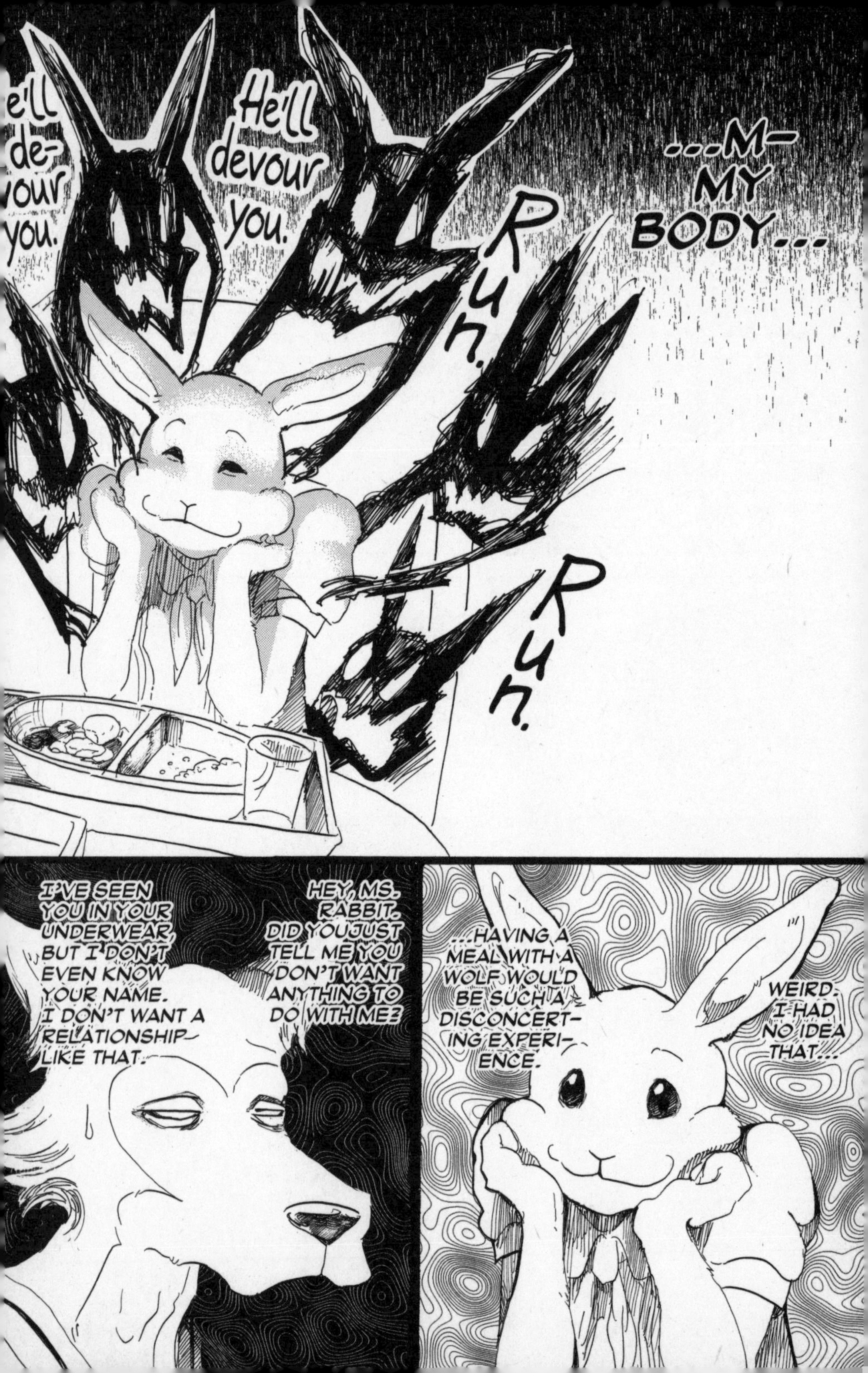
...M- MY BODY...
Run.
Run.
He'll devour you.
e'll de-vour you.
WEIRD. I HAD NO IDEA THAT...
...HAVING A MEAL WITH A WOLF WOULD BE SUCH A DISCONCERT-ING EXPERI-ENCE.
HEY, MS. RABBIT. DID YOU JUST TELL ME YOU DON'T WANT ANYTHING TO DO WITH ME?
I'VE SEEN YOU IN YOUR UNDERWEAR, BUT I DON'T EVEN KNOW YOUR NAME. I DON'T WANT A RELATIONSHIP LIKE THAT.

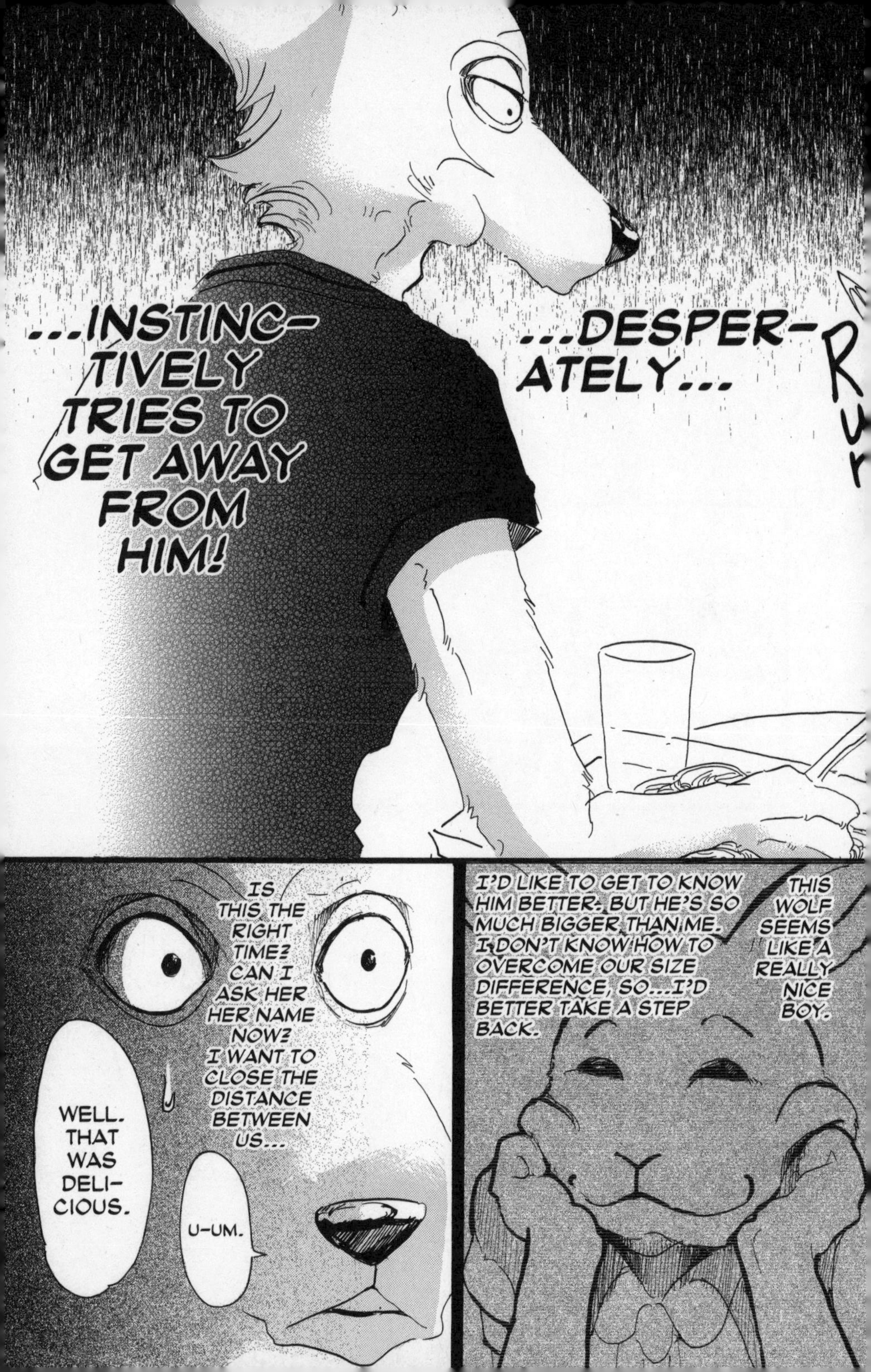
...DESPER-ATELY...
...INSTINC-TIVELY TRIES TO GET AWAY FROM HIM!
THIS WOLF SEEMS LIKE A REALLY NICE BOY.
I'D LIKE TO GET TO KNOW HIM BETTER. BUT HE'S SO MUCH BIGGER THAN ME. I DON'T KNOW HOW TO OVERCOME OUR SIZE DIFFERENCE, SO...I'D BETTER TAKE A STEP BACK.
IS THIS THE RIGHT TIME? CAN I ASK HER HER NAME NOW? I WANT TO CLOSE THE DISTANCE BETWEEN US...
U-UM.
WELL. THAT WAS DELICIOUS.

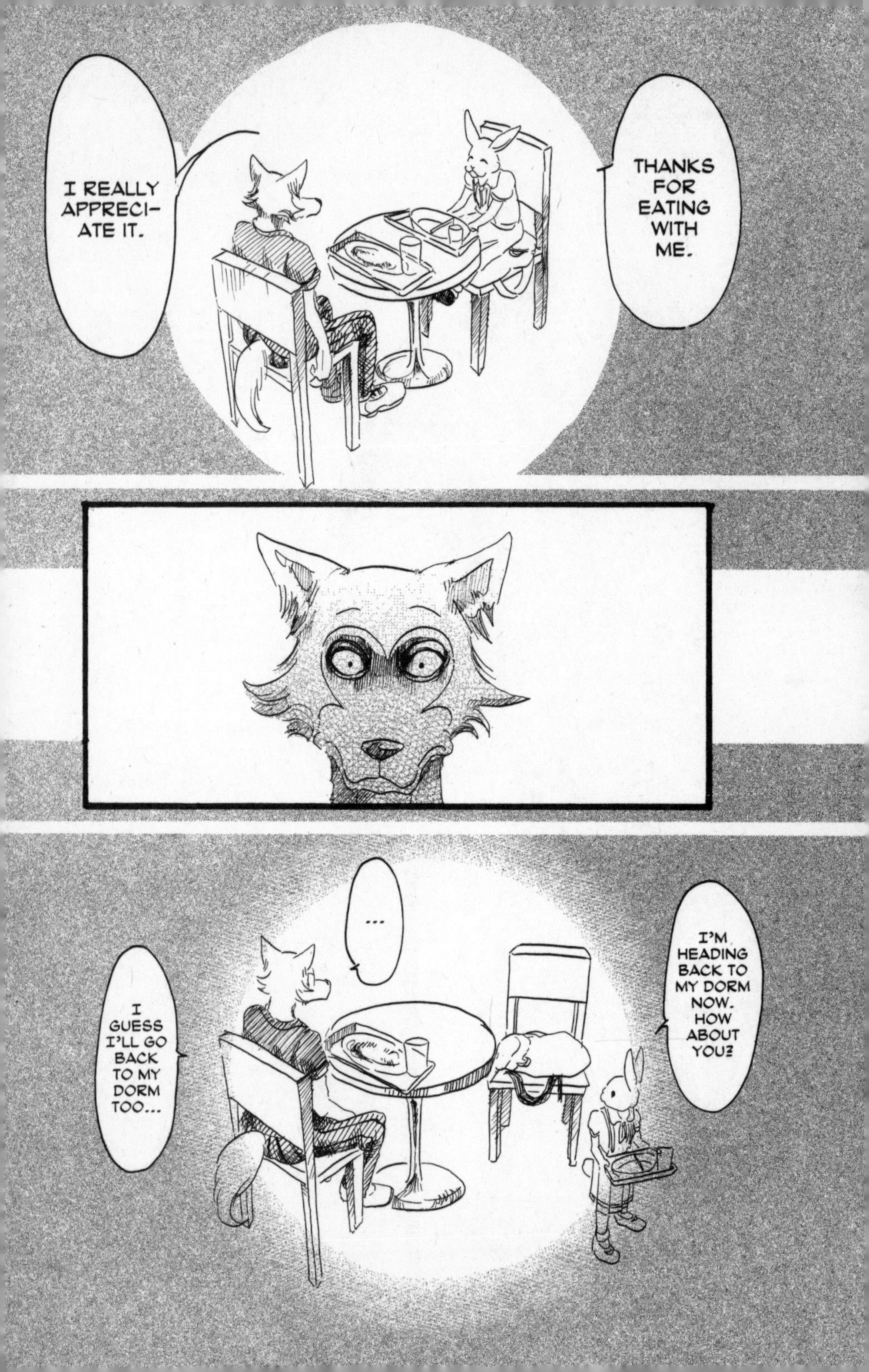
THANKS FOR EATING WITH ME.
I REALLY APPRECIATE IT.
I'M HEADING BACK TO MY DORM NOW. HOW ABOUT YOU?
...
I GUESS I'LL GO BACK TO MY DORM TOO...

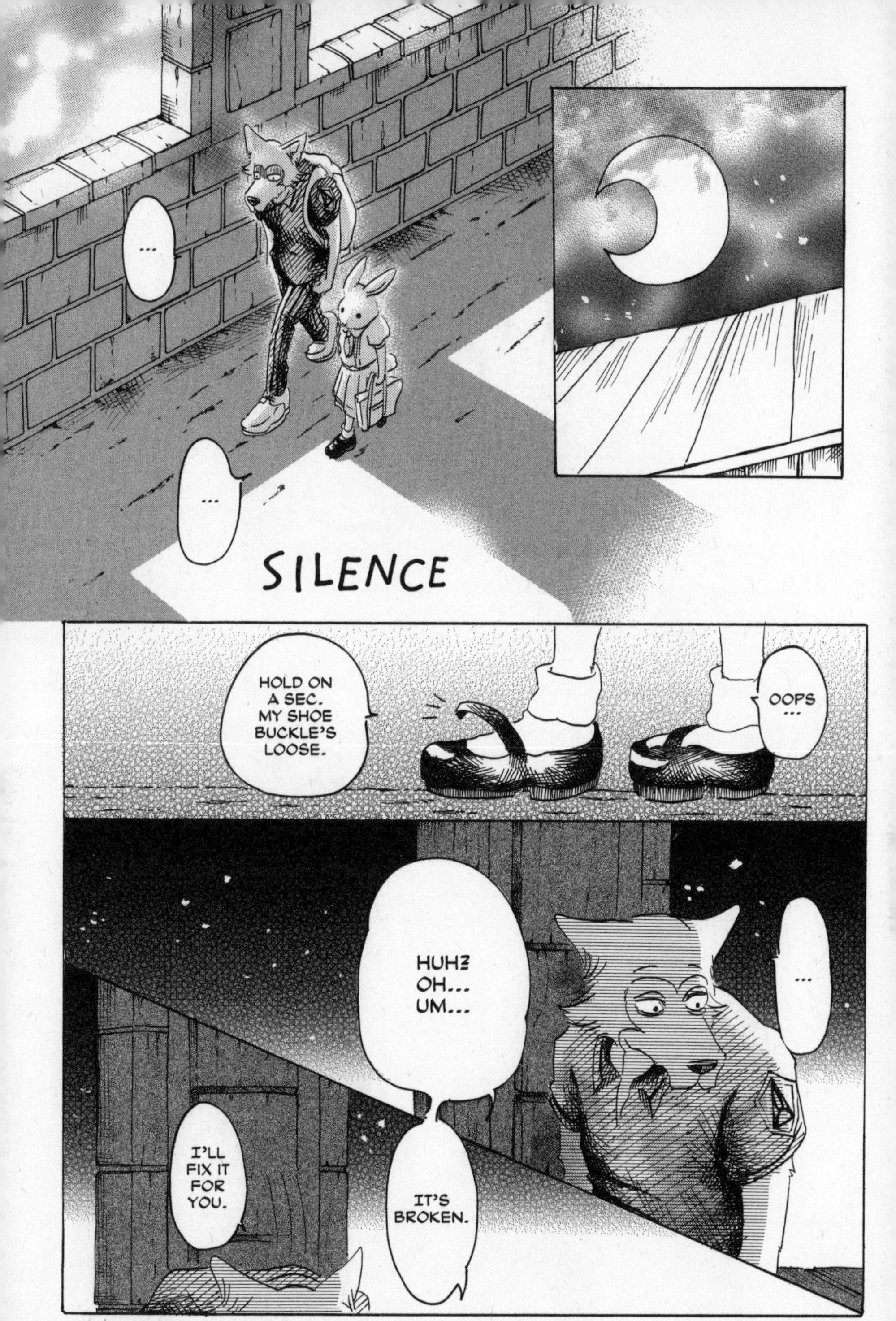
...
...
SILENCE
OOPS ...
HOLD ON A SEC. MY SHOE BUCKLE'S LOOSE.
...
HUH? OH... UM...
IT'S BROKEN.
I'LL FIX IT FOR YOU.

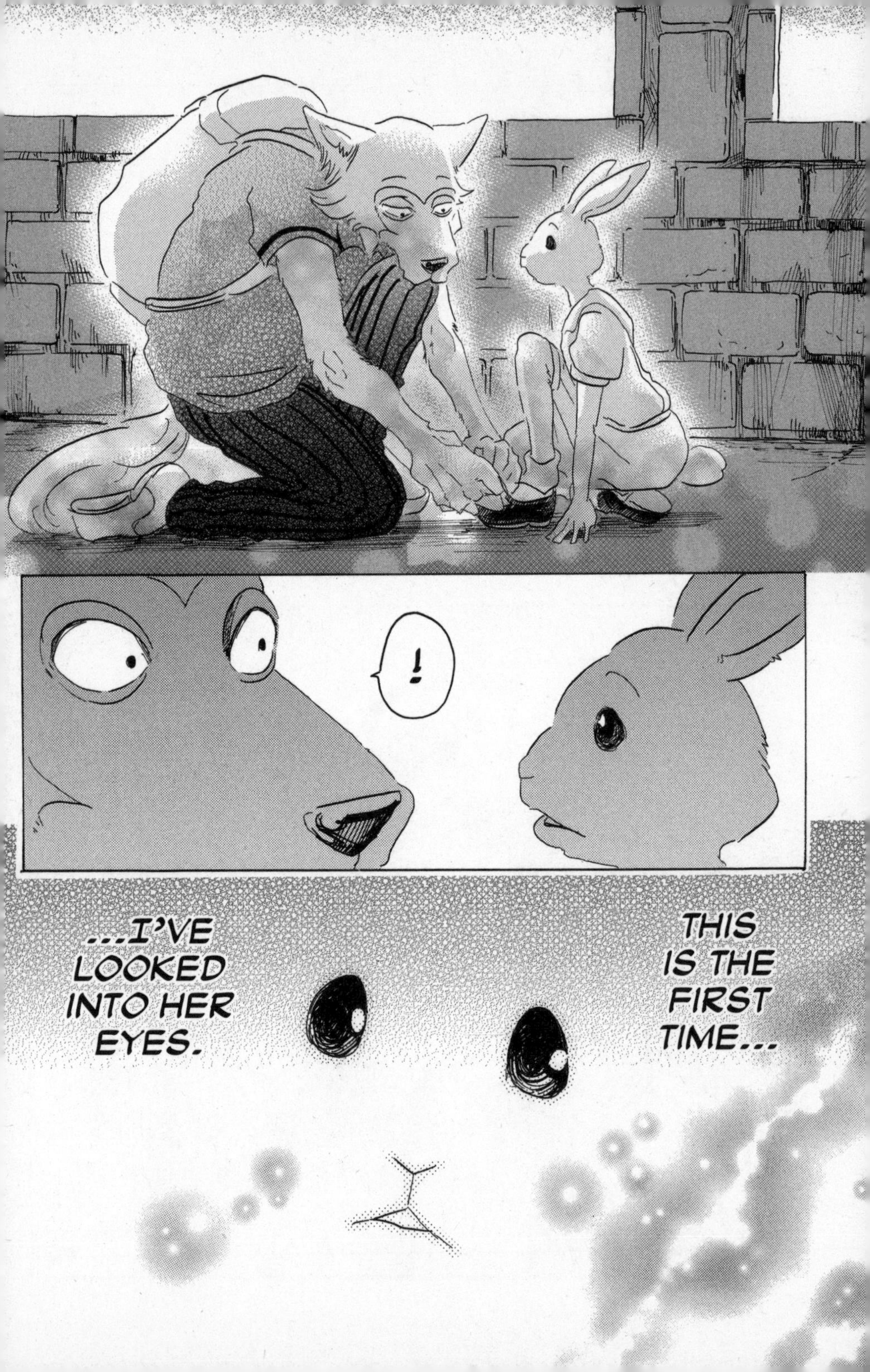
!
THIS IS THE FIRST TIME...
...I'VE LOOKED INTO HER EYES.

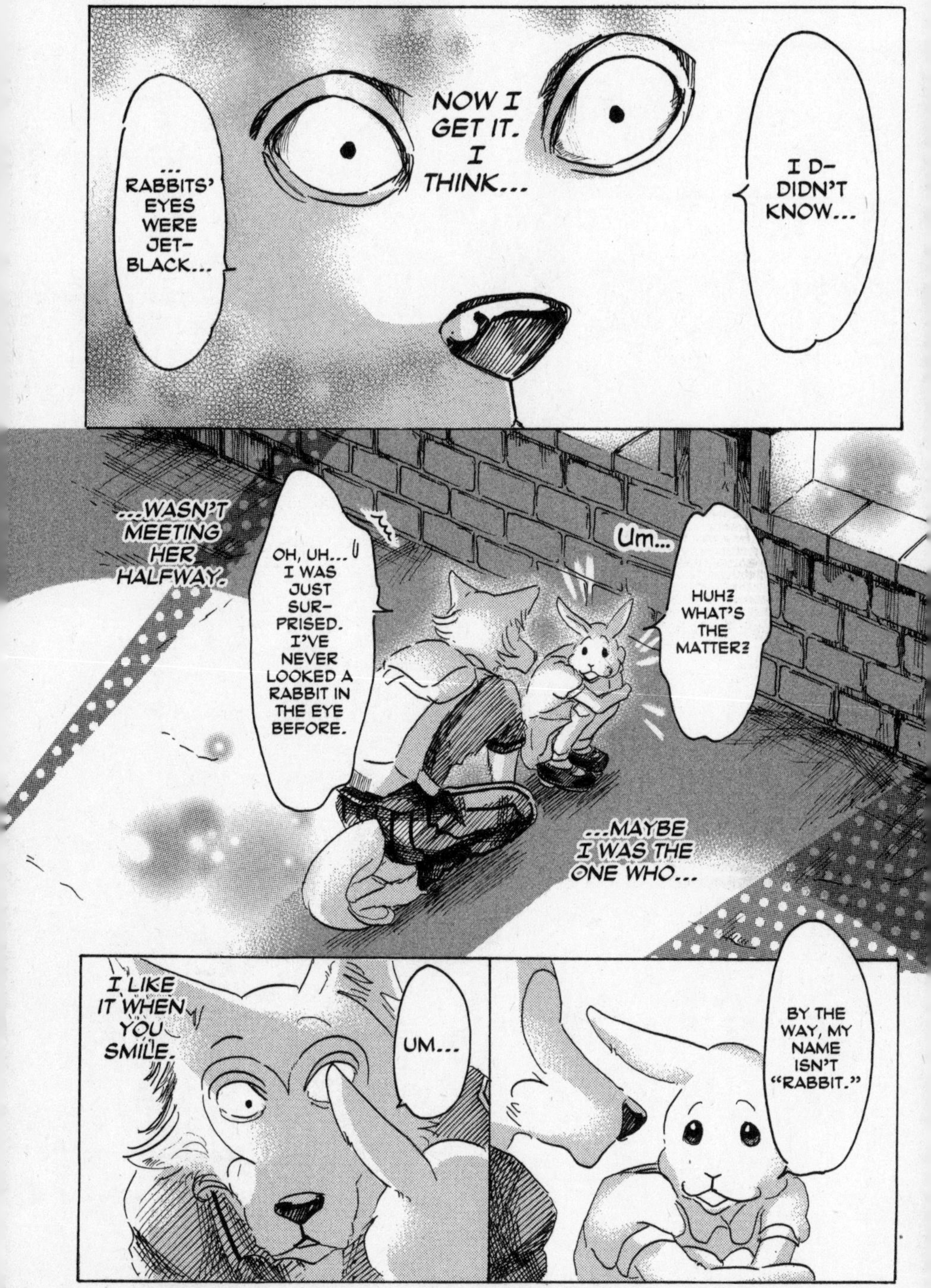
I D-DIDN'T KNOW...
NOW I GET IT. I THINK...
...RABBITS' EYES WERE JET-BLACK...
Um...
HUH? WHAT'S THE MATTER?
OH, UH... I WAS JUST SUR-PRISED. I'VE NEVER LOOKED A RABBIT IN THE EYE BEFORE.
...MAYBE I WAS THE ONE WHO...
...WASN'T MEETING HER HALFWAY.
BY THE WAY, MY NAME ISN'T "RABBIT."
UM...
I LIKE IT WHEN YOU SMILE.

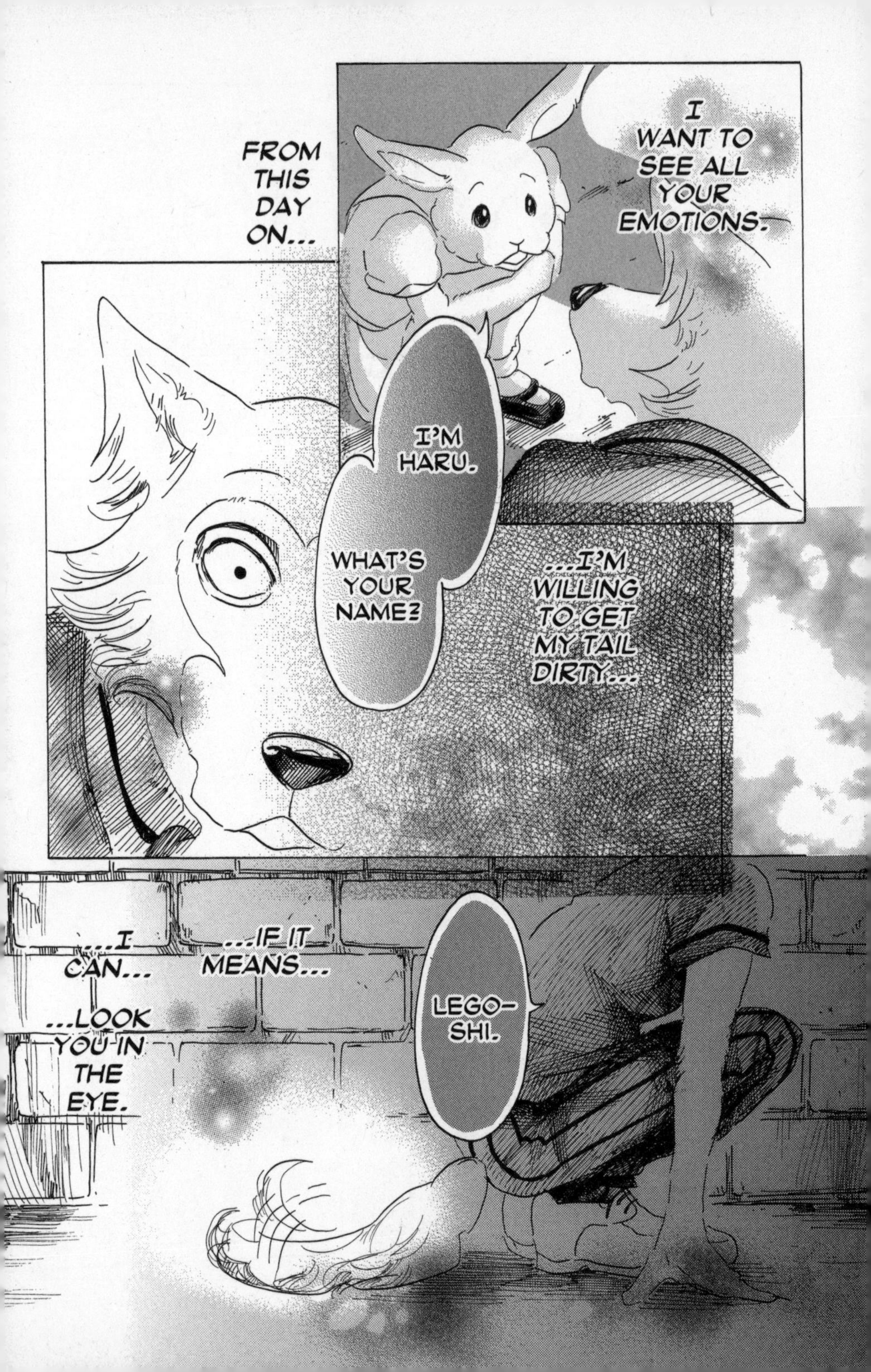

I WANT TO SEE ALL YOUR EMOTIONS.
FROM THIS DAY ON...
I'M HARU.
WHAT'S YOUR NAME?
...I'M WILLING TO GET MY TAIL DIRTY...
LEGO-SHI.
...IF IT MEANS...
...I CAN...
...LOOK YOU IN THE EYE.

Chapter 20: The Client Next Door

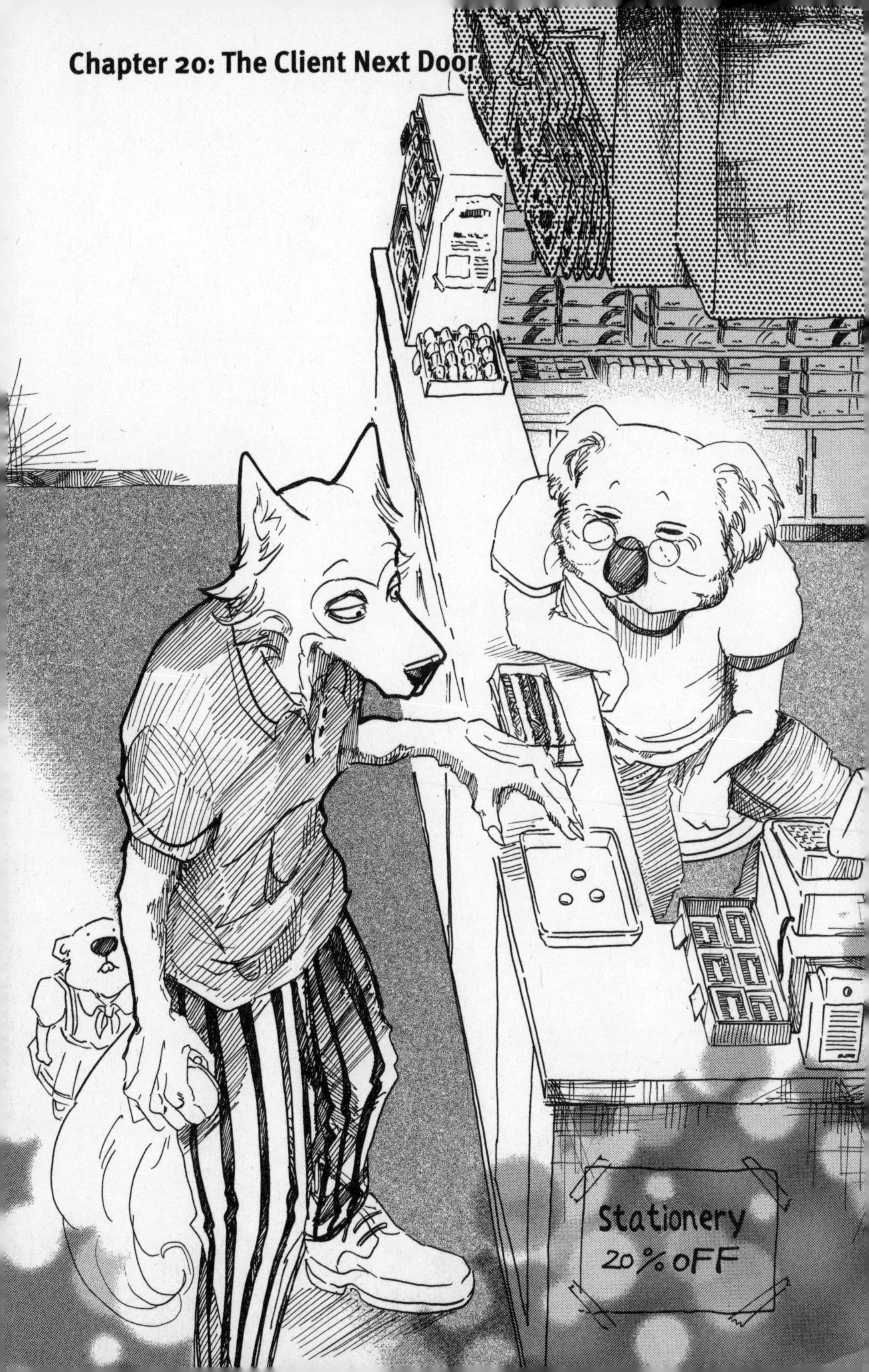
Stationery
20% OFF

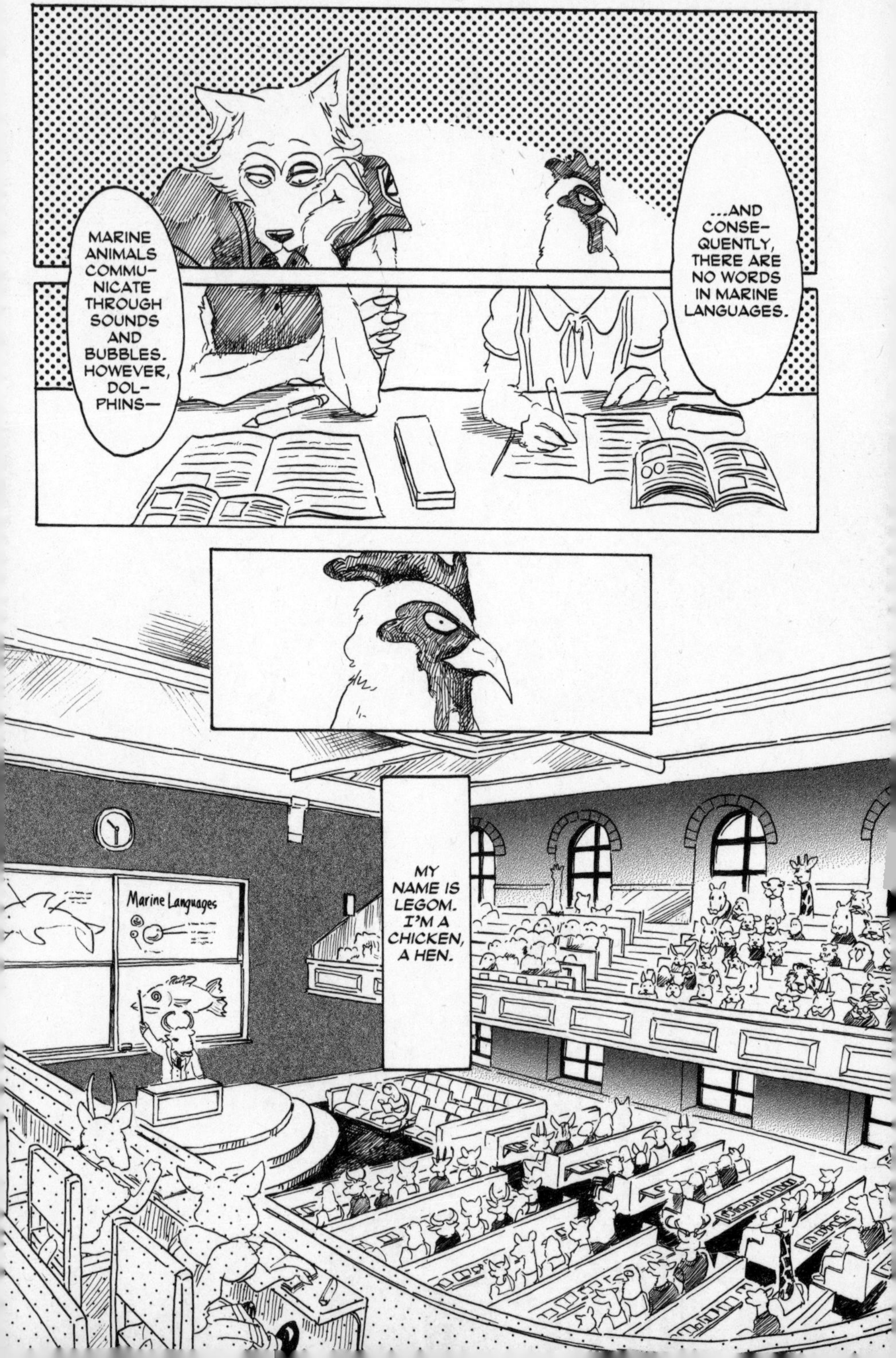
...AND CONSEQUENTLY, THERE ARE NO WORDS IN MARINE LANGUAGES.
MARINE ANIMALS COMMUNICATE THROUGH SOUNDS AND BUBBLES. HOWEVER, DOLPHINS—
MY NAME IS LEGOM. I'M A CHICKEN, A HEN.
Marine Languages

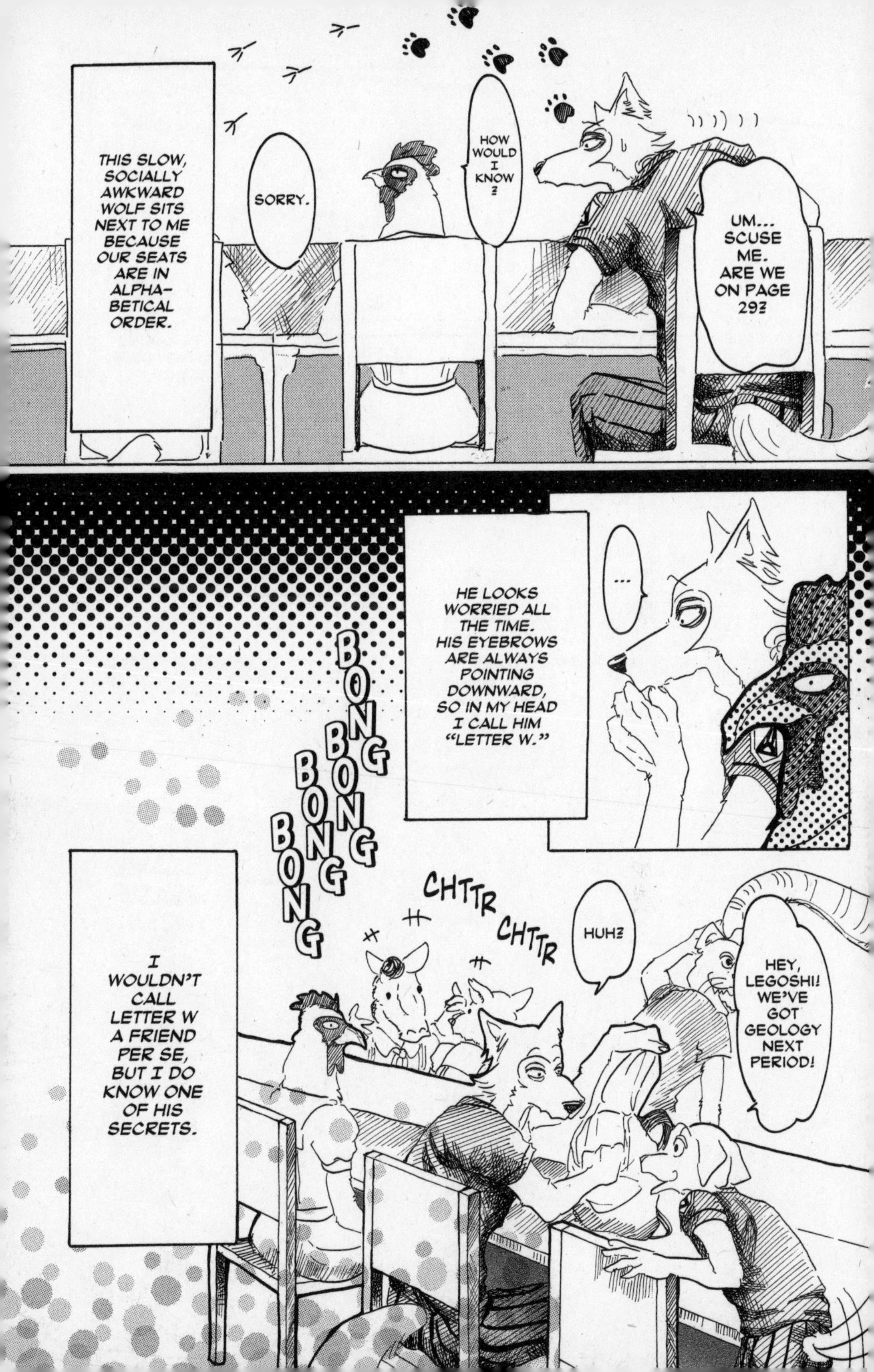
UM... SCUSE ME. ARE WE ON PAGE 29?
HOW WOULD I KNOW?
SORRY.
THIS SLOW, SOCIALLY AWKWARD WOLF SITS NEXT TO ME BECAUSE OUR SEATS ARE IN ALPHA-BETICAL ORDER.
...
HE LOOKS WORRIED ALL THE TIME. HIS EYEBROWS ARE ALWAYS POINTING DOWNWARD, SO IN MY HEAD I CALL HIM "LETTER W."
BONG BONG BONG BONG
HEY, LEGOSHI! WE'VE GOT GEOLOGY NEXT PERIOD!
HUH?
CHTTR CHTTR
I WOULDN'T CALL LETTER W A FRIEND PER SE, BUT I DO KNOW ONE OF HIS SECRETS.

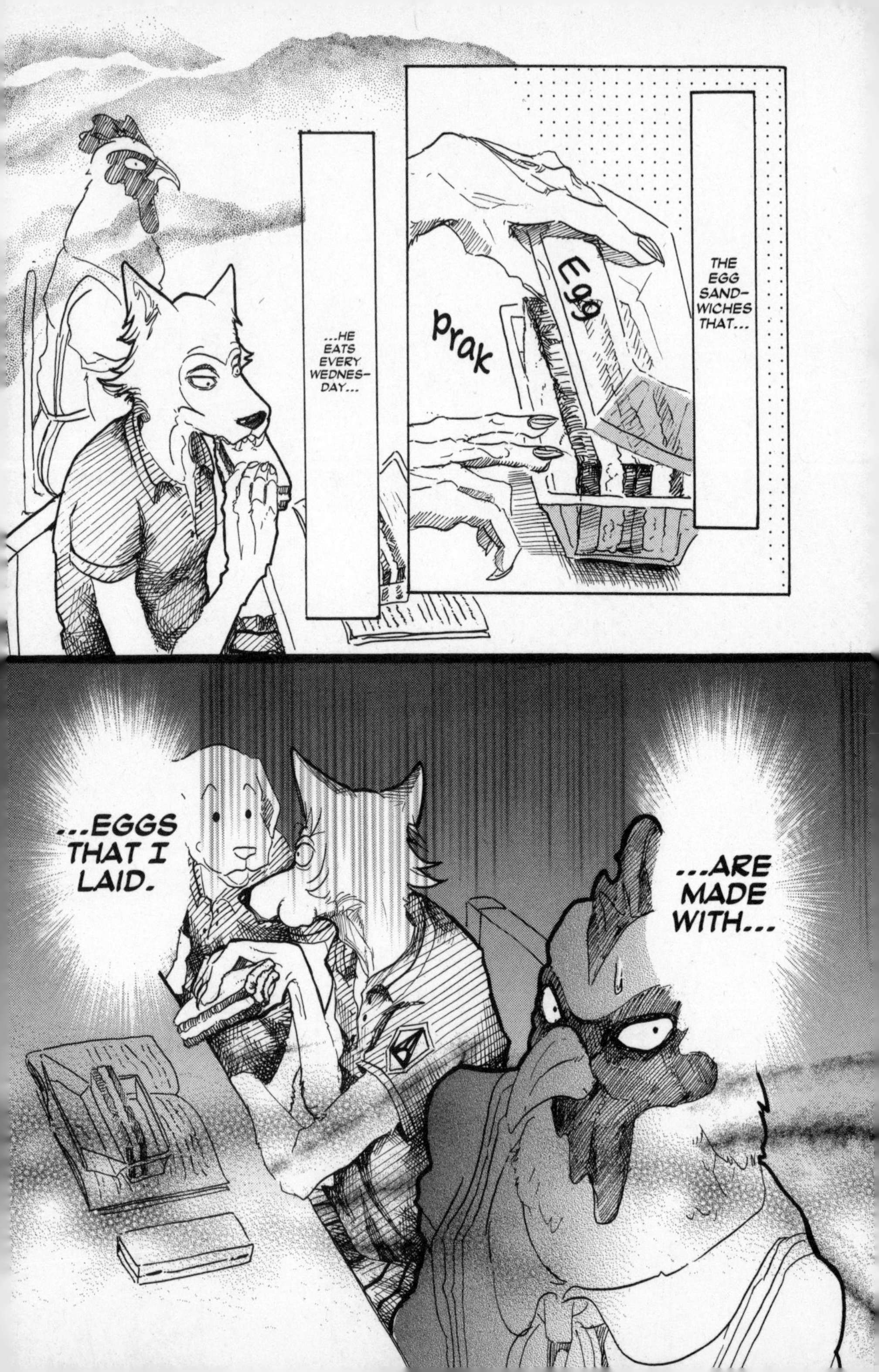
THE EGG SANDWICHES THAT...
Egg
prak
...HE EATS EVERY WEDNESDAY...
...ARE MADE WITH...
...EGGS THAT I LAID.

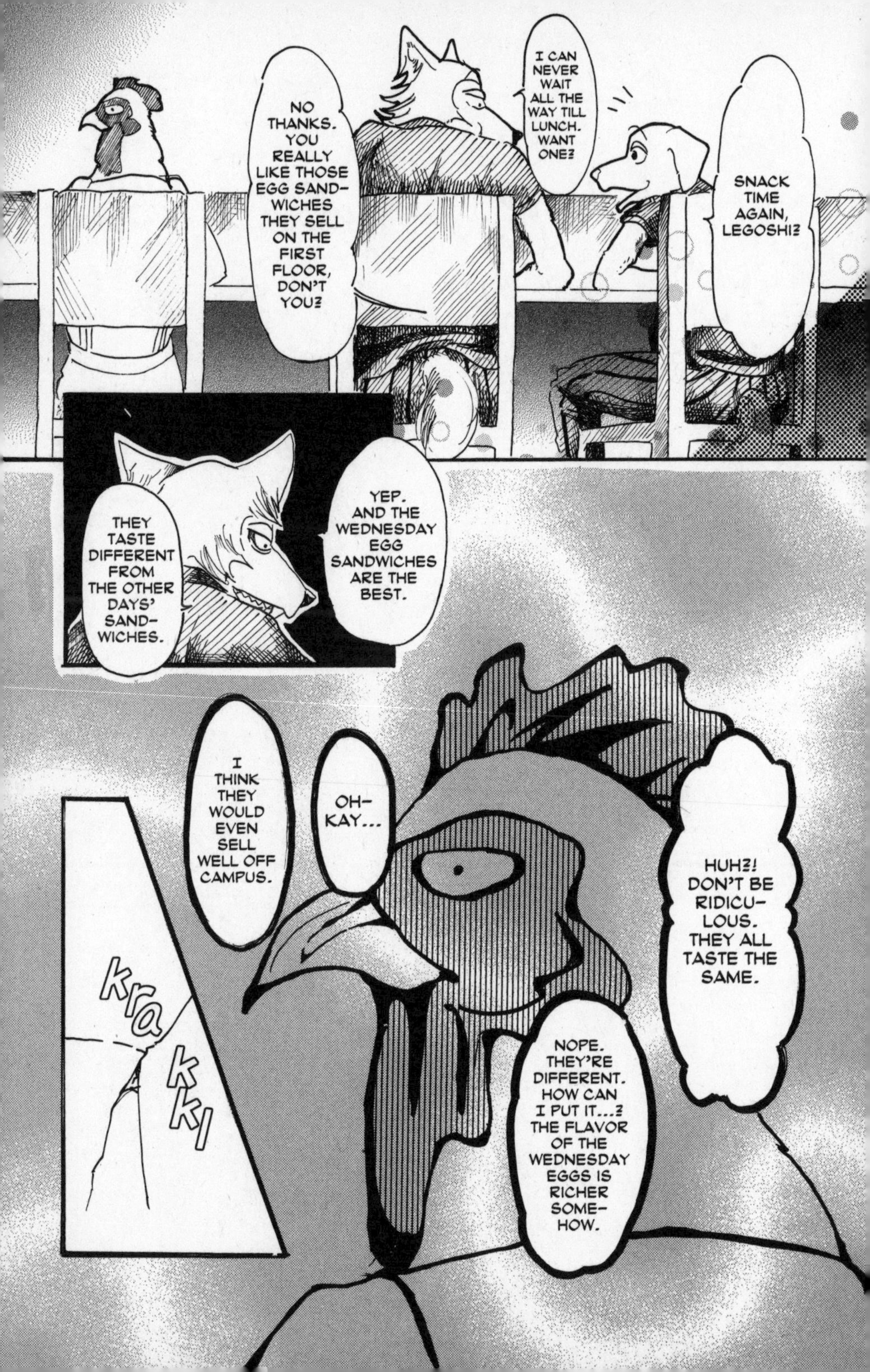
SNACK TIME AGAIN, LEGOSHI?
I CAN NEVER WAIT ALL THE WAY TILL LUNCH. WANT ONE?
NO THANKS. YOU REALLY LIKE THOSE EGG SANDWICHES THEY SELL ON THE FIRST FLOOR, DON'T YOU?
YEP. AND THE WEDNESDAY EGG SANDWICHES ARE THE BEST.
THEY TASTE DIFFERENT FROM THE OTHER DAYS' SANDWICHES.
HUH?! DON'T BE RIDICULOUS. THEY ALL TASTE THE SAME.
NOPE. THEY'RE DIFFERENT. HOW CAN I PUT IT...? THE FLAVOR OF THE WEDNESDAY EGGS IS RICHER SOMEHOW.
OH-KAY...
I THINK THEY WOULD EVEN SELL WELL OFF CAMPUS.
krakki

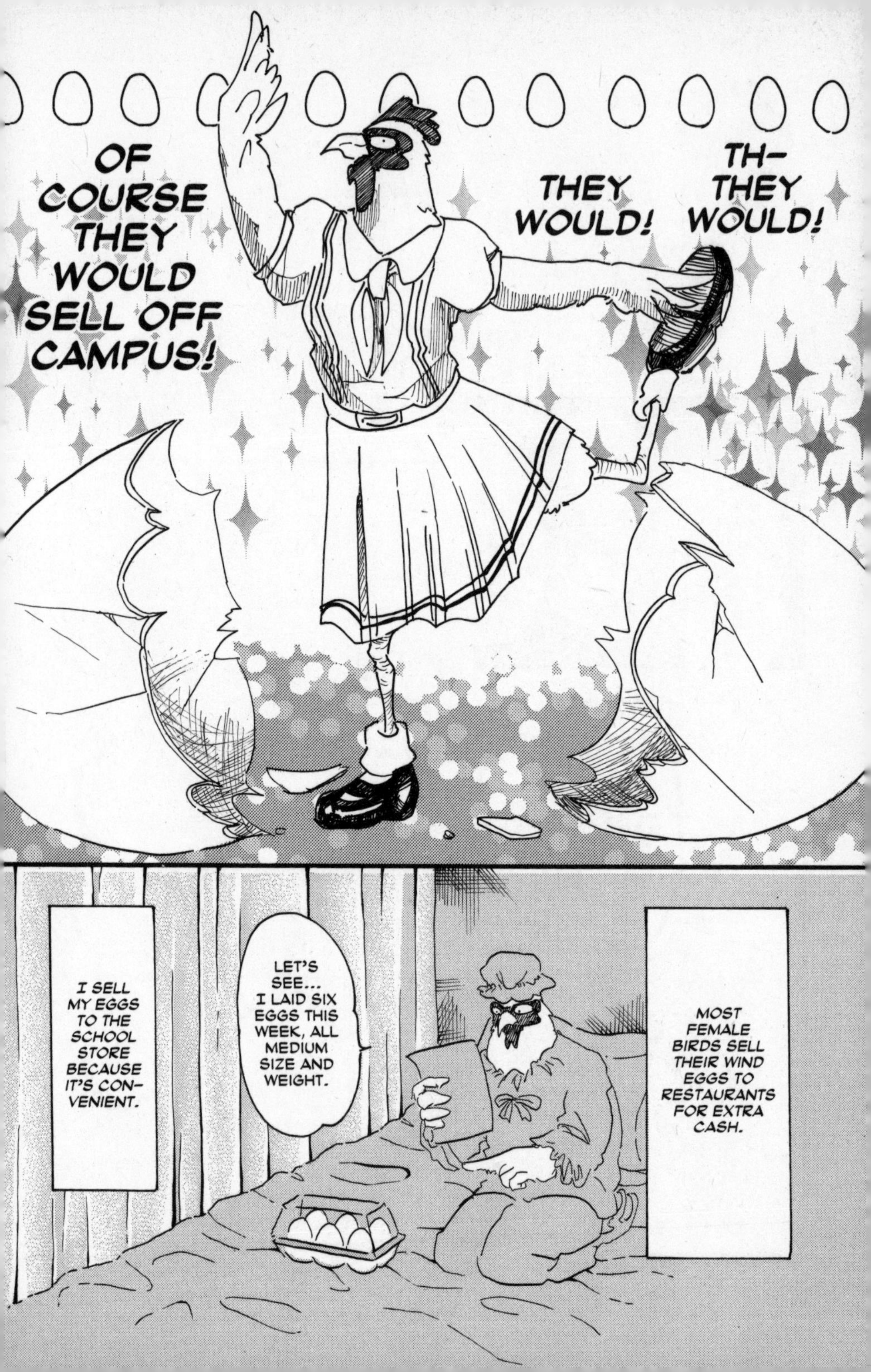
TH- THEY WOULD!
THEY WOULD!
OF COURSE THEY WOULD SELL OFF CAMPUS!
MOST FEMALE BIRDS SELL THEIR WIND EGGS TO RESTAURANTS FOR EXTRA CASH.
LET'S SEE... I LAID SIX EGGS THIS WEEK, ALL MEDIUM SIZE AND WEIGHT.
I SELL MY EGGS TO THE SCHOOL STORE BECAUSE IT'S CONVENIENT.

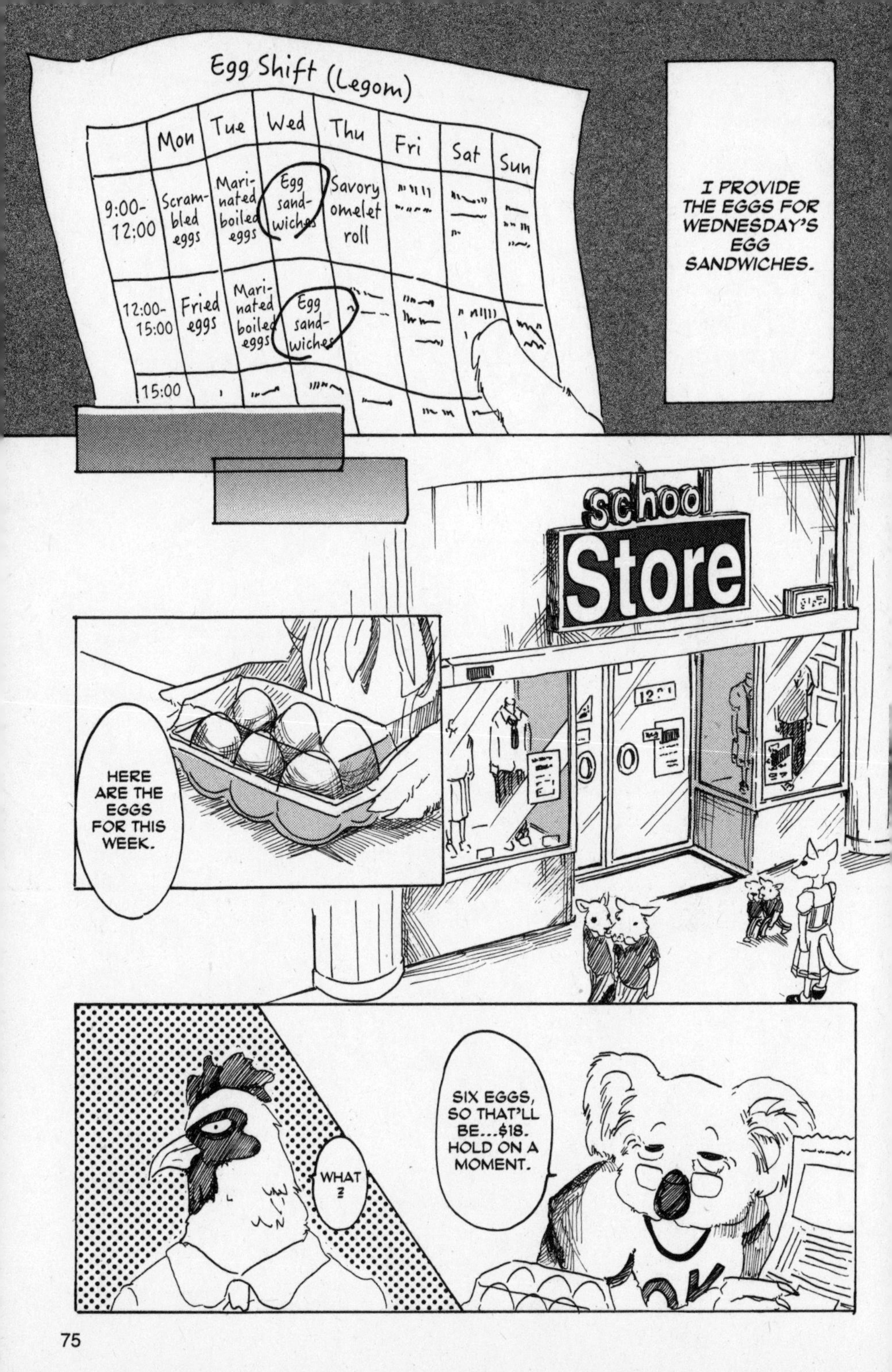
I PROVIDE THE EGGS FOR WEDNESDAY'S EGG SANDWICHES.
Egg Shift (Legom)
Mon Tue Wed Thu Fri Sat Sun
9:00-12:00 Scram-bled eggs Mari-nated boiled eggs Egg sand-wiches Savory omelet roll
12:00-15:00 Fried eggs Mari-nated boiled eggs Egg sand-wiches
15:00
school Store
HERE ARE THE EGGS FOR THIS WEEK.
SIX EGGS, SO THAT'LL BE...$18. HOLD ON A MOMENT.
WHAT?

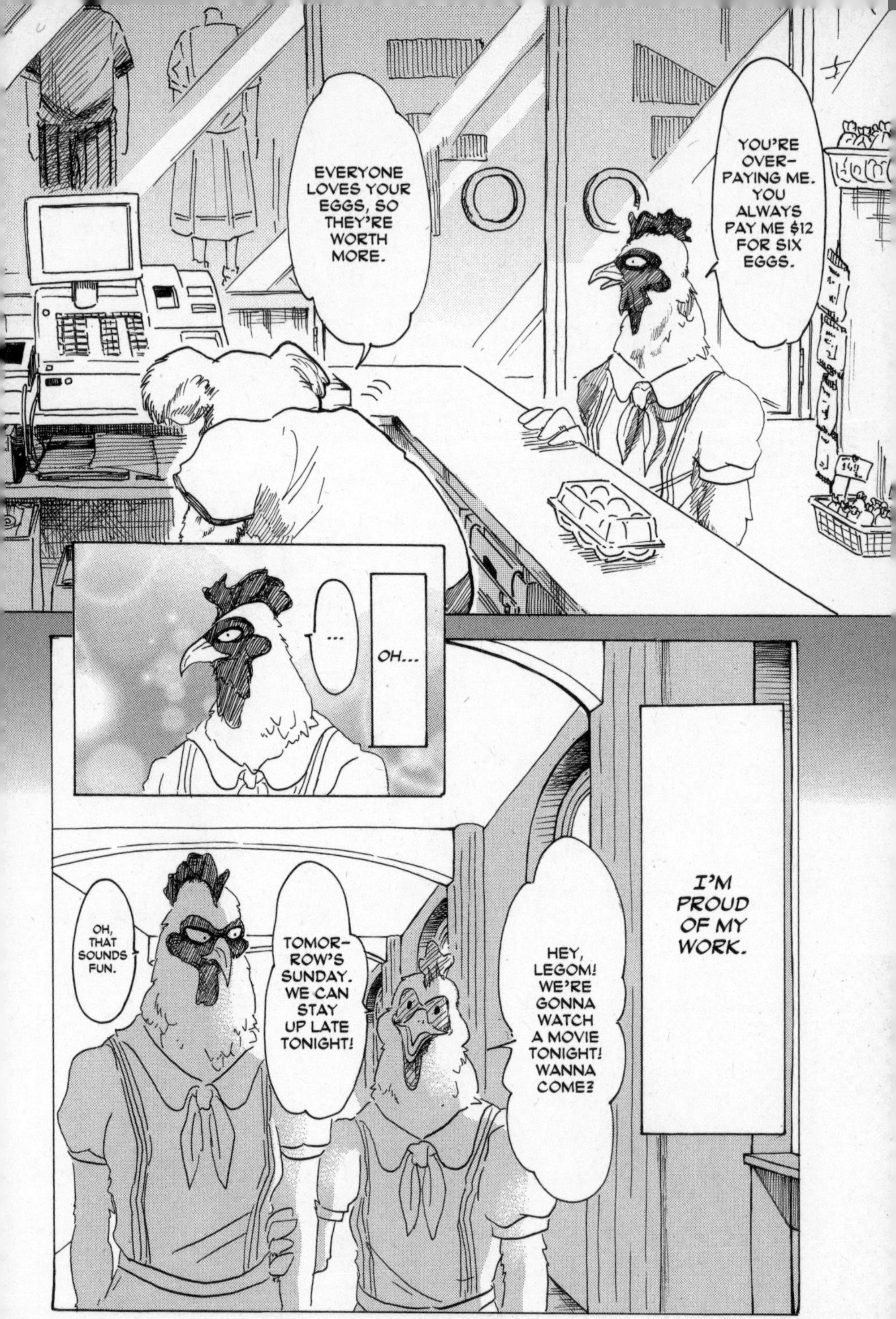
YOU'RE OVER-PAYING ME. YOU ALWAYS PAY ME $12 FOR SIX EGGS.
EVERYONE LOVES YOUR EGGS, SO THEY'RE WORTH MORE.
OH...
...
I'M PROUD OF MY WORK.
HEY, LEGOM! WE'RE GONNA WATCH A MOVIE TONIGHT! WANNA COME?
TOMOR-ROW'S SUNDAY. WE CAN STAY UP LATE TONIGHT!
OH, THAT SOUNDS FUN.

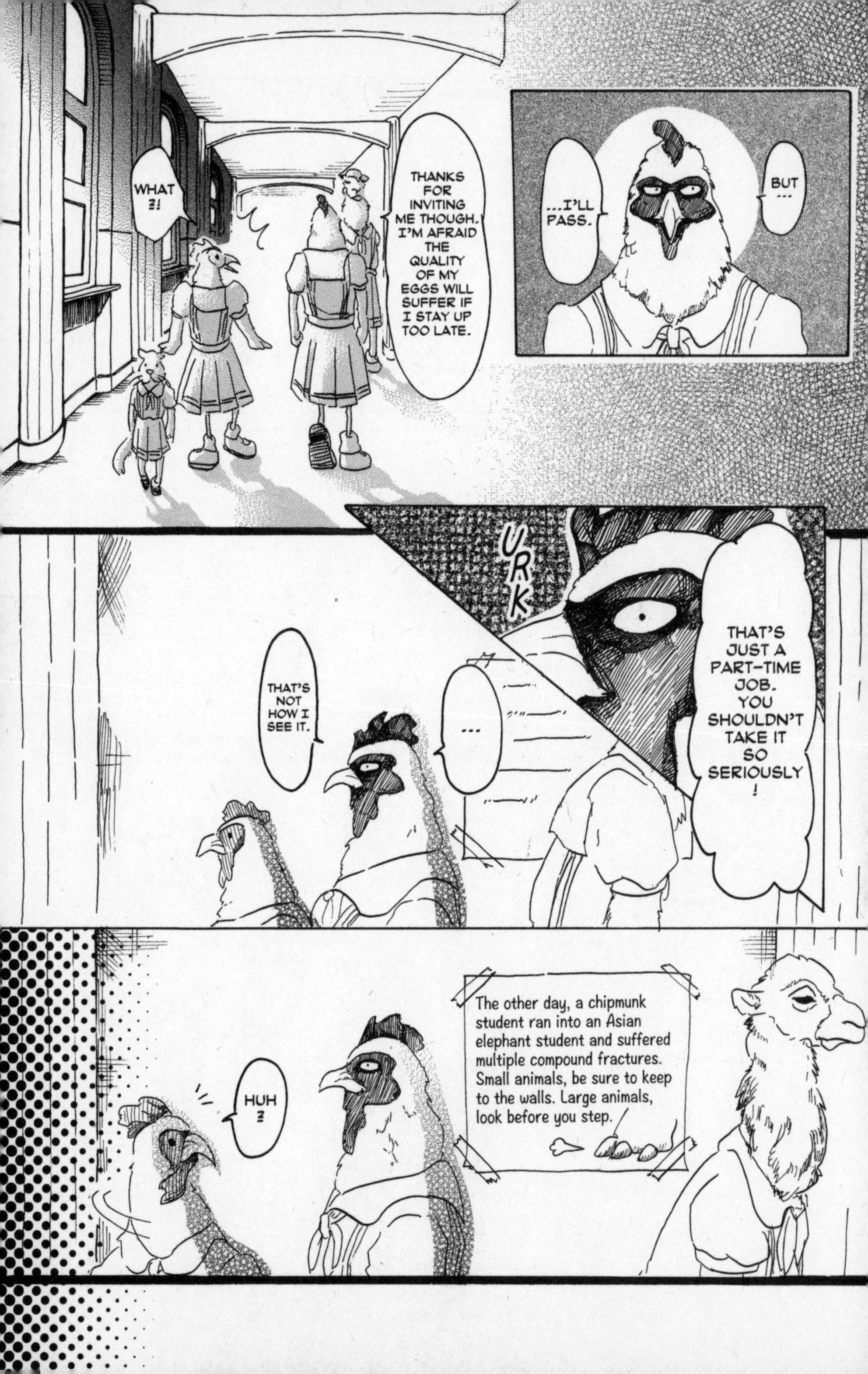
BUT ---
...I'LL PASS.
THANKS FOR INVITING ME THOUGH. I'M AFRAID THE QUALITY OF MY EGGS WILL SUFFER IF I STAY UP TOO LATE.
WHAT ?!
URK
THAT'S JUST A PART-TIME JOB. YOU SHOULDN'T TAKE IT SO SERIOUSLY !
...
THAT'S NOT HOW I SEE IT.
The other day, a chipmunk student ran into an Asian elephant student and suffered multiple compound fractures. Small animals, be sure to keep to the walls. Large animals, look before you step.
HUH ?

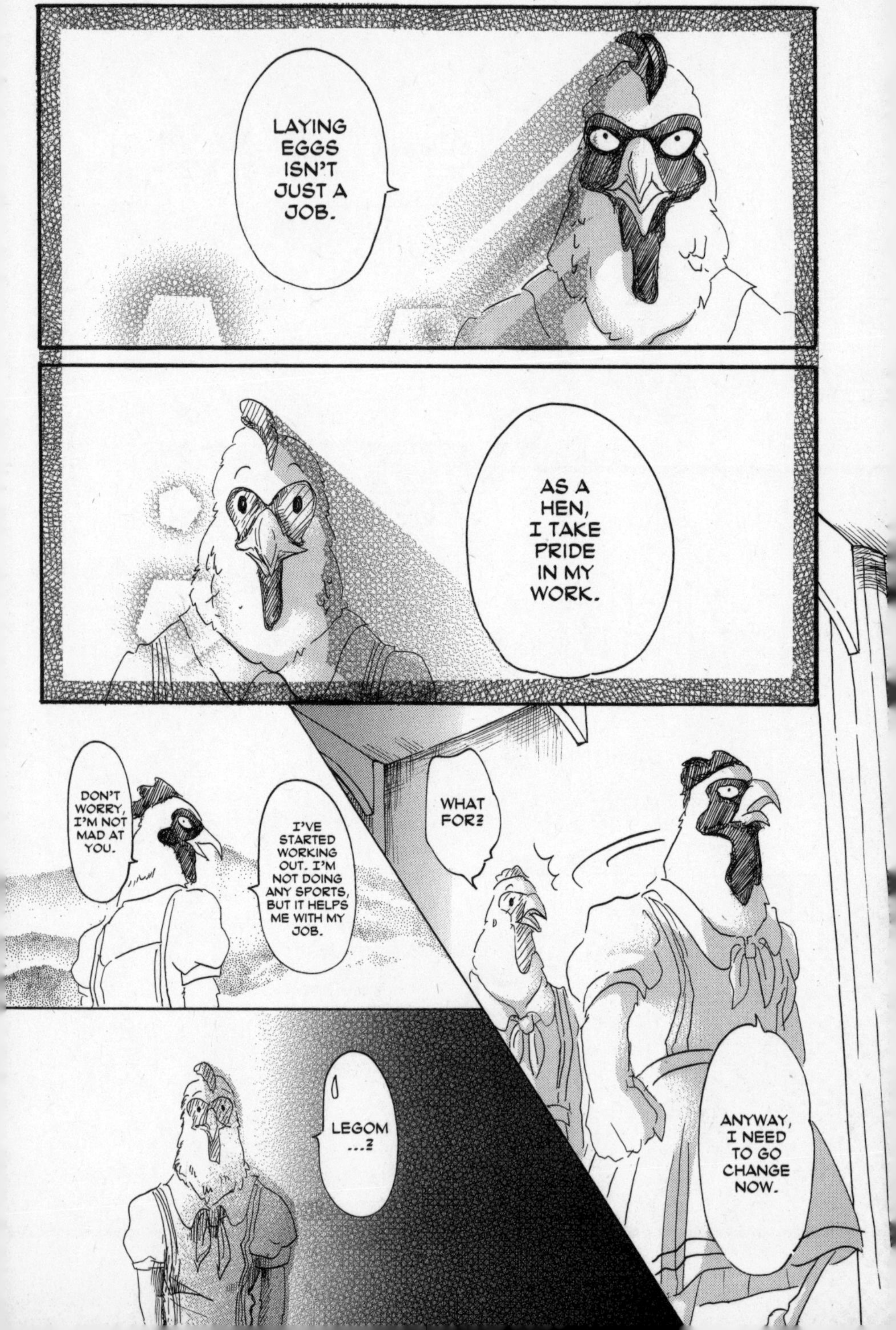
LAYING EGGS ISN'T JUST A JOB.
AS A HEN, I TAKE PRIDE IN MY WORK.
WHAT FOR?
ANYWAY, I NEED TO GO CHANGE NOW.
I'VE STARTED WORKING OUT. I'M NOT DOING ANY SPORTS, BUT IT HELPS ME WITH MY JOB.
DON'T WORRY, I'M NOT MAD AT YOU.
LEGOM ...?

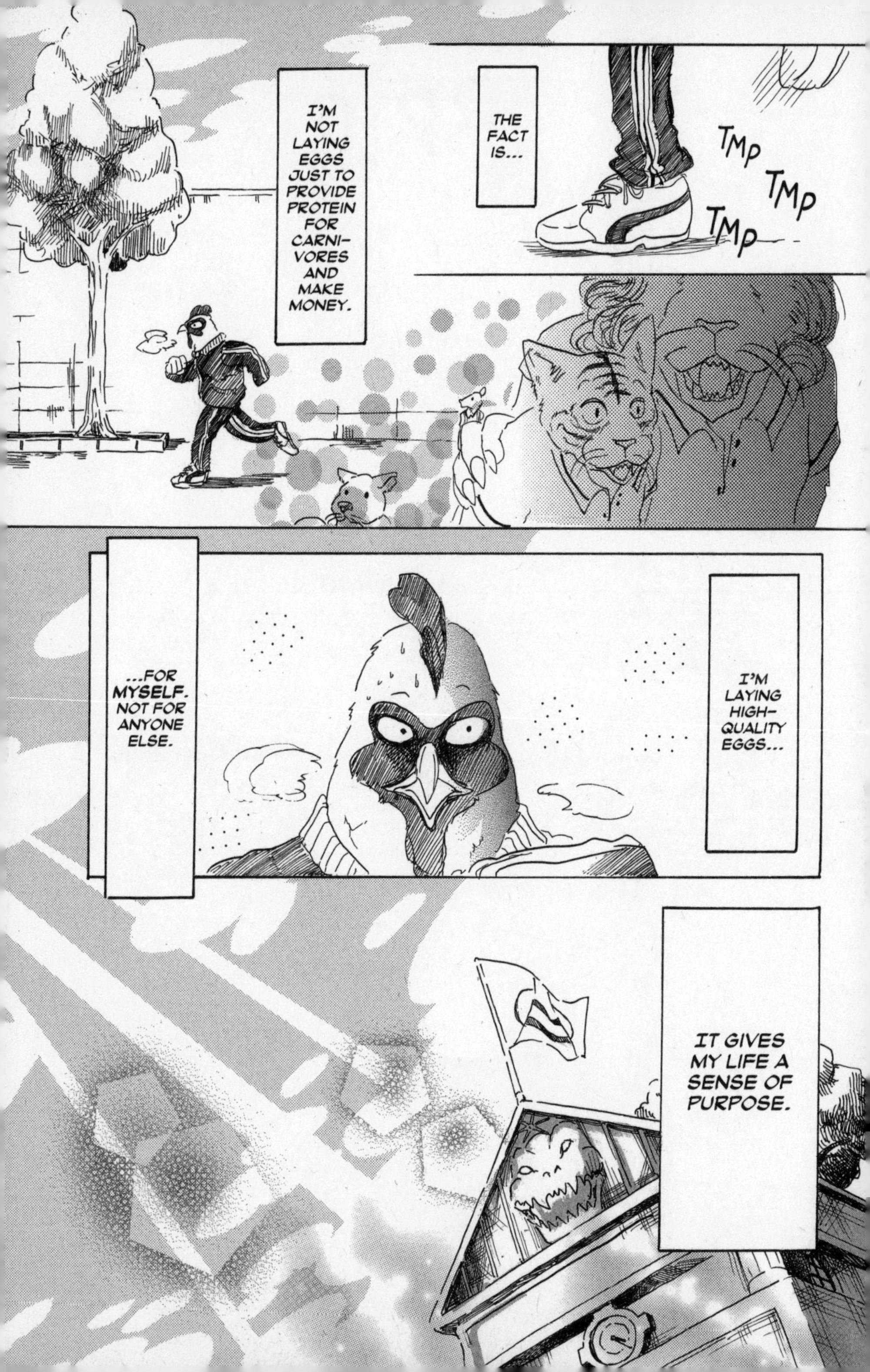

THE FACT IS...
TMP TMP TMP
I'M NOT LAYING EGGS JUST TO PROVIDE PROTEIN FOR CARNIVORES AND MAKE MONEY.
I'M LAYING HIGH-QUALITY EGGS...
...FOR MYSELF. NOT FOR ANYONE ELSE.
IT GIVES MY LIFE A SENSE OF PURPOSE.

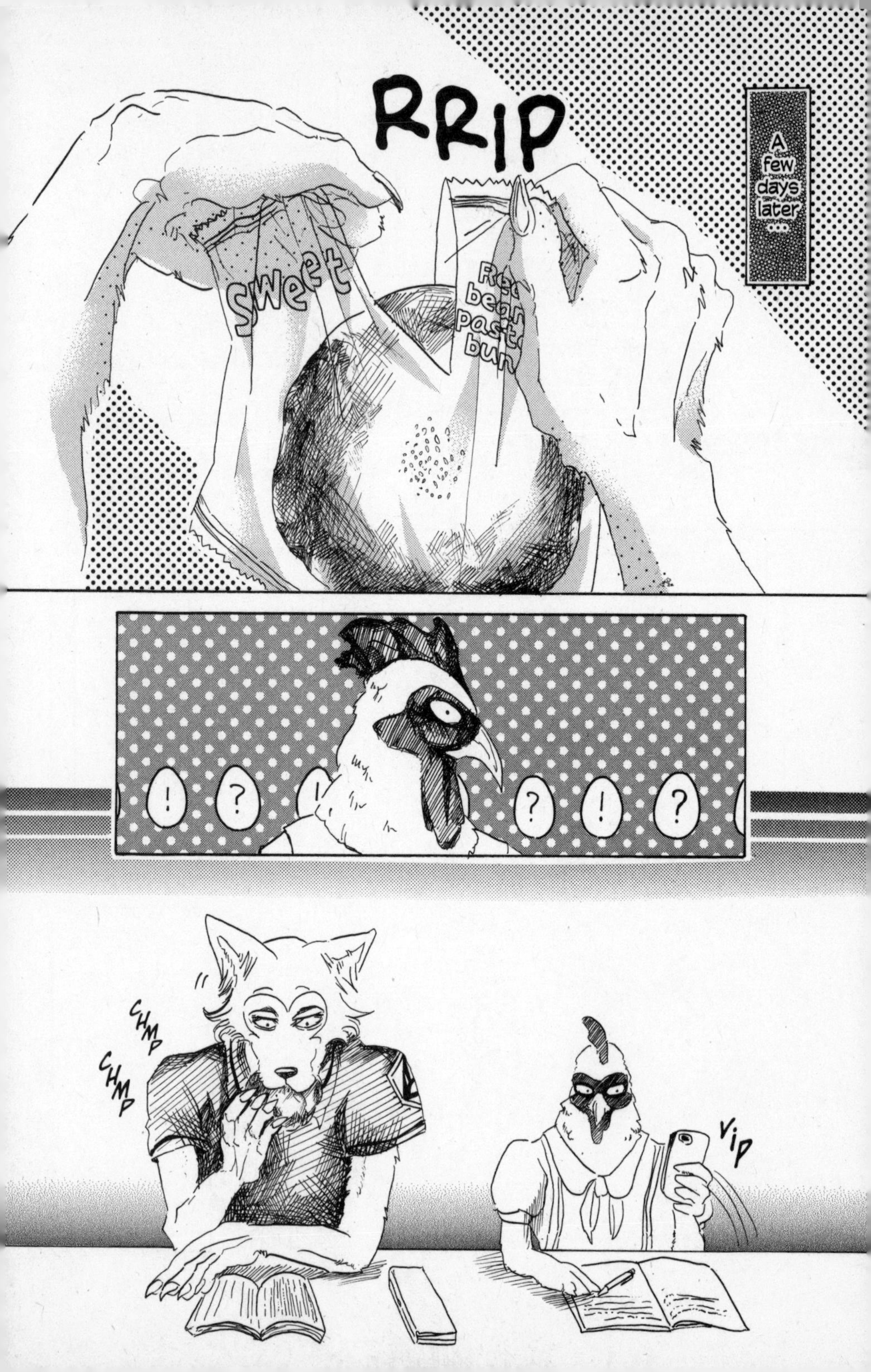
A few days later...
RRIP
Sweet
! ? ! ? ! ?
vip
CHMP CHMP

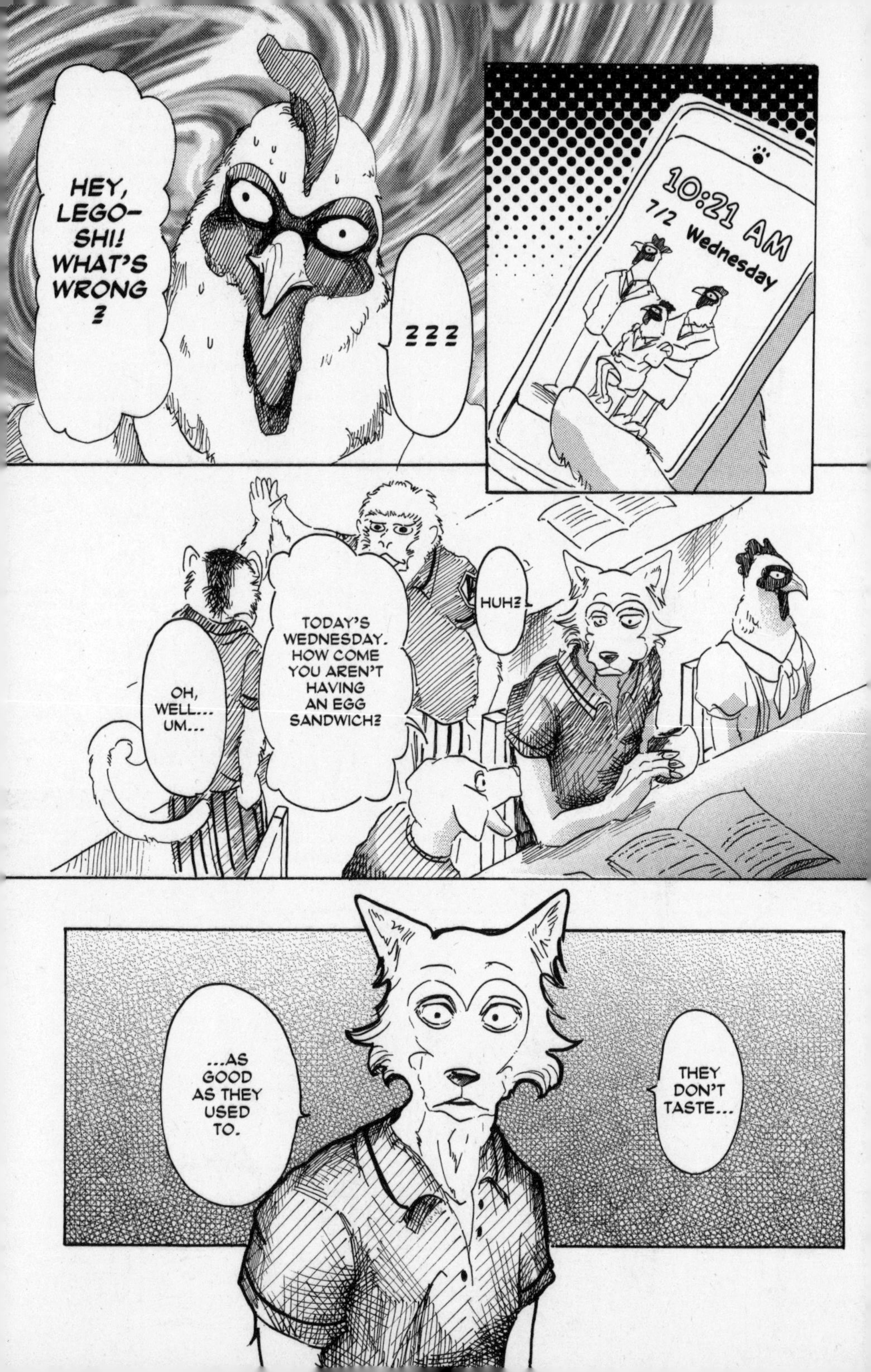
10:21 AM
7/2 Wednesday
HEY, LEGOSHI! WHAT'S WRONG?
???
HUH?
TODAY'S WEDNESDAY. HOW COME YOU AREN'T HAVING AN EGG SANDWICH?
OH, WELL... UM...
THEY DON'T TASTE...
...AS GOOD AS THEY USED TO.

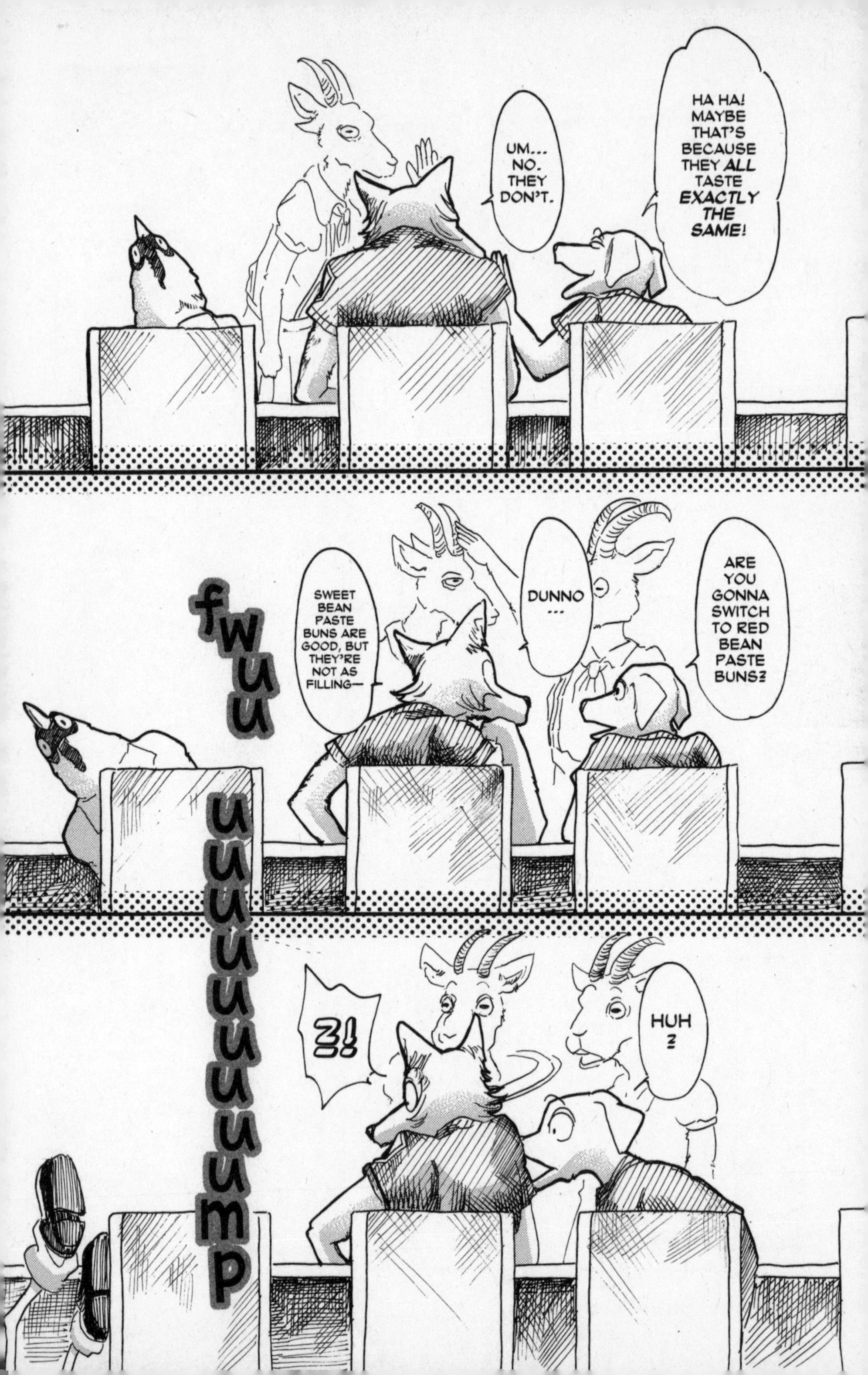
HA HA! MAYBE THAT'S BECAUSE THEY *ALL* TASTE ***EXACTLY THE SAME!***
UM... NO. THEY DON'T.
ARE YOU GONNA SWITCH TO RED BEAN PASTE BUNS?
DUNNO...
SWEET BEAN PASTE BUNS ARE GOOD, BUT THEY'RE NOT AS FILLING—
fwuu
uuuuuuuump
HUH?
?!

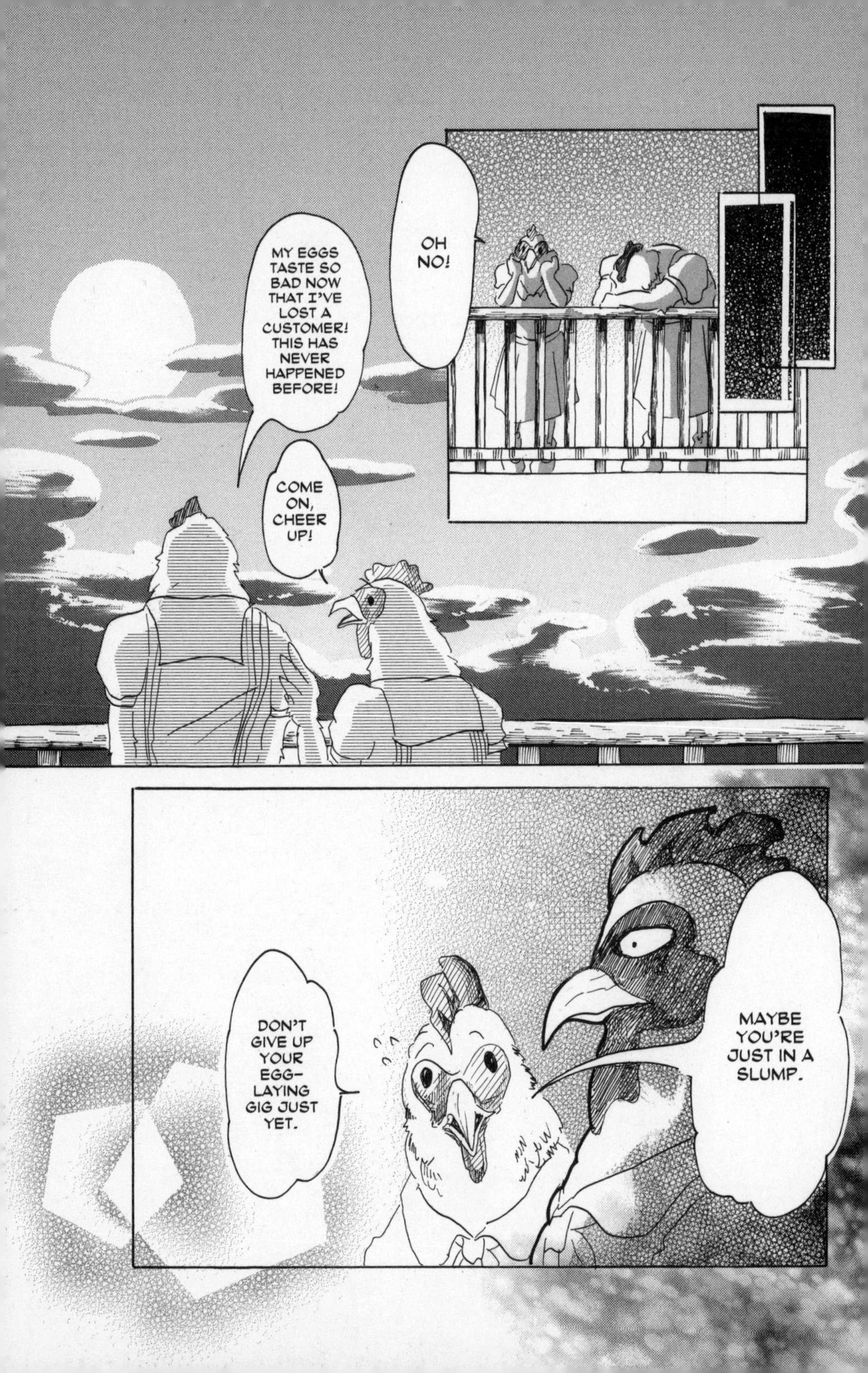
OH NO!
MY EGGS TASTE SO BAD NOW THAT I'VE LOST A CUSTOMER! THIS HAS NEVER HAPPENED BEFORE!
COME ON, CHEER UP!
MAYBE YOU'RE JUST IN A SLUMP.
DON'T GIVE UP YOUR EGG-LAYING GIG JUST YET.

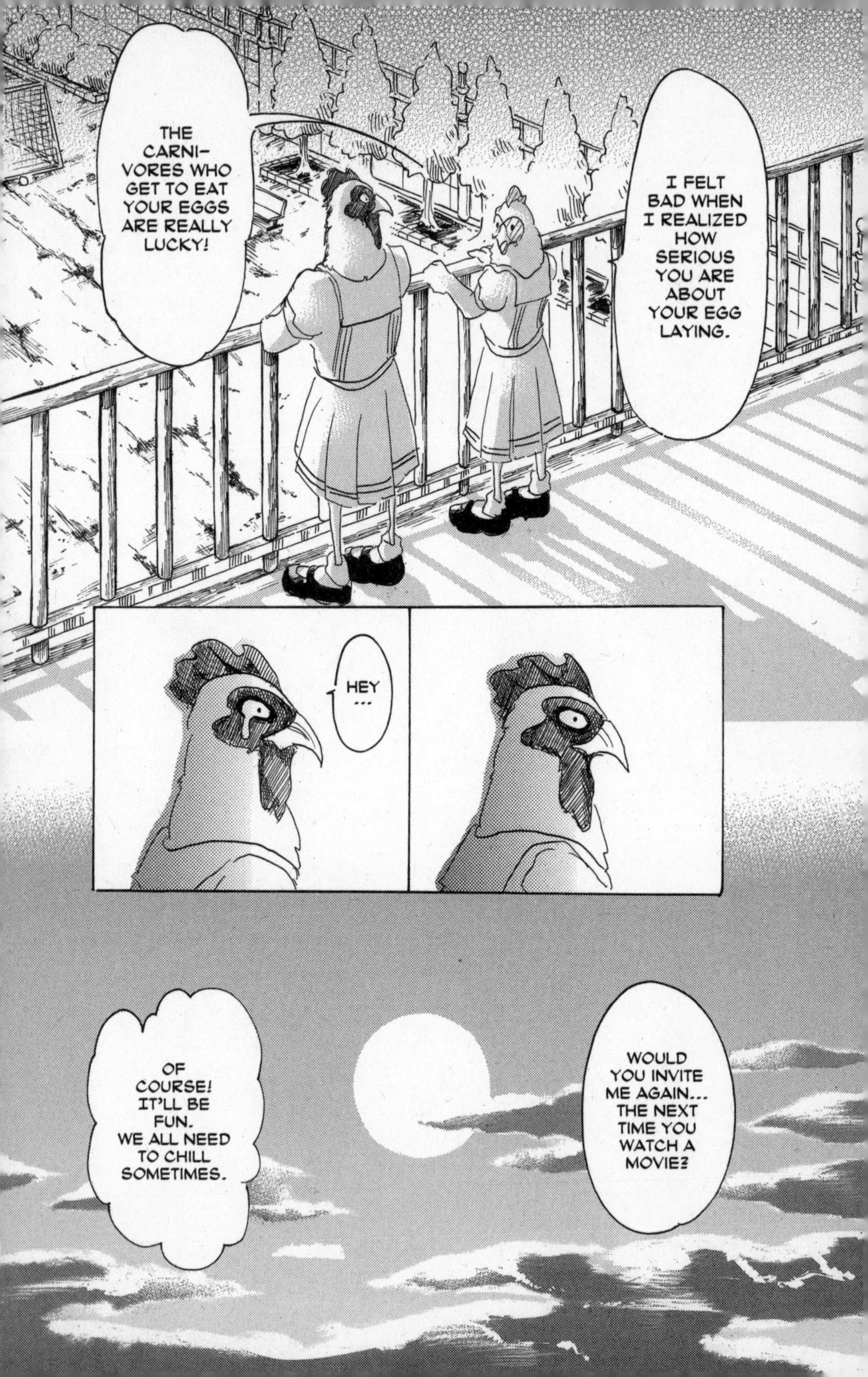
I FELT BAD WHEN I REALIZED HOW SERIOUS YOU ARE ABOUT YOUR EGG LAYING.
THE CARNI-VORES WHO GET TO EAT YOUR EGGS ARE REALLY LUCKY!
HEY...
WOULD YOU INVITE ME AGAIN... THE NEXT TIME YOU WATCH A MOVIE?
OF COURSE! IT'LL BE FUN. WE ALL NEED TO CHILL SOMETIMES.

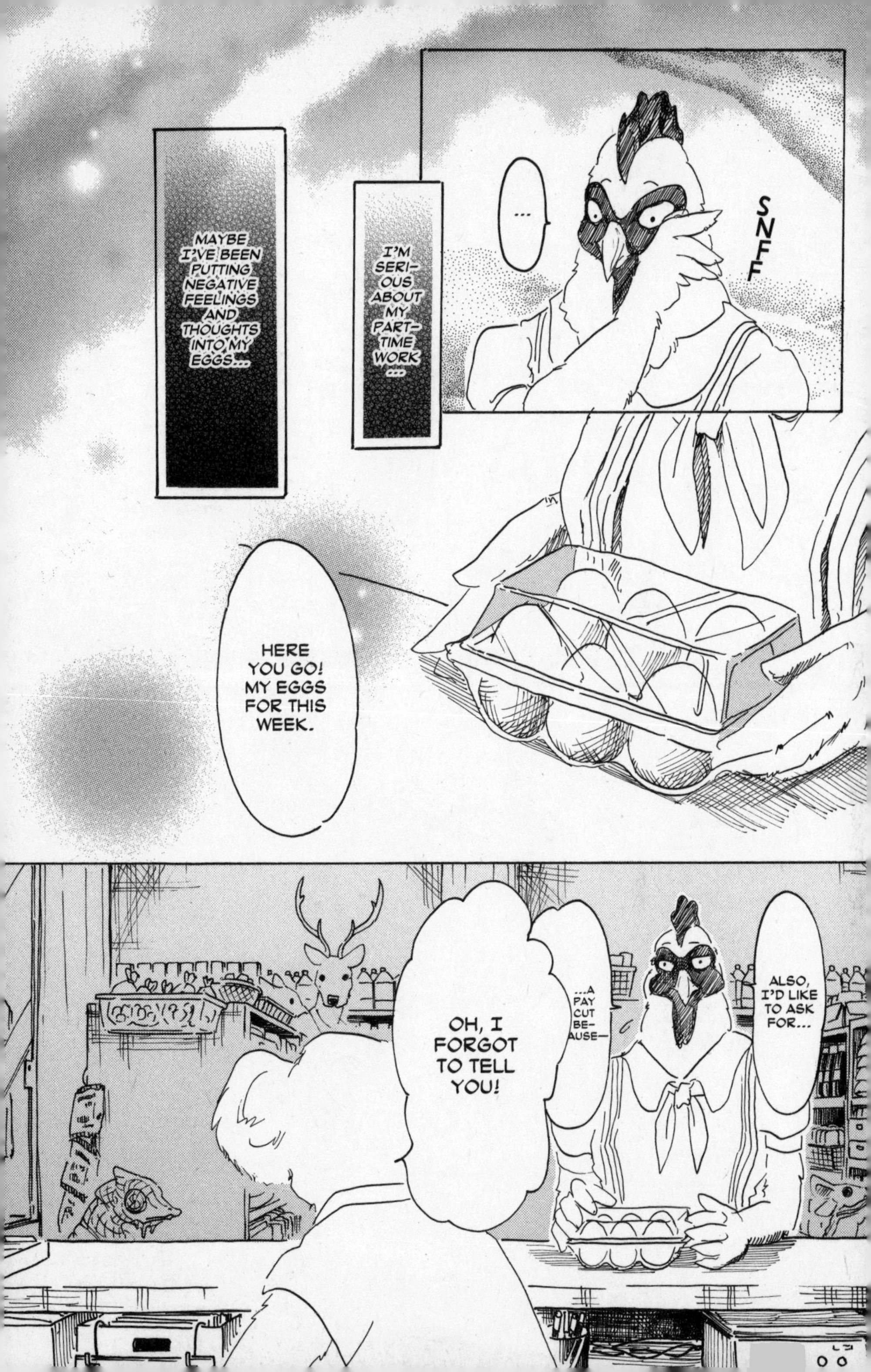
...
SNFF
I'M SERI-OUS ABOUT MY PART-TIME WORK ...
MAYBE I'VE BEEN PUTTING NEGATIVE FEELINGS AND THOUGHTS INTO MY EGGS...
HERE YOU GO! MY EGGS FOR THIS WEEK.
ALSO, I'D LIKE TO ASK FOR...
...A PAY CUT BE-AUSE—
OH, I FORGOT TO TELL YOU!

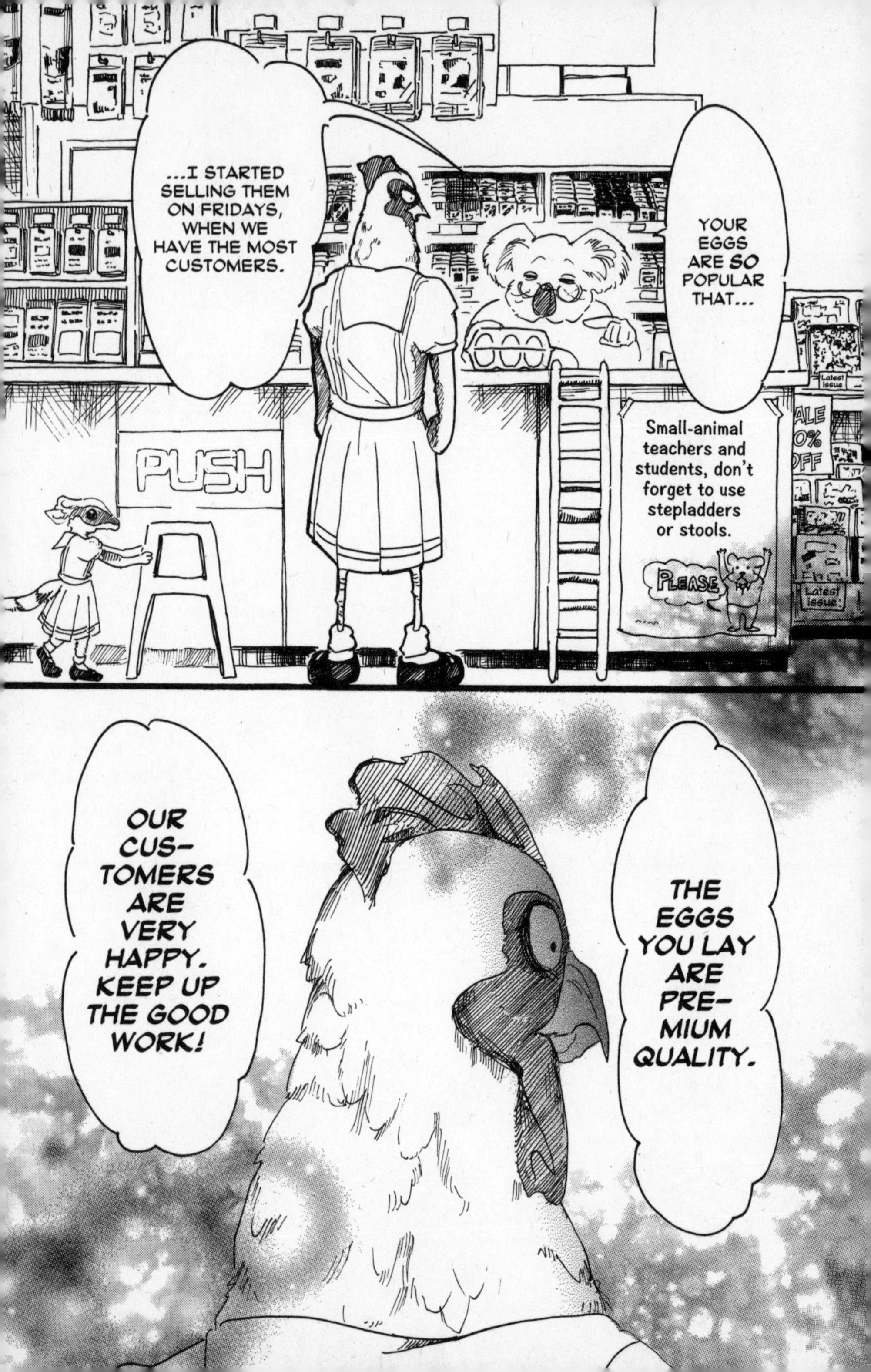
YOUR EGGS ARE SO POPULAR THAT...
...I STARTED SELLING THEM ON FRIDAYS, WHEN WE HAVE THE MOST CUSTOMERS.
PUSH
Small-animal teachers and students, don't forget to use stepladders or stools.
PLEASE
Latest issue
Latest issue
THE EGGS YOU LAY ARE PRE-MIUM QUALITY.
OUR CUS-TOMERS ARE VERY HAPPY. KEEP UP THE GOOD WORK!

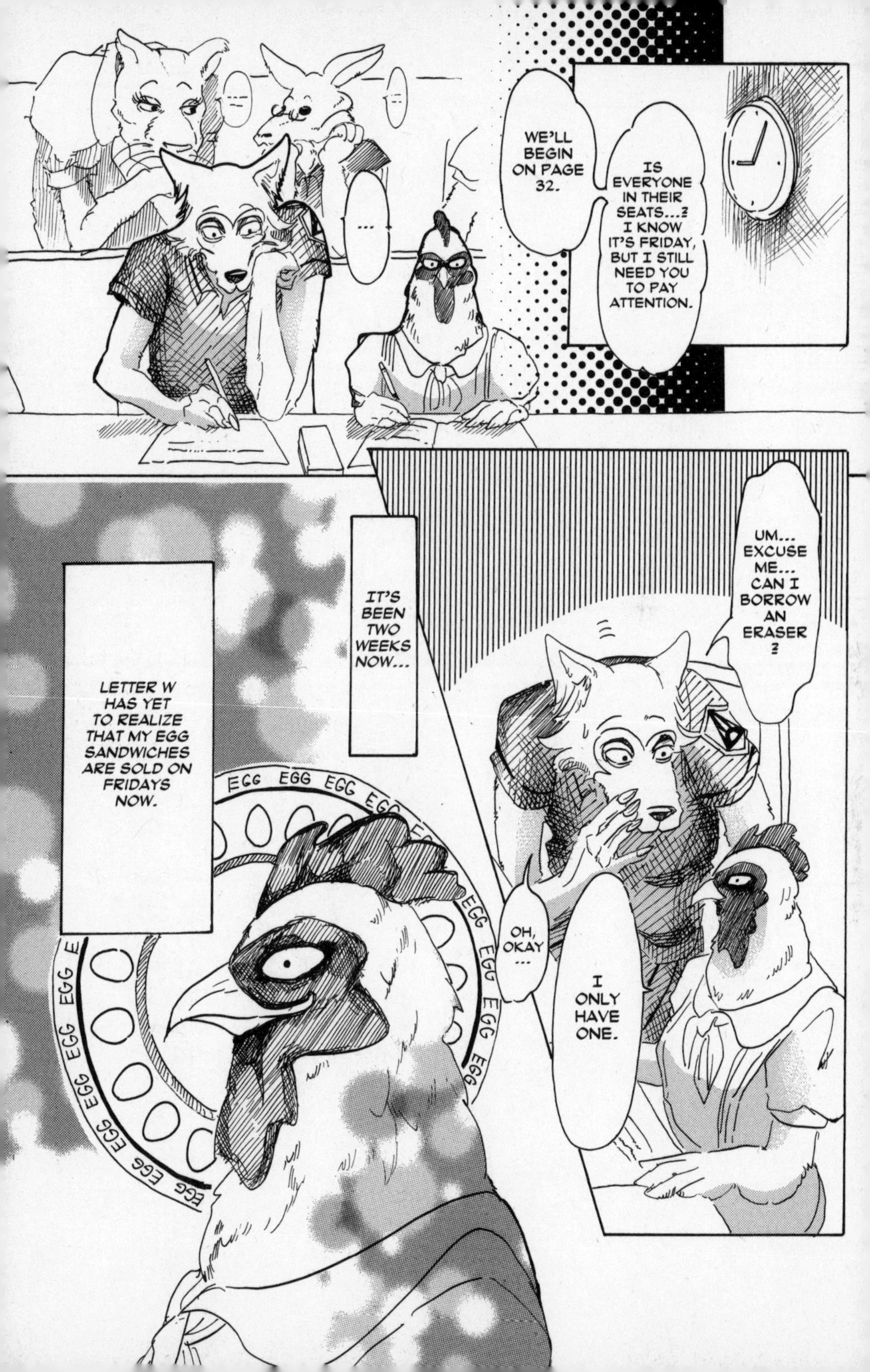

IS EVERYONE IN THEIR SEATS...? I KNOW IT'S FRIDAY, BUT I STILL NEED YOU TO PAY ATTENTION.
WE'LL BEGIN ON PAGE 32.
...
...
...
UM... EXCUSE ME... CAN I BORROW AN ERASER?
I ONLY HAVE ONE.
OH, OKAY...
IT'S BEEN TWO WEEKS NOW...
LETTER W HAS YET TO REALIZE THAT MY EGG SANDWICHES ARE SOLD ON FRIDAYS NOW.
EGG EGG EGG EGG EGG EGG EGG EGG EGG EGG EGG EGG EGG

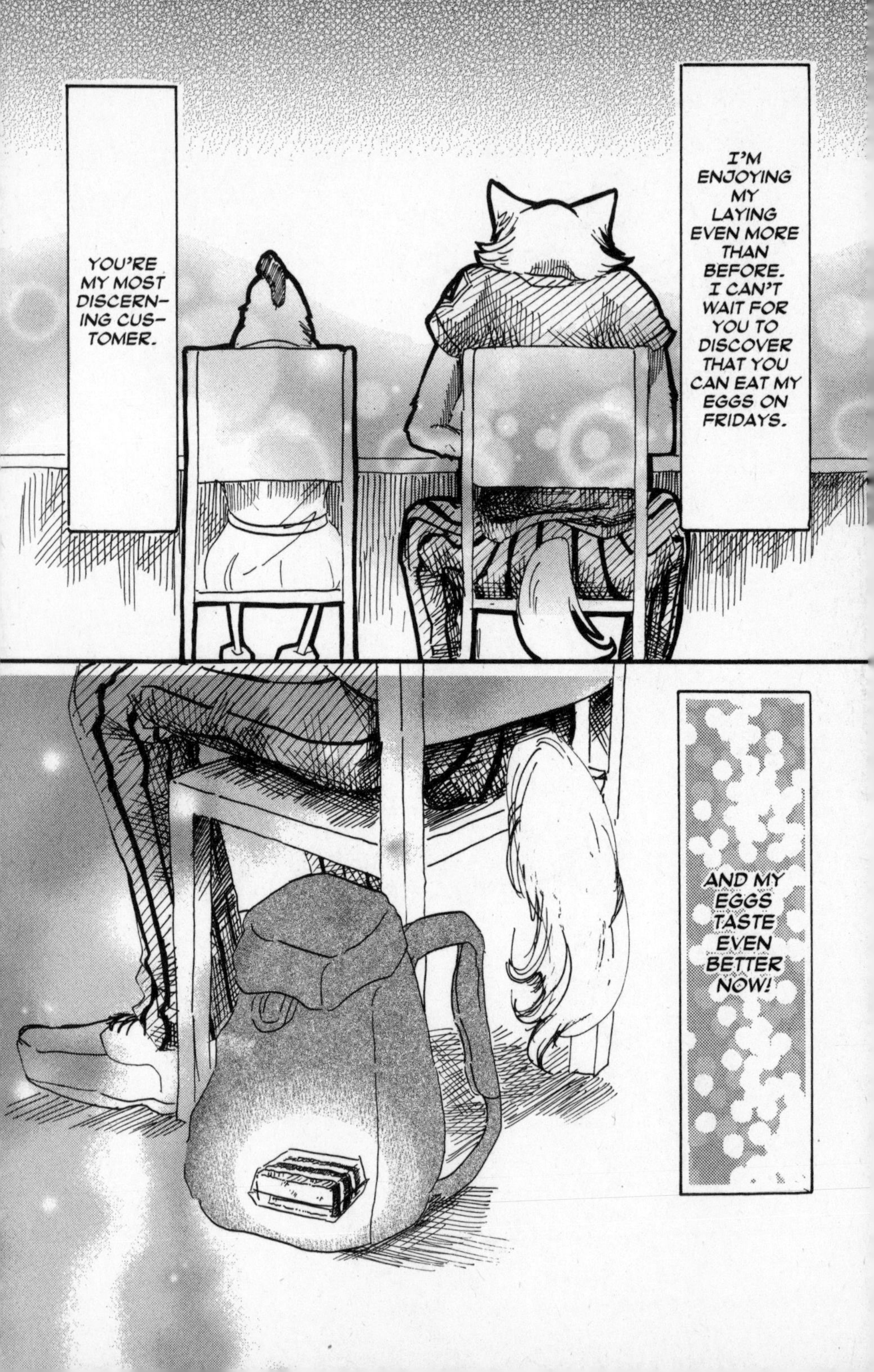
I'M ENJOYING MY LAYING EVEN MORE THAN BEFORE. I CAN'T WAIT FOR YOU TO DISCOVER THAT YOU CAN EAT MY EGGS ON FRIDAYS.
YOU'RE MY MOST DISCERNING CUSTOMER.
AND MY EGGS TASTE EVEN BETTER NOW!

Chapter 21: Resonating with the Outside World

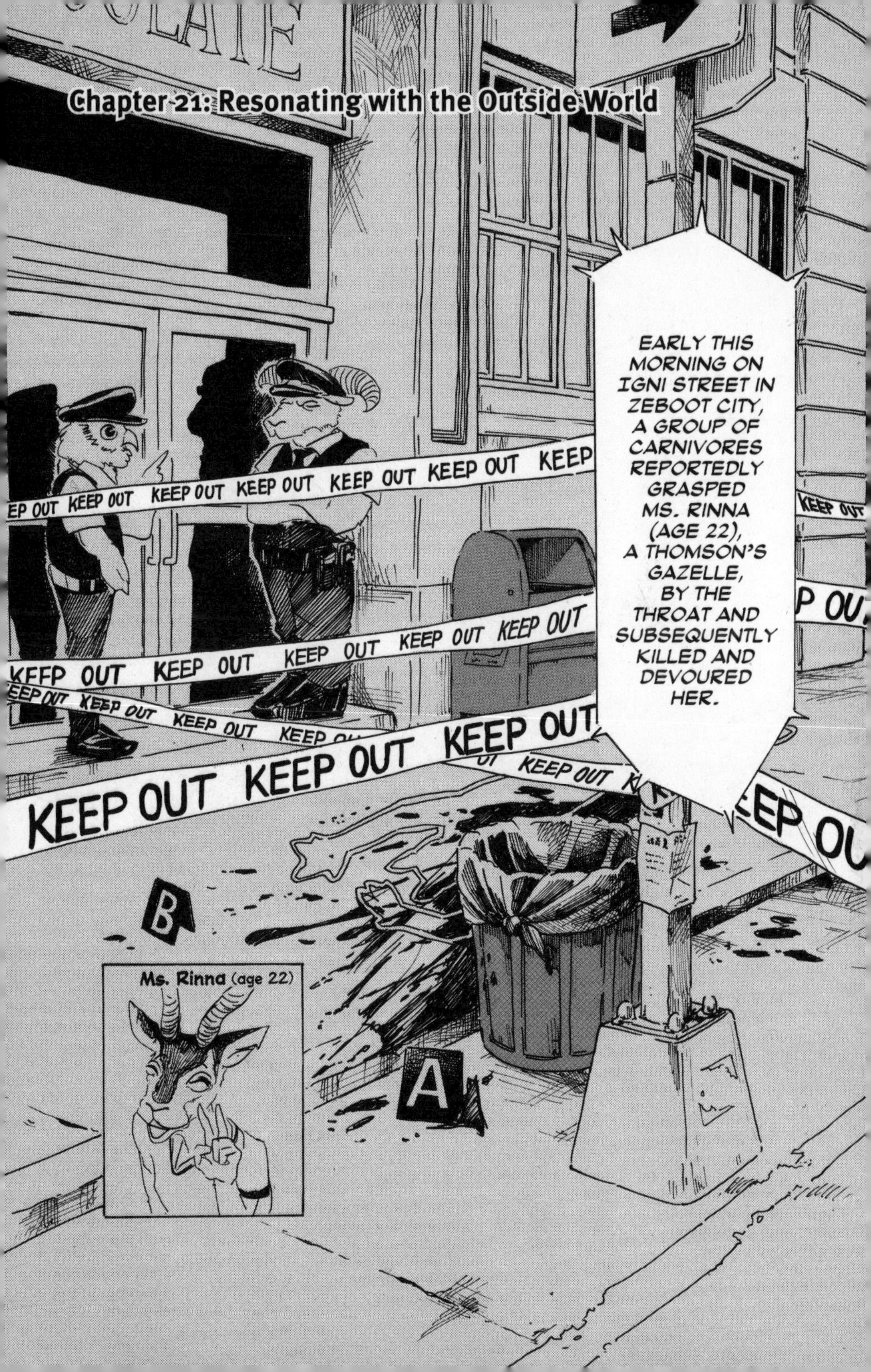
EARLY THIS MORNING ON IGNI STREET IN ZEBOOT CITY, A GROUP OF CARNIVORES REPORTEDLY GRASPED MS. RINNA (AGE 22), A THOMSON'S GAZELLE, BY THE THROAT AND SUBSEQUENTLY KILLED AND DEVOURED HER.
KEEP OUT KEEP OUT KEEP OUT KEEP OUT KEEP OUT KEEP
KEEP OUT KEEP OUT KEEP OUT KEEP OUT
KEEP OUT KEEP OUT
KEEP OUT
B
A
Ms. Rinna (age 22)

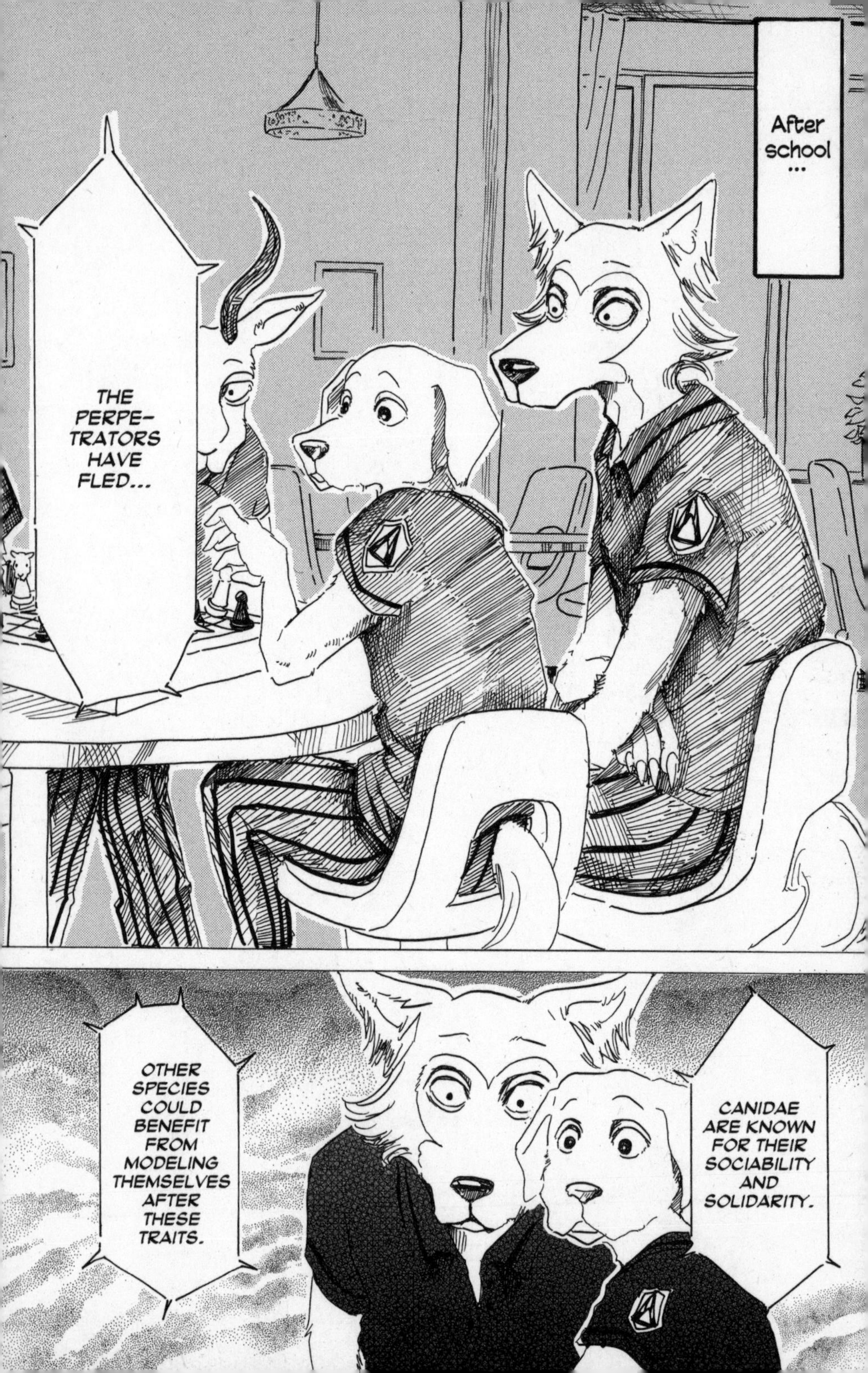
After school...
THE PERPETRATORS HAVE FLED...
CANIDAE ARE KNOWN FOR THEIR SOCIABILITY AND SOLIDARITY.
OTHER SPECIES COULD BENEFIT FROM MODELING THEMSELVES AFTER THESE TRAITS.

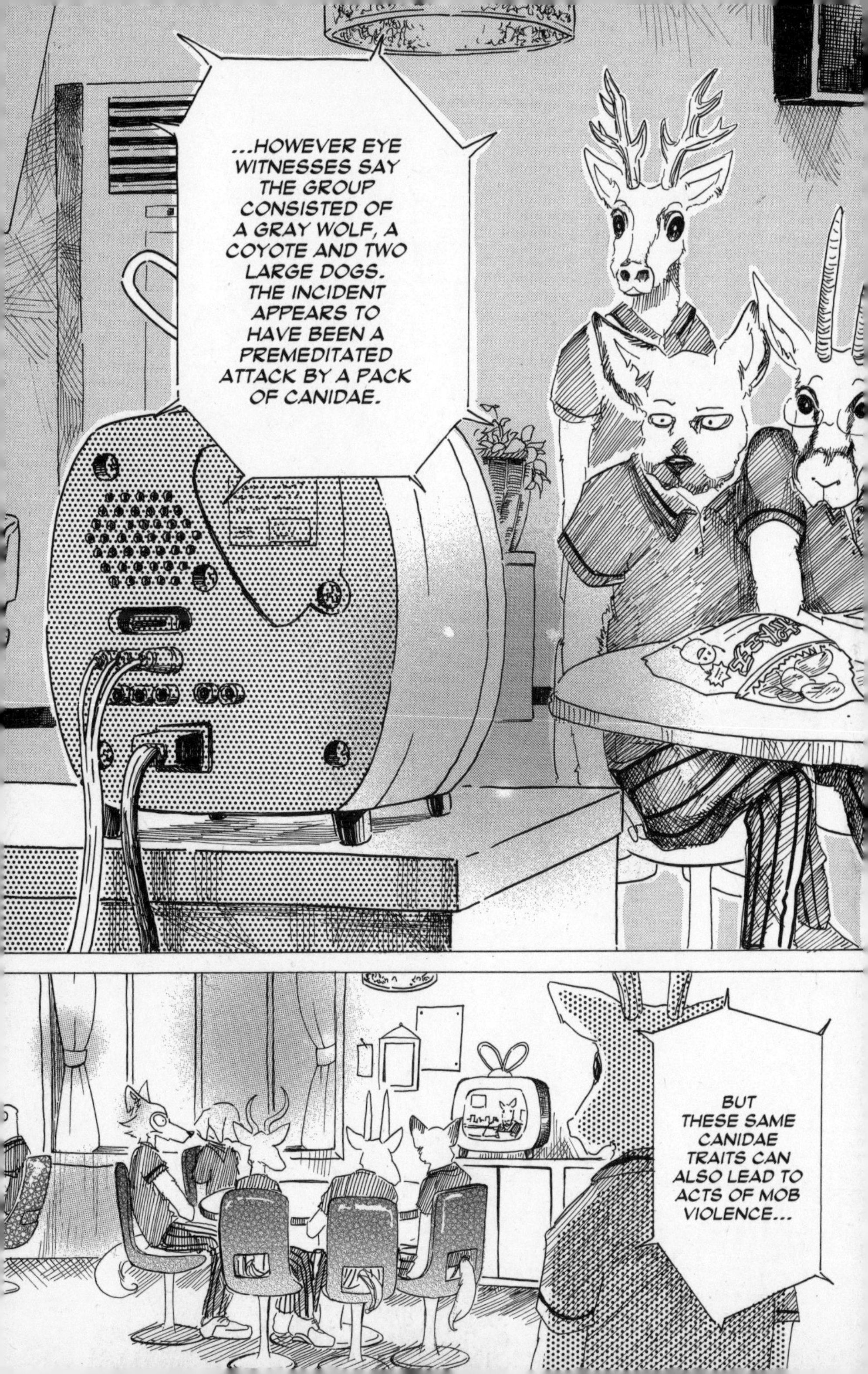
...HOWEVER EYE WITNESSES SAY THE GROUP CONSISTED OF A GRAY WOLF, A COYOTE AND TWO LARGE DOGS. THE INCIDENT APPEARS TO HAVE BEEN A PREMEDITATED ATTACK BY A PACK OF CANIDAE.
BUT THESE SAME CANIDAE TRAITS CAN ALSO LEAD TO ACTS OF MOB VIOLENCE...

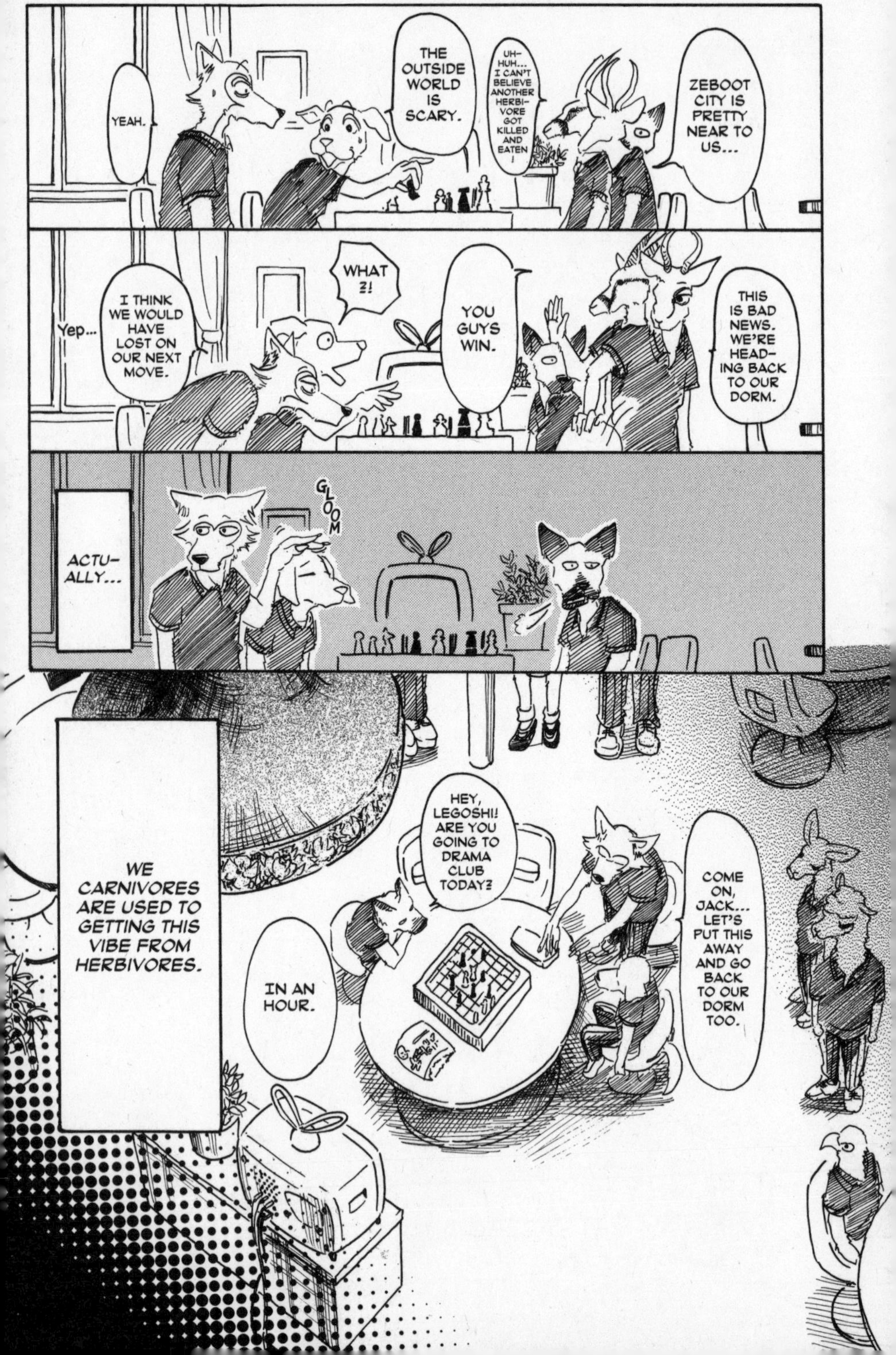
ZEBOOT CITY IS PRETTY NEAR TO US...
UH-HUH... I CAN'T BELIEVE ANOTHER HERBI-VORE GOT KILLED AND EATEN!
THE OUTSIDE WORLD IS SCARY.
YEAH.
THIS IS BAD NEWS. WE'RE HEAD-ING BACK TO OUR DORM.
YOU GUYS WIN.
WHAT?!
I THINK WE WOULD HAVE LOST ON OUR NEXT MOVE.
Yep...
GLOOM
ACTU-ALLY...
HEY, LEGOSHI! ARE YOU GOING TO DRAMA CLUB TODAY?
IN AN HOUR.
COME ON, JACK... LET'S PUT THIS AWAY AND GO BACK TO OUR DORM TOO.
WE CARNIVORES ARE USED TO GETTING THIS VIBE FROM HERBIVORES.

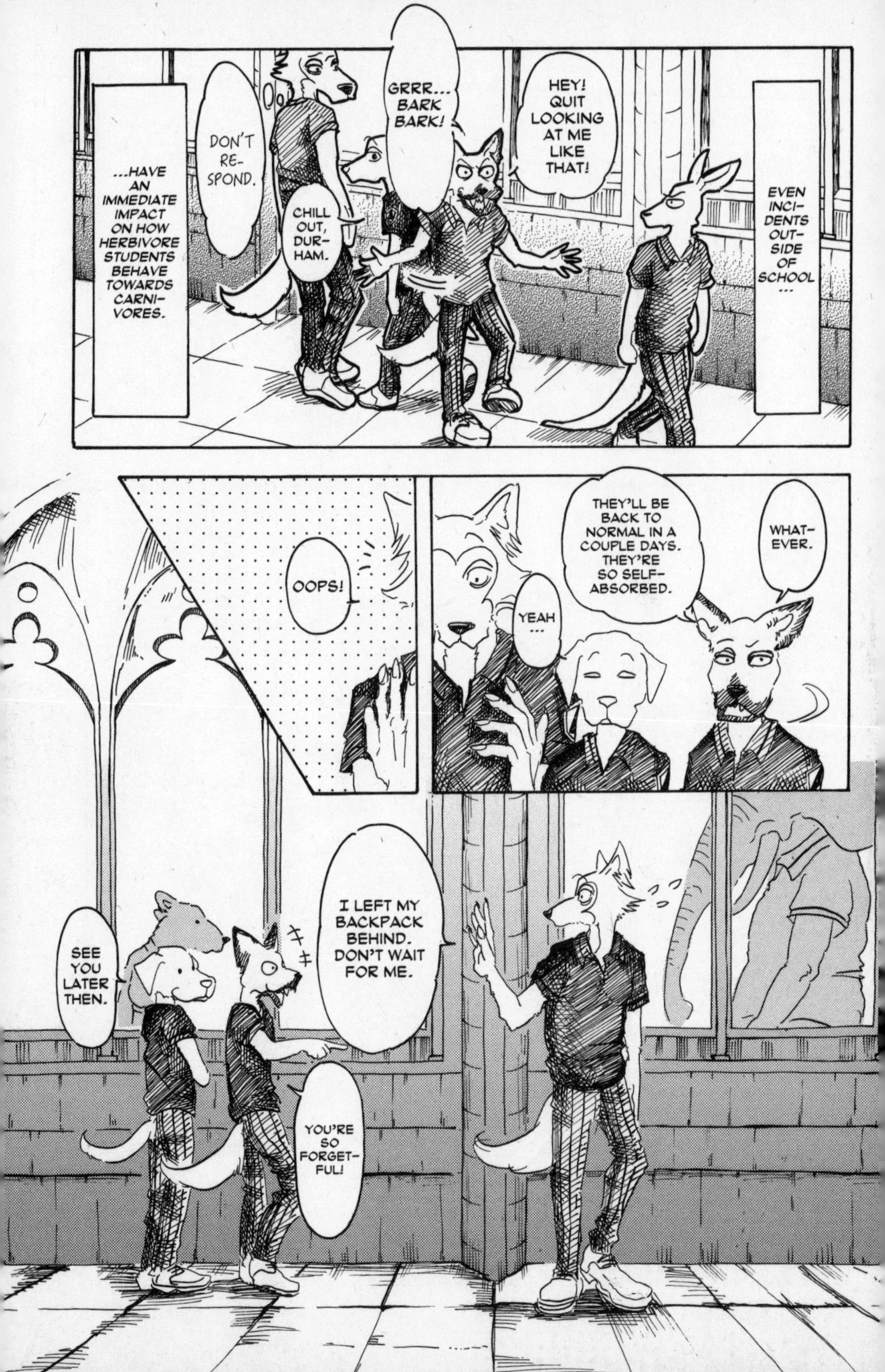
EVEN INCIDENTS OUTSIDE OF SCHOOL...
HEY! QUIT LOOKING AT ME LIKE THAT!
GRRR... BARK BARK!
CHILL OUT, DURHAM.
DON'T RESPOND.
...HAVE AN IMMEDIATE IMPACT ON HOW HERBIVORE STUDENTS BEHAVE TOWARDS CARNIVORES.
WHATEVER.
THEY'LL BE BACK TO NORMAL IN A COUPLE DAYS. THEY'RE SO SELF-ABSORBED.
YEAH...
OOPS!
I LEFT MY BACKPACK BEHIND. DON'T WAIT FOR ME.
SEE YOU LATER THEN.
YOU'RE SO FORGETFUL!

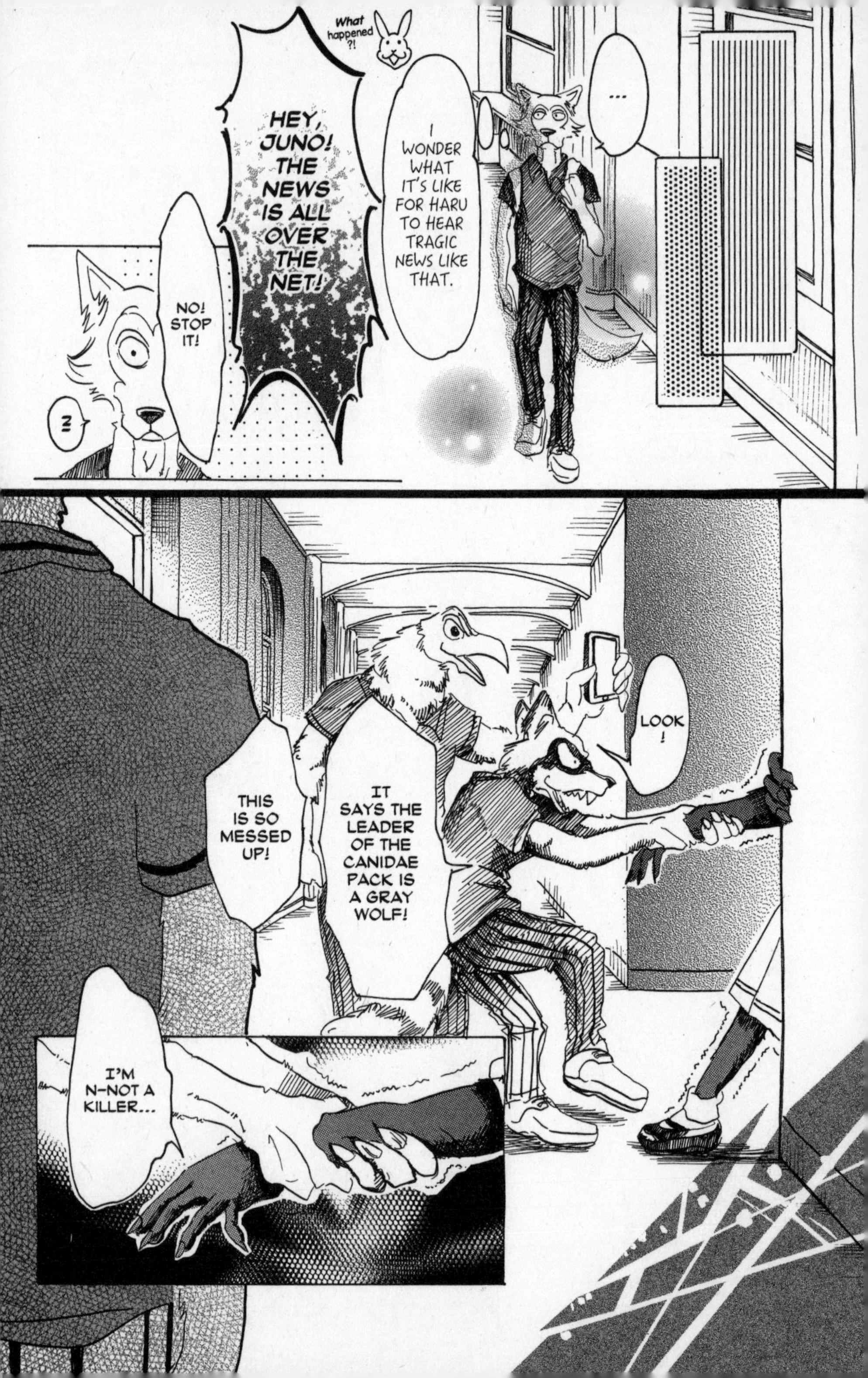
...
I WONDER WHAT IT'S LIKE FOR HARU TO HEAR TRAGIC NEWS LIKE THAT.
HEY, JUNO! THE NEWS IS ALL OVER THE NET!
What happened ?!
NO! STOP IT!
LOOK!
IT SAYS THE LEADER OF THE CANIDAE PACK IS A GRAY WOLF!
THIS IS SO MESSED UP!
I'M N-NOT A KILLER...

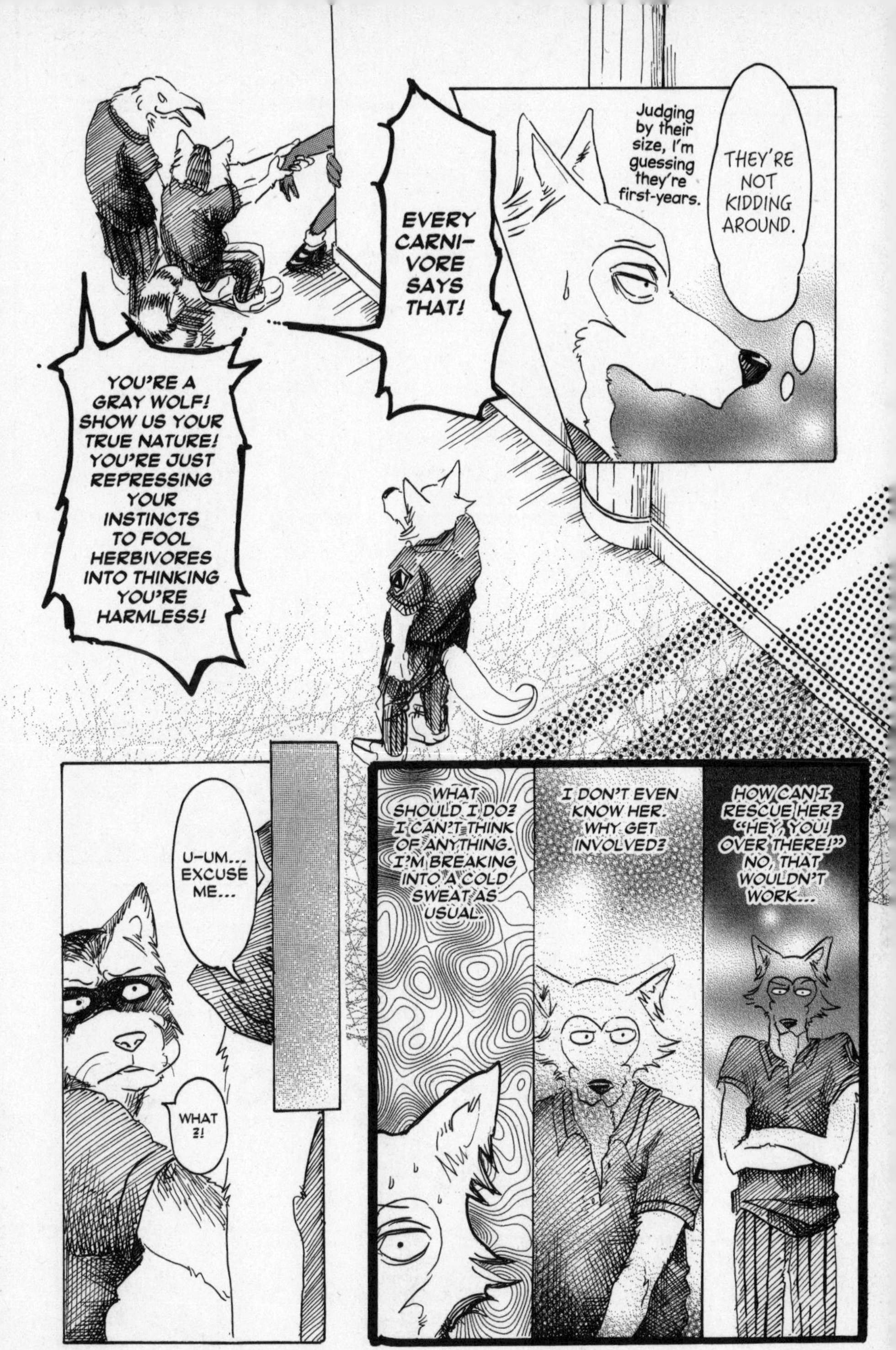
THEY'RE NOT KIDDING AROUND.
Judging by their size, I'm guessing they're first-years.
EVERY CARNIVORE SAYS THAT!
YOU'RE A GRAY WOLF! SHOW US YOUR TRUE NATURE! YOU'RE JUST REPRESSING YOUR INSTINCTS TO FOOL HERBIVORES INTO THINKING YOU'RE HARMLESS!
HOW CAN I RESCUE HER? "HEY, YOU! OVER THERE!" NO, THAT WOULDN'T WORK...
I DON'T EVEN KNOW HER. WHY GET INVOLVED?
WHAT SHOULD I DO? I CAN'T THINK OF ANYTHING. I'M BREAKING INTO A COLD SWEAT AS USUAL.
U-UM... EXCUSE ME...
WHAT?!

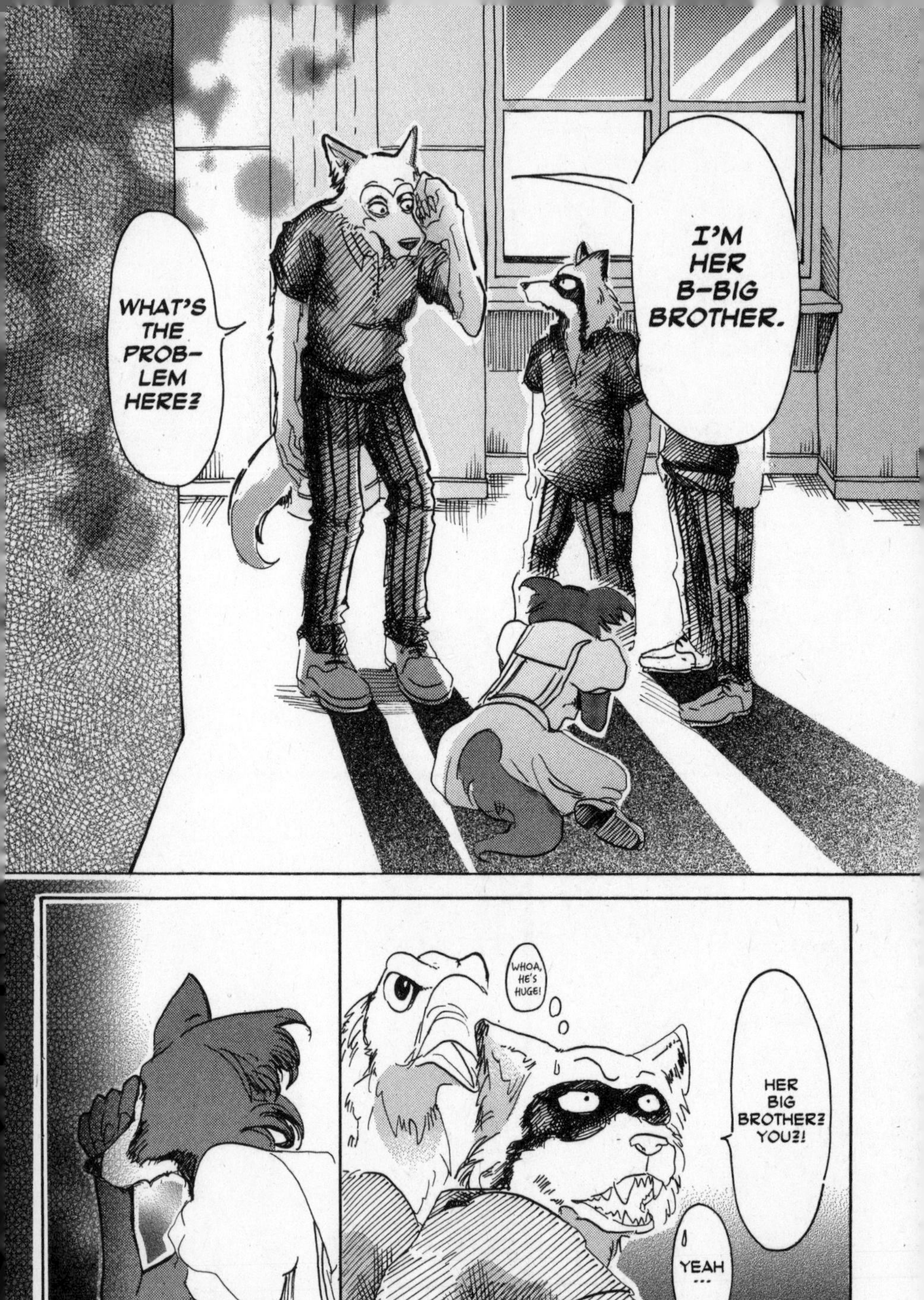
I'M HER B-BIG BROTHER.
WHAT'S THE PROB-LEM HERE?
HER BIG BROTHER? YOU?!
WHOA, HE'S HUGE!
YEAH...

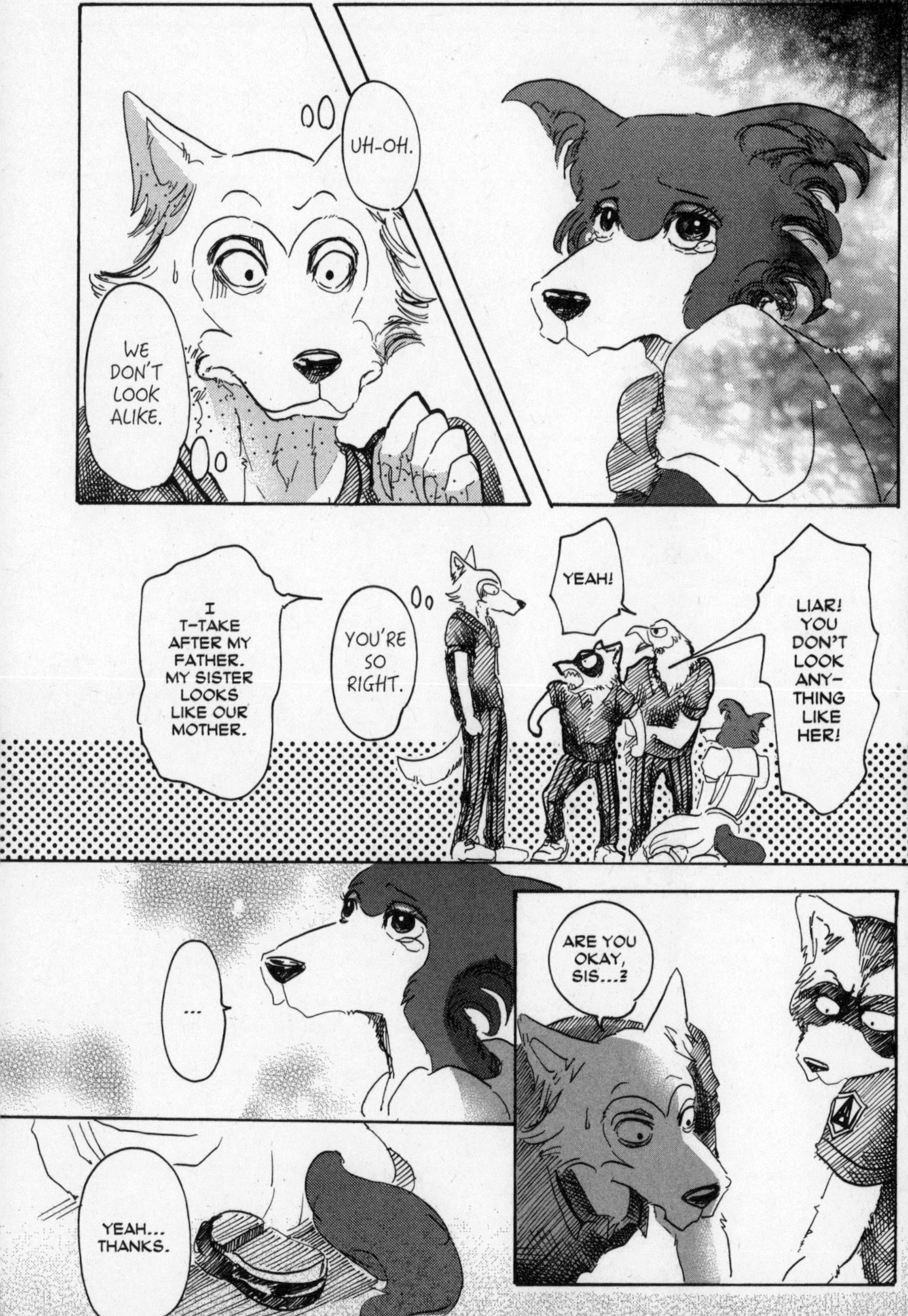
UH-OH.
WE DON'T LOOK ALIKE.
LIAR! YOU DON'T LOOK ANY-THING LIKE HER!
YEAH!
YOU'RE SO RIGHT.
I T-TAKE AFTER MY FATHER. MY SISTER LOOKS LIKE OUR MOTHER.
ARE YOU OKAY, SIS...?
...
YEAH... THANKS.

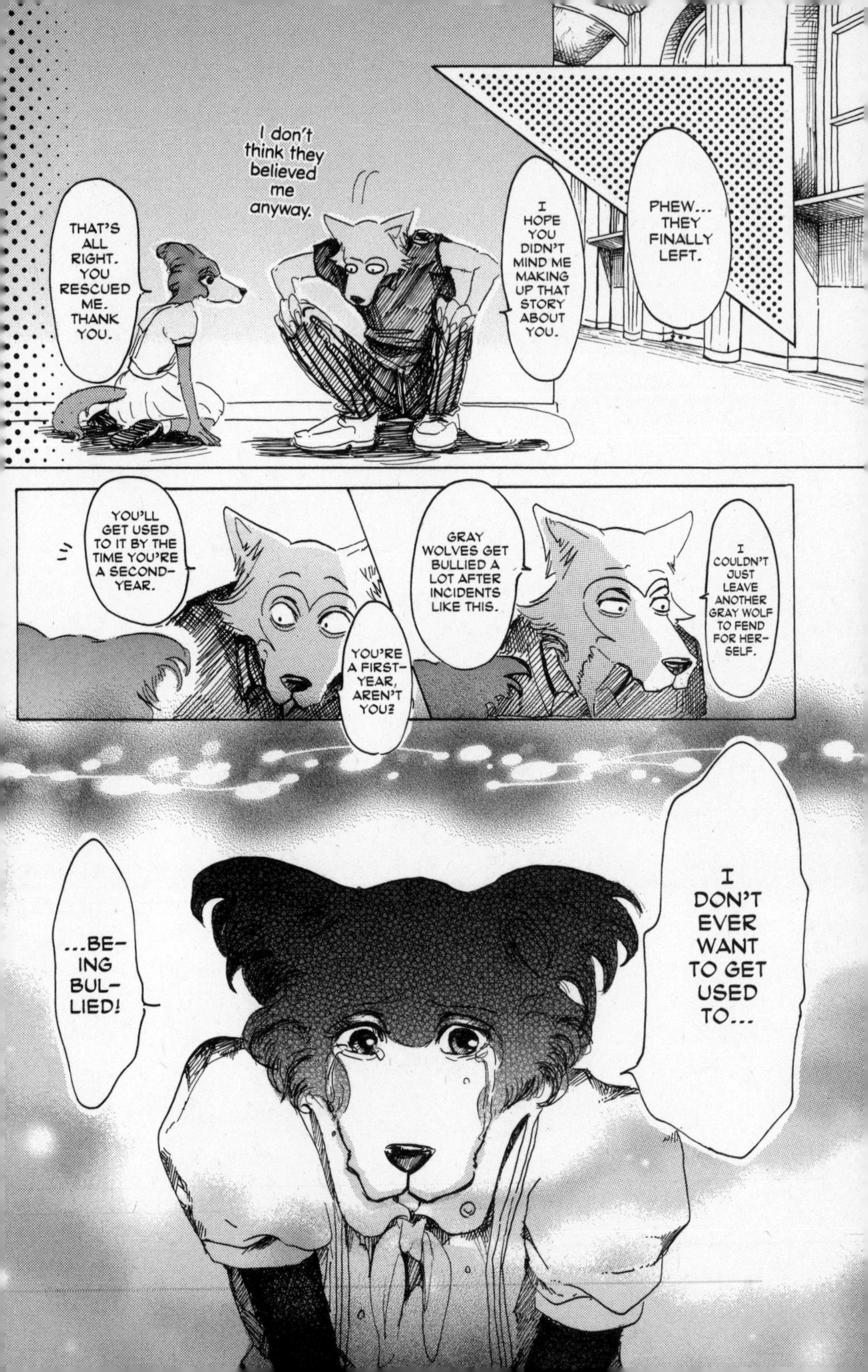
PHEW... THEY FINALLY LEFT.
I HOPE YOU DIDN'T MIND ME MAKING UP THAT STORY ABOUT YOU.
I don't think they believed me anyway.
THAT'S ALL RIGHT. YOU RESCUED ME. THANK YOU.
I COULDN'T JUST LEAVE ANOTHER GRAY WOLF TO FEND FOR HER-SELF.
GRAY WOLVES GET BULLIED A LOT AFTER INCIDENTS LIKE THIS.
YOU'RE A FIRST-YEAR, AREN'T YOU?
YOU'LL GET USED TO IT BY THE TIME YOU'RE A SECOND-YEAR.
I DON'T EVER WANT TO GET USED TO...
...BE-ING BUL-LIED!

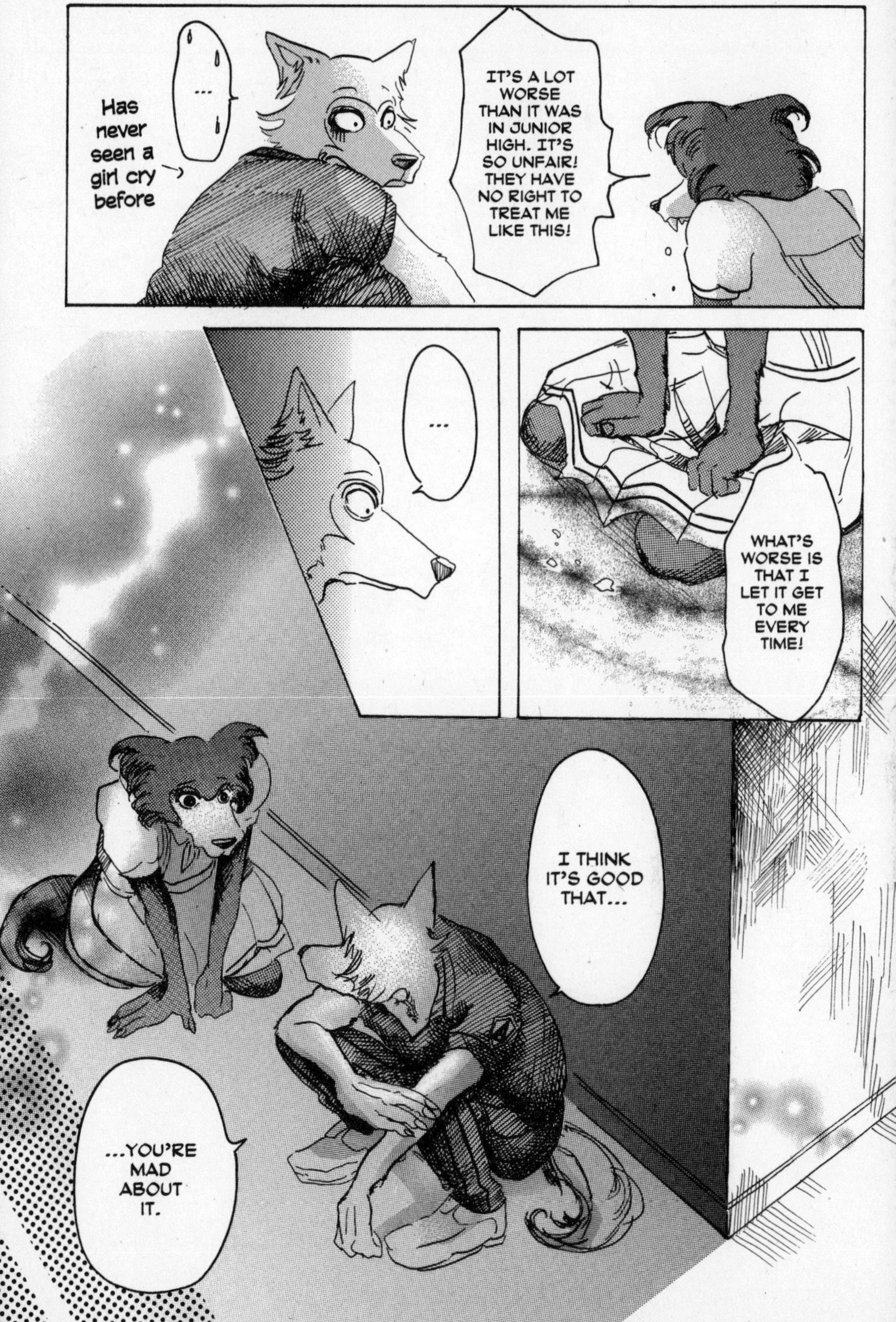
IT'S A LOT WORSE THAN IT WAS IN JUNIOR HIGH. IT'S SO UNFAIR! THEY HAVE NO RIGHT TO TREAT ME LIKE THIS!
...
Has never seen a girl cry before
WHAT'S WORSE IS THAT I LET IT GET TO ME EVERY TIME!
...
I THINK IT'S GOOD THAT...
...YOU'RE MAD ABOUT IT.

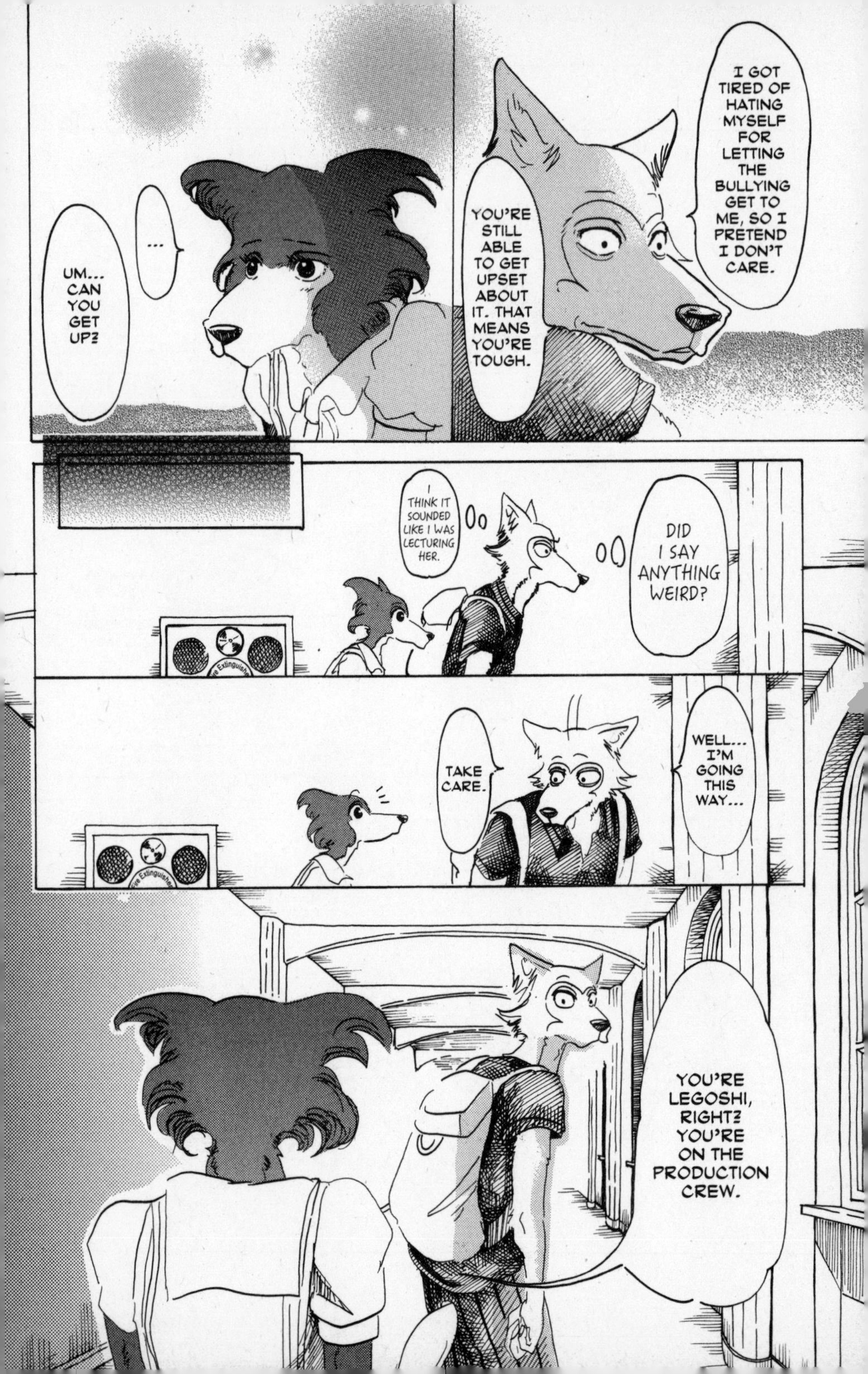
I GOT TIRED OF HATING MYSELF FOR LETTING THE BULLYING GET TO ME, SO I PRETEND I DON'T CARE.
YOU'RE STILL ABLE TO GET UPSET ABOUT IT. THAT MEANS YOU'RE TOUGH.
...
UM... CAN YOU GET UP?
DID I SAY ANYTHING WEIRD?
I THINK IT SOUNDED LIKE I WAS LECTURING HER.
WELL... I'M GOING THIS WAY...
TAKE CARE.
YOU'RE LEGOSHI, RIGHT? YOU'RE ON THE PRODUCTION CREW.

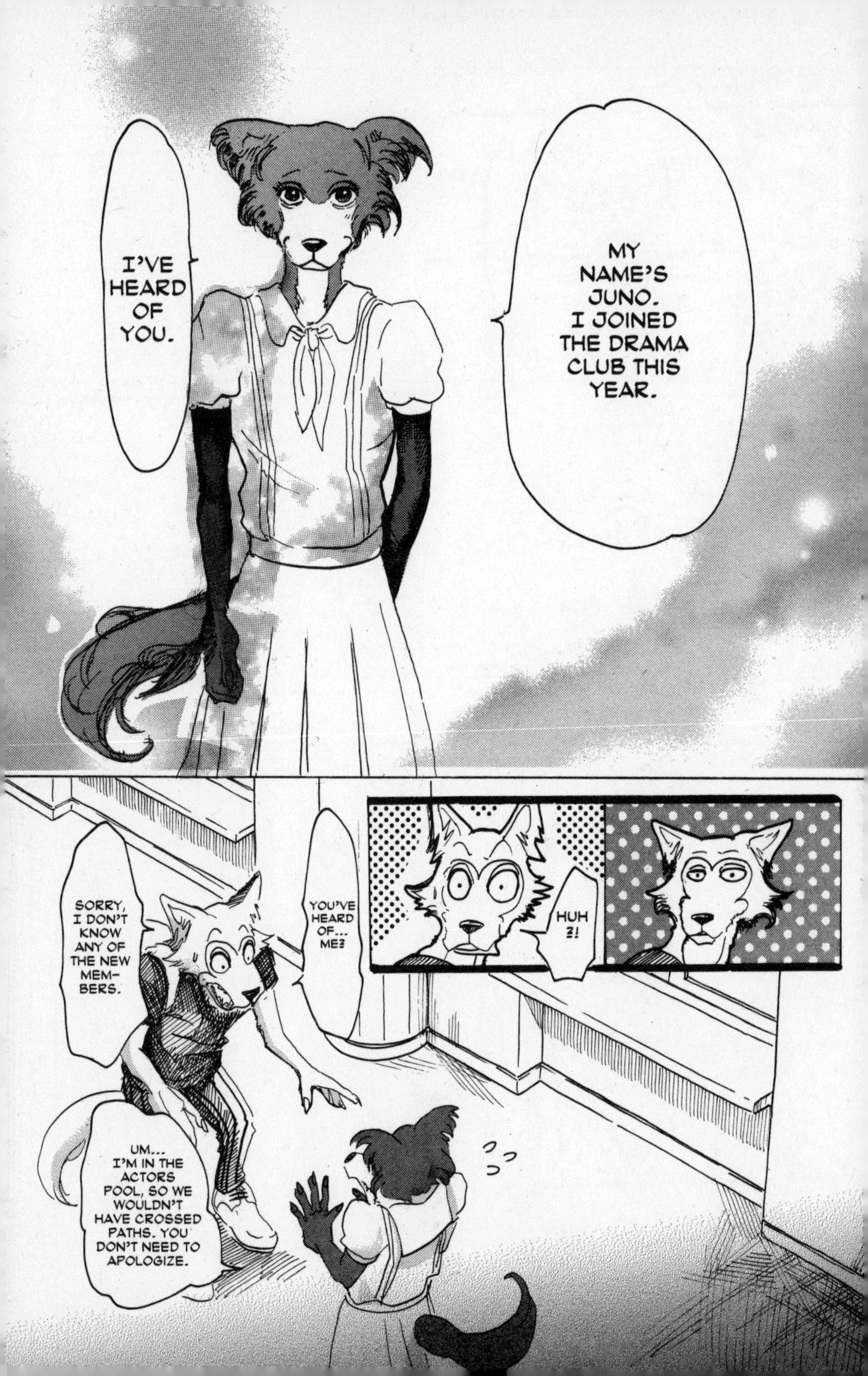
MY NAME'S JUNO. I JOINED THE DRAMA CLUB THIS YEAR.
I'VE HEARD OF YOU.
HUH ?!
YOU'VE HEARD OF... ME?
SORRY, I DON'T KNOW ANY OF THE NEW MEM-BERS.
UM... I'M IN THE ACTORS POOL, SO WE WOULDN'T HAVE CROSSED PATHS. YOU DON'T NEED TO APOLOGIZE.

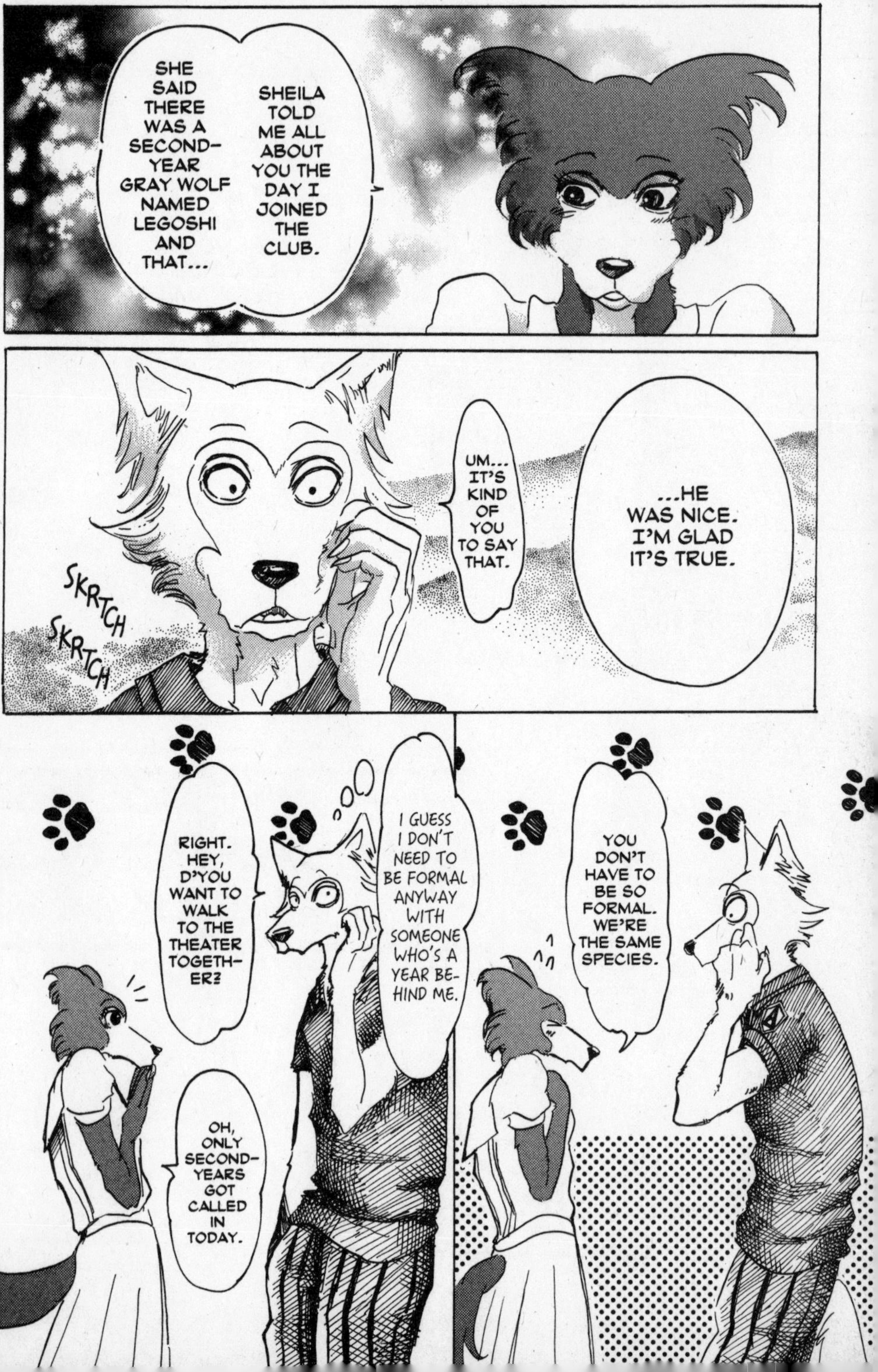
SHEILA TOLD ME ALL ABOUT YOU THE DAY I JOINED THE CLUB.
SHE SAID THERE WAS A SECOND-YEAR GRAY WOLF NAMED LEGOSHI AND THAT...
...HE WAS NICE. I'M GLAD IT'S TRUE.
UM... IT'S KIND OF YOU TO SAY THAT.
SKRTCH SKRTCH
YOU DON'T HAVE TO BE SO FORMAL. WE'RE THE SAME SPECIES.
I GUESS I DON'T NEED TO BE FORMAL ANYWAY WITH SOMEONE WHO'S A YEAR BEHIND ME.
RIGHT. HEY, D'YOU WANT TO WALK TO THE THEATER TOGETHER?
OH, ONLY SECOND-YEARS GOT CALLED IN TODAY.

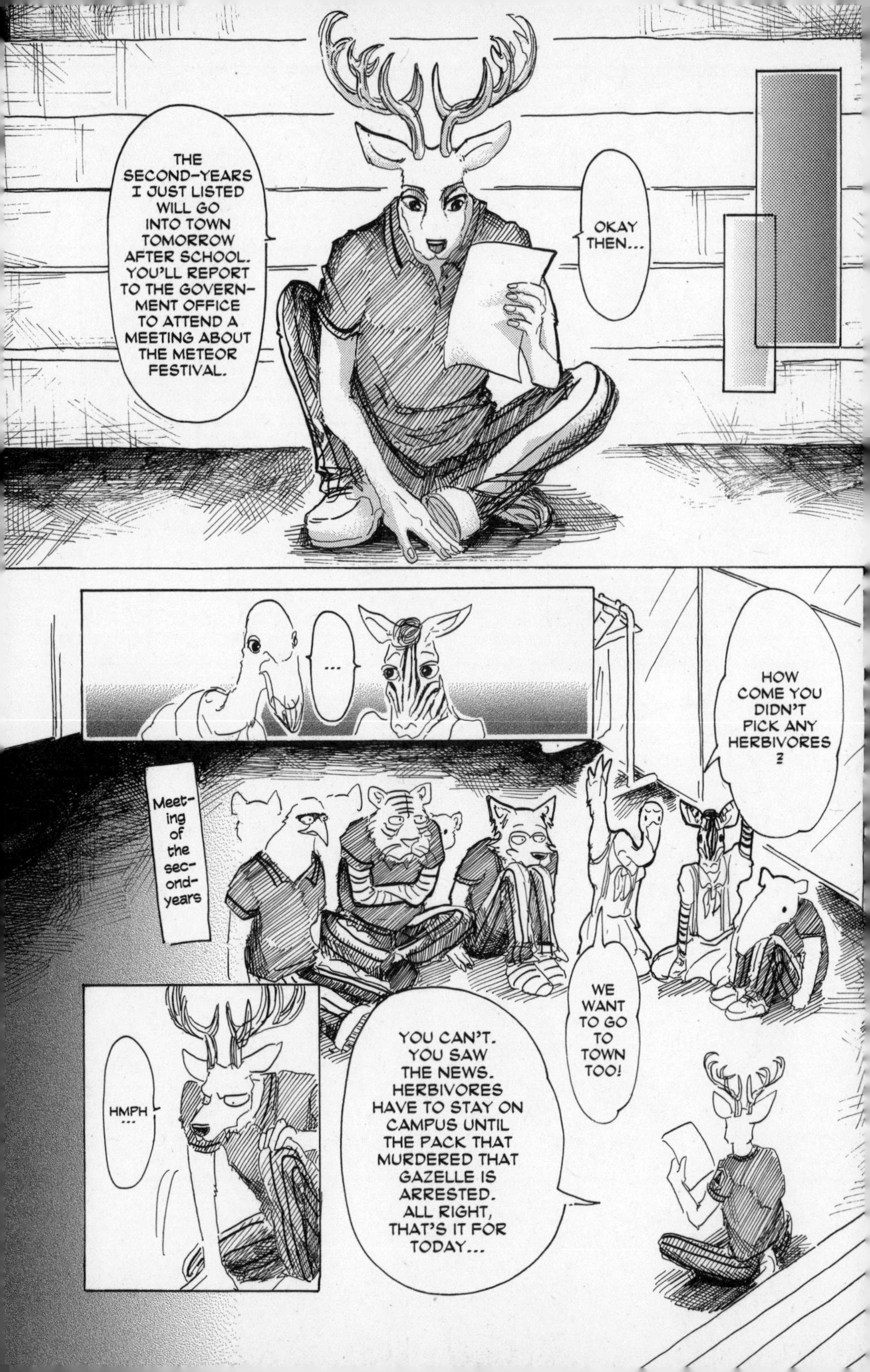
OKAY THEN...
THE SECOND-YEARS I JUST LISTED WILL GO INTO TOWN TOMORROW AFTER SCHOOL. YOU'LL REPORT TO THE GOVERNMENT OFFICE TO ATTEND A MEETING ABOUT THE METEOR FESTIVAL.
HOW COME YOU DIDN'T PICK ANY HERBIVORES?
...
Meeting of the second-years
WE WANT TO GO TO TOWN TOO!
YOU CAN'T. YOU SAW THE NEWS. HERBIVORES HAVE TO STAY ON CAMPUS UNTIL THE PACK THAT MURDERED THAT GAZELLE IS ARRESTED. ALL RIGHT, THAT'S IT FOR TODAY...
HMPH...

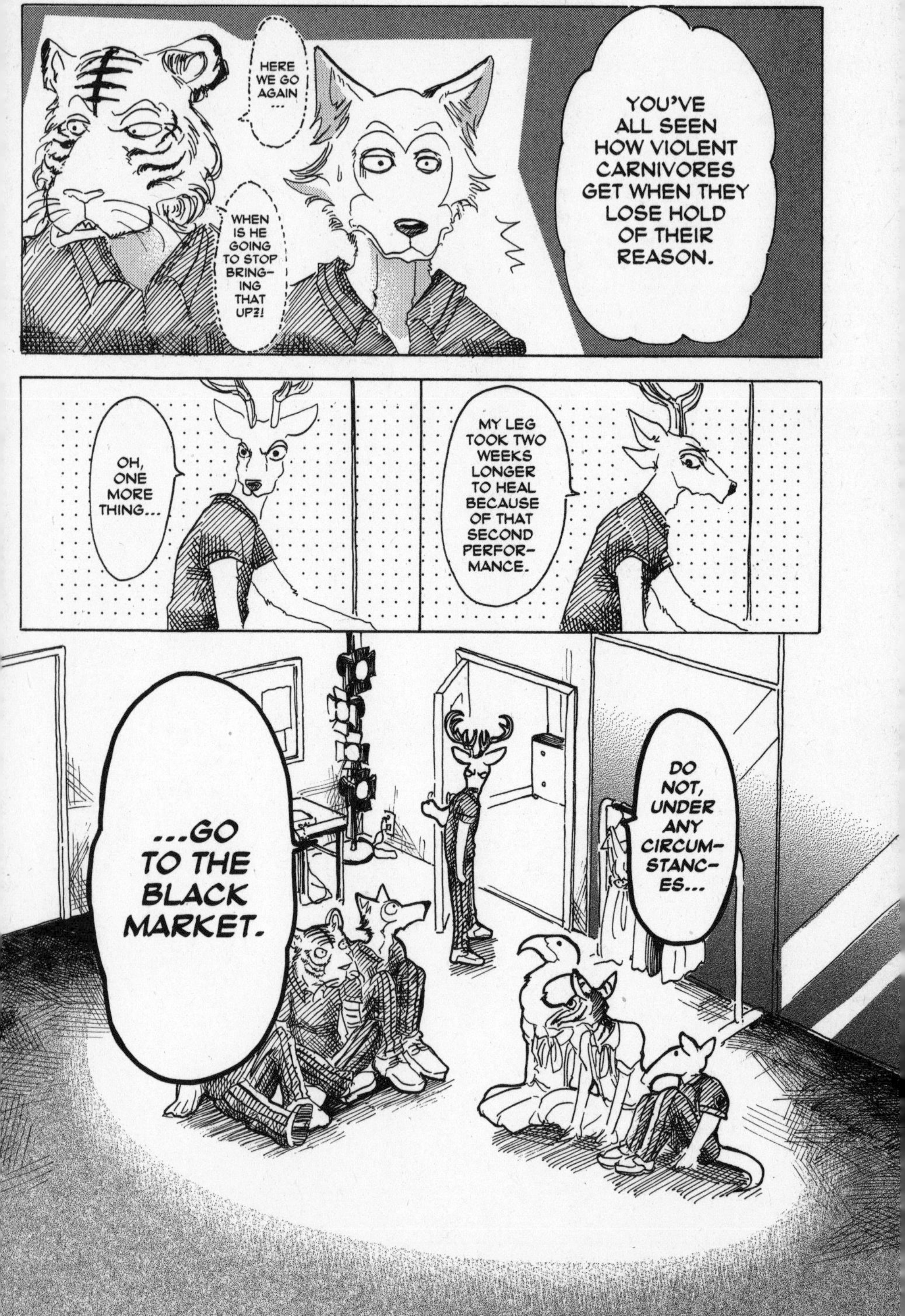
YOU'VE ALL SEEN HOW VIOLENT CARNIVORES GET WHEN THEY LOSE HOLD OF THEIR REASON.
HERE WE GO AGAIN...
WHEN IS HE GOING TO STOP BRING-ING THAT UP?!
MY LEG TOOK TWO WEEKS LONGER TO HEAL BECAUSE OF THAT SECOND PERFOR-MANCE.
OH, ONE MORE THING...
DO NOT, UNDER ANY CIRCUM-STANC-ES...
...GO TO THE BLACK MARKET.

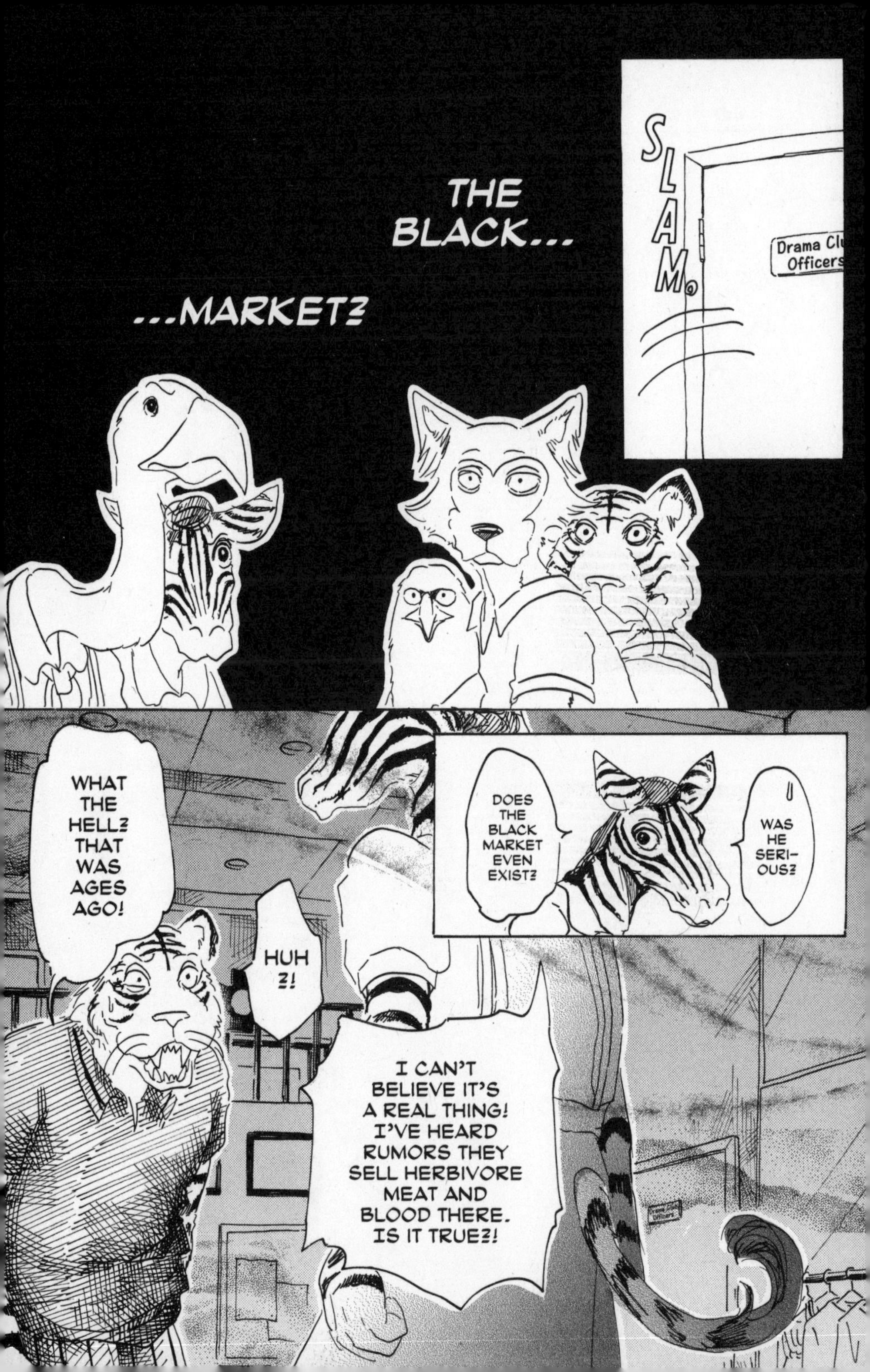
SLAM
Drama Clu
Officers
THE BLACK...
...MARKET?
WAS HE SERIOUS?
DOES THE BLACK MARKET EVEN EXIST?
WHAT THE HELL? THAT WAS AGES AGO!
HUH?!
I CAN'T BELIEVE IT'S A REAL THING! I'VE HEARD RUMORS THEY SELL HERBIVORE MEAT AND BLOOD THERE. IS IT TRUE?!

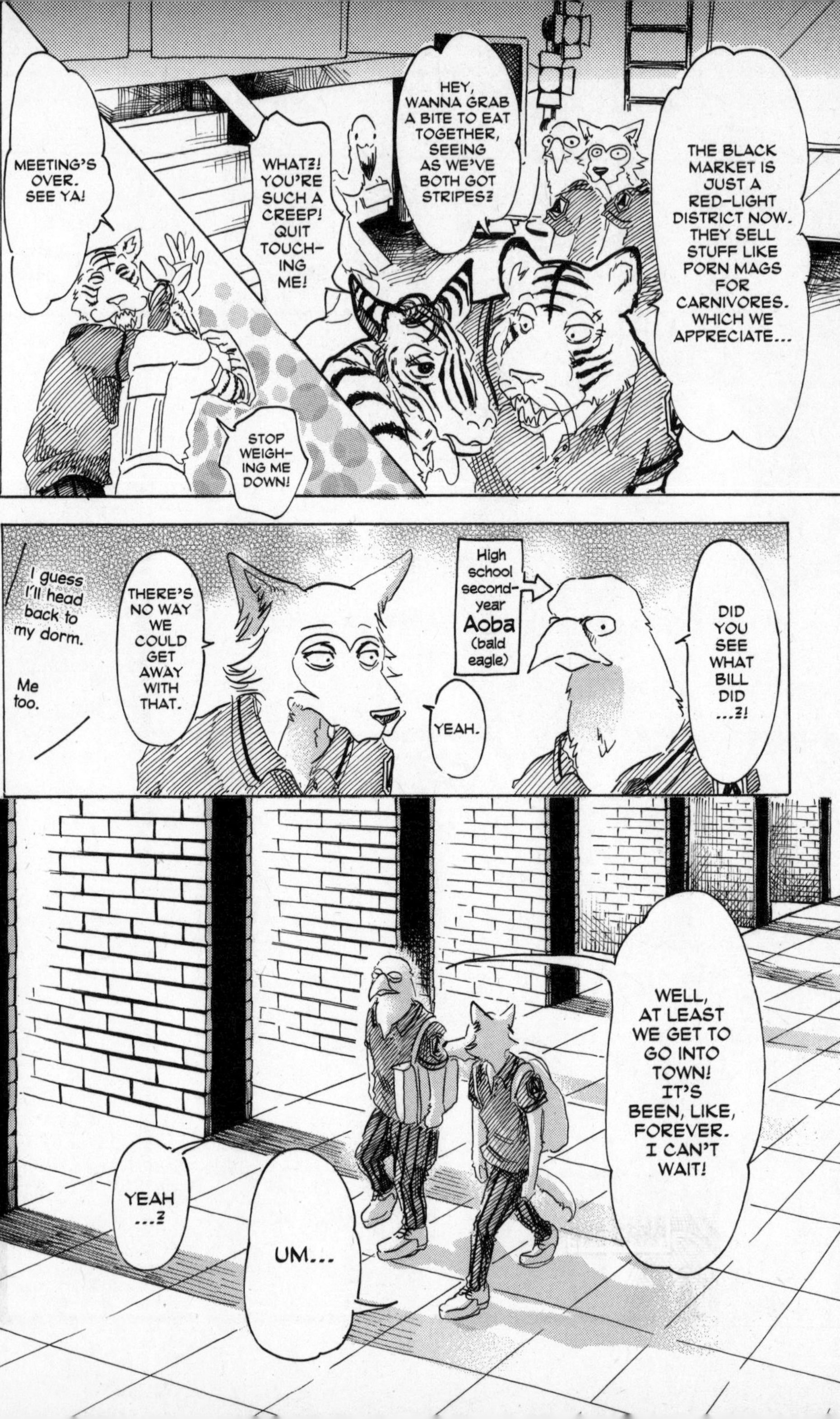
THE BLACK MARKET IS JUST A RED-LIGHT DISTRICT NOW. THEY SELL STUFF LIKE PORN MAGS FOR CARNIVORES. WHICH WE APPRECIATE...
HEY, WANNA GRAB A BITE TO EAT TOGETHER, SEEING AS WE'VE BOTH GOT STRIPES?
WHAT?! YOU'RE SUCH A CREEP! QUIT TOUCHING ME!
MEETING'S OVER. SEE YA!
STOP WEIGHING ME DOWN!
DID YOU SEE WHAT BILL DID ...?!
High school second-year Aoba (bald eagle)
YEAH.
THERE'S NO WAY WE COULD GET AWAY WITH THAT.
I guess I'll head back to my dorm.
Me too.
WELL, AT LEAST WE GET TO GO INTO TOWN! IT'S BEEN, LIKE, FOREVER. I CAN'T WAIT!
UM...
YEAH ...?

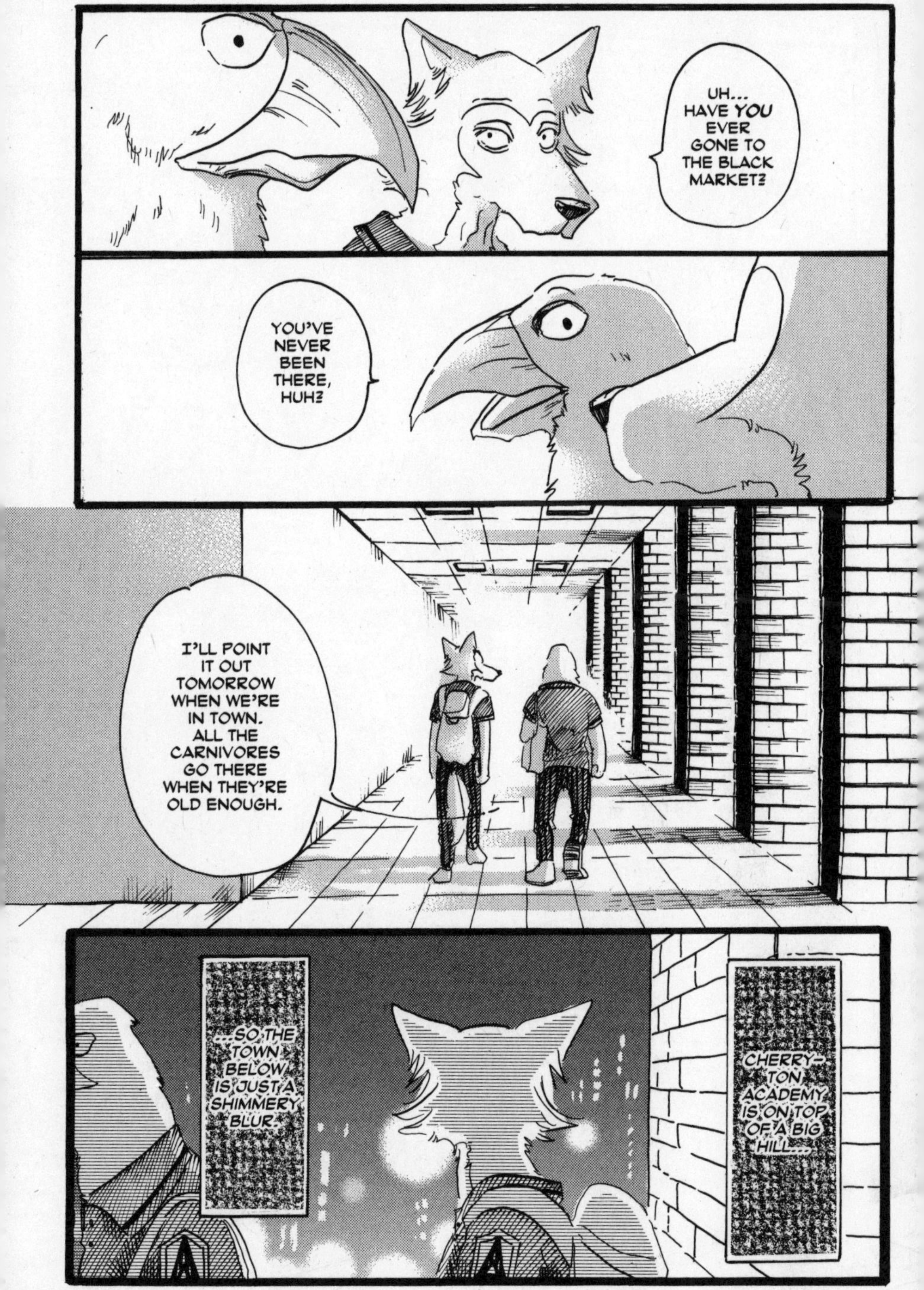
UH... HAVE YOU EVER GONE TO THE BLACK MARKET?
YOU'VE NEVER BEEN THERE, HUH?
I'LL POINT IT OUT TOMORROW WHEN WE'RE IN TOWN. ALL THE CARNIVORES GO THERE WHEN THEY'RE OLD ENOUGH.
CHERRY-TON ACADEMY IS ON TOP OF A BIG HILL...
...SO THE TOWN BELOW IS JUST A SHIMMERY BLUR.

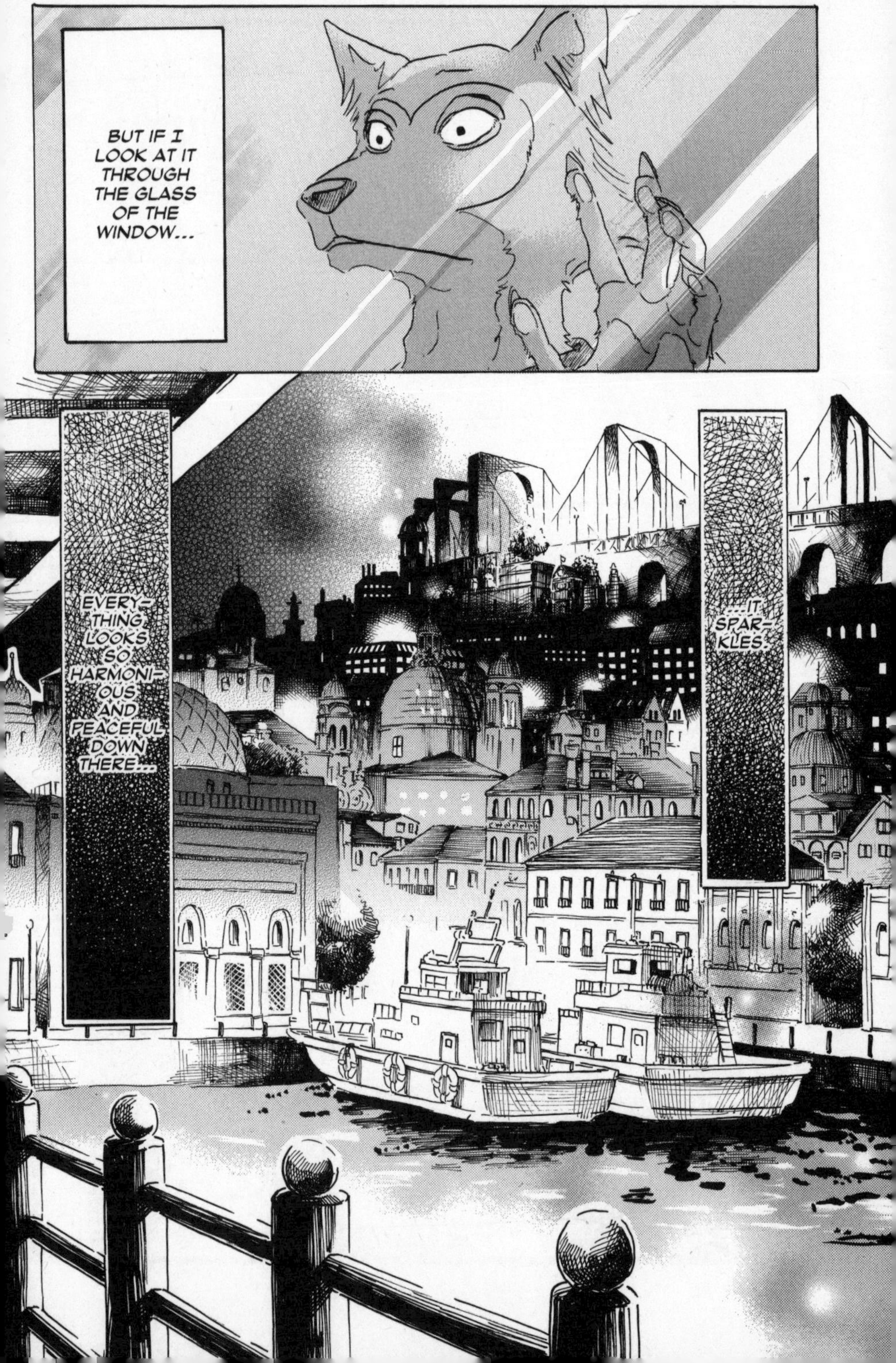
BUT IF I LOOK AT IT THROUGH THE GLASS OF THE WINDOW...
EVERY-THING LOOKS SO HARMONI-OUS AND PEACEFUL DOWN THERE...
...IT SPAR-KLES.

Chapter 22: Shadows of Tall Buildings

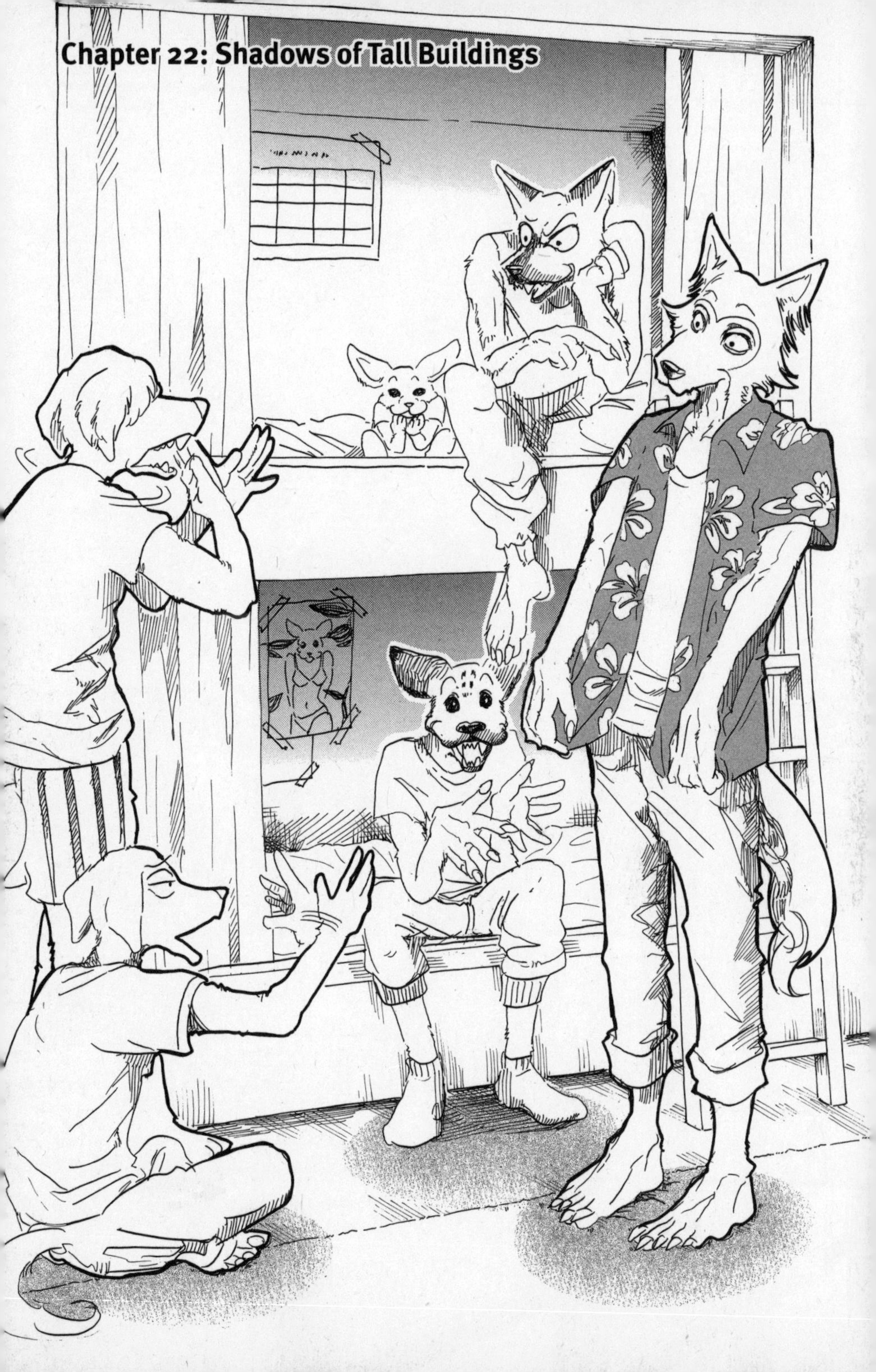

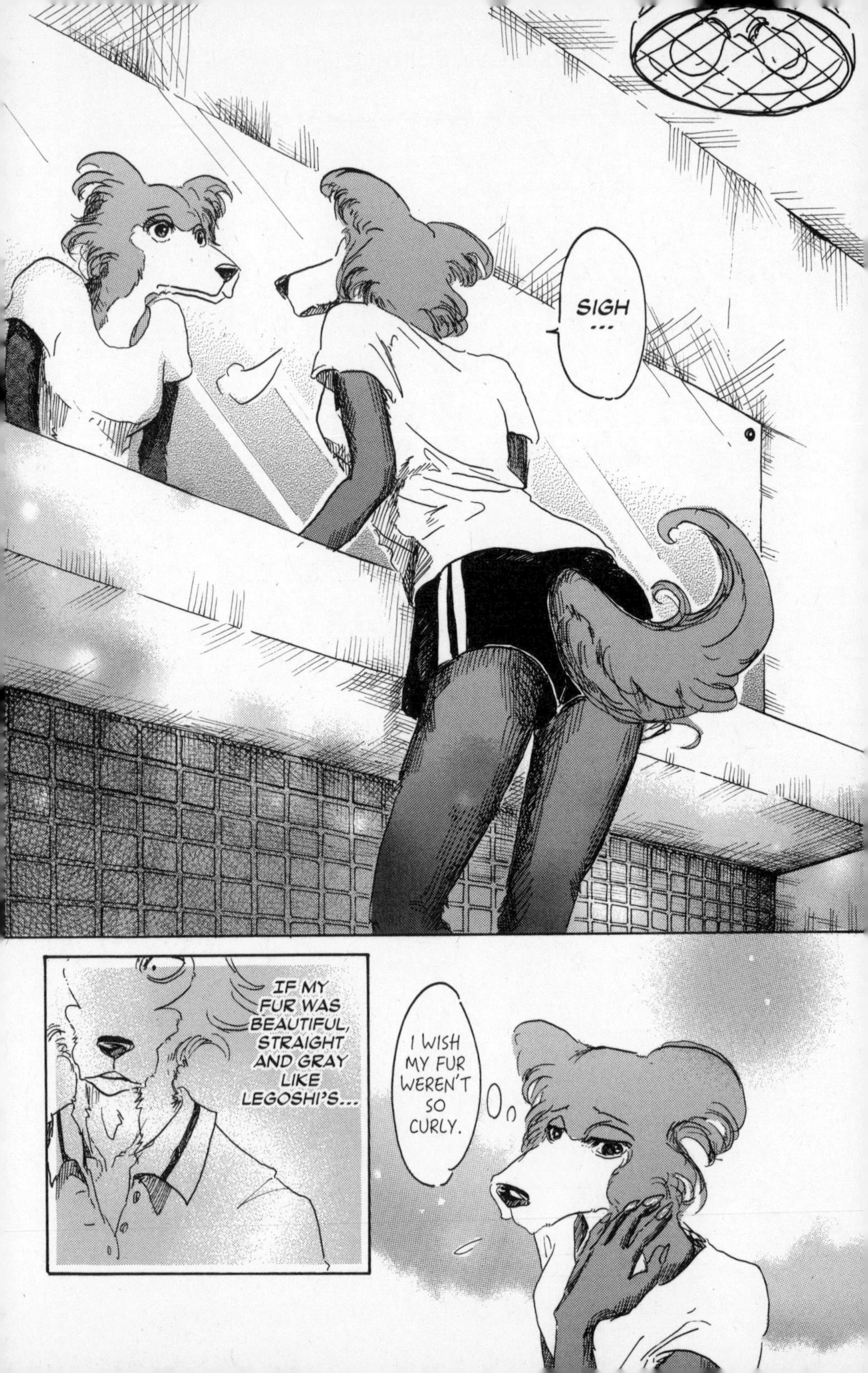
SIGH...
I WISH MY FUR WEREN'T SO CURLY.
IF MY FUR WAS BEAUTIFUL, STRAIGHT AND GRAY LIKE LEGOSHI'S...

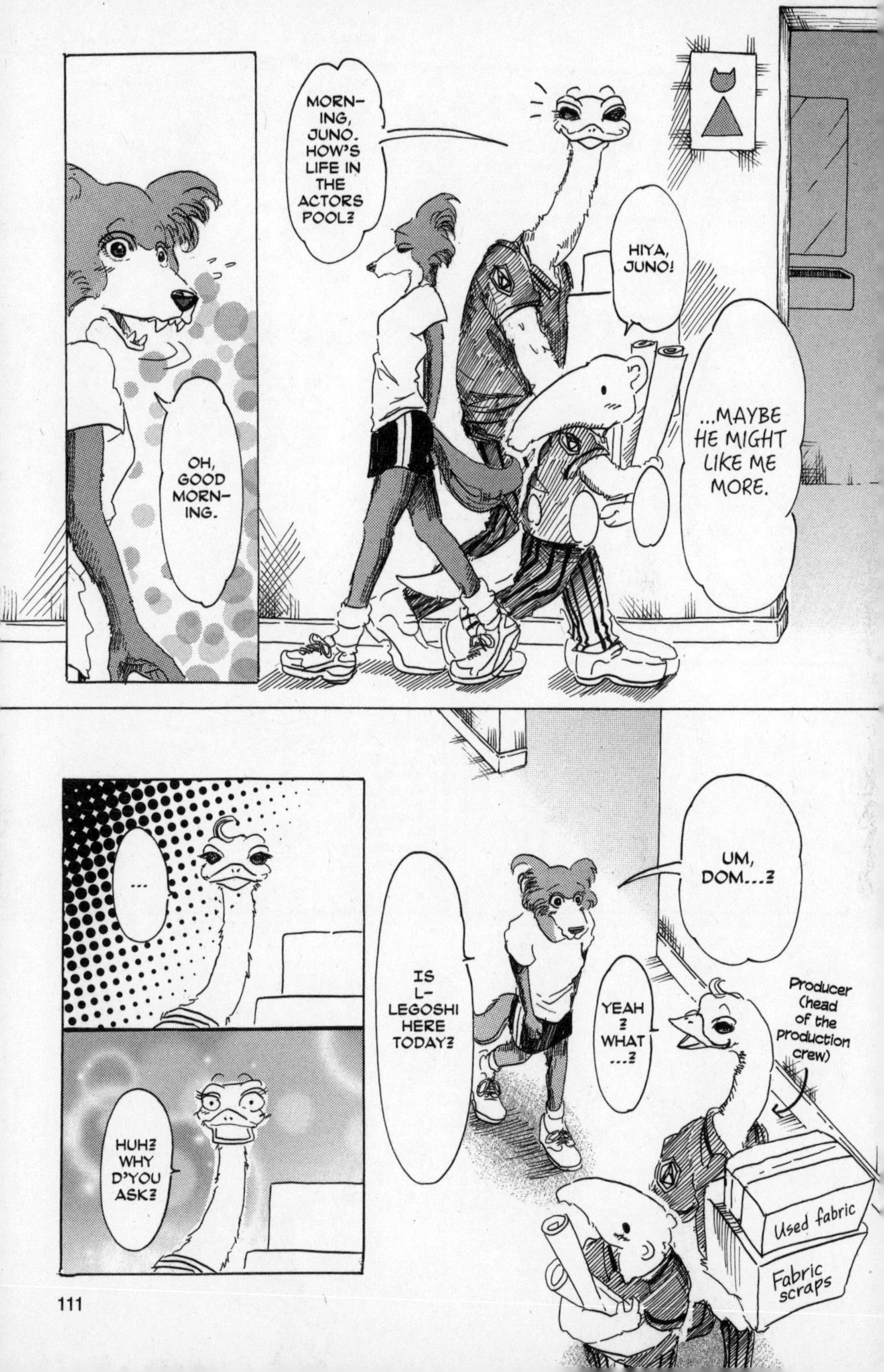
MORNING, JUNO. HOW'S LIFE IN THE ACTORS POOL?
HIYA, JUNO!
...MAYBE HE MIGHT LIKE ME MORE.
OH, GOOD MORNING.
UM, DOM...?
YEAH? WHAT...?
IS L-LEGOSHI HERE TODAY?
Producer (head of the production crew)
Used fabric
Fabric scraps
...
HUH? WHY D'YOU ASK?

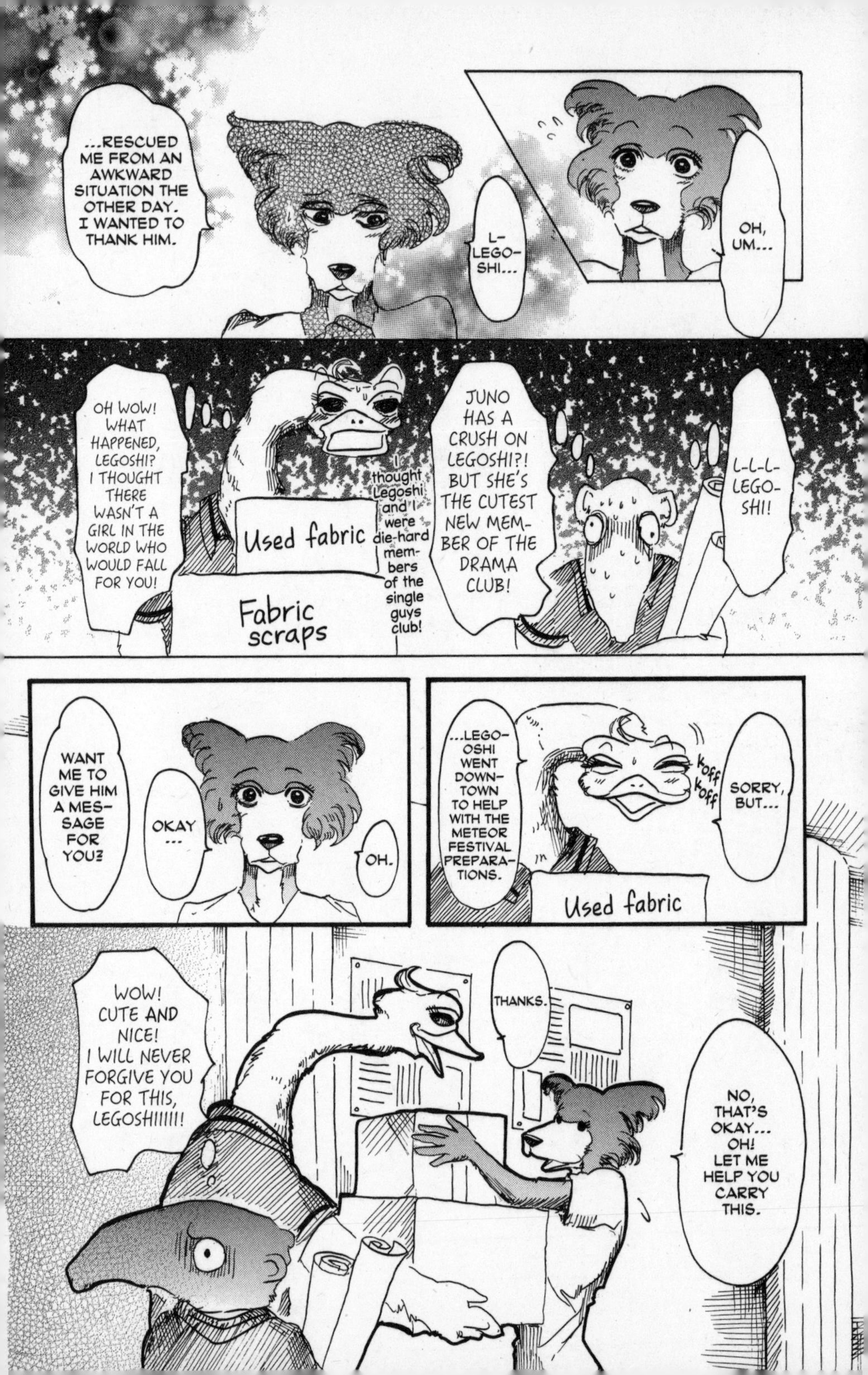
OH, UM...
L-LEGO-SHI...
...RESCUED ME FROM AN AWKWARD SITUATION THE OTHER DAY. I WANTED TO THANK HIM.
L-L-L-LEGO-SHI!
JUNO HAS A CRUSH ON LEGOSHI?! BUT SHE'S THE CUTEST NEW MEM-BER OF THE DRAMA CLUB!
I thought Legoshi and I were die-hard mem-bers of the single guys club!
OH WOW! WHAT HAPPENED, LEGOSHI? I THOUGHT THERE WASN'T A GIRL IN THE WORLD WHO WOULD FALL FOR YOU!
Used fabric
Fabric scraps
SORRY, BUT...
koff koff
...LEGO-OSHI WENT DOWN-TOWN TO HELP WITH THE METEOR FESTIVAL PREPARA-TIONS.
Used fabric
OH.
OKAY...
WANT ME TO GIVE HIM A MES-SAGE FOR YOU?
NO, THAT'S OKAY... OH! LET ME HELP YOU CARRY THIS.
THANKS.
WOW! CUTE AND NICE! I WILL NEVER FORGIVE YOU FOR THIS, LEGOSHIIIIII!

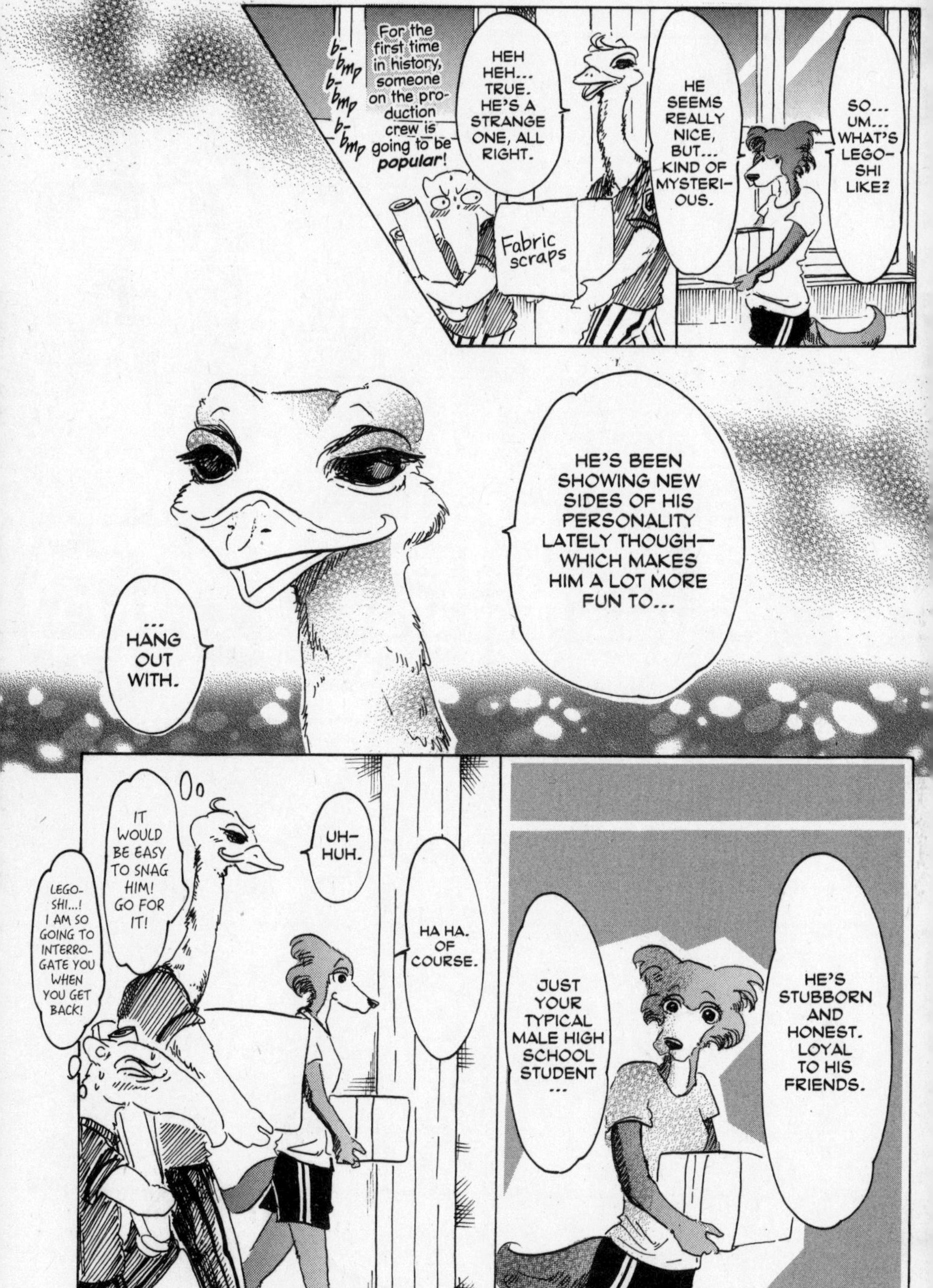
SO... UM... WHAT'S LEGO-SHI LIKE?
HE SEEMS REALLY NICE, BUT... KIND OF MYSTERI-OUS.
HEH HEH... TRUE. HE'S A STRANGE ONE, ALL RIGHT.
Fabric scraps
For the first time in history, someone on the pro-duction crew is going to be ***popular***!
b-bmp b-bmp b-bmp
HE'S BEEN SHOWING NEW SIDES OF HIS PERSONALITY LATELY THOUGH—WHICH MAKES HIM A LOT MORE FUN TO...
...HANG OUT WITH.
HE'S STUBBORN AND HONEST. LOYAL TO HIS FRIENDS.
JUST YOUR TYPICAL MALE HIGH SCHOOL STUDENT...
HA HA. OF COURSE.
UH-HUH.
IT WOULD BE EASY TO SNAG HIM! GO FOR IT!
LEGO-SHI...! I AM SO GOING TO INTERROGATE YOU WHEN YOU GET BACK!

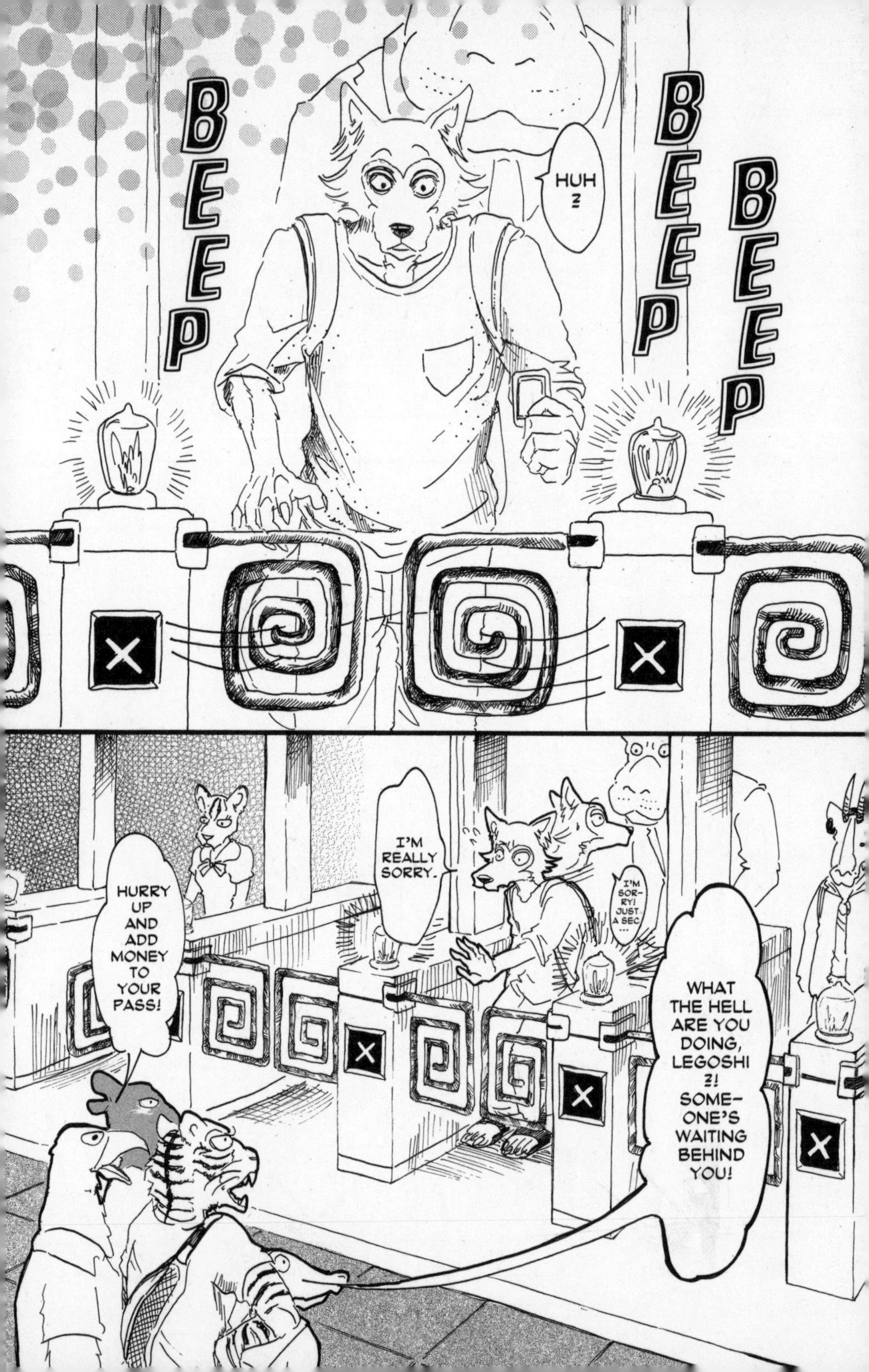
BEEP
BEEP
BEEP
HUH?
WHAT THE HELL ARE YOU DOING, LEGOSHI?! SOMEONE'S WAITING BEHIND YOU!
I'M SORRY! JUST A SEC...
I'M REALLY SORRY.
HURRY UP AND ADD MONEY TO YOUR PASS!

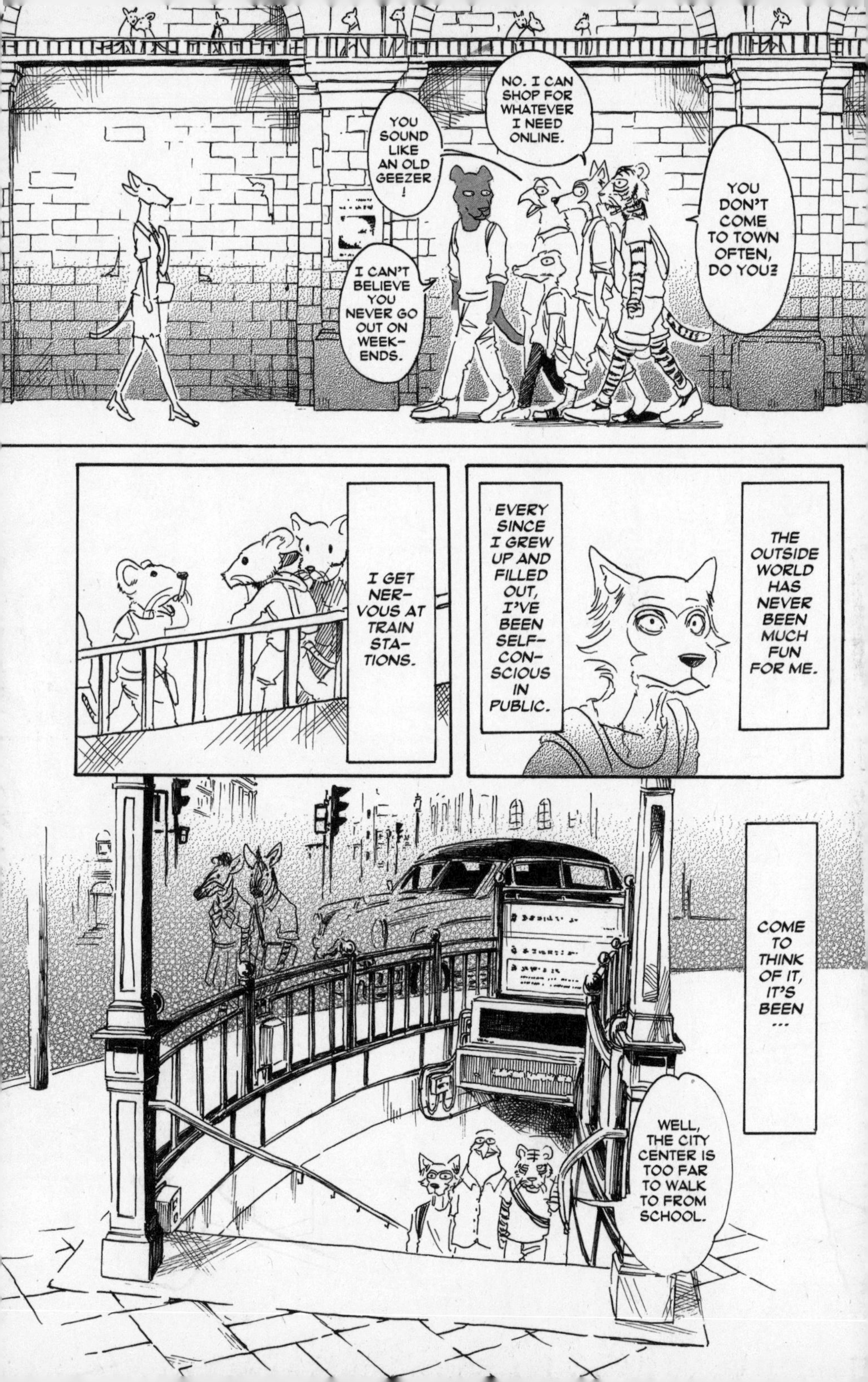
YOU DON'T COME TO TOWN OFTEN, DO YOU?
NO. I CAN SHOP FOR WHATEVER I NEED ONLINE.
YOU SOUND LIKE AN OLD GEEZER!
I CAN'T BELIEVE YOU NEVER GO OUT ON WEEKENDS.
THE OUTSIDE WORLD HAS NEVER BEEN MUCH FUN FOR ME.
EVERY SINCE I GREW UP AND FILLED OUT, I'VE BEEN SELF-CONSCIOUS IN PUBLIC.
I GET NERVOUS AT TRAIN STATIONS.
COME TO THINK OF IT, IT'S BEEN ...
WELL, THE CITY CENTER IS TOO FAR TO WALK TO FROM SCHOOL.

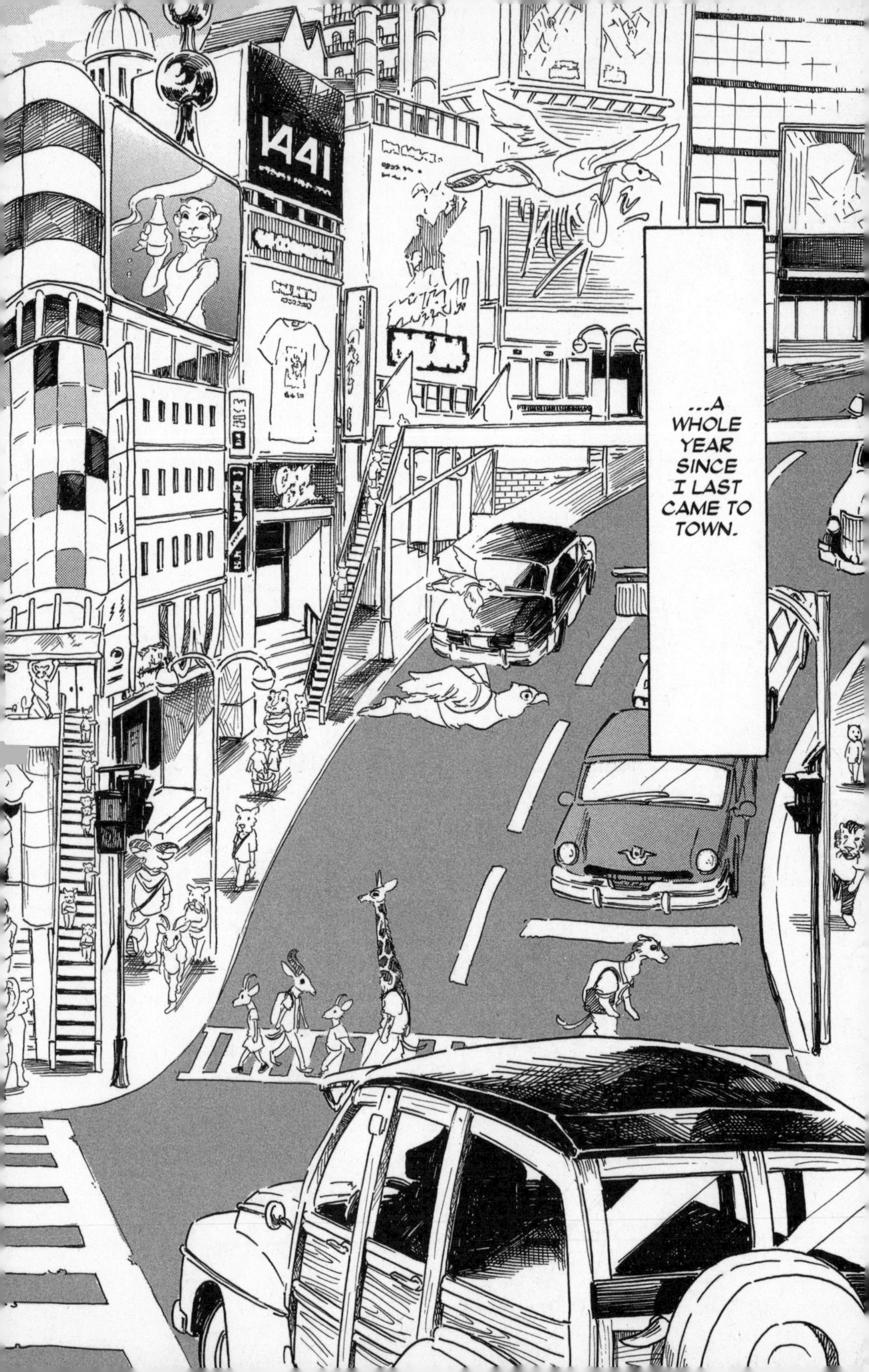
...A WHOLE YEAR SINCE I LAST CAME TO TOWN.

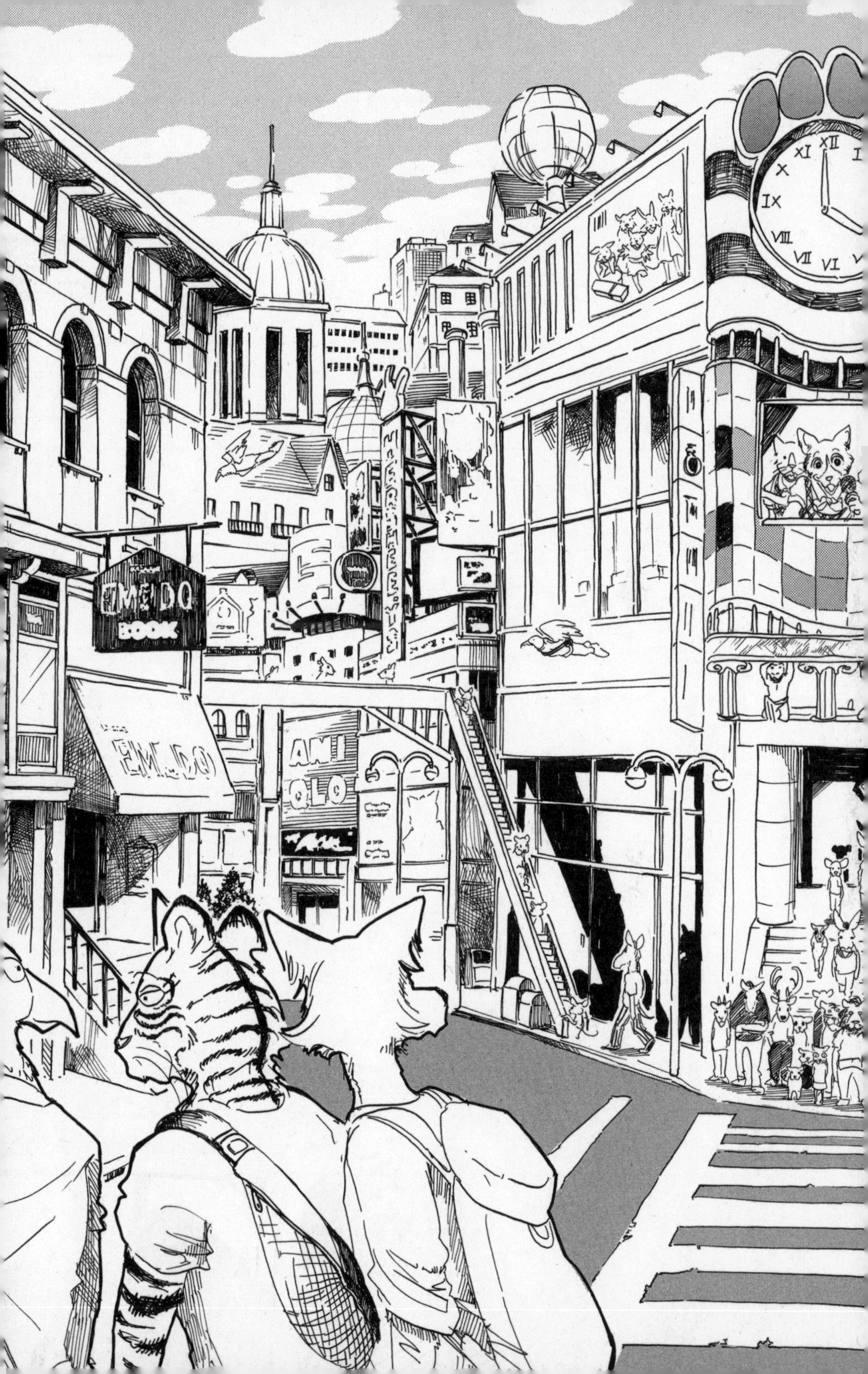
BOOK
ANI
QLO

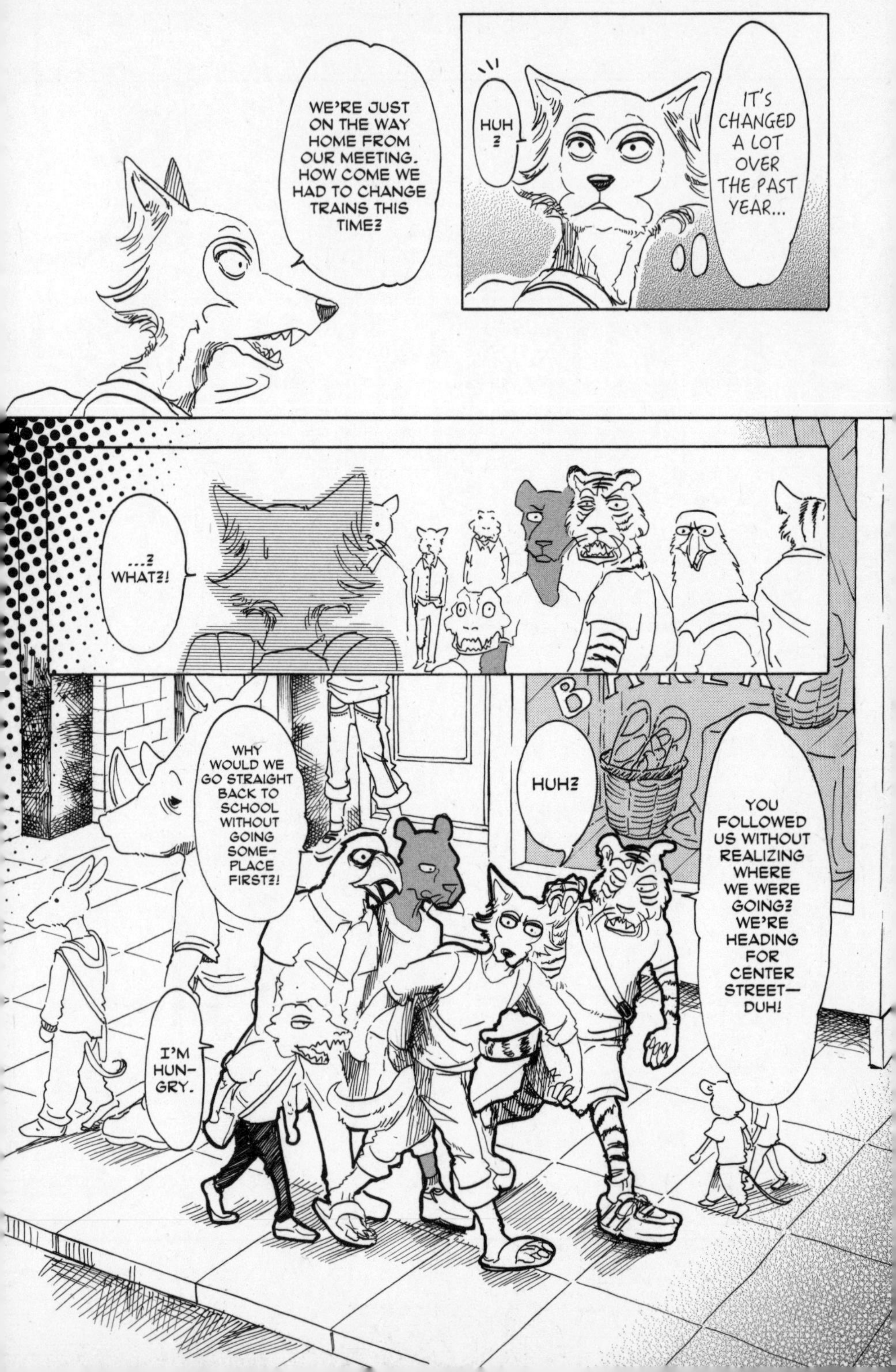
IT'S CHANGED A LOT OVER THE PAST YEAR...
HUH?
WE'RE JUST ON THE WAY HOME FROM OUR MEETING. HOW COME WE HAD TO CHANGE TRAINS THIS TIME?
...? WHAT?!
YOU FOLLOWED US WITHOUT REALIZING WHERE WE WERE GOING? WE'RE HEADING FOR CENTER STREET—DUH!
HUH?
WHY WOULD WE GO STRAIGHT BACK TO SCHOOL WITHOUT GOING SOME-PLACE FIRST?!
I'M HUN-GRY.

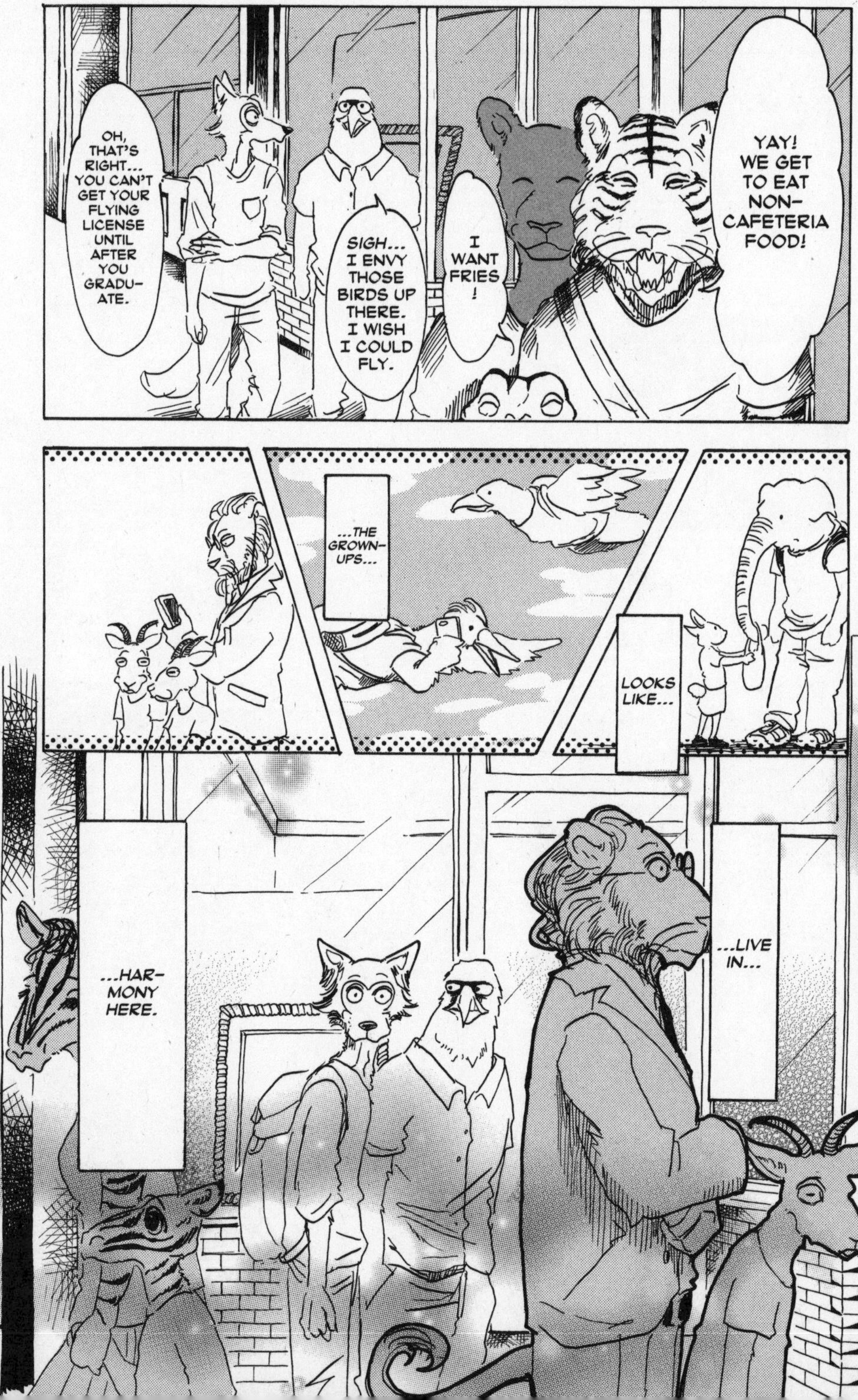
YAY! WE GET TO EAT NON-CAFETERIA FOOD!
I WANT FRIES!
SIGH... I ENVY THOSE BIRDS UP THERE. I WISH I COULD FLY.
OH, THAT'S RIGHT... YOU CAN'T GET YOUR FLYING LICENSE UNTIL AFTER YOU GRADUATE.
LOOKS LIKE...
...THE GROWN-UPS...
...LIVE IN...
...HARMONY HERE.

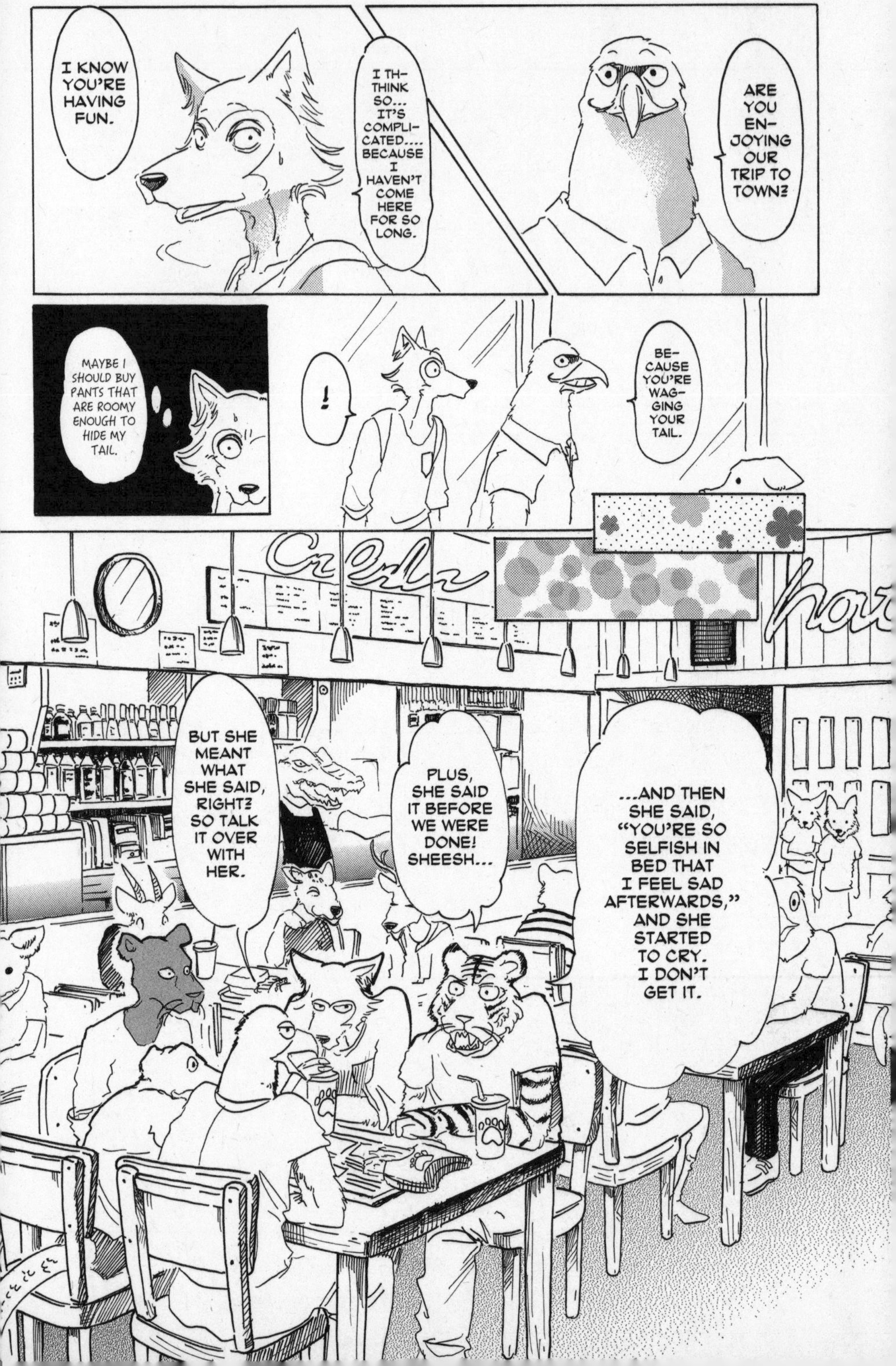

ARE YOU EN-JOYING OUR TRIP TO TOWN?
I TH-THINK SO... IT'S COMPLICATED.... BECAUSE I HAVEN'T COME HERE FOR SO LONG.
I KNOW YOU'RE HAVING FUN.
BE-CAUSE YOU'RE WAG-GING YOUR TAIL.
!
MAYBE I SHOULD BUY PANTS THAT ARE ROOMY ENOUGH TO HIDE MY TAIL.
...AND THEN SHE SAID, "YOU'RE SO SELFISH IN BED THAT I FEEL SAD AFTERWARDS," AND SHE STARTED TO CRY. I DON'T GET IT.
PLUS, SHE SAID IT BEFORE WE WERE DONE! SHEESH...
BUT SHE MEANT WHAT SHE SAID, RIGHT? SO TALK IT OVER WITH HER.

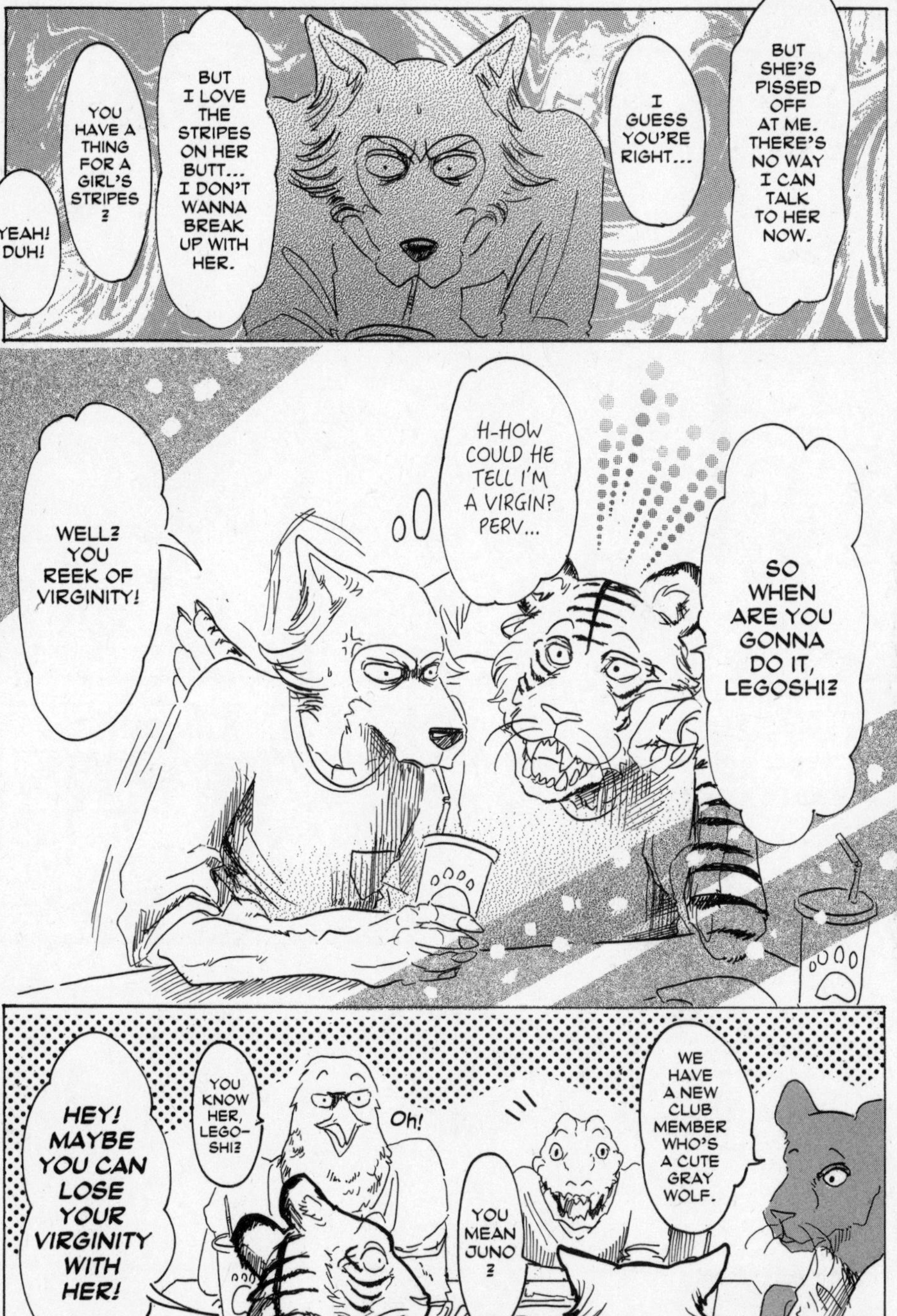
BUT SHE'S PISSED OFF AT ME. THERE'S NO WAY I CAN TALK TO HER NOW.
I GUESS YOU'RE RIGHT...
BUT I LOVE THE STRIPES ON HER BUTT... I DON'T WANNA BREAK UP WITH HER.
YOU HAVE A THING FOR A GIRL'S STRIPES?
YEAH! DUH!
SO WHEN ARE YOU GONNA DO IT, LEGOSHI?
H-HOW COULD HE TELL I'M A VIRGIN? PERV...
WELL? YOU REEK OF VIRGINITY!
WE HAVE A NEW CLUB MEMBER WHO'S A CUTE GRAY WOLF.
YOU MEAN JUNO?
Oh!
YOU KNOW HER, LEGO-SHI?
HEY! MAYBE YOU CAN LOSE YOUR VIRGINITY WITH HER!

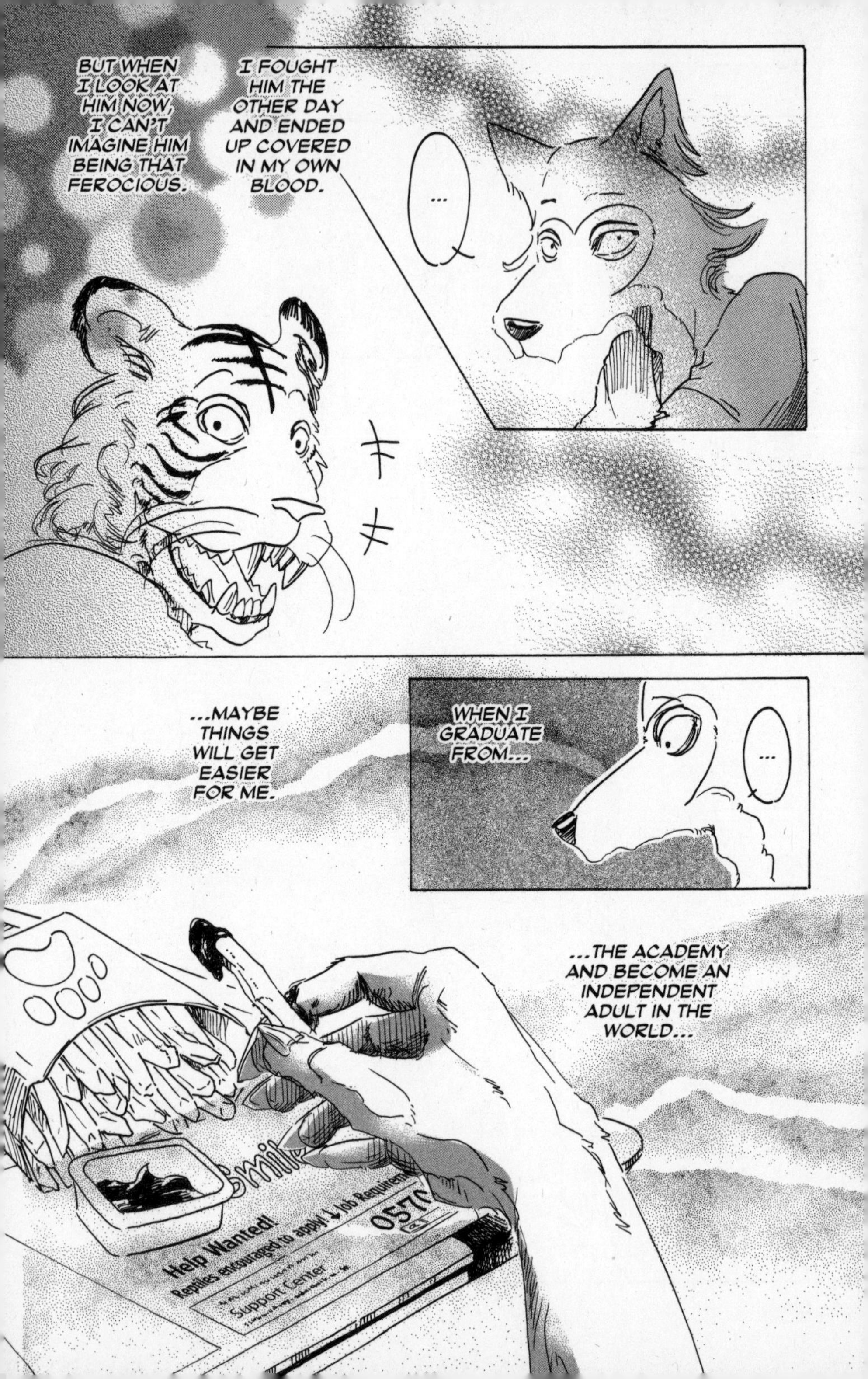

I FOUGHT HIM THE OTHER DAY AND ENDED UP COVERED IN MY OWN BLOOD.
BUT WHEN I LOOK AT HIM NOW, I CAN'T IMAGINE HIM BEING THAT FEROCIOUS.
...
WHEN I GRADUATE FROM...
...
...THE ACADEMY AND BECOME AN INDEPENDENT ADULT IN THE WORLD...
...MAYBE THINGS WILL GET EASIER FOR ME.
Help Wanted!
Reptiles encouraged to apply!
0570
Support Center

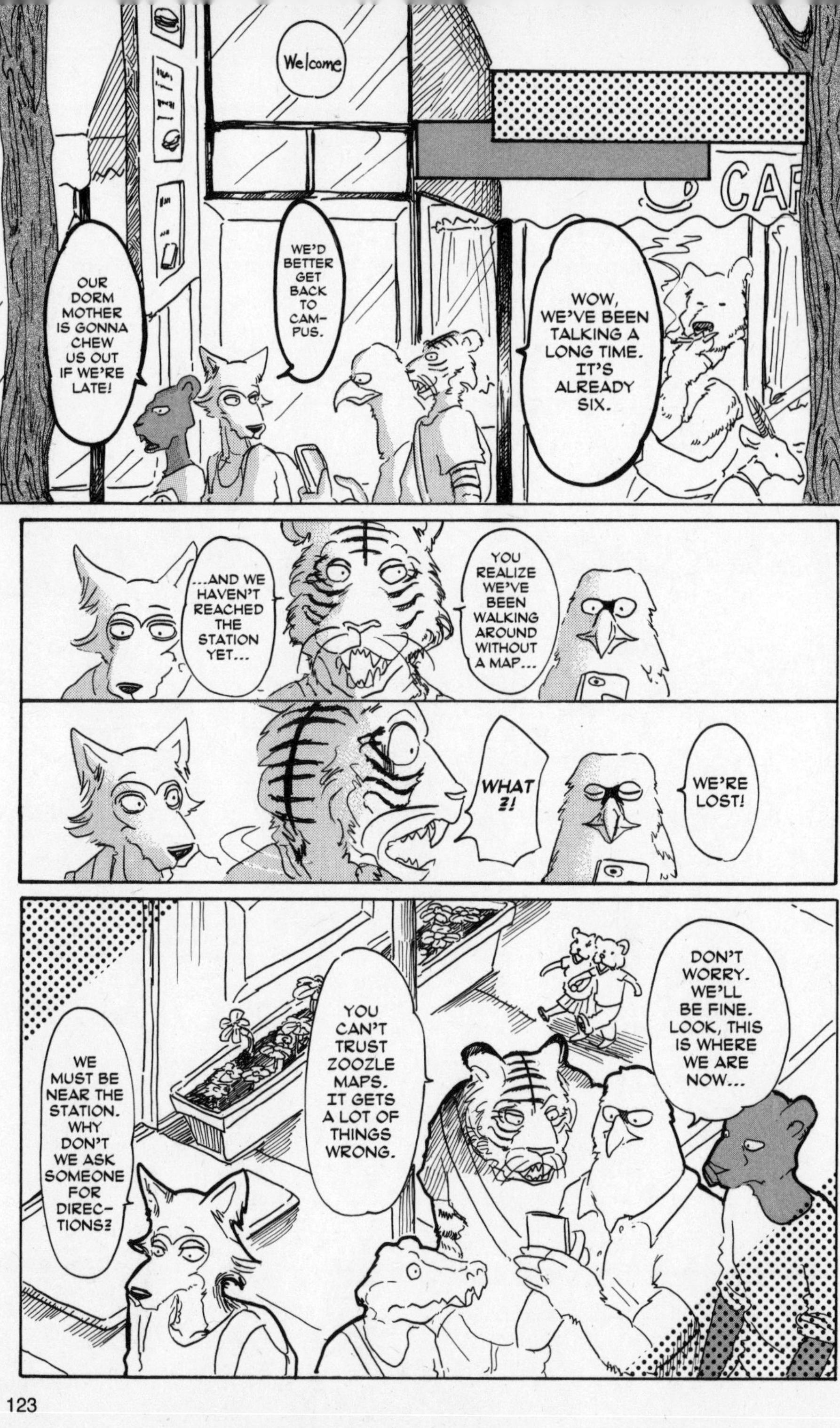
CAF
Welcome
WOW, WE'VE BEEN TALKING A LONG TIME. IT'S ALREADY SIX.
WE'D BETTER GET BACK TO CAM-PUS.
OUR DORM MOTHER IS GONNA CHEW US OUT IF WE'RE LATE!
YOU REALIZE WE'VE BEEN WALKING AROUND WITHOUT A MAP...
...AND WE HAVEN'T REACHED THE STATION YET...
WE'RE LOST!
WHAT?!
DON'T WORRY. WE'LL BE FINE. LOOK, THIS IS WHERE WE ARE NOW...
YOU CAN'T TRUST ZOOZLE MAPS. IT GETS A LOT OF THINGS WRONG.
WE MUST BE NEAR THE STATION. WHY DON'T WE ASK SOMEONE FOR DIRECTIONS?

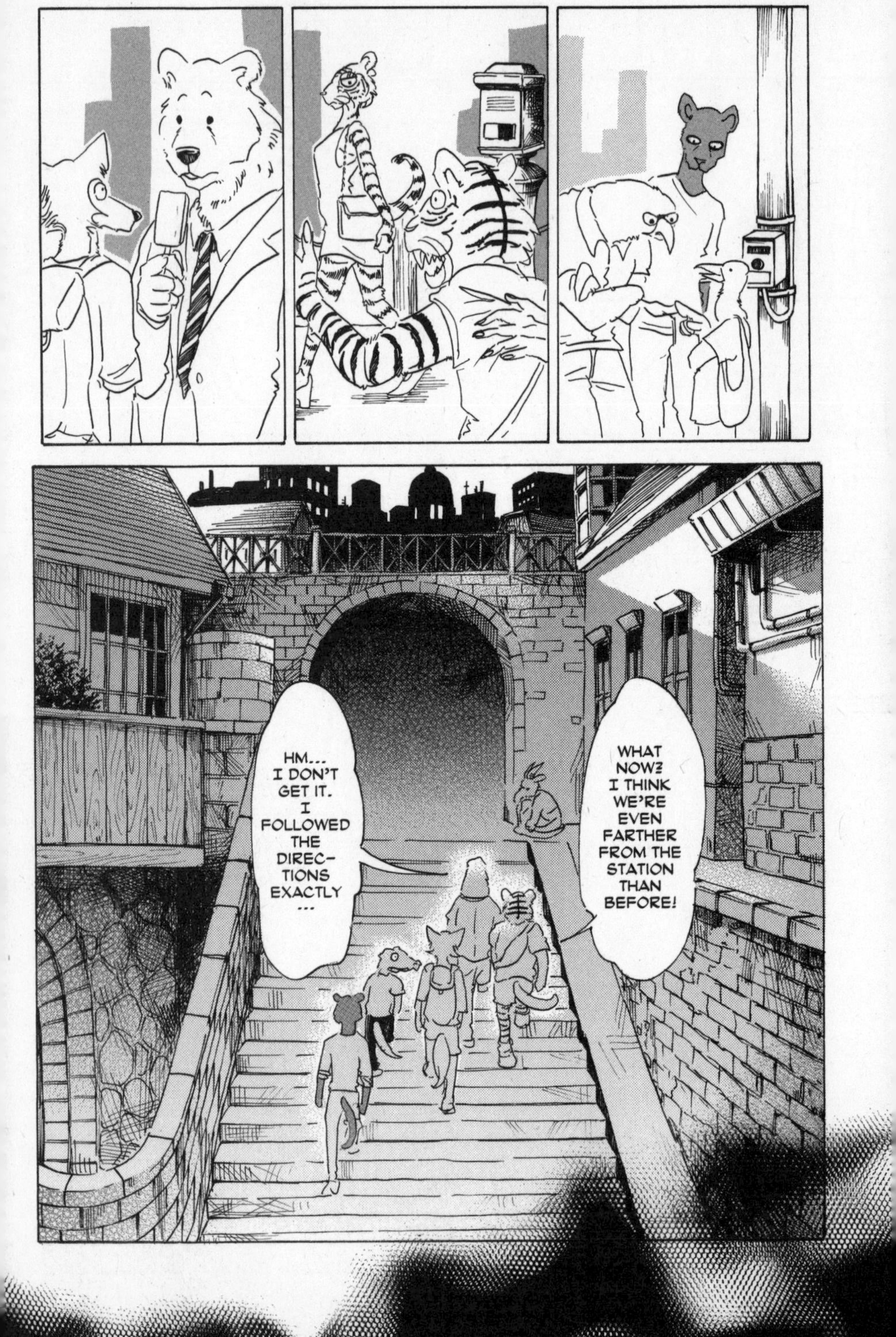
WHAT NOW? I THINK WE'RE EVEN FARTHER FROM THE STATION THAN BEFORE!
HM... I DON'T GET IT. I FOLLOWED THE DIRECTIONS EXACTLY...

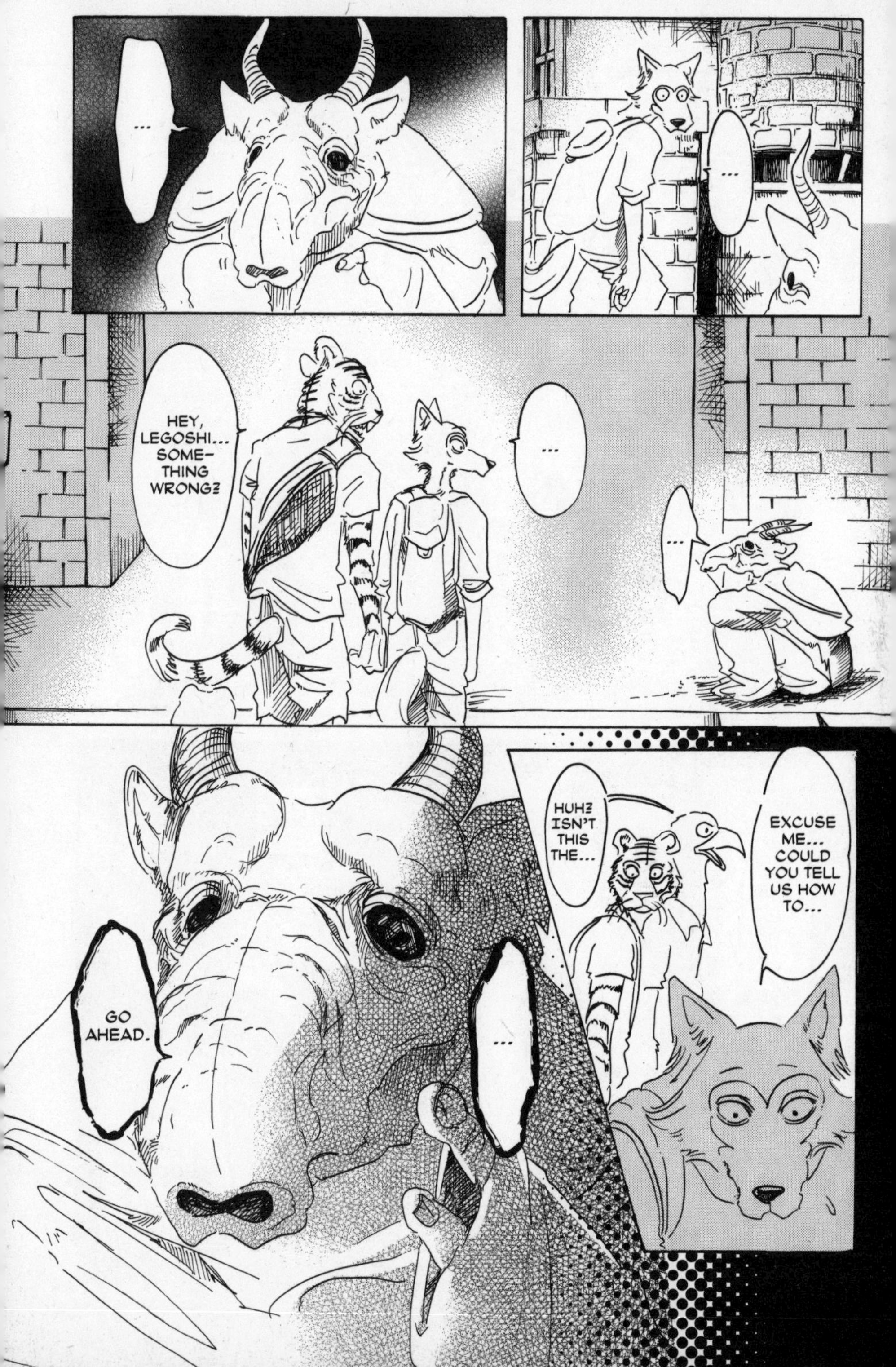
...
...
HEY, LEGOSHI... SOMETHING WRONG?
...
...
EXCUSE ME... COULD YOU TELL US HOW TO...
HUH? ISN'T THIS THE...
...
GO AHEAD.

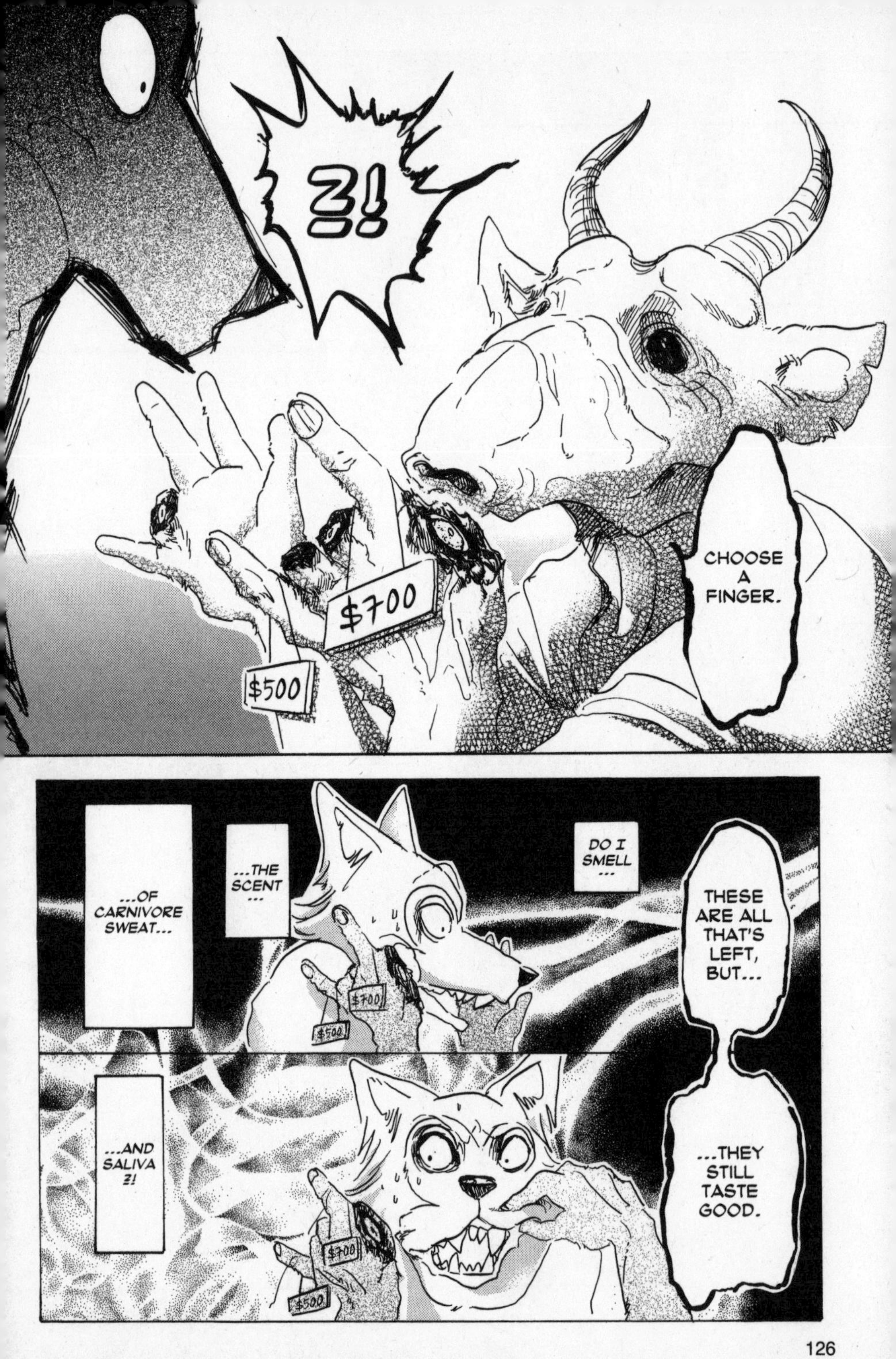
?!
CHOOSE A FINGER.
THESE ARE ALL THAT'S LEFT, BUT...
DO I SMELL...
...THE SCENT...
...OF CARNIVORE SWEAT...
$700
$500
...THEY STILL TASTE GOOD.
...AND SALIVA ?!

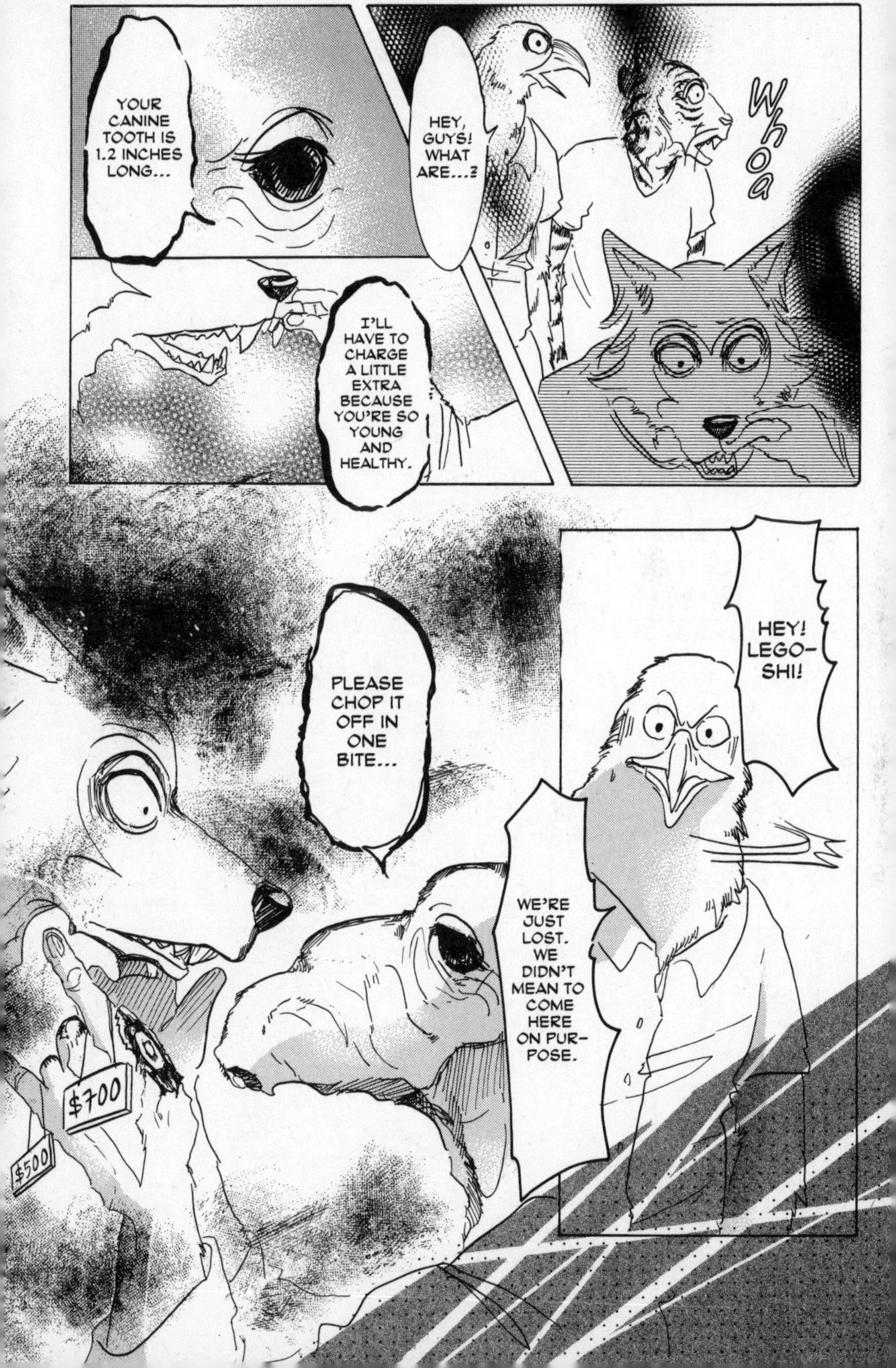
HEY, GUYS! WHAT ARE...?
Whoa
YOUR CANINE TOOTH IS 1.2 INCHES LONG...
I'LL HAVE TO CHARGE A LITTLE EXTRA BECAUSE YOU'RE SO YOUNG AND HEALTHY.
HEY! LEGO-SHI!
WE'RE JUST LOST. WE DIDN'T MEAN TO COME HERE ON PUR-POSE.
PLEASE CHOP IT OFF IN ONE BITE...
$700
$500

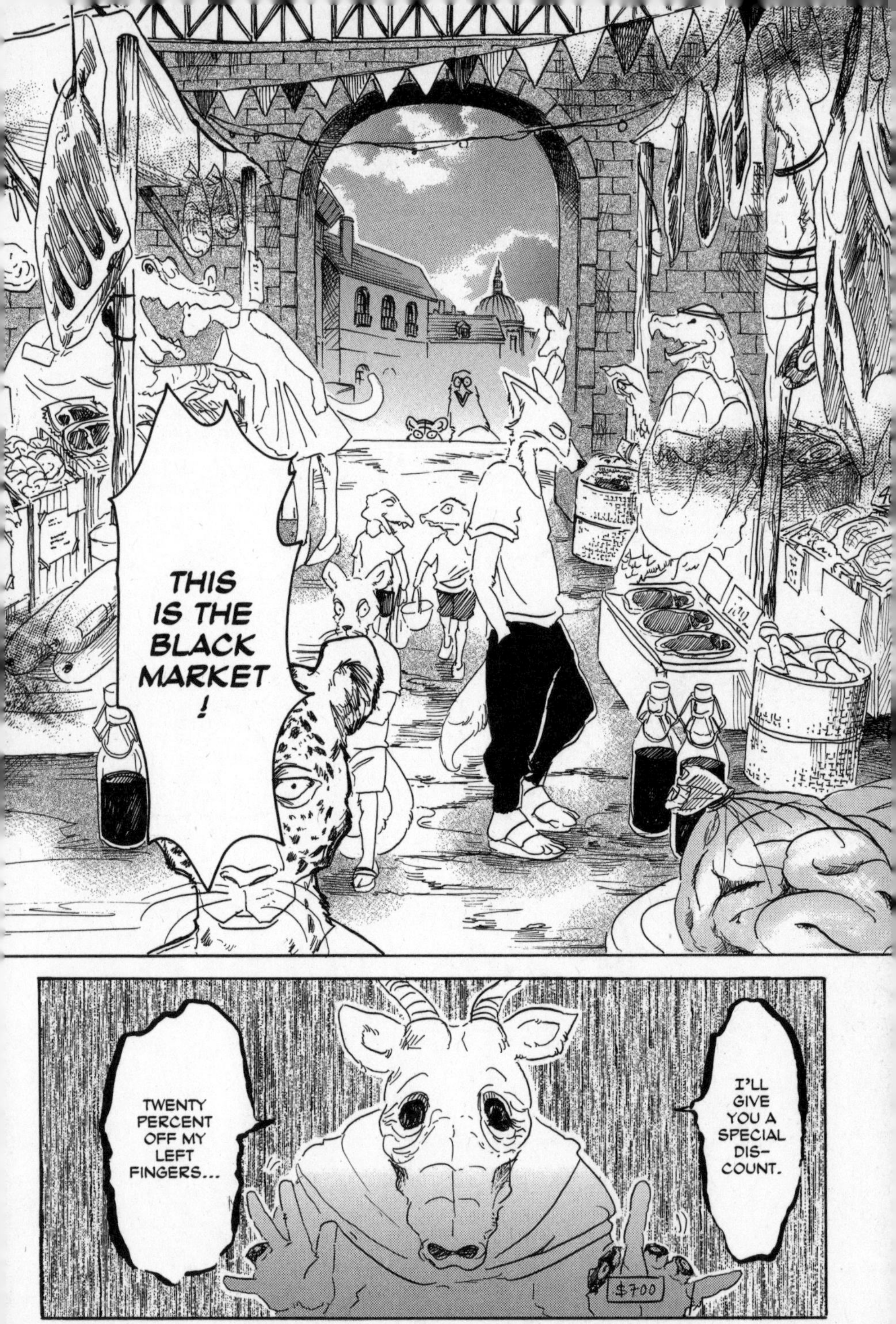
THIS IS THE BLACK MARKET!
I'LL GIVE YOU A SPECIAL DIS-COUNT.
TWENTY PERCENT OFF MY LEFT FINGERS...
$700

Chapter 23:
Shattered on the Stairway to Adulthood

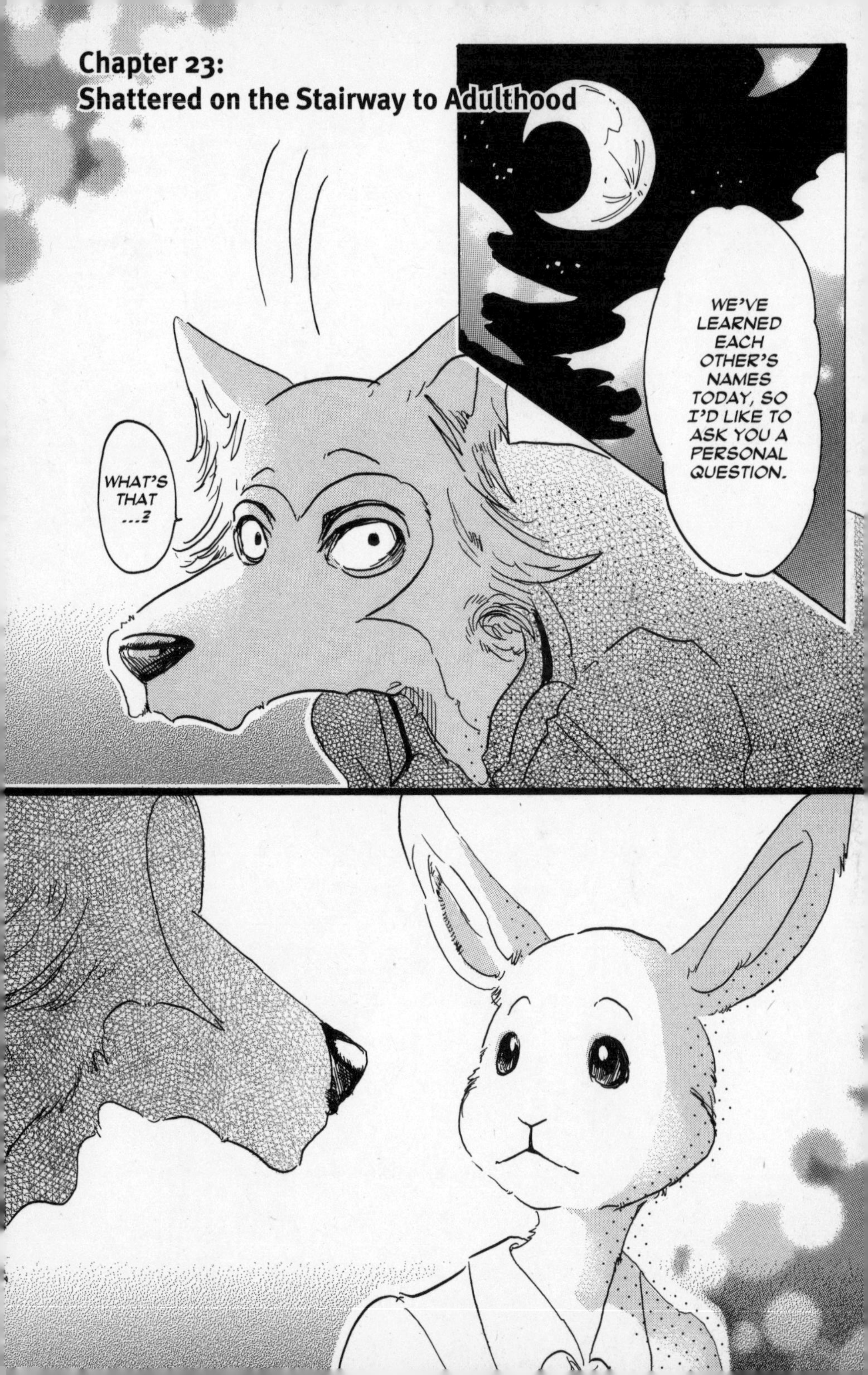
WE'VE LEARNED EACH OTHER'S NAMES TODAY, SO I'D LIKE TO ASK YOU A PERSONAL QUESTION.
WHAT'S THAT ...?

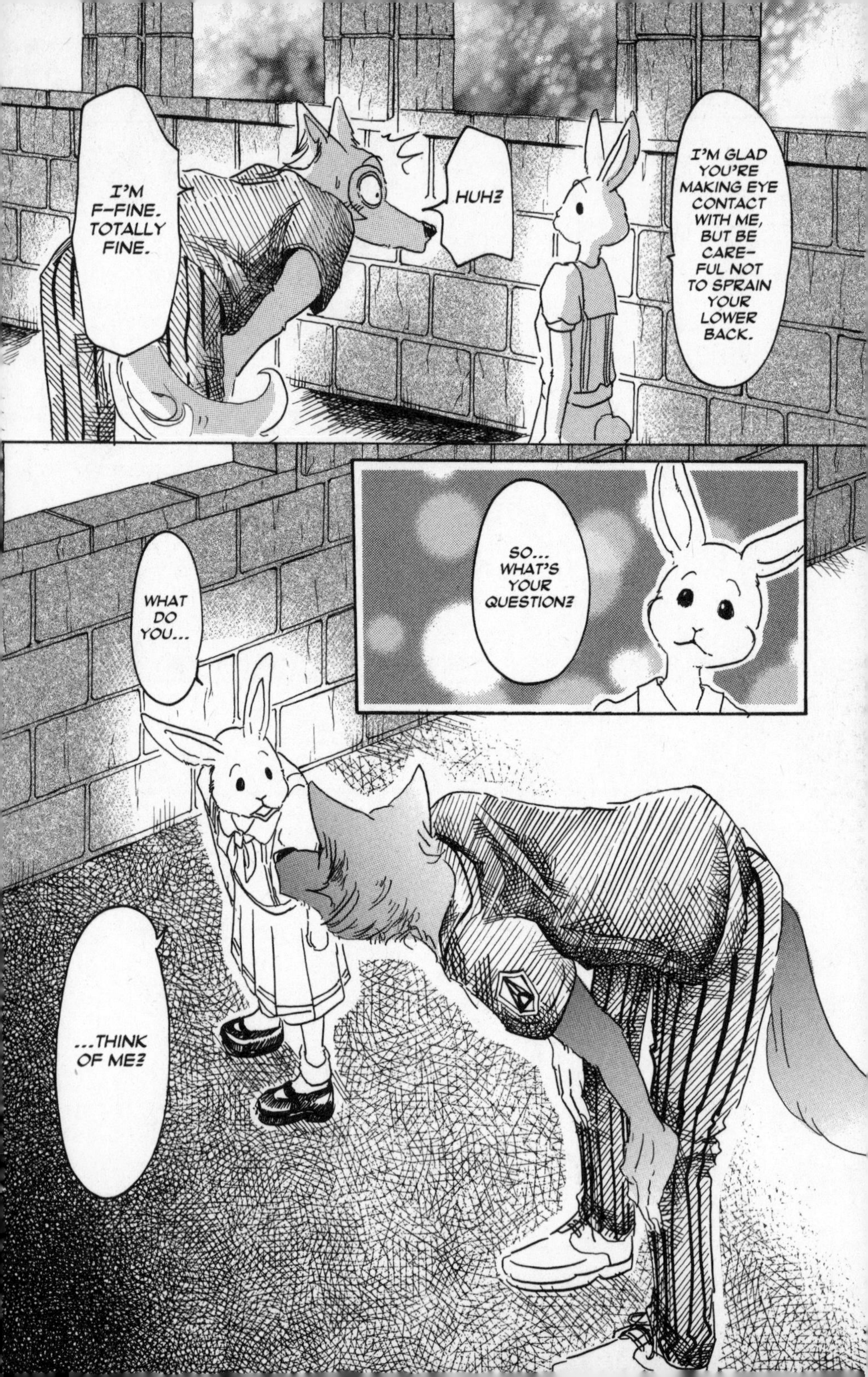
I'M GLAD YOU'RE MAKING EYE CONTACT WITH ME, BUT BE CARE-FUL NOT TO SPRAIN YOUR LOWER BACK.
HUH?
I'M F-FINE. TOTALLY FINE.
SO... WHAT'S YOUR QUESTION?
WHAT DO YOU...
...THINK OF ME?

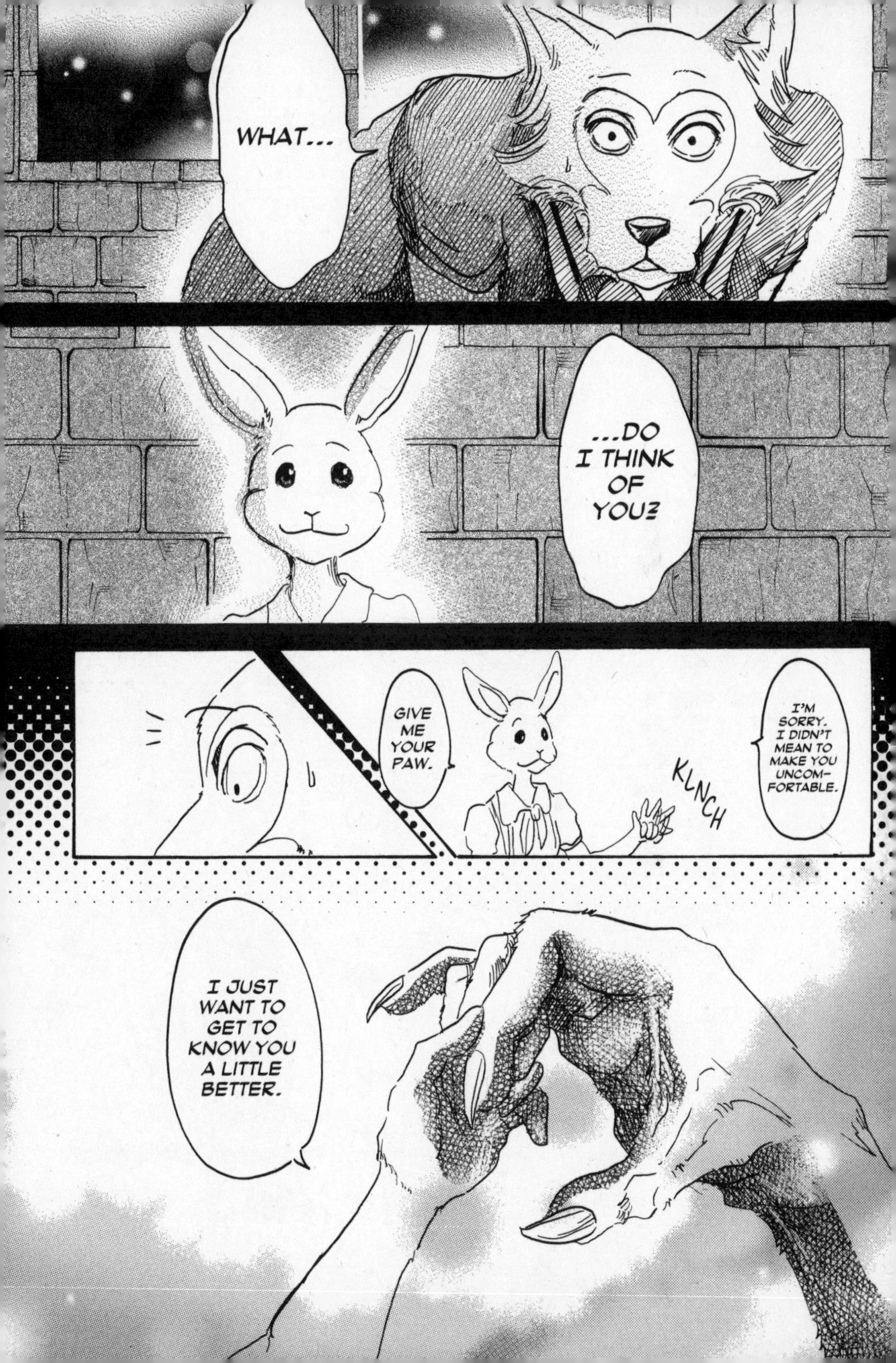
WHAT...
...DO I THINK OF YOU?
I'M SORRY. I DIDN'T MEAN TO MAKE YOU UNCOMFORTABLE.
KLNCH
GIVE ME YOUR PAW.
I JUST WANT TO GET TO KNOW YOU A LITTLE BETTER.

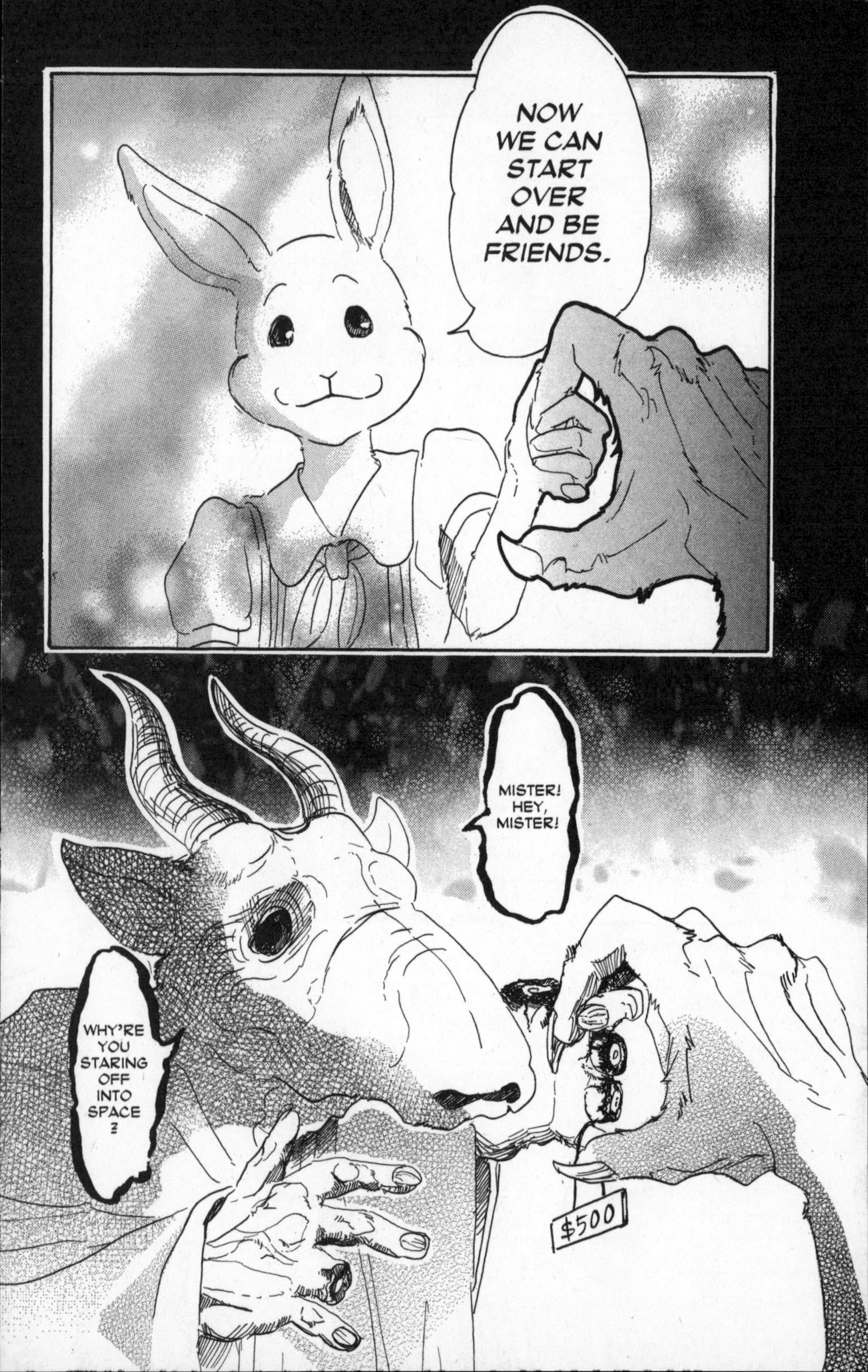
NOW WE CAN START OVER AND BE FRIENDS.
MISTER! HEY, MISTER!
WHY'RE YOU STARING OFF INTO SPACE?
$500

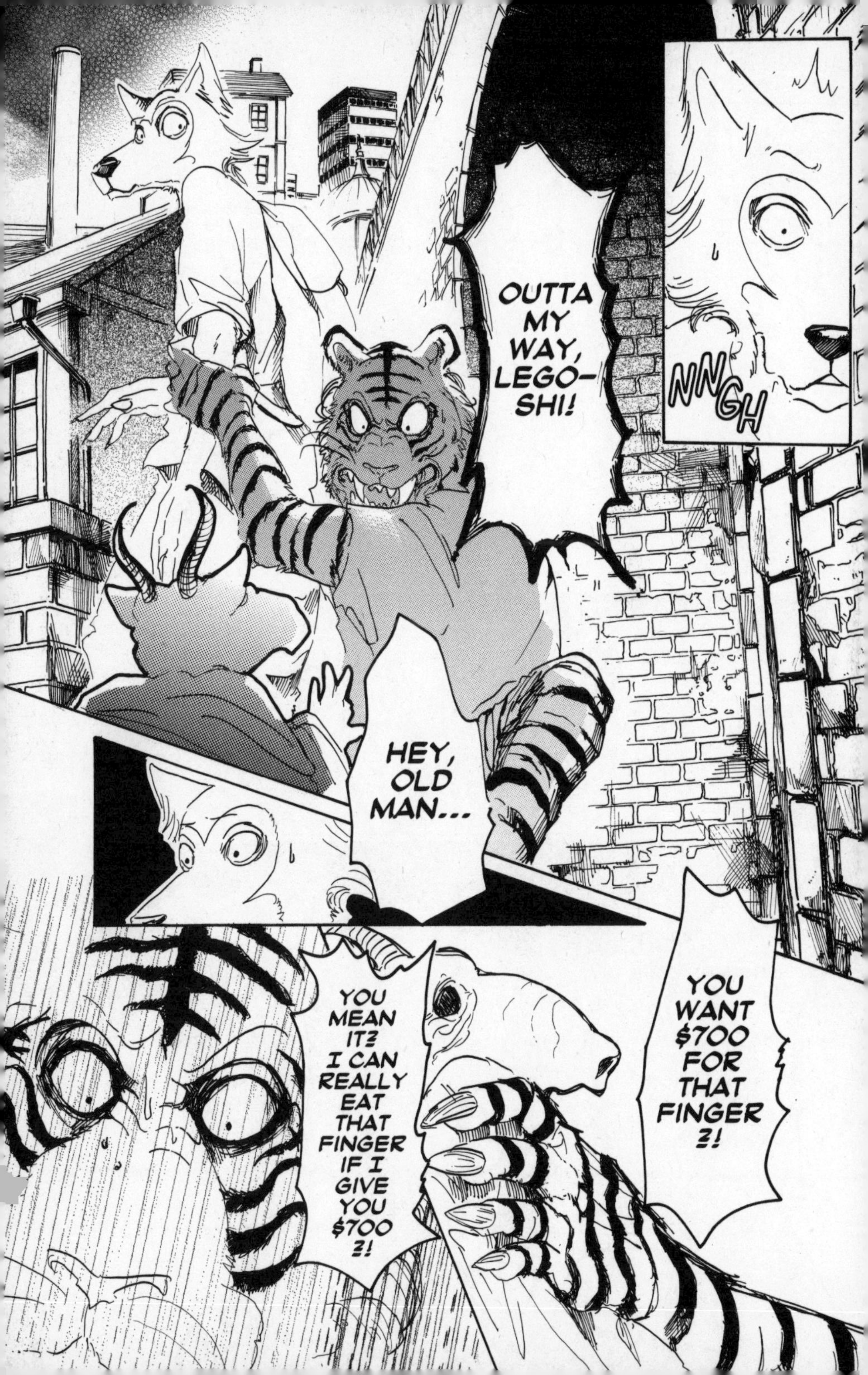
NNGH
OUTTA MY WAY, LEGOSHI!
HEY, OLD MAN...
YOU WANT $700 FOR THAT FINGER?!
YOU MEAN IT? I CAN REALLY EAT THAT FINGER IF I GIVE YOU $700?!

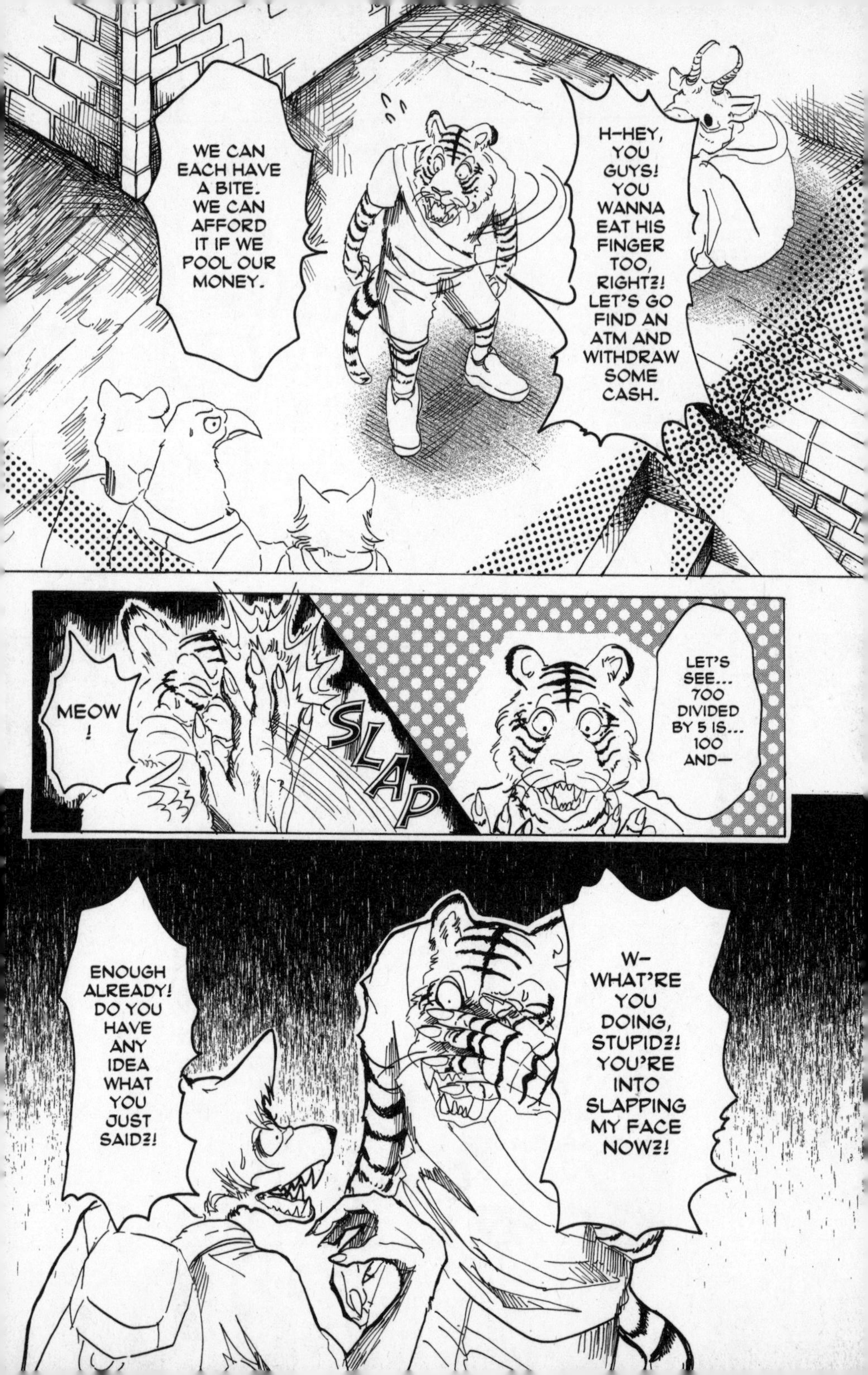
H-HEY, YOU GUYS! YOU WANNA EAT HIS FINGER TOO, RIGHT?! LET'S GO FIND AN ATM AND WITHDRAW SOME CASH.
WE CAN EACH HAVE A BITE. WE CAN AFFORD IT IF WE POOL OUR MONEY.
LET'S SEE... 700 DIVIDED BY 5 IS... 100 AND—
SLAP
MEOW !
W-WHAT'RE YOU DOING, STUPID?! YOU'RE INTO SLAPPING MY FACE NOW?!
ENOUGH ALREADY! DO YOU HAVE ANY IDEA WHAT YOU JUST SAID?!

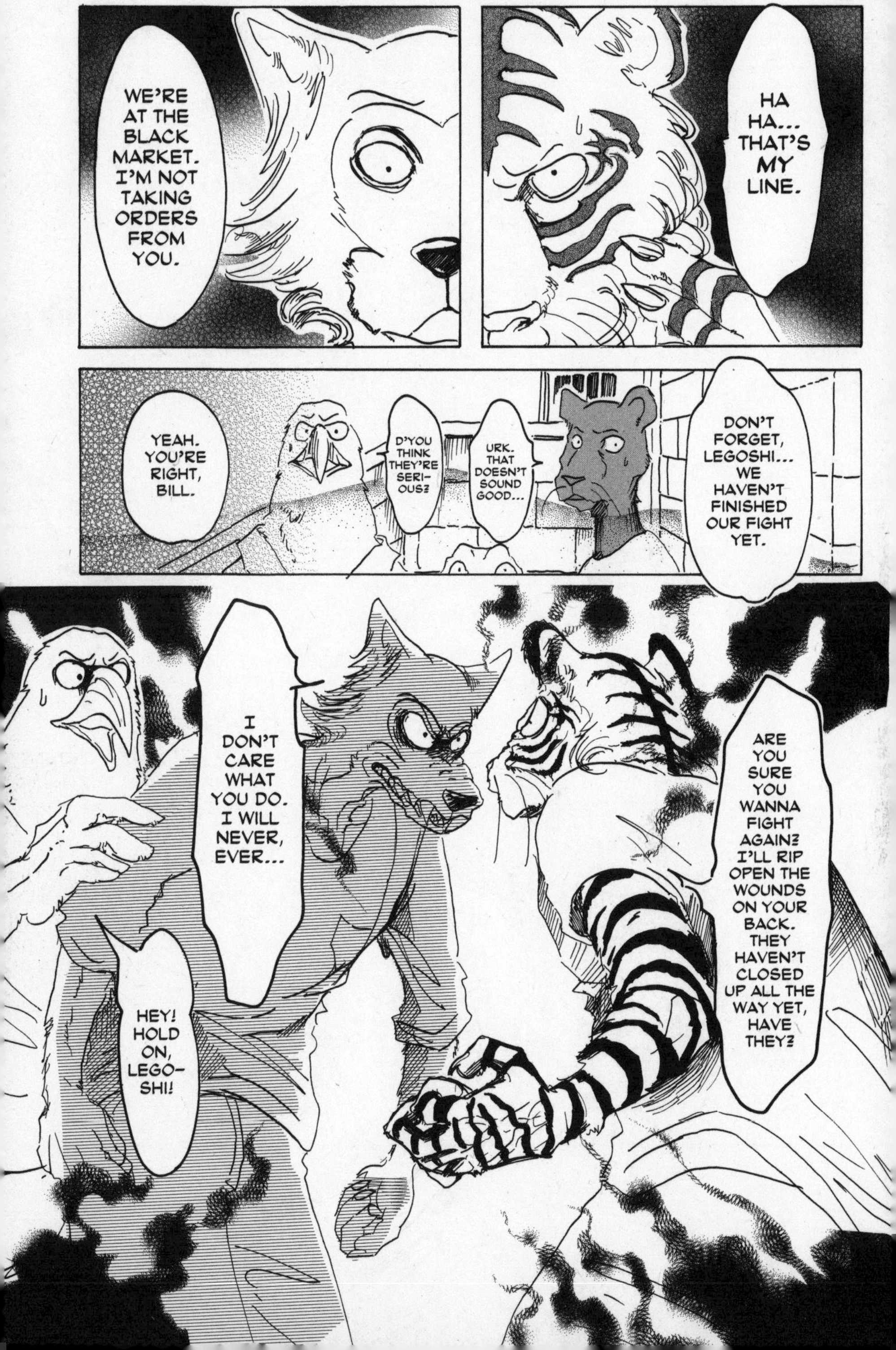
HA HA... THAT'S MY LINE.
WE'RE AT THE BLACK MARKET. I'M NOT TAKING ORDERS FROM YOU.
DON'T FORGET, LEGOSHI... WE HAVEN'T FINISHED OUR FIGHT YET.
URK. THAT DOESN'T SOUND GOOD...
D'YOU THINK THEY'RE SERI-OUS?
YEAH. YOU'RE RIGHT, BILL.
ARE YOU SURE YOU WANNA FIGHT AGAIN? I'LL RIP OPEN THE WOUNDS ON YOUR BACK. THEY HAVEN'T CLOSED UP ALL THE WAY YET, HAVE THEY?
I DON'T CARE WHAT YOU DO. I WILL NEVER, EVER...
HEY! HOLD ON, LEGO-SHI!

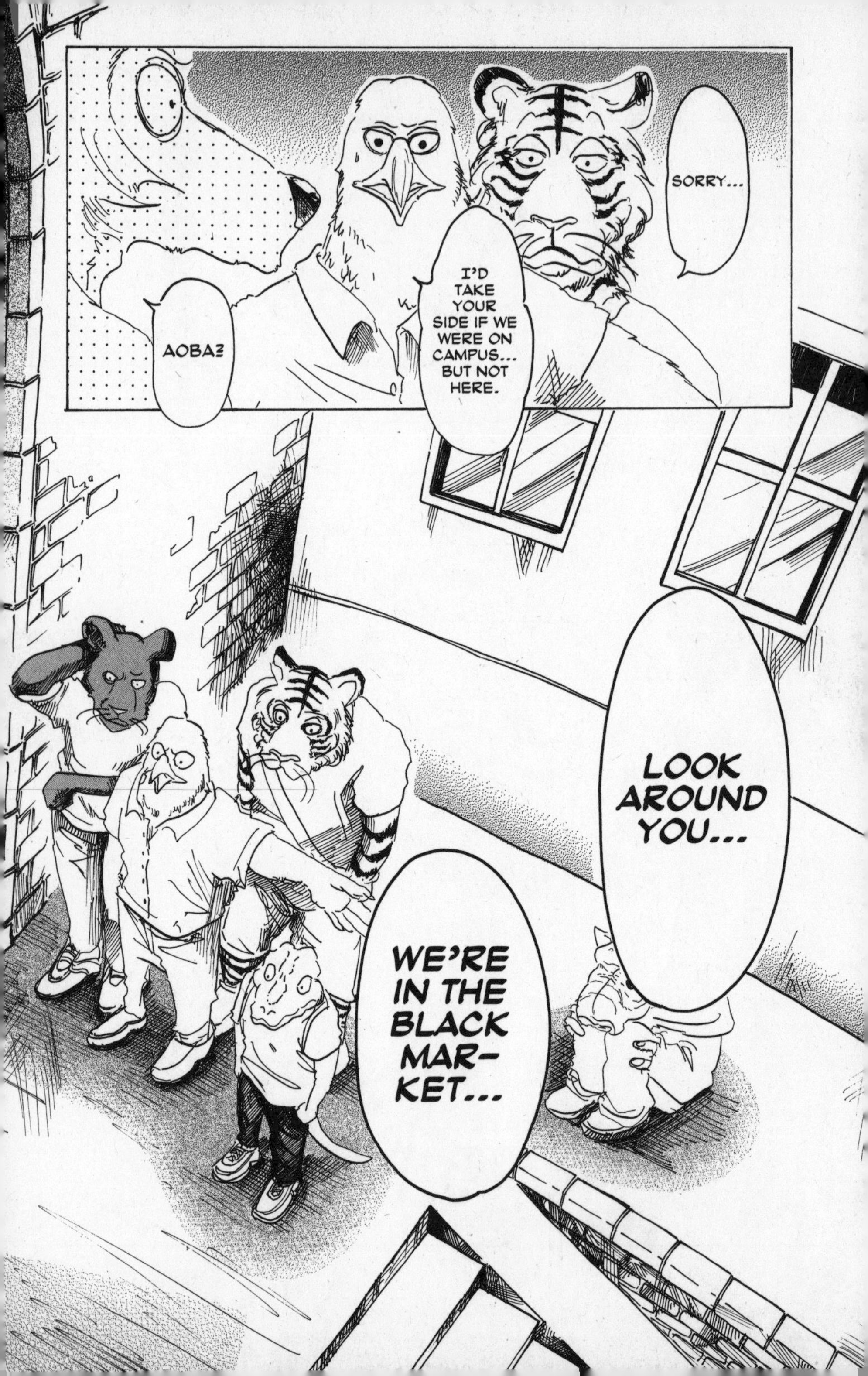
SORRY...
I'D TAKE YOUR SIDE IF WE WERE ON CAMPUS... BUT NOT HERE.
AOBA?
LOOK AROUND YOU...
WE'RE IN THE BLACK MAR-KET...

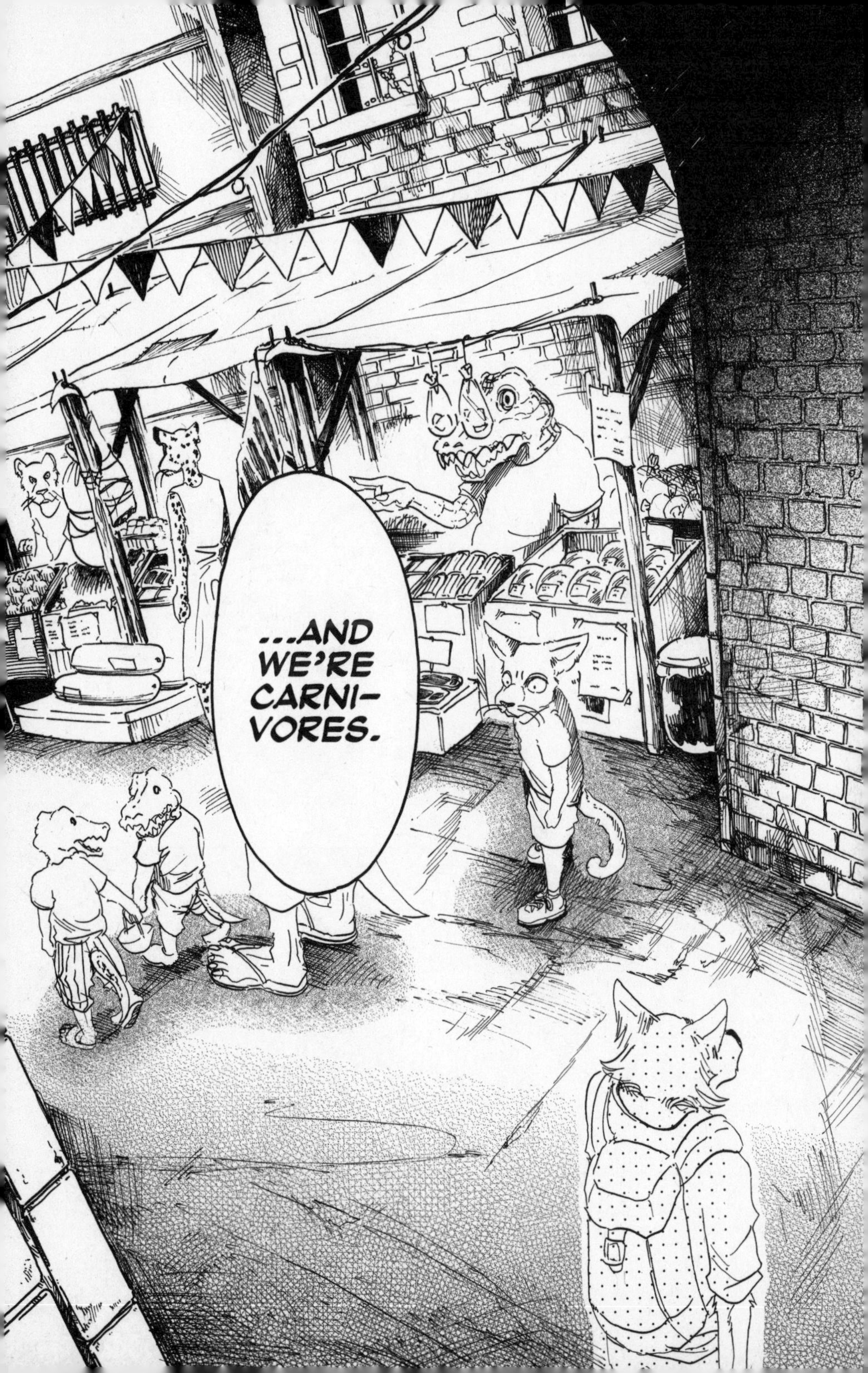
...AND WE'RE CARNI- VORES.

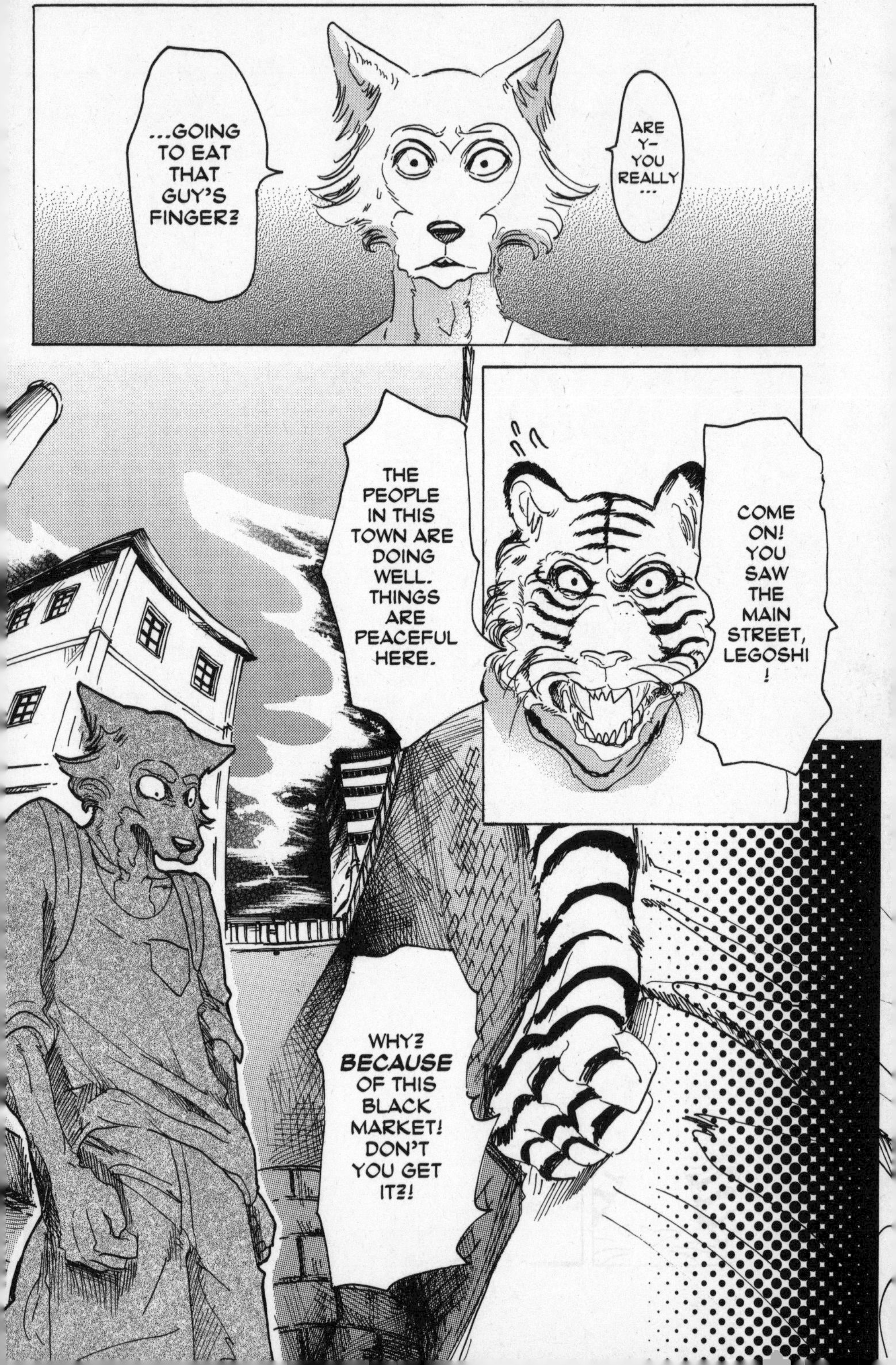
ARE Y-YOU REALLY...
...GOING TO EAT THAT GUY'S FINGER?
COME ON! YOU SAW THE MAIN STREET, LEGOSHI!
THE PEOPLE IN THIS TOWN ARE DOING WELL. THINGS ARE PEACEFUL HERE.
WHY? *BECAUSE* OF THIS BLACK MARKET! DON'T YOU GET IT?!

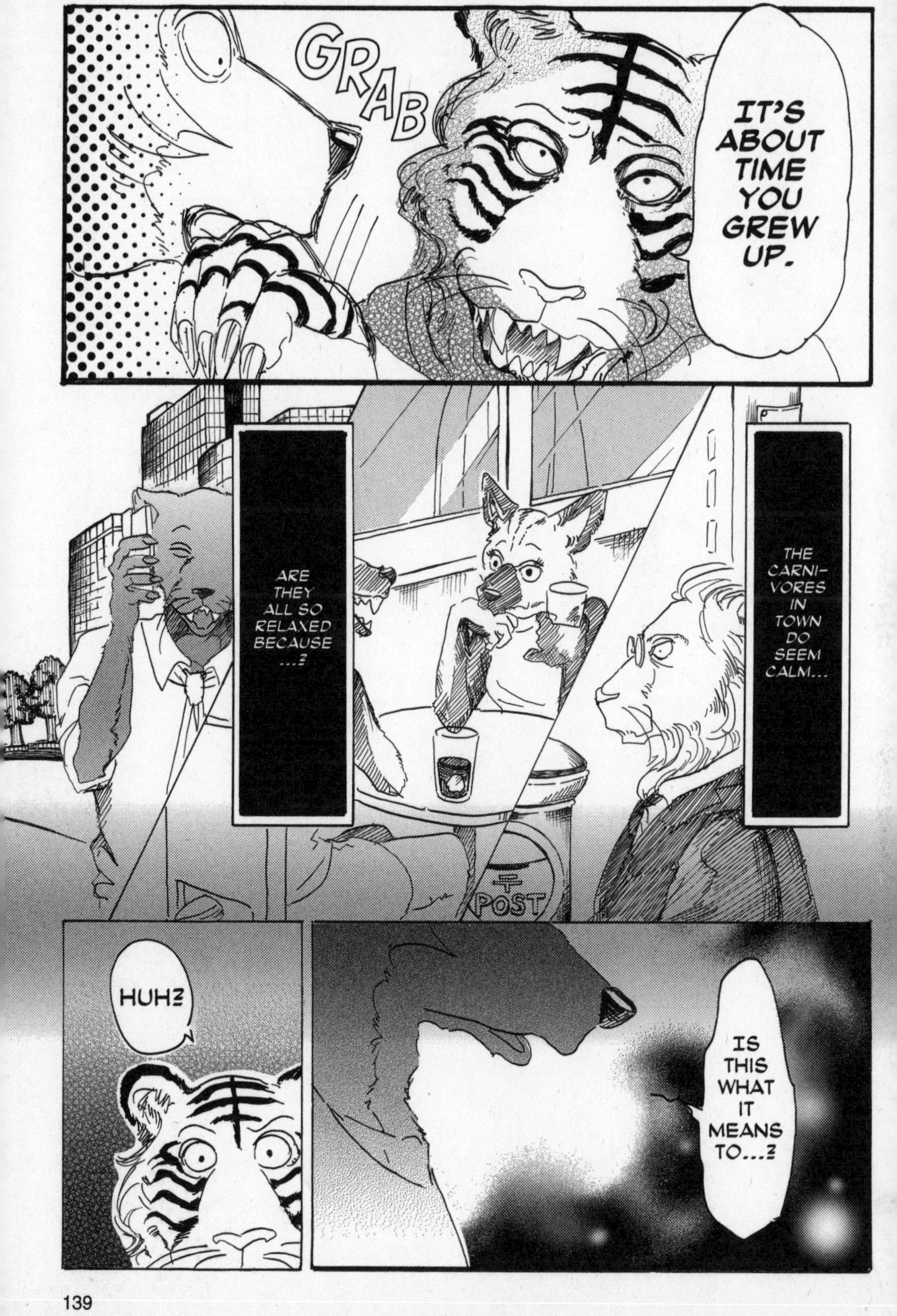
IT'S ABOUT TIME YOU GREW UP.
GRAB
THE CARNIVORES IN TOWN DO SEEM CALM...
ARE THEY ALL SO RELAXED BECAUSE...?
IS THIS WHAT IT MEANS TO...?
HUH?

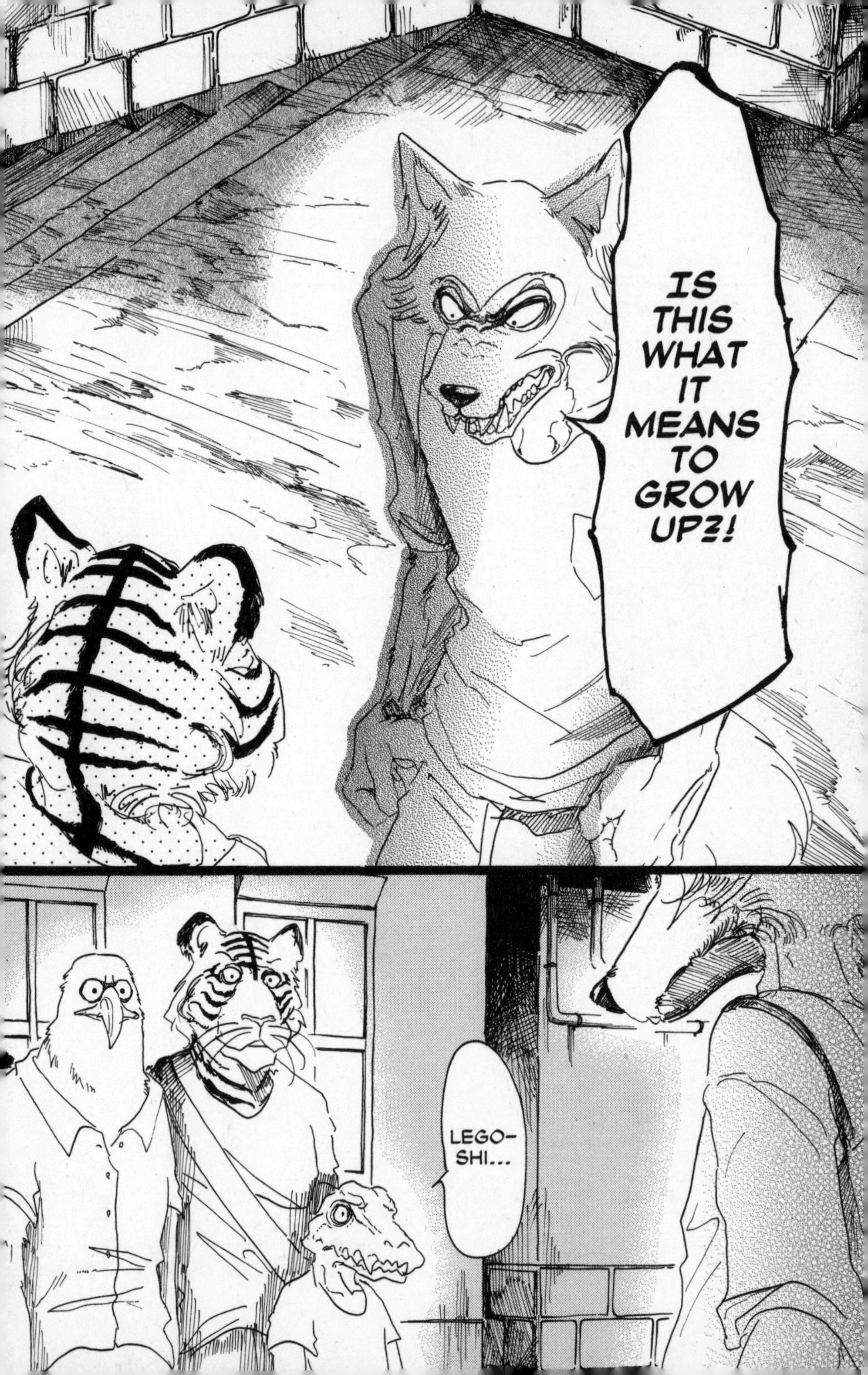
IS THIS WHAT IT MEANS TO GROW UP?!
LEGO-SHI...

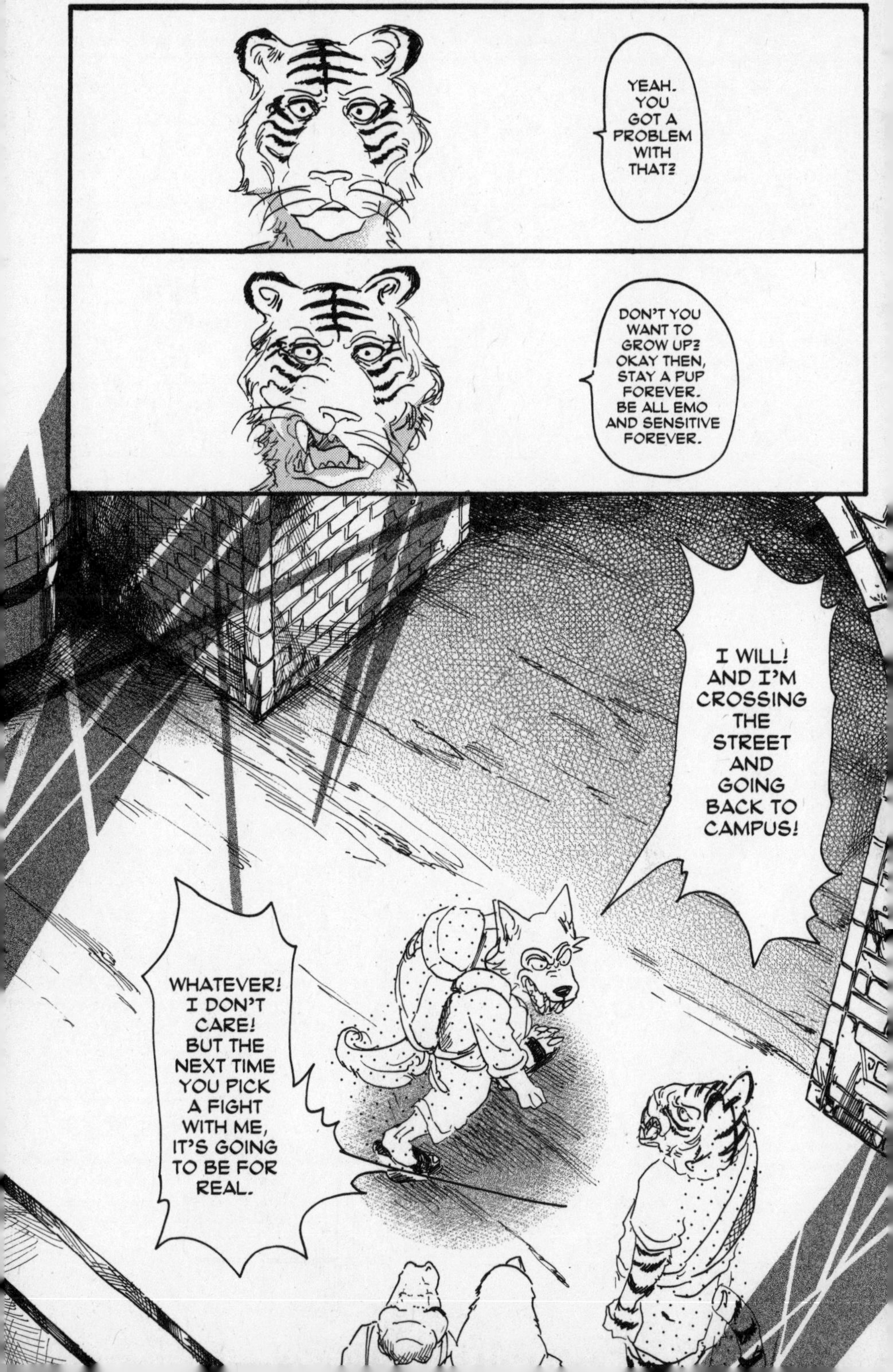
YEAH. YOU GOT A PROBLEM WITH THAT?
DON'T YOU WANT TO GROW UP? OKAY THEN, STAY A PUP FOREVER. BE ALL EMO AND SENSITIVE FOREVER.
I WILL! AND I'M CROSSING THE STREET AND GOING BACK TO CAMPUS!
WHATEVER! I DON'T CARE! BUT THE NEXT TIME YOU PICK A FIGHT WITH ME, IT'S GOING TO BE FOR REAL.

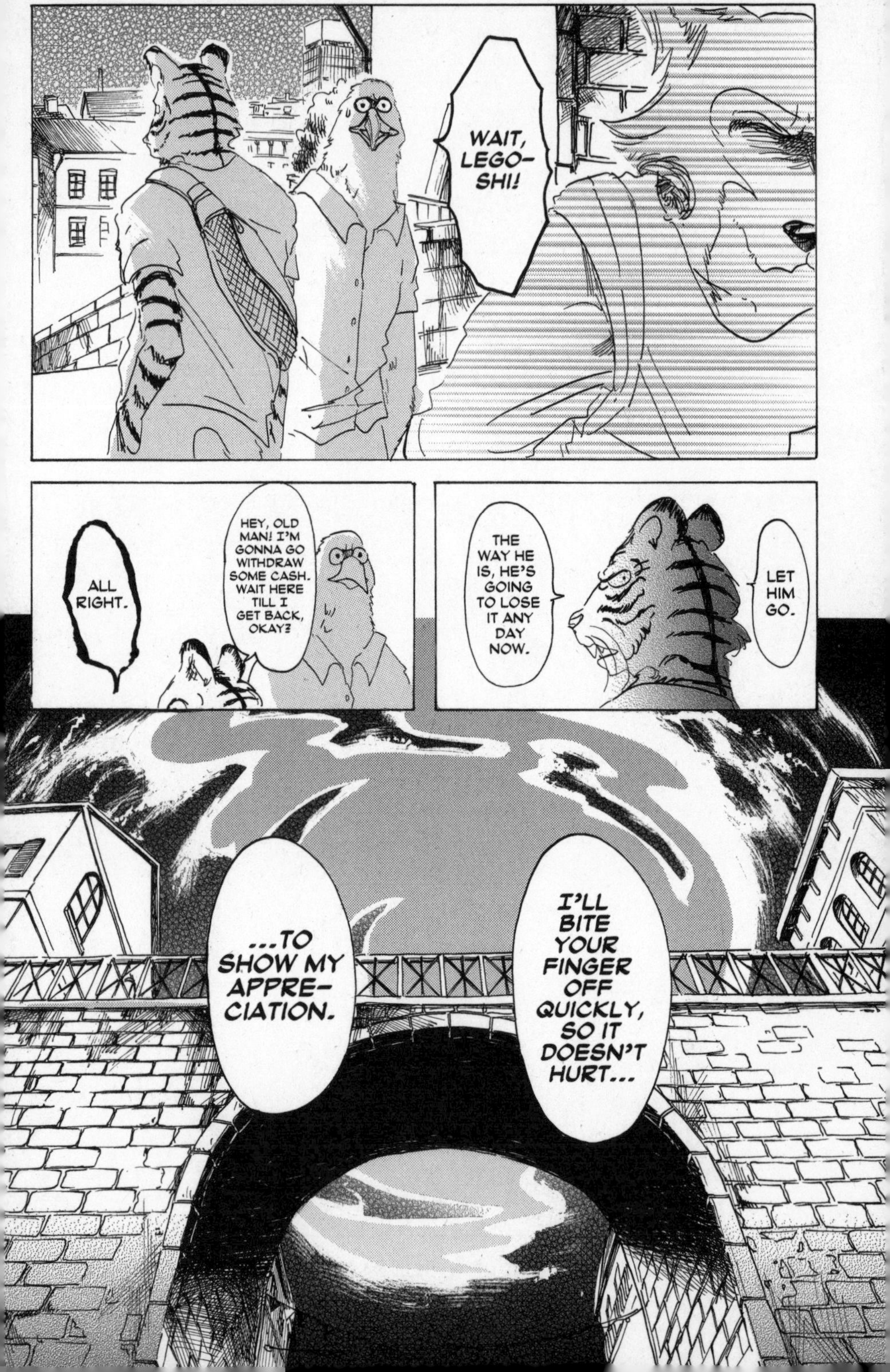
WAIT, LEGOSHI!
LET HIM GO.
THE WAY HE IS, HE'S GOING TO LOSE IT ANY DAY NOW.
HEY, OLD MAN! I'M GONNA GO WITHDRAW SOME CASH. WAIT HERE TILL I GET BACK, OKAY?
ALL RIGHT.
I'LL BITE YOUR FINGER OFF QUICKLY, SO IT DOESN'T HURT...
...TO SHOW MY APPRECIATION.

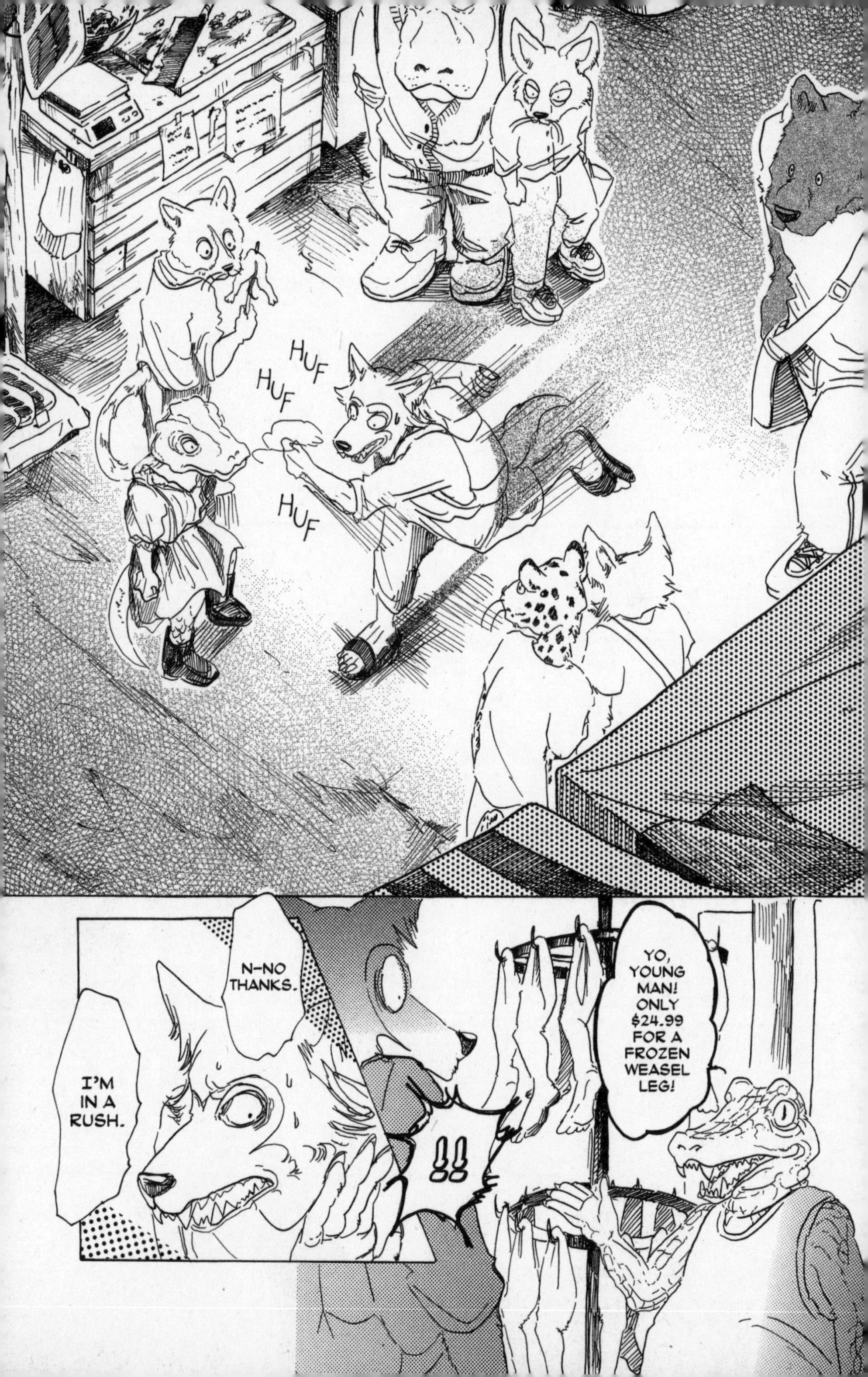
HUF
HUF
HUF
YO, YOUNG MAN! ONLY $24.99 FOR A FROZEN WEASEL LEG!
!!
N-NO THANKS.
I'M IN A RUSH.

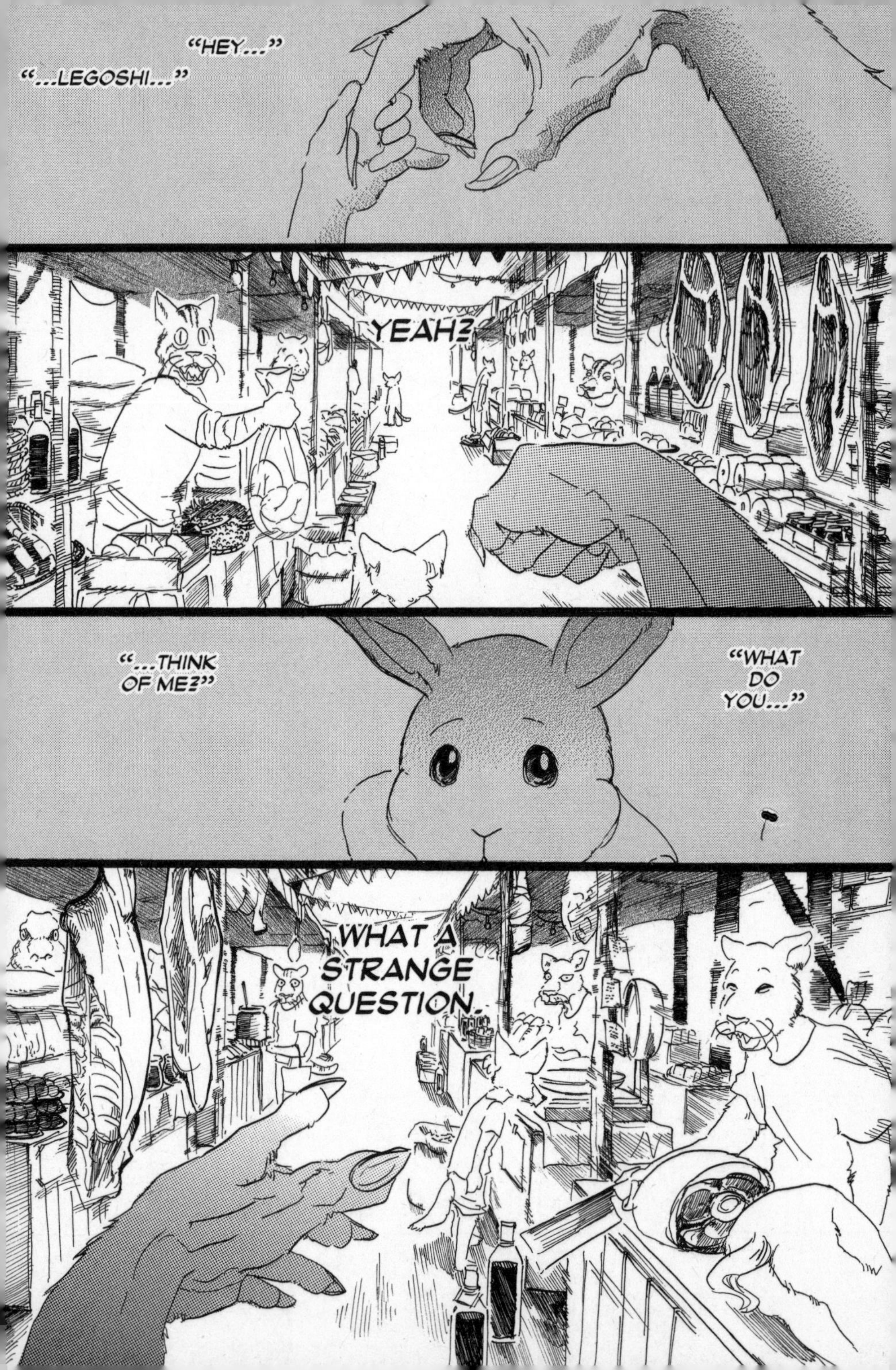
"HEY..."
"...LEGOSHI..."
YEAH?
"WHAT DO YOU..."
"...THINK OF ME?"
WHAT A STRANGE QUESTION.

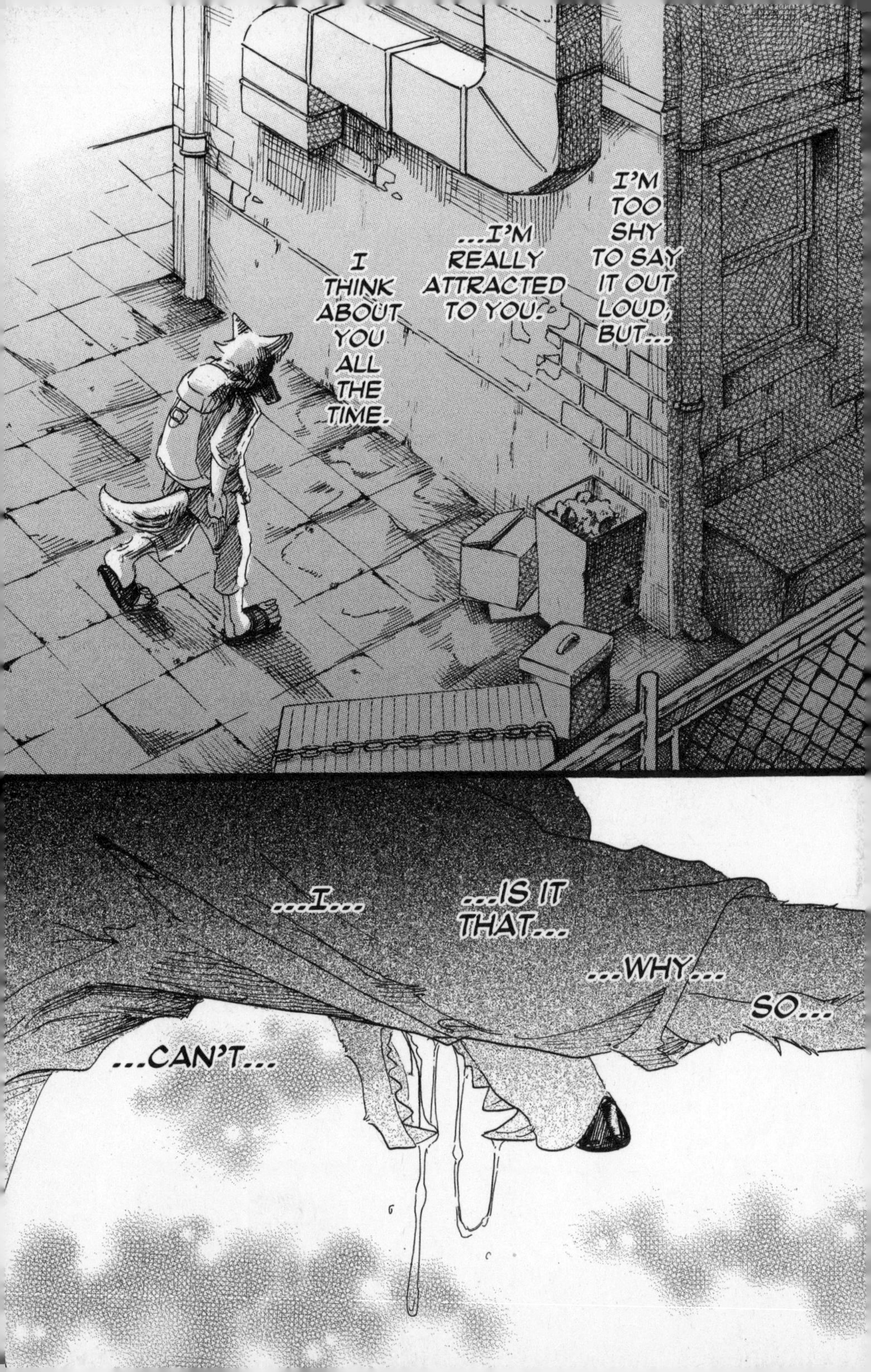
I'M TOO SHY TO SAY IT OUT LOUD, BUT...
...I'M REALLY ATTRACTED TO YOU.
I THINK ABOUT YOU ALL THE TIME.
...IS IT THAT...
...I...
...WHY...
SO...
...CAN'T...

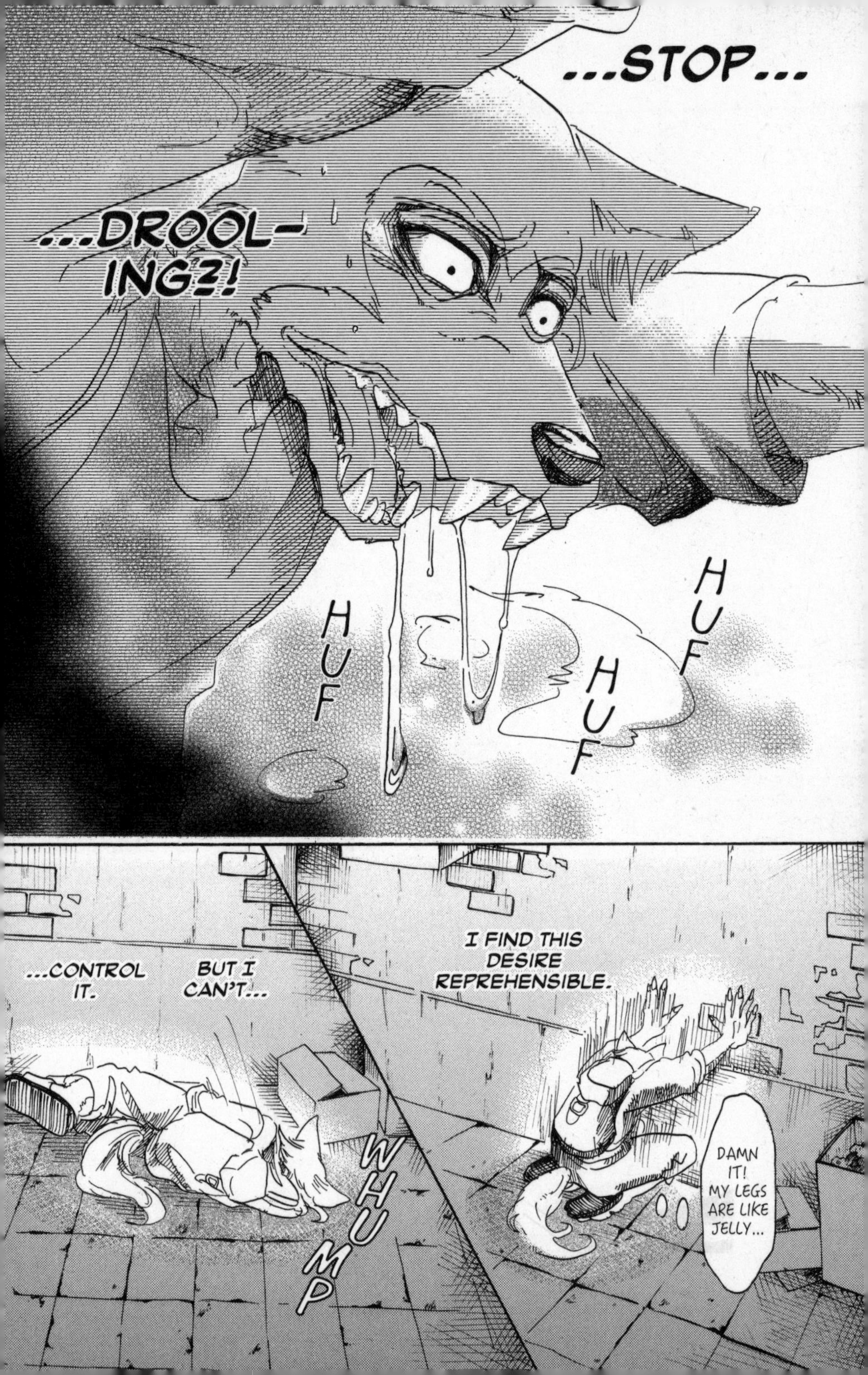
...STOP...
...DROOL-ING?!
HUF HUF
HUF HUF
HUF
I FIND THIS DESIRE REPREHENSIBLE.
DAMN IT! MY LEGS ARE LIKE JELLY...
BUT I CAN'T...
...CONTROL IT.
WHUMP

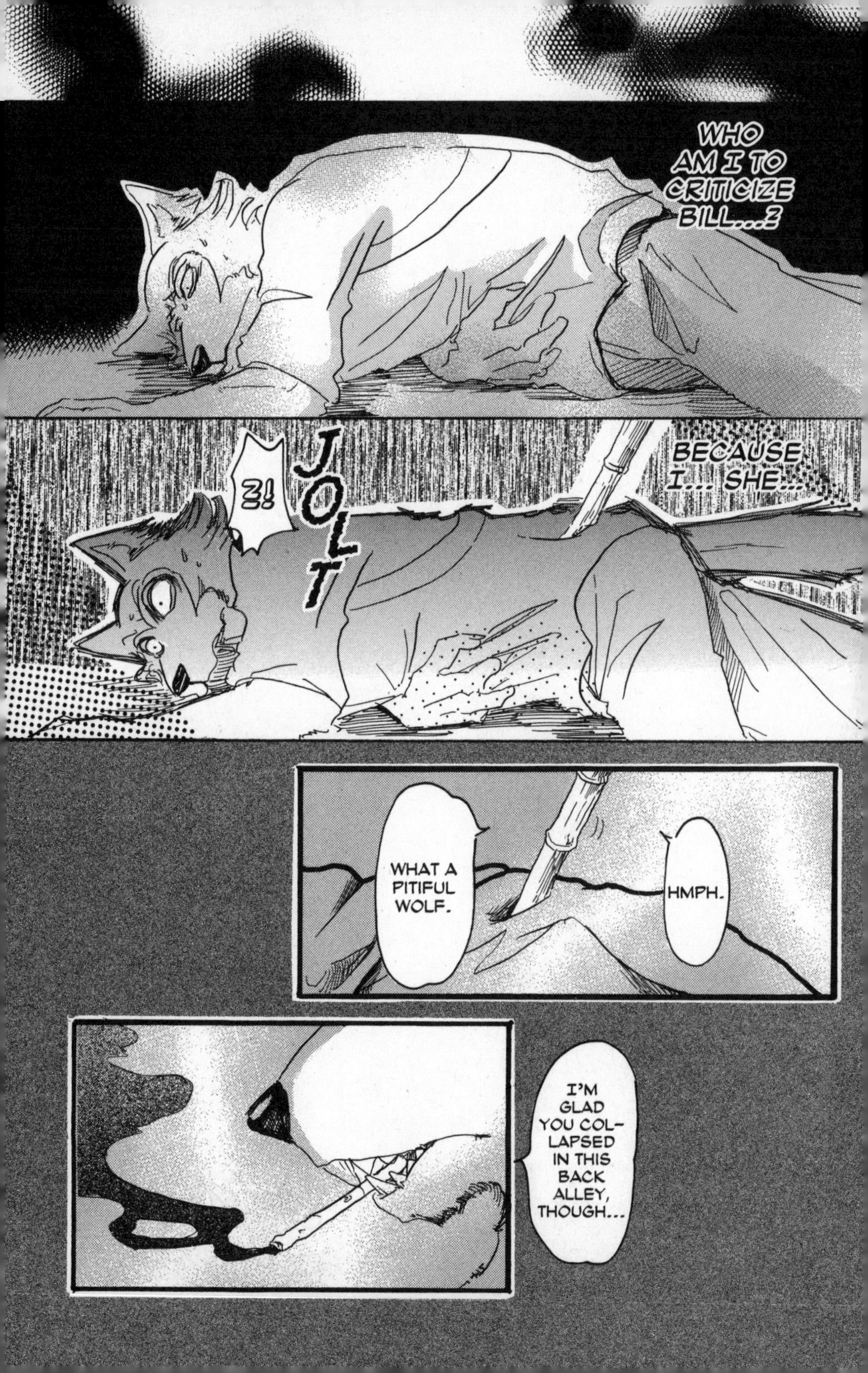
WHO AM I TO CRITICIZE BILL...?
BECAUSE I... SHE...
JOLT
HMPH.
WHAT A PITIFUL WOLF.
I'M GLAD YOU COL-LAPSED IN THIS BACK ALLEY, THOUGH...

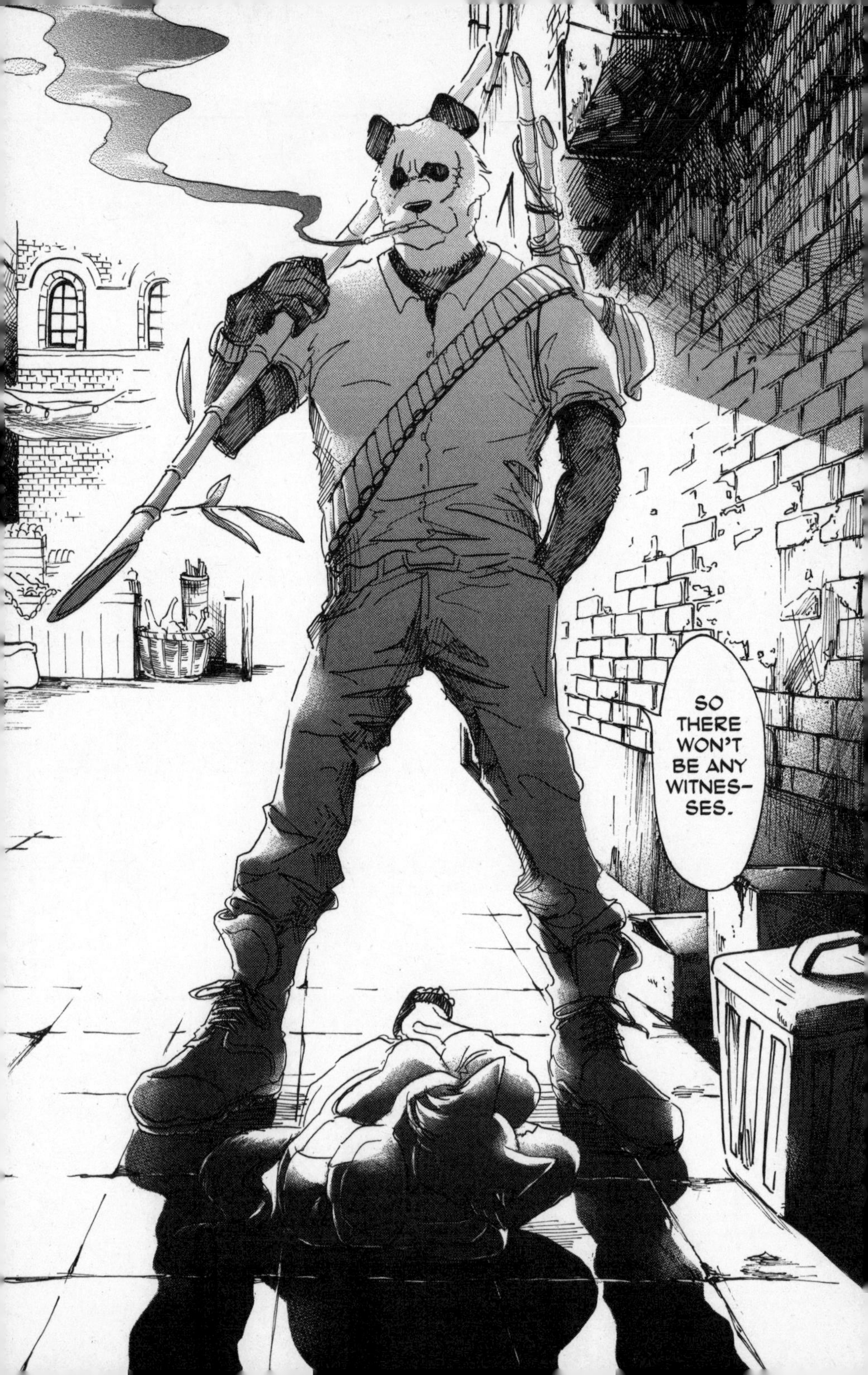
SO THERE WON'T BE ANY WITNESSES.

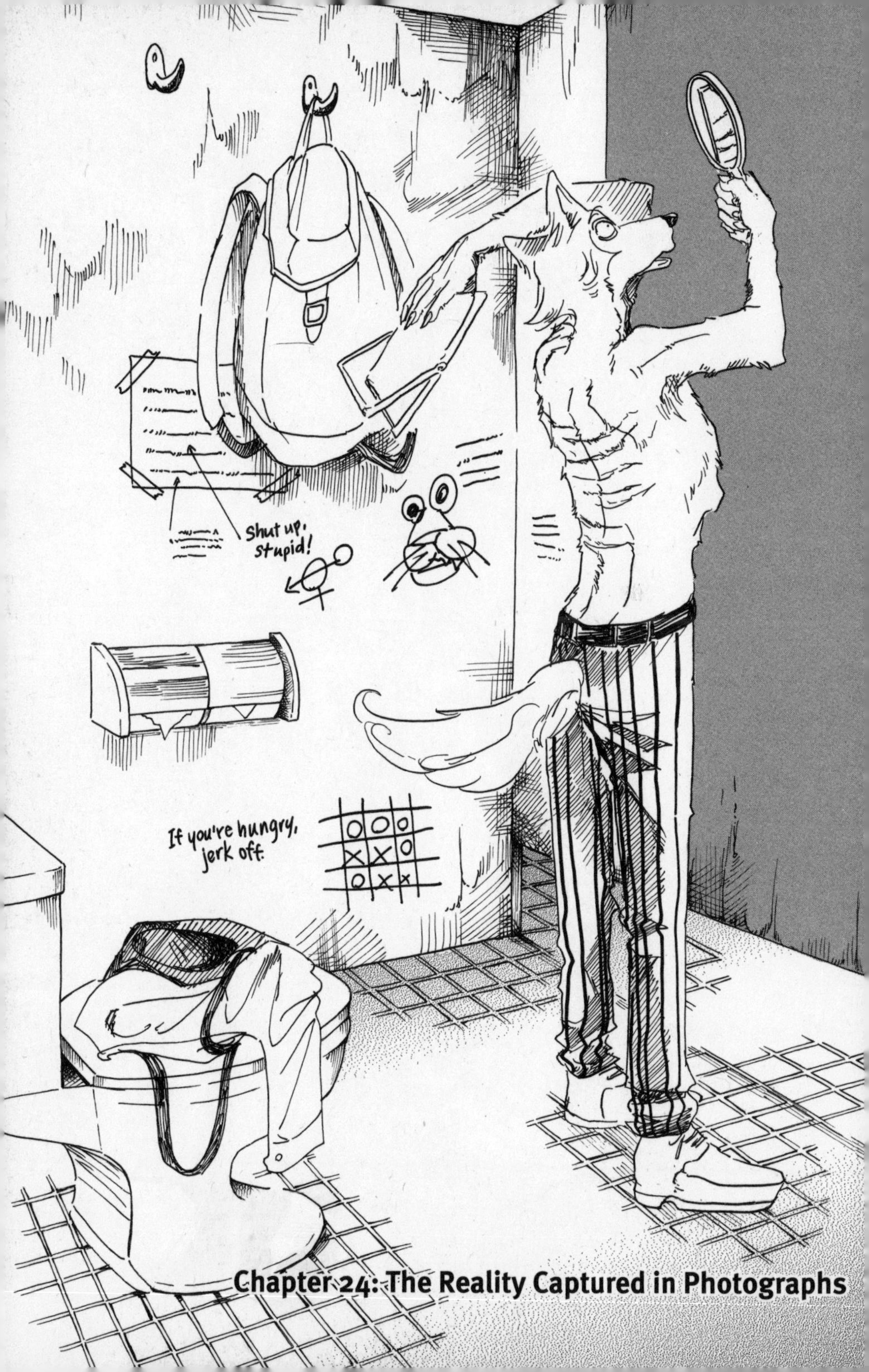
Shut up, stupid!
If you're hungry, jerk off.

Chapter 24: The Reality Captured in Photographs

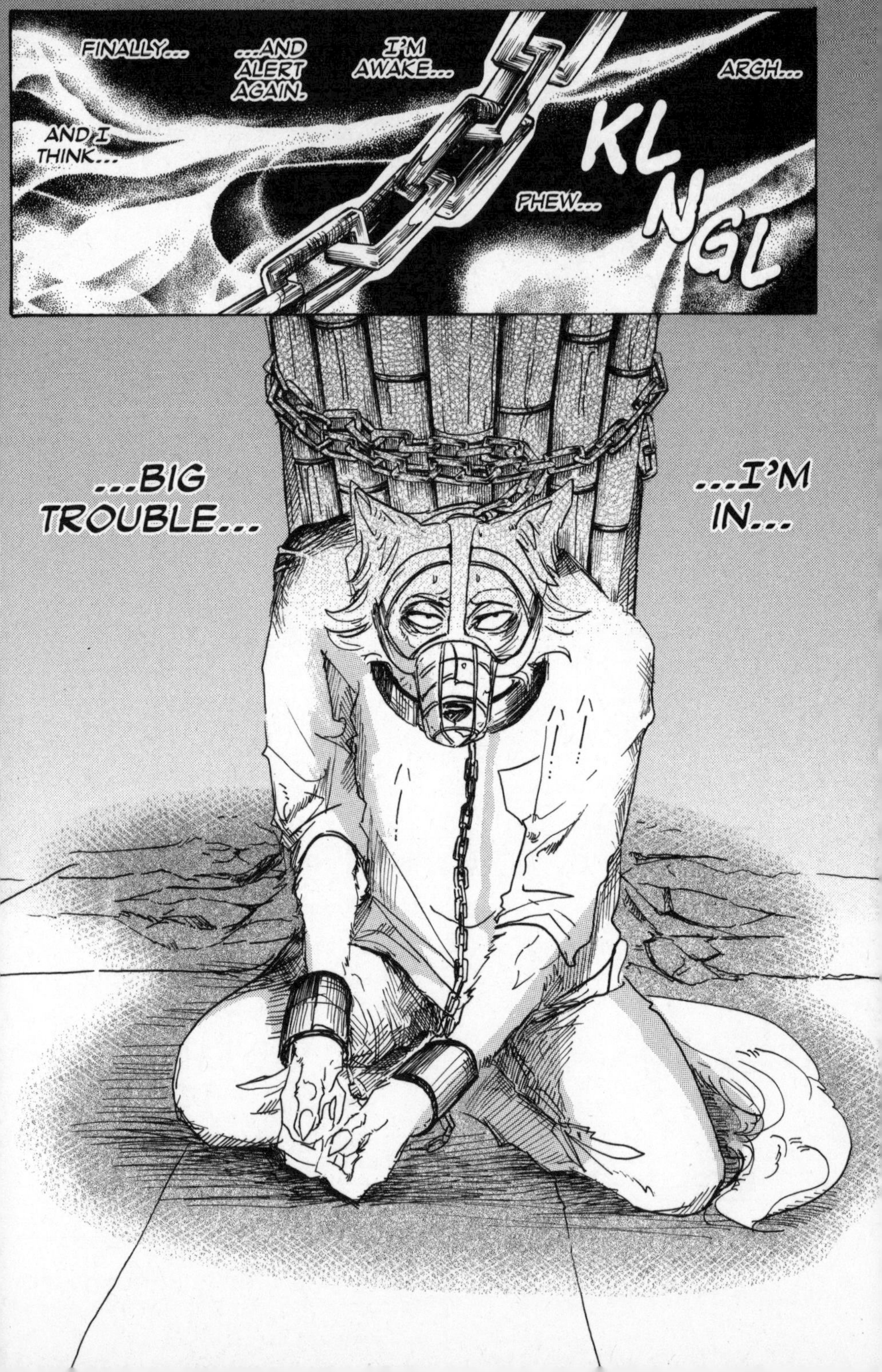
ARGH...
KL NGL
PHEW...
I'M AWAKE...
...AND ALERT AGAIN.
FINALLY...
AND I THINK...
...I'M IN...
...BIG TROUBLE...

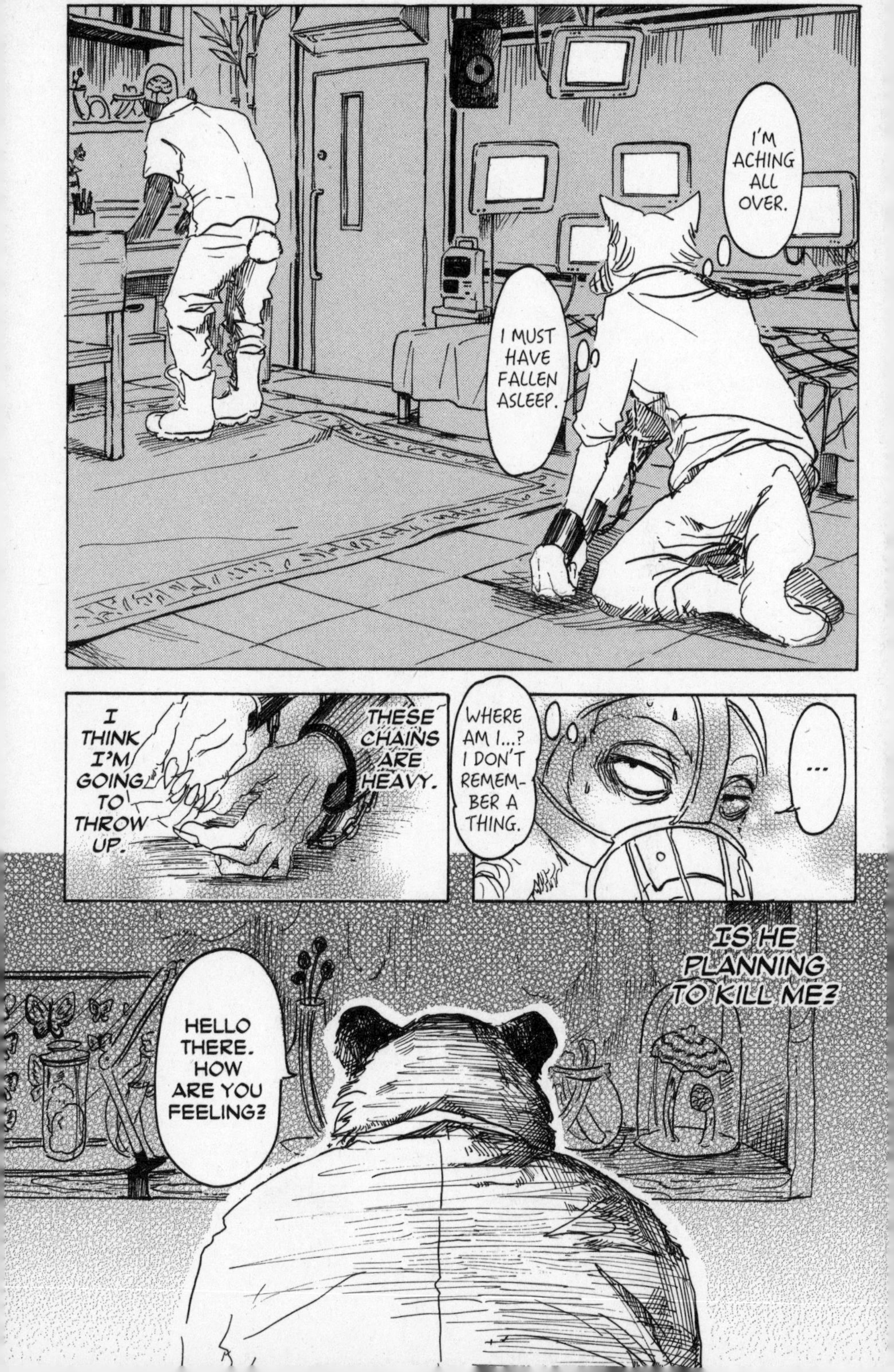
I'M ACHING ALL OVER.
I MUST HAVE FALLEN ASLEEP.
...
WHERE AM I...? I DON'T REMEMBER A THING.
THESE CHAINS ARE HEAVY.
I THINK I'M GOING TO THROW UP.
IS HE PLANNING TO KILL ME?
HELLO THERE. HOW ARE YOU FEELING?

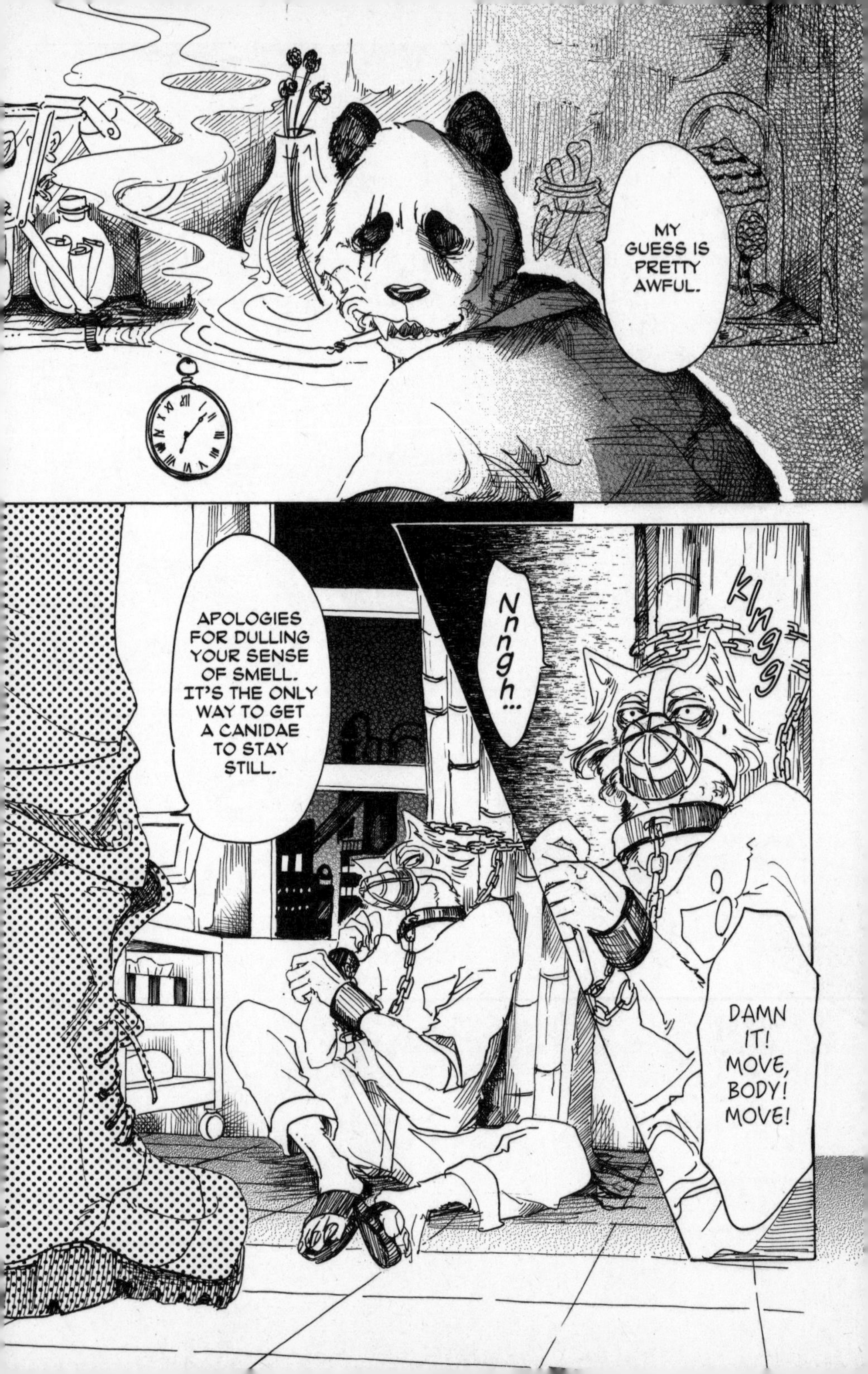
MY GUESS IS PRETTY AWFUL.
Klingg
Nnngh...
DAMN IT! MOVE, BODY! MOVE!
APOLOGIES FOR DULLING YOUR SENSE OF SMELL. IT'S THE ONLY WAY TO GET A CANIDAE TO STAY STILL.

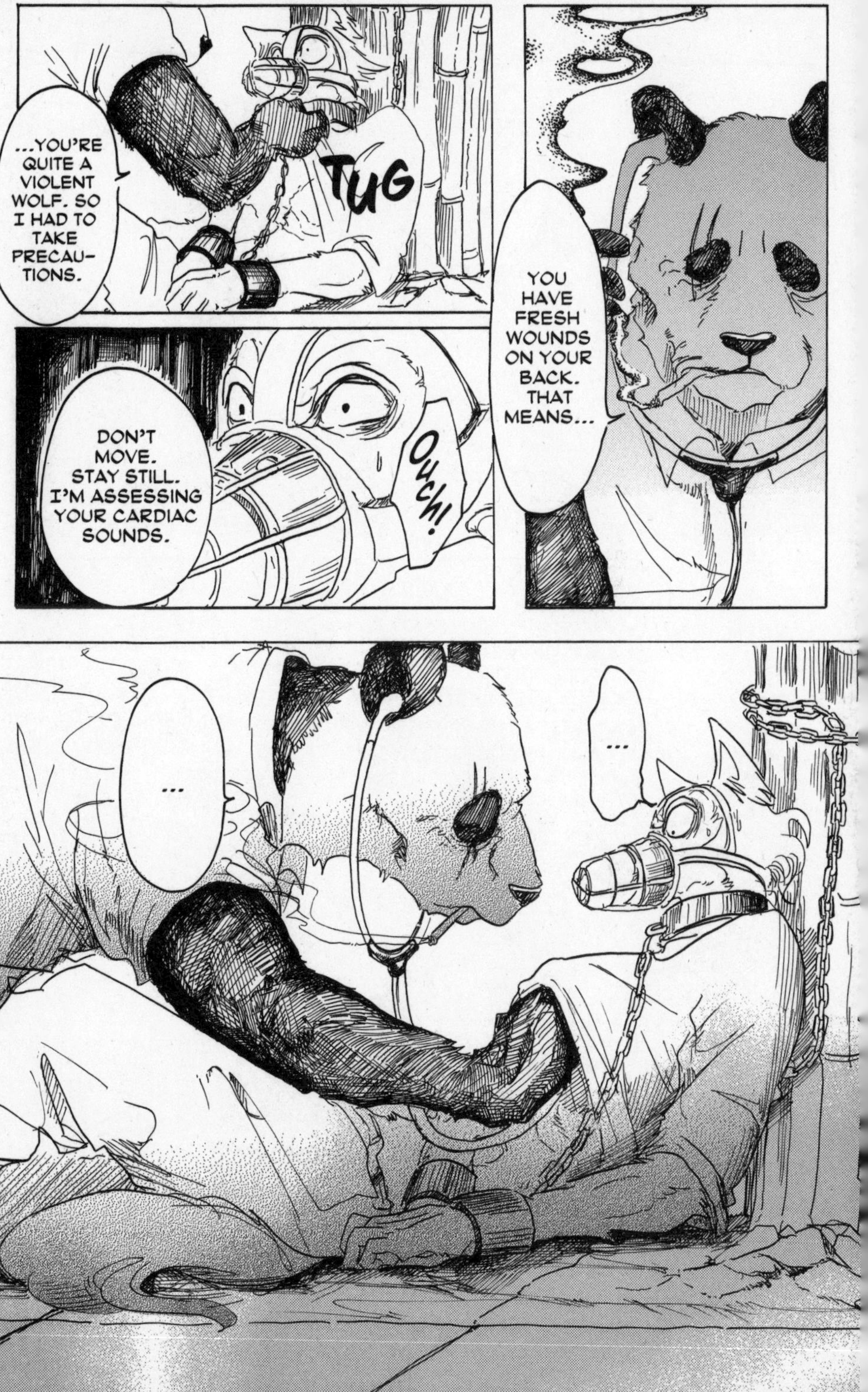

YOU HAVE FRESH WOUNDS ON YOUR BACK. THAT MEANS...
...YOU'RE QUITE A VIOLENT WOLF. SO I HAD TO TAKE PRECAU-TIONS.
TUG
DON'T MOVE. STAY STILL. I'M ASSESSING YOUR CARDIAC SOUNDS.
OUCH!
...
...

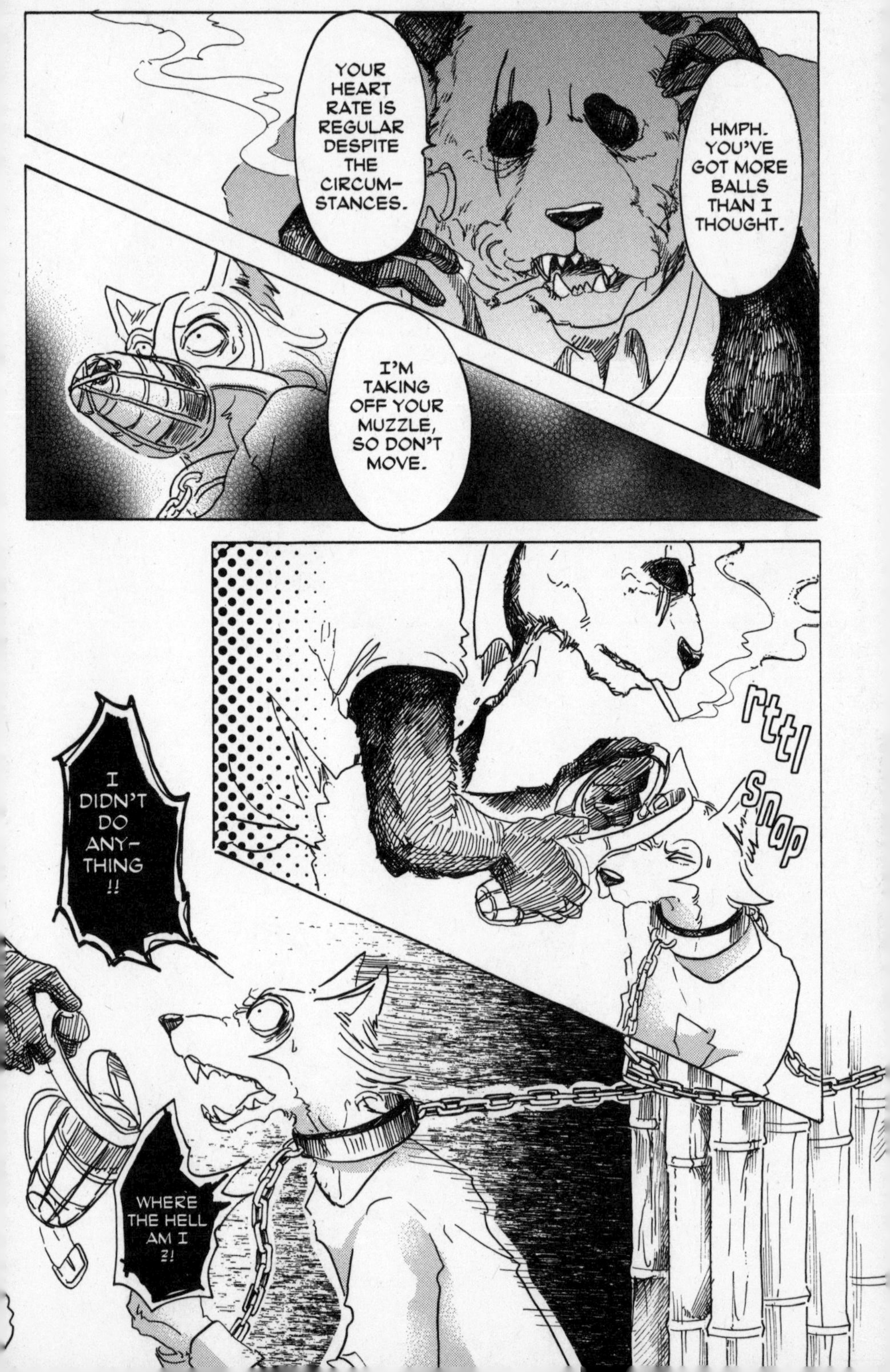
HMPH. YOU'VE GOT MORE BALLS THAN I THOUGHT.
YOUR HEART RATE IS REGULAR DESPITE THE CIRCUM- STANCES.
I'M TAKING OFF YOUR MUZZLE, SO DON'T MOVE.
rttl
snap
I DIDN'T DO ANY- THING !!
WHERE THE HELL AM I ?!

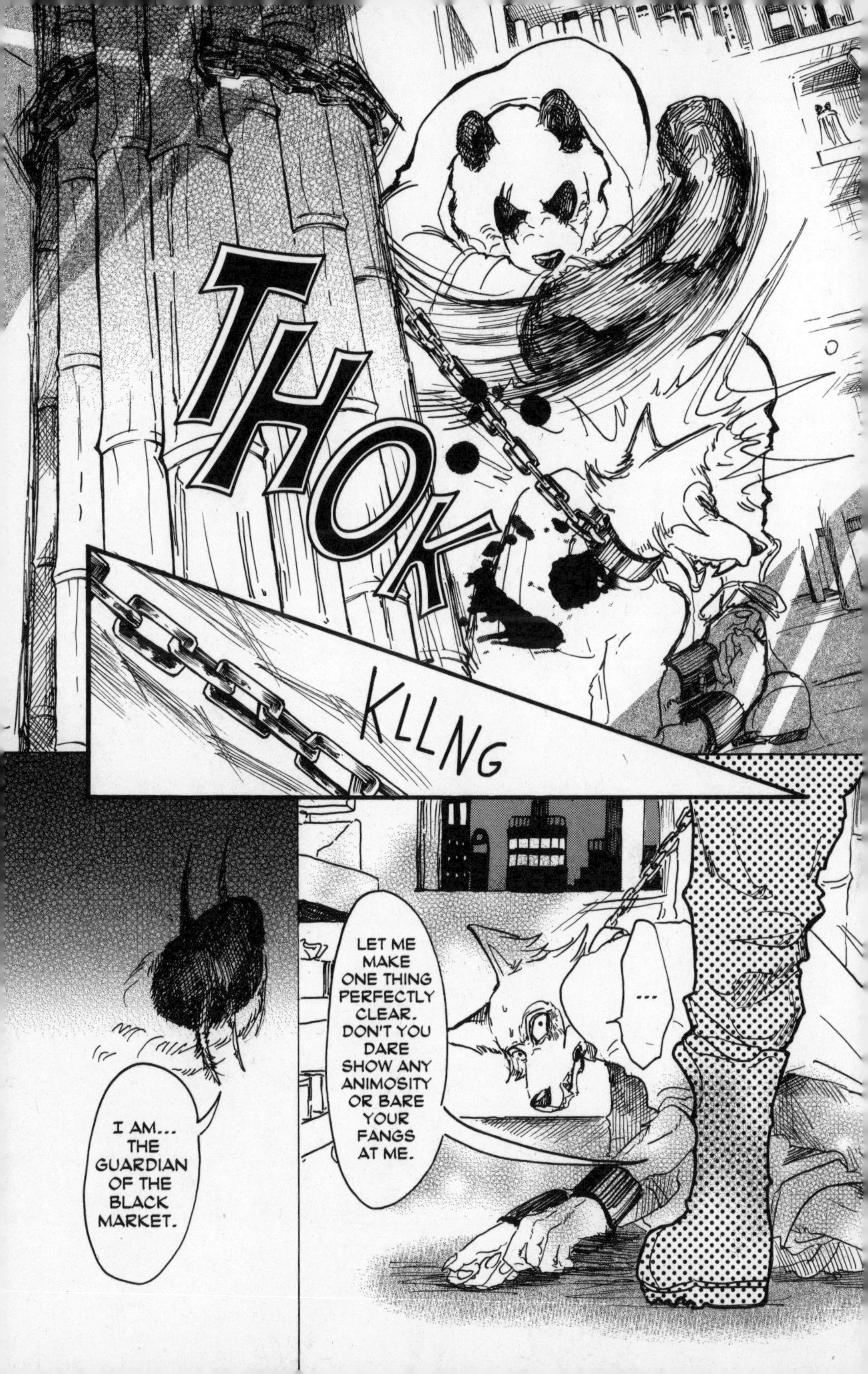
THOK
KLLNG
...
LET ME MAKE ONE THING PERFECTLY CLEAR. DON'T YOU DARE SHOW ANY ANIMOSITY OR BARE YOUR FANGS AT ME.
I AM... THE GUARDIAN OF THE BLACK MARKET.

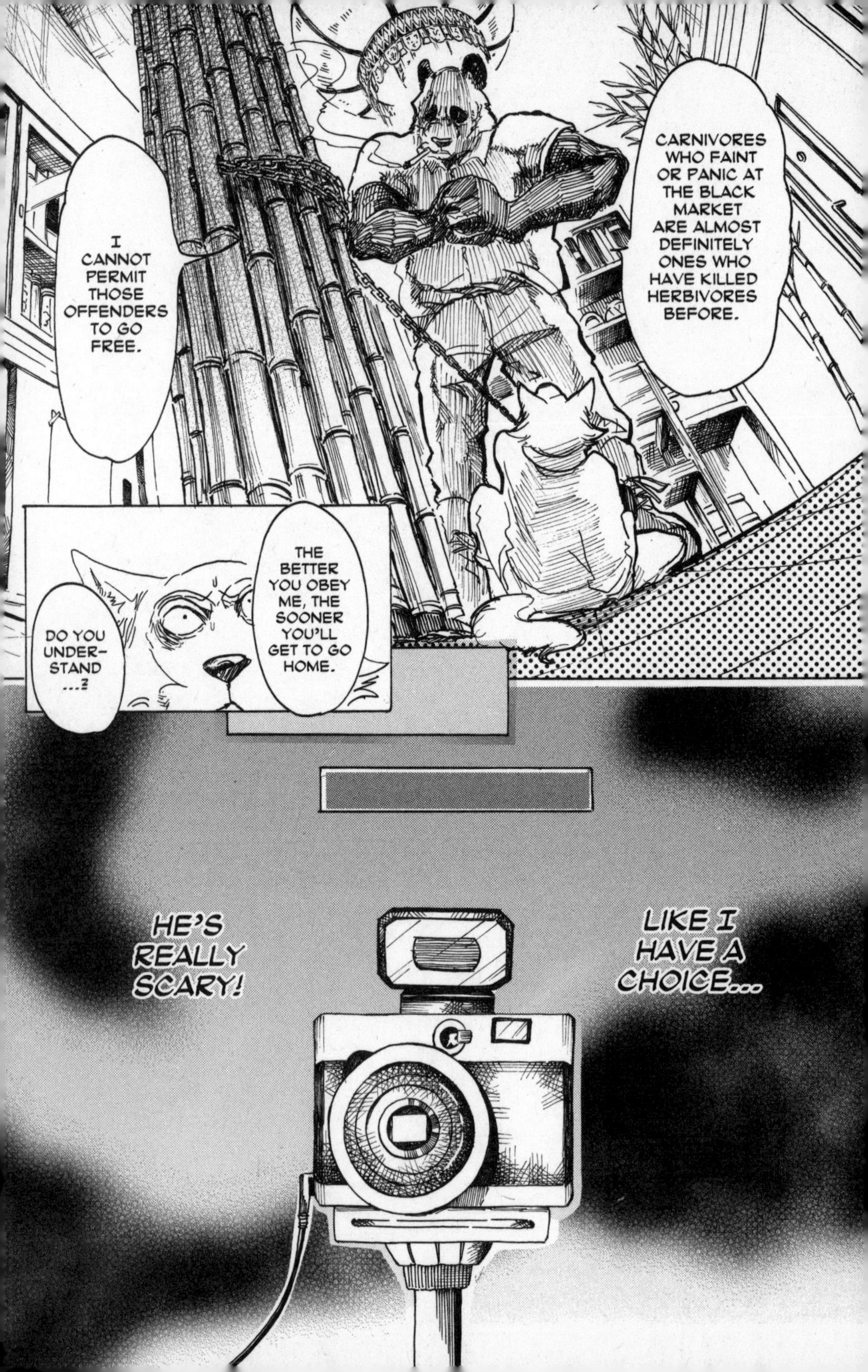
CARNIVORES WHO FAINT OR PANIC AT THE BLACK MARKET ARE ALMOST DEFINITELY ONES WHO HAVE KILLED HERBIVORES BEFORE.
I CANNOT PERMIT THOSE OFFENDERS TO GO FREE.
THE BETTER YOU OBEY ME, THE SOONER YOU'LL GET TO GO HOME.
DO YOU UNDER-STAND ...?
LIKE I HAVE A CHOICE...
HE'S REALLY SCARY!

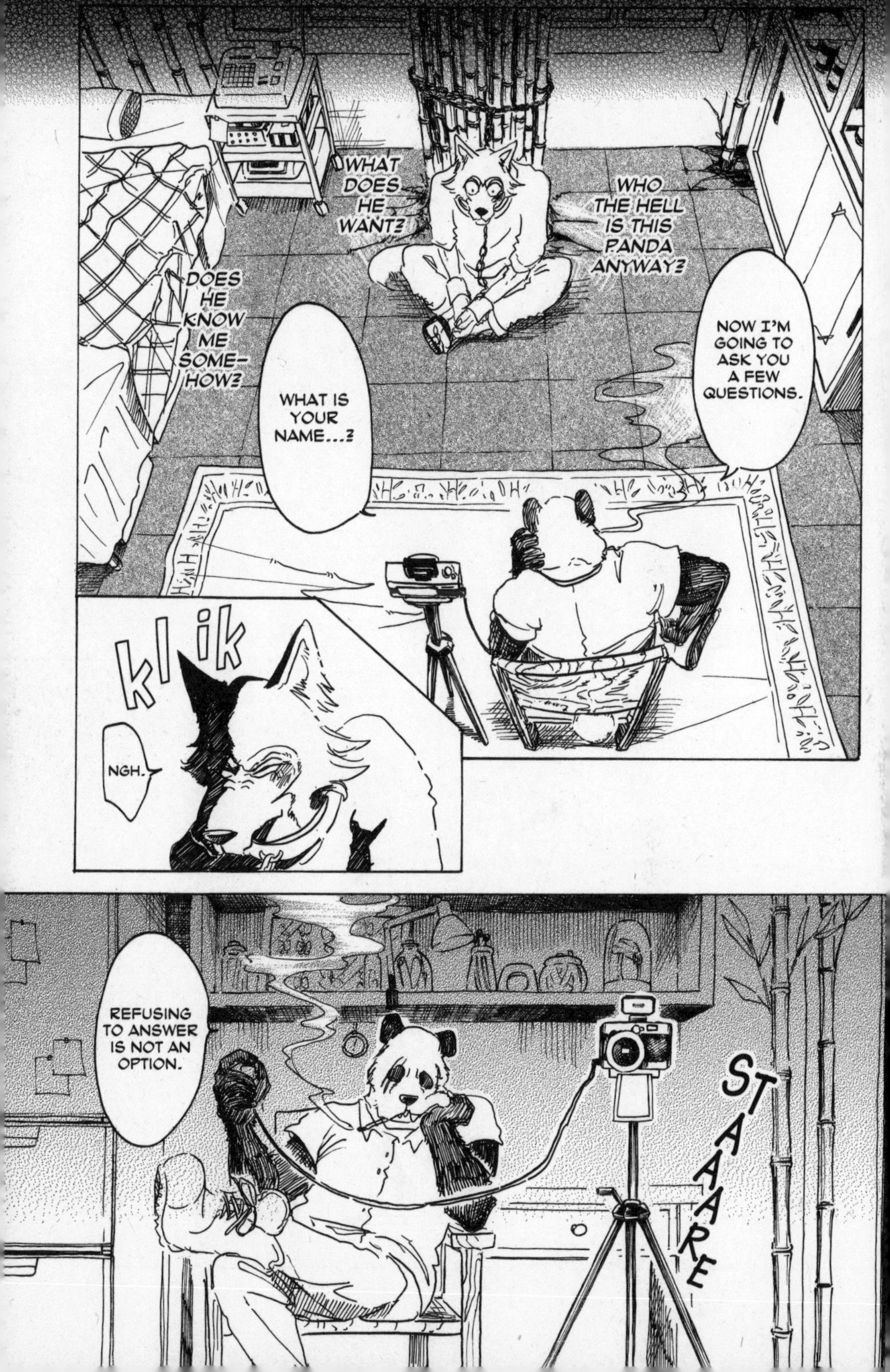
WHO THE HELL IS THIS PANDA ANYWAY?
WHAT DOES HE WANT?
DOES HE KNOW ME SOMEHOW?
NOW I'M GOING TO ASK YOU A FEW QUESTIONS.
WHAT IS YOUR NAME...?
klik
NGH.
STAAARE
REFUSING TO ANSWER IS NOT AN OPTION.

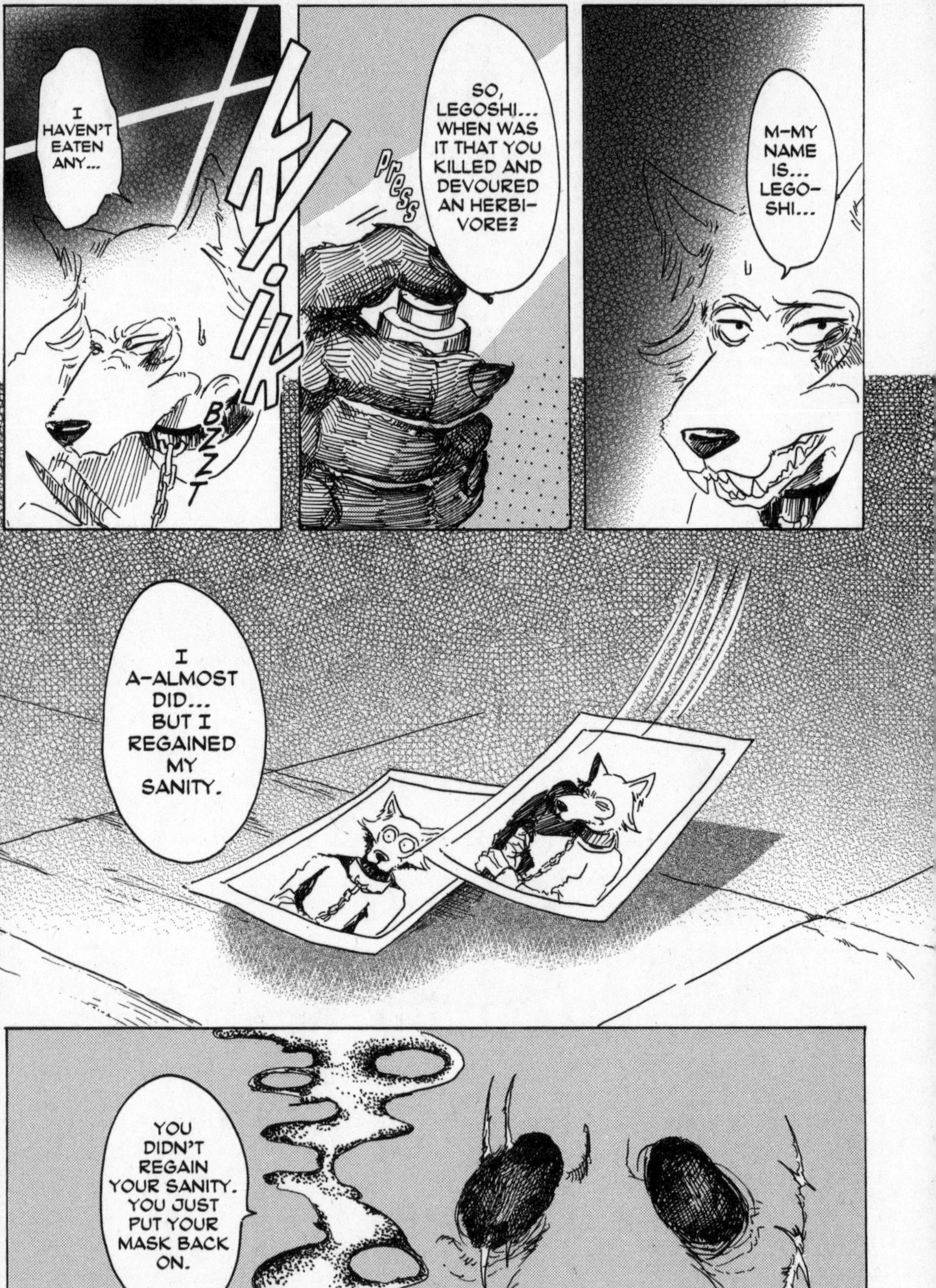
M-MY NAME IS... LEGO-SHI...
SO, LEGOSHI... WHEN WAS IT THAT YOU KILLED AND DEVOURED AN HERBI-VORE?
Press
I HAVEN'T EATEN ANY...
KLIK
BZZZT
I A-ALMOST DID... BUT I REGAINED MY SANITY.
YOU DIDN'T REGAIN YOUR SANITY. YOU JUST PUT YOUR MASK BACK ON.

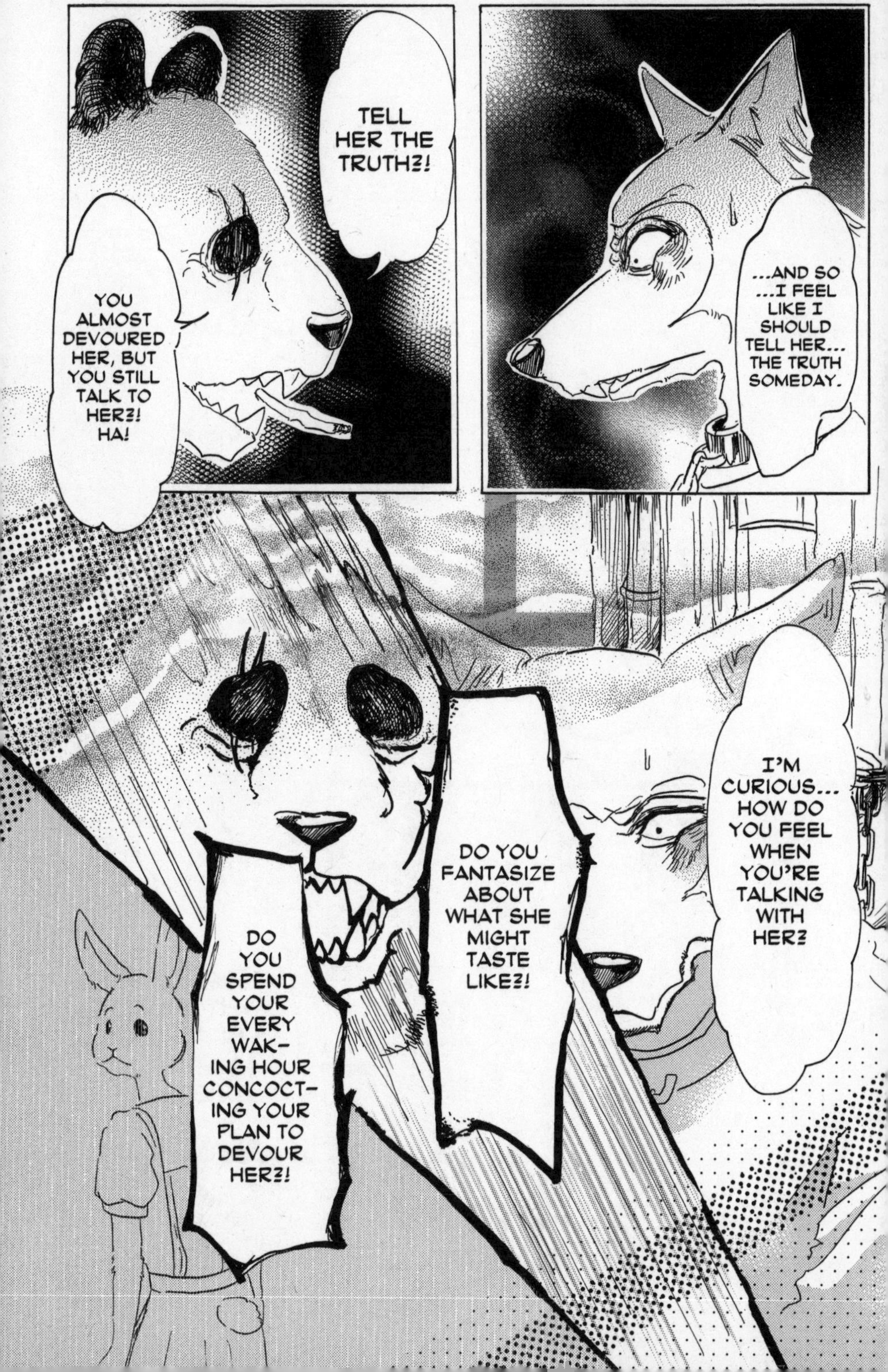
...AND SO ...I FEEL LIKE I SHOULD TELL HER... THE TRUTH SOMEDAY.
TELL HER THE TRUTH?!
YOU ALMOST DEVOURED HER, BUT YOU STILL TALK TO HER?! HA!
I'M CURIOUS... HOW DO YOU FEEL WHEN YOU'RE TALKING WITH HER?
DO YOU FANTASIZE ABOUT WHAT SHE MIGHT TASTE LIKE?!
DO YOU SPEND YOUR EVERY WAK-ING HOUR CONCOCT-ING YOUR PLAN TO DEVOUR HER?!

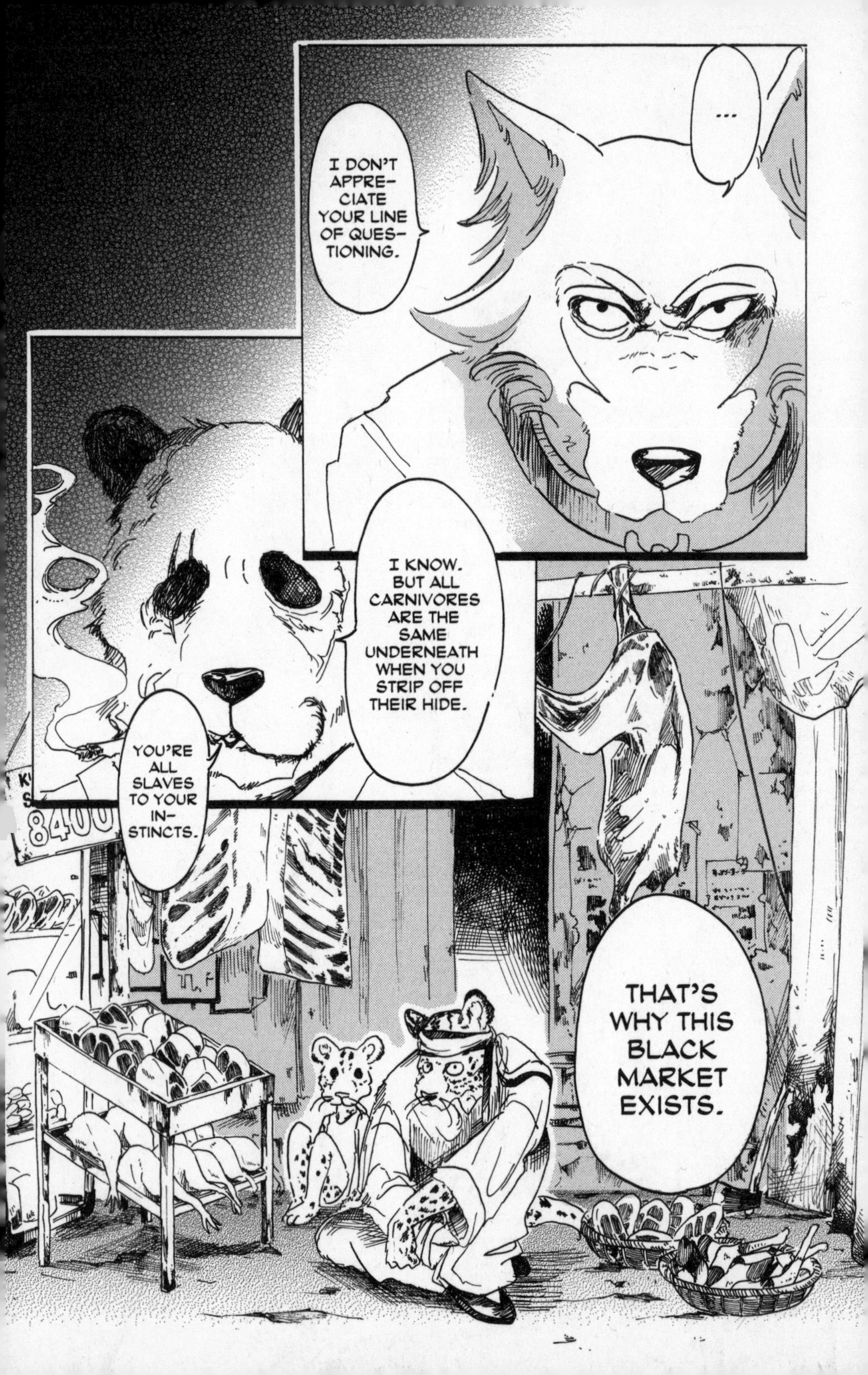
...
I DON'T APPRECIATE YOUR LINE OF QUESTIONING.
I KNOW. BUT ALL CARNIVORES ARE THE SAME UNDERNEATH WHEN YOU STRIP OFF THEIR HIDE.
YOU'RE ALL SLAVES TO YOUR INSTINCTS.
THAT'S WHY THIS BLACK MARKET EXISTS.

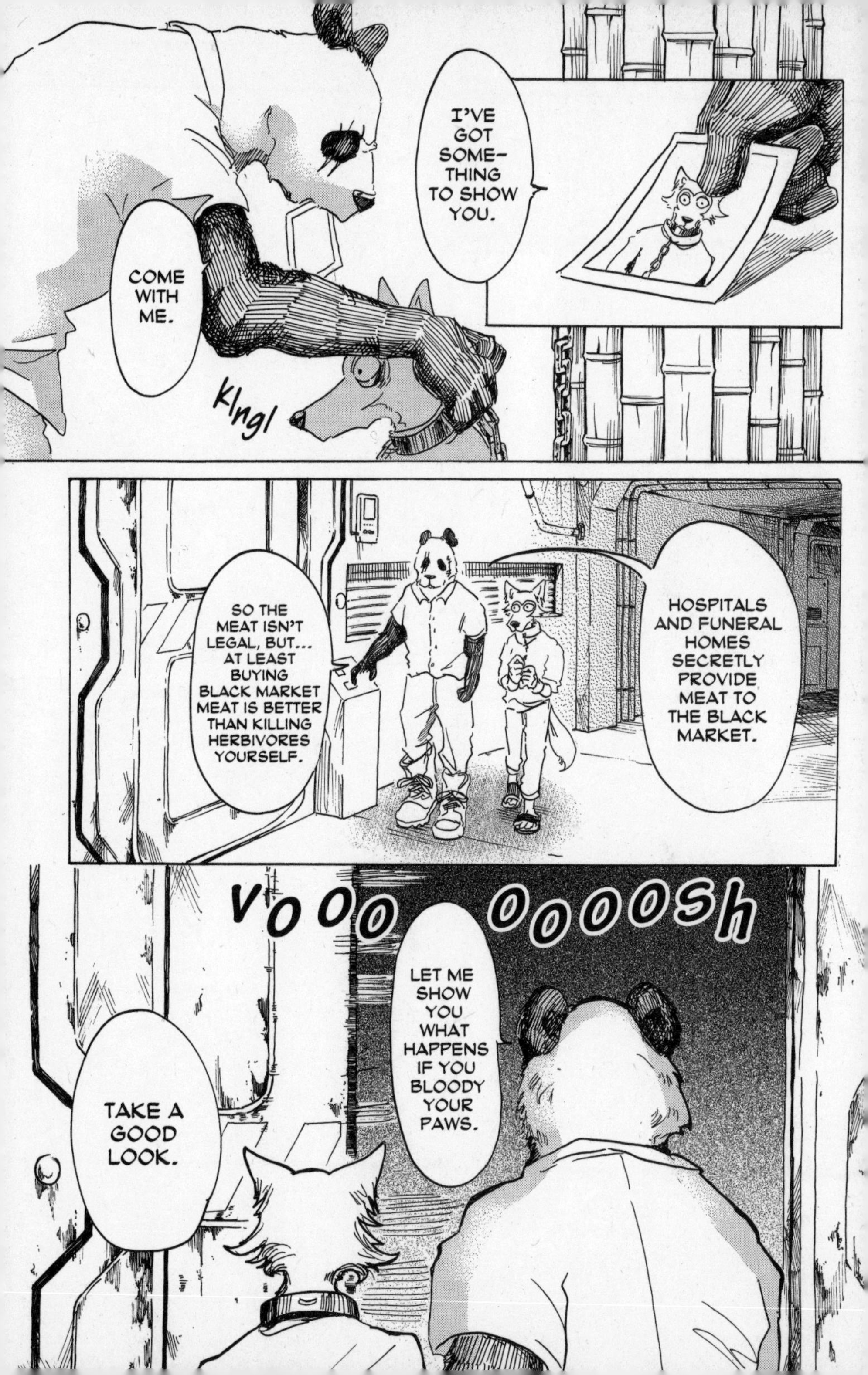
I'VE GOT SOME-THING TO SHOW YOU.
COME WITH ME.
Klng!
HOSPITALS AND FUNERAL HOMES SECRETLY PROVIDE MEAT TO THE BLACK MARKET.
SO THE MEAT ISN'T LEGAL, BUT... AT LEAST BUYING BLACK MARKET MEAT IS BETTER THAN KILLING HERBIVORES YOURSELF.
VOOO OOOOSh
LET ME SHOW YOU WHAT HAPPENS IF YOU BLOODY YOUR PAWS.
TAKE A GOOD LOOK.

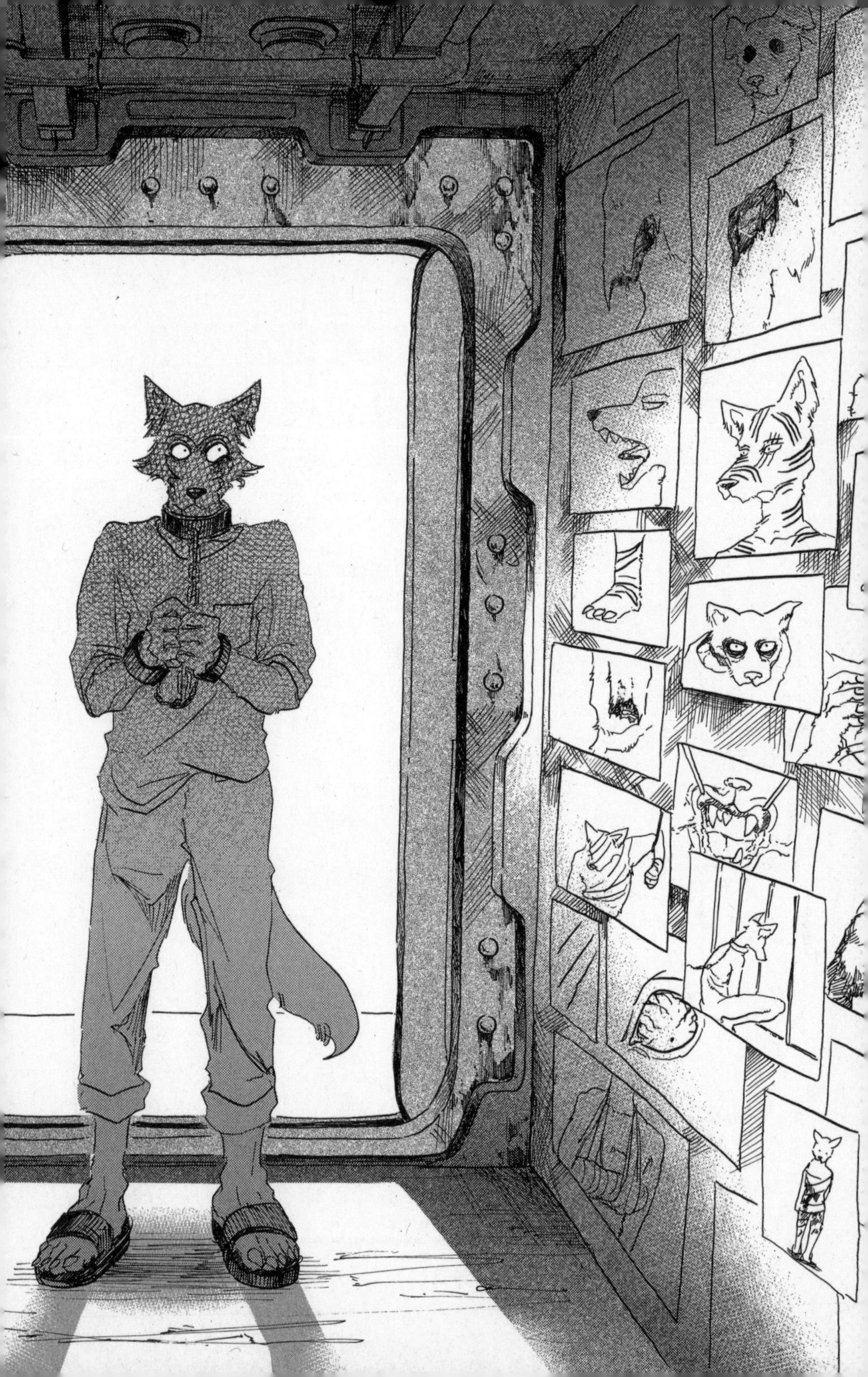

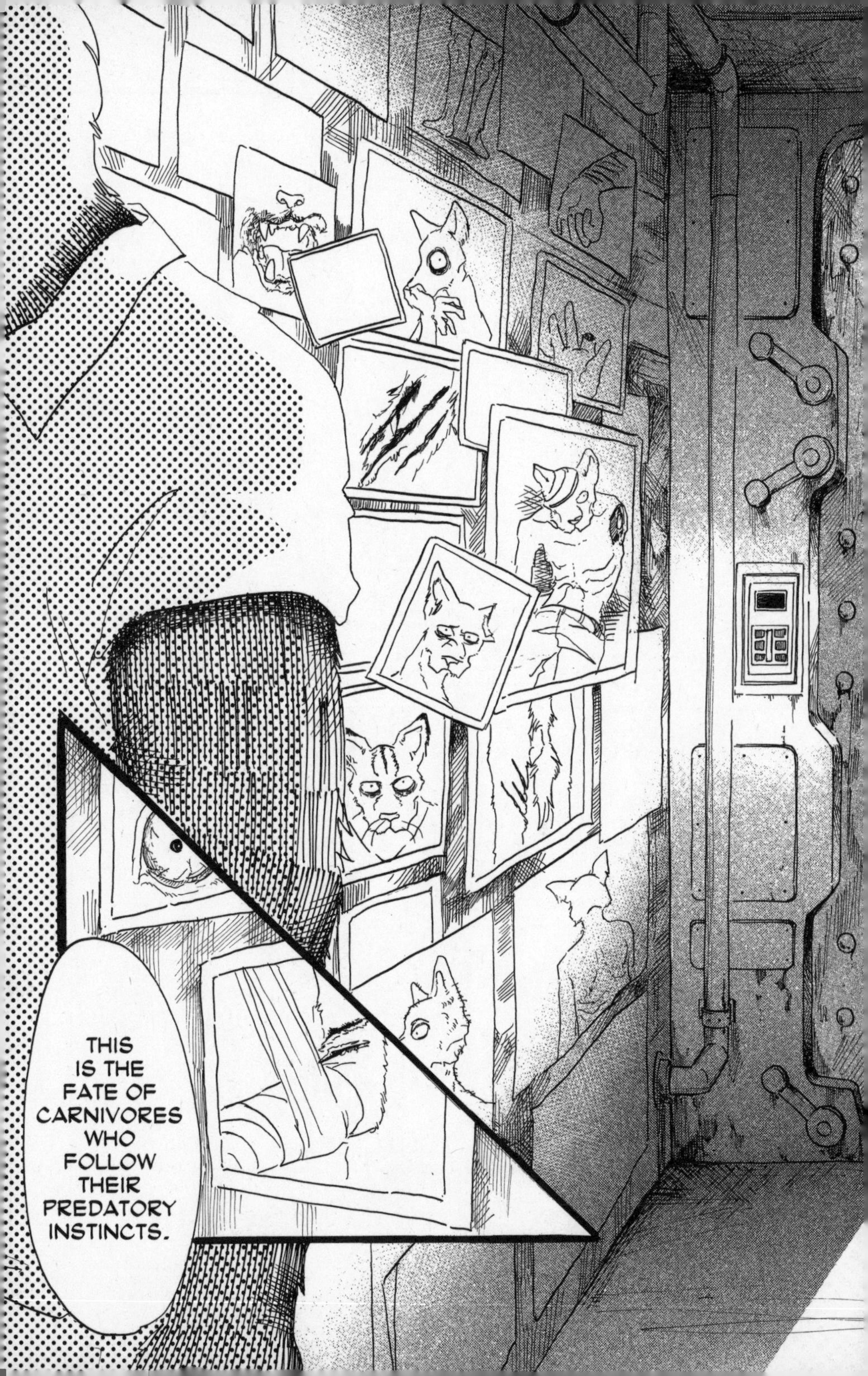
THIS IS THE FATE OF CARNIVORES WHO FOLLOW THEIR PREDATORY INSTINCTS.

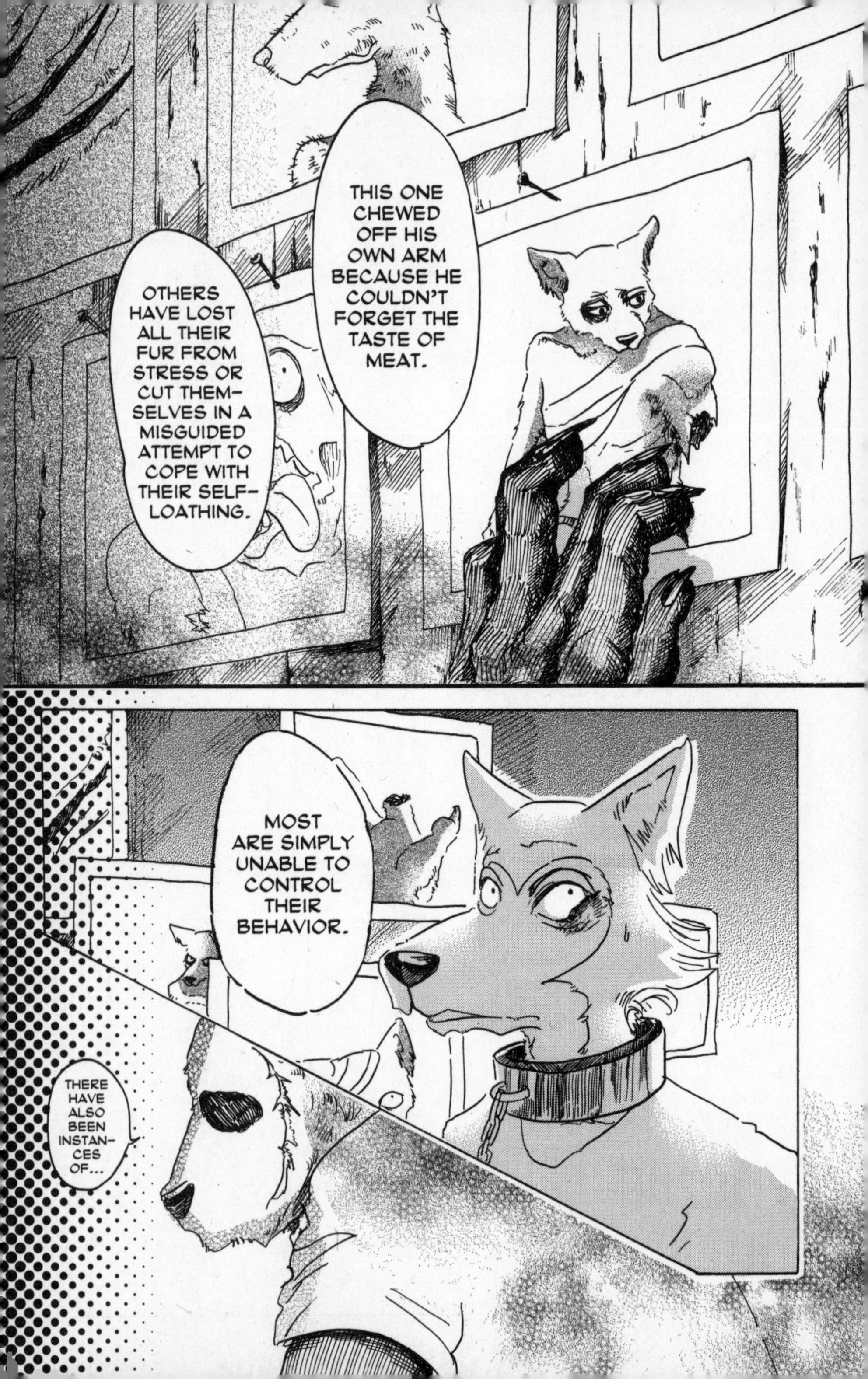
THIS ONE CHEWED OFF HIS OWN ARM BECAUSE HE COULDN'T FORGET THE TASTE OF MEAT.
OTHERS HAVE LOST ALL THEIR FUR FROM STRESS OR CUT THEM-SELVES IN A MISGUIDED ATTEMPT TO COPE WITH THEIR SELF-LOATHING.
MOST ARE SIMPLY UNABLE TO CONTROL THEIR BEHAVIOR.
THERE HAVE ALSO BEEN INSTAN-CES OF...

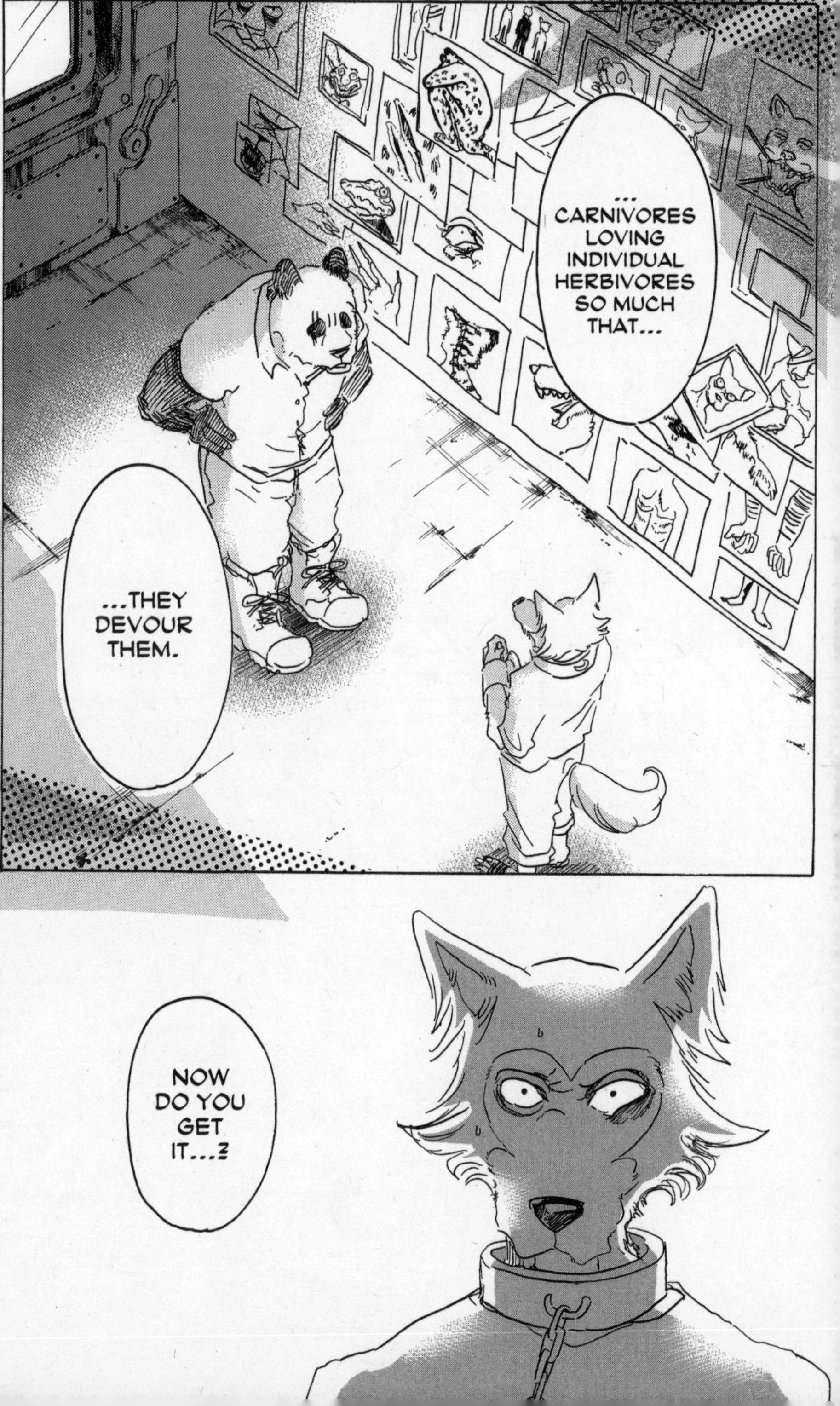
...CARNIVORES LOVING INDIVIDUAL HERBIVORES SO MUCH THAT...
...THEY DEVOUR THEM.
NOW DO YOU GET IT...?

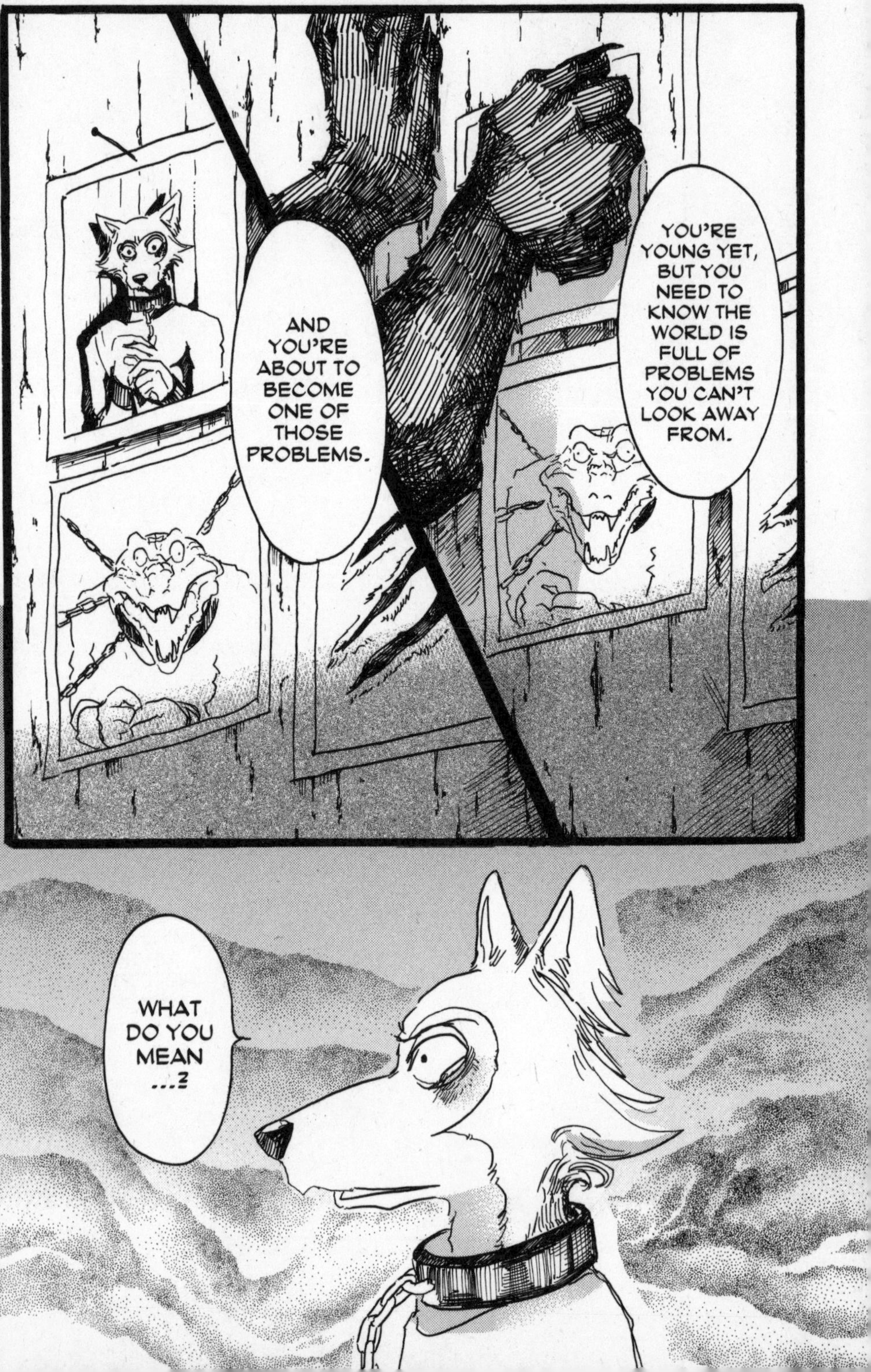
YOU'RE YOUNG YET, BUT YOU NEED TO KNOW THE WORLD IS FULL OF PROBLEMS YOU CAN'T LOOK AWAY FROM.
AND YOU'RE ABOUT TO BECOME ONE OF THOSE PROBLEMS.
WHAT DO YOU MEAN ...?

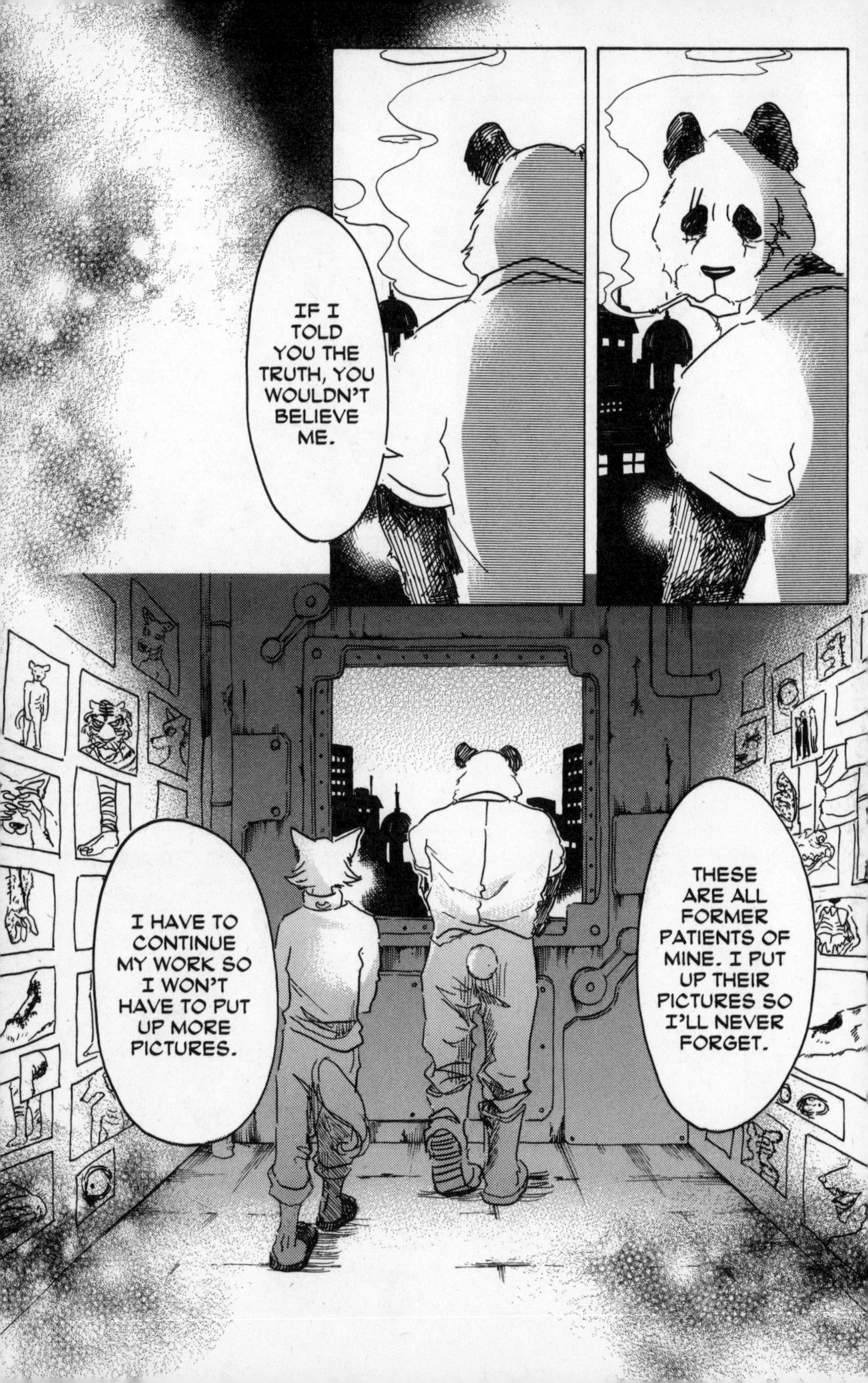
IF I TOLD YOU THE TRUTH, YOU WOULDN'T BELIEVE ME.
THESE ARE ALL FORMER PATIENTS OF MINE. I PUT UP THEIR PICTURES SO I'LL NEVER FORGET.
I HAVE TO CONTINUE MY WORK SO I WON'T HAVE TO PUT UP MORE PICTURES.

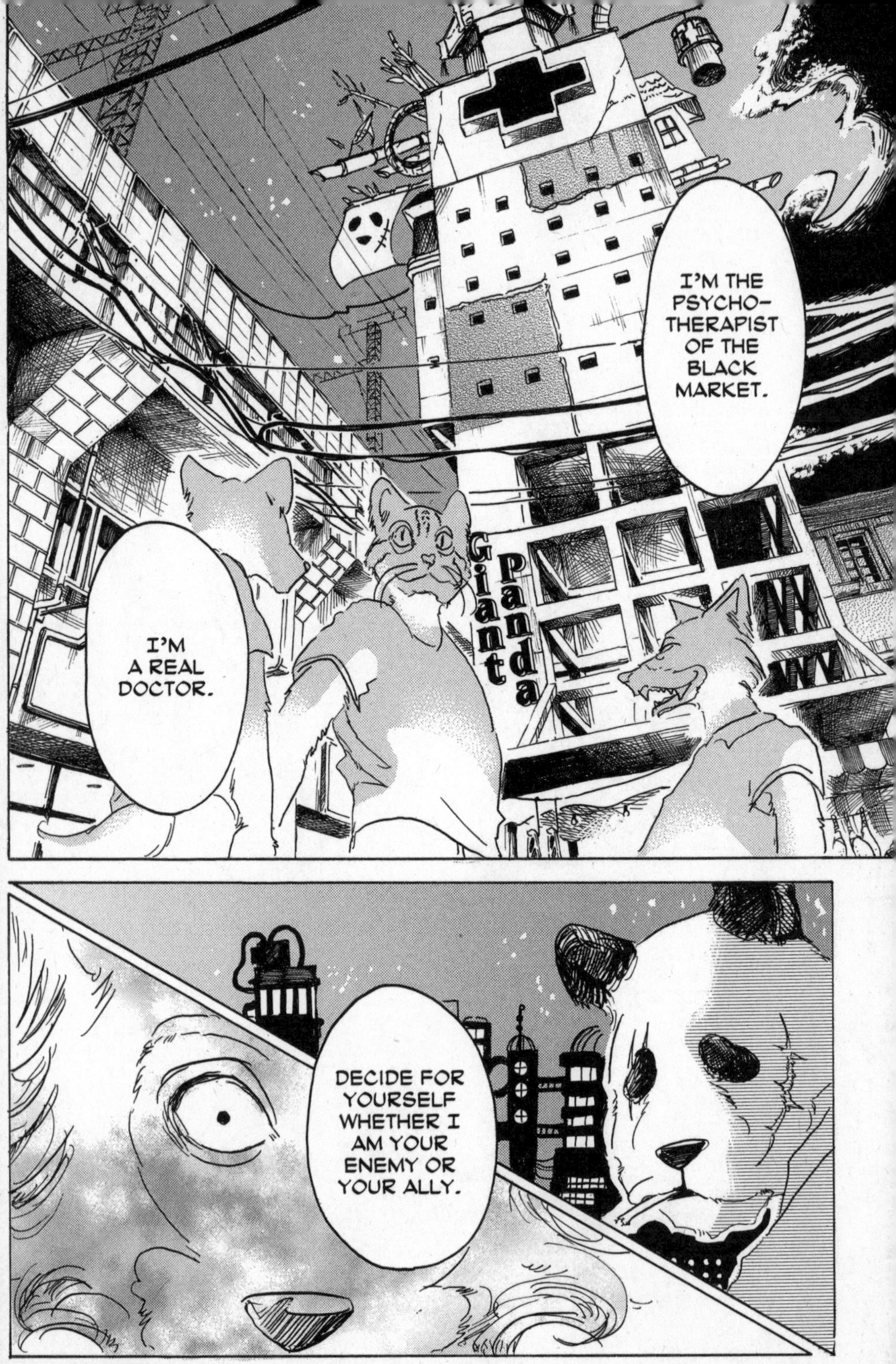
I'M THE PSYCHO-THERAPIST OF THE BLACK MARKET.
Giant Panda
I'M A REAL DOCTOR.
DECIDE FOR YOURSELF WHETHER I AM YOUR ENEMY OR YOUR ALLY.

Chapter 25: I'm in Tears and I Hate Everything

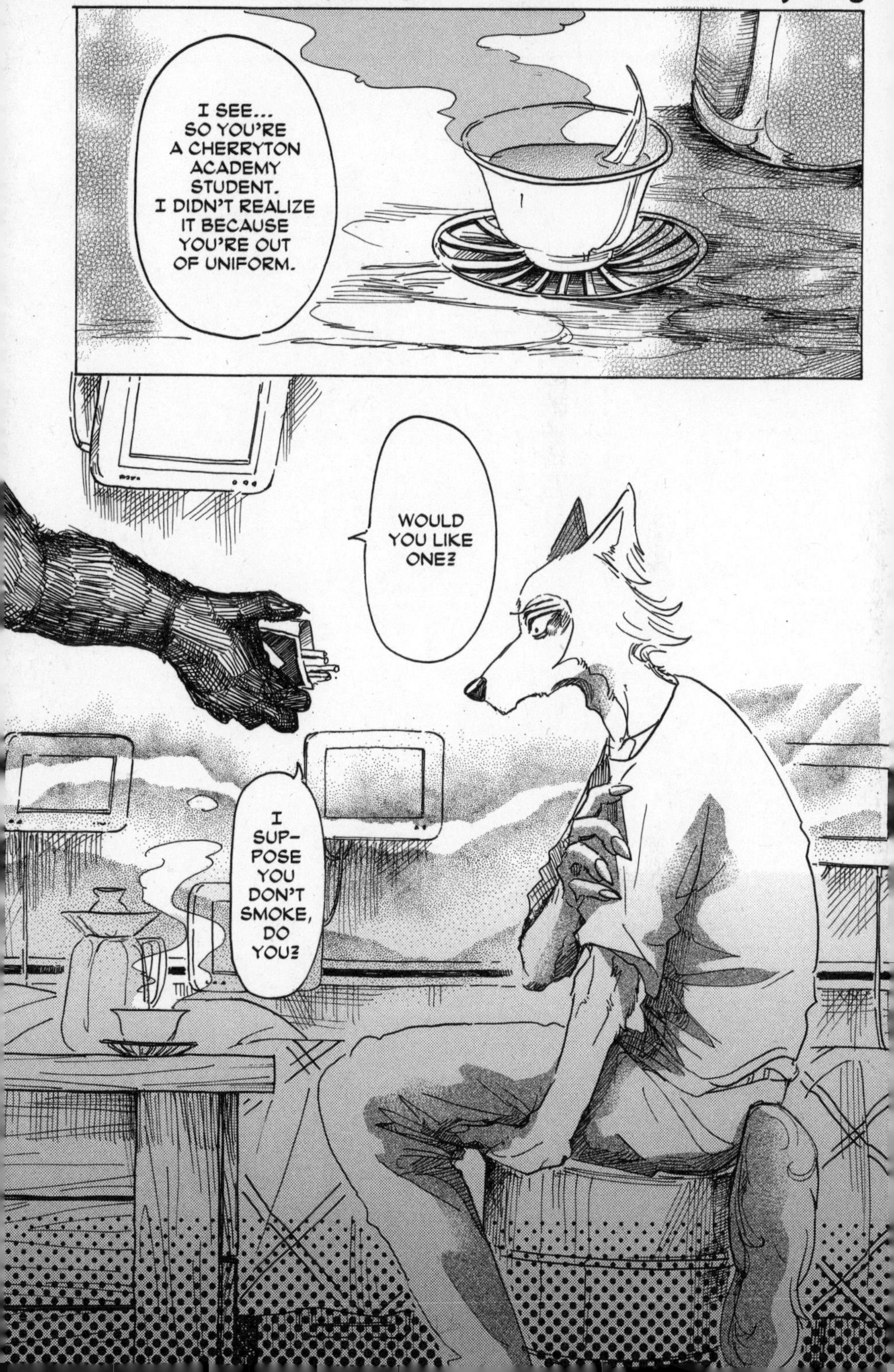
I SEE... SO YOU'RE A CHERRYTON ACADEMY STUDENT. I DIDN'T REALIZE IT BECAUSE YOU'RE OUT OF UNIFORM.
WOULD YOU LIKE ONE?
I SUPPOSE YOU DON'T SMOKE, DO YOU?

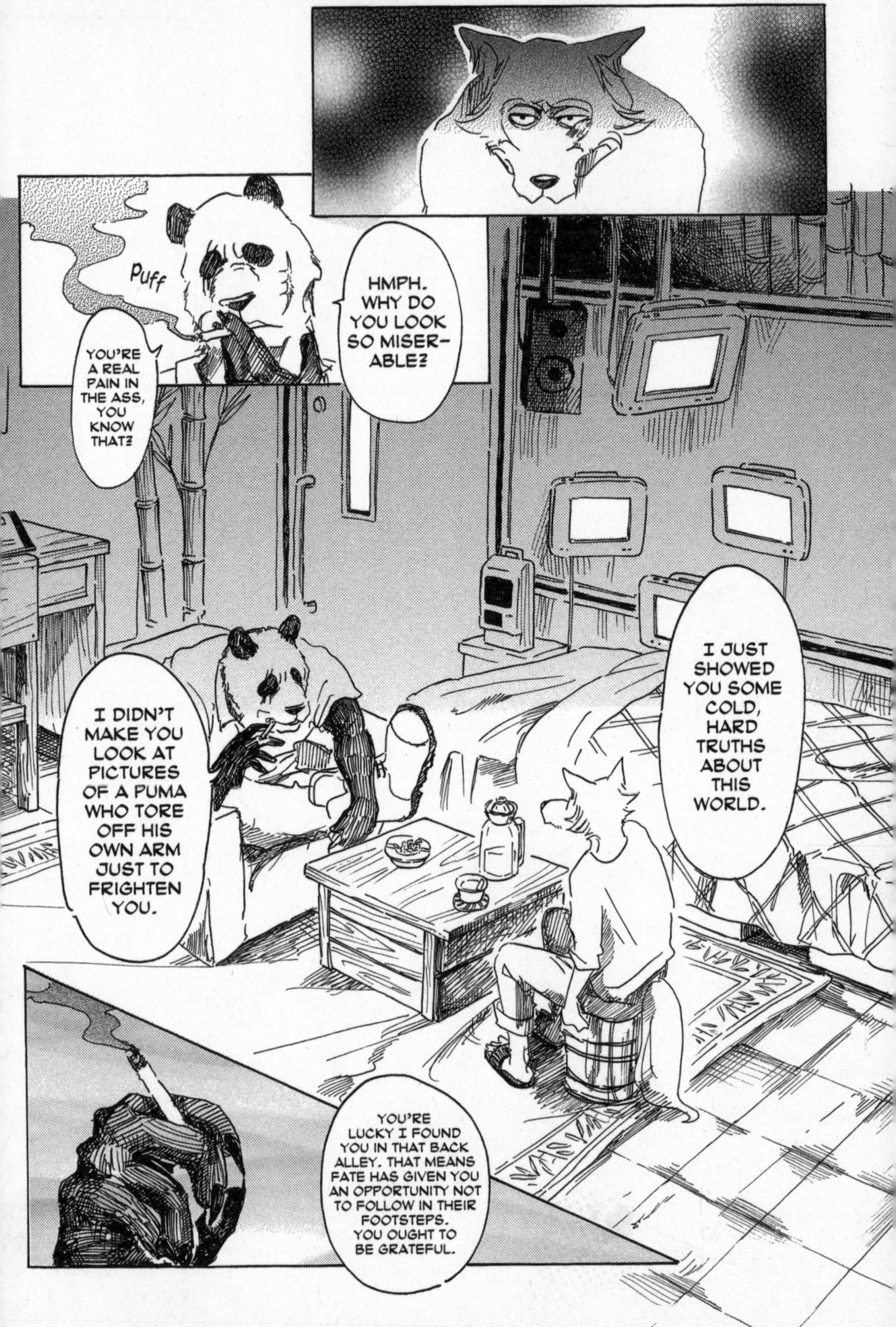
HMPH. WHY DO YOU LOOK SO MISER-ABLE?
Puff
YOU'RE A REAL PAIN IN THE ASS, YOU KNOW THAT?
I JUST SHOWED YOU SOME COLD, HARD TRUTHS ABOUT THIS WORLD.
I DIDN'T MAKE YOU LOOK AT PICTURES OF A PUMA WHO TORE OFF HIS OWN ARM JUST TO FRIGHTEN YOU.
YOU'RE LUCKY I FOUND YOU IN THAT BACK ALLEY. THAT MEANS FATE HAS GIVEN YOU AN OPPORTUNITY NOT TO FOLLOW IN THEIR FOOTSTEPS. YOU OUGHT TO BE GRATEFUL.

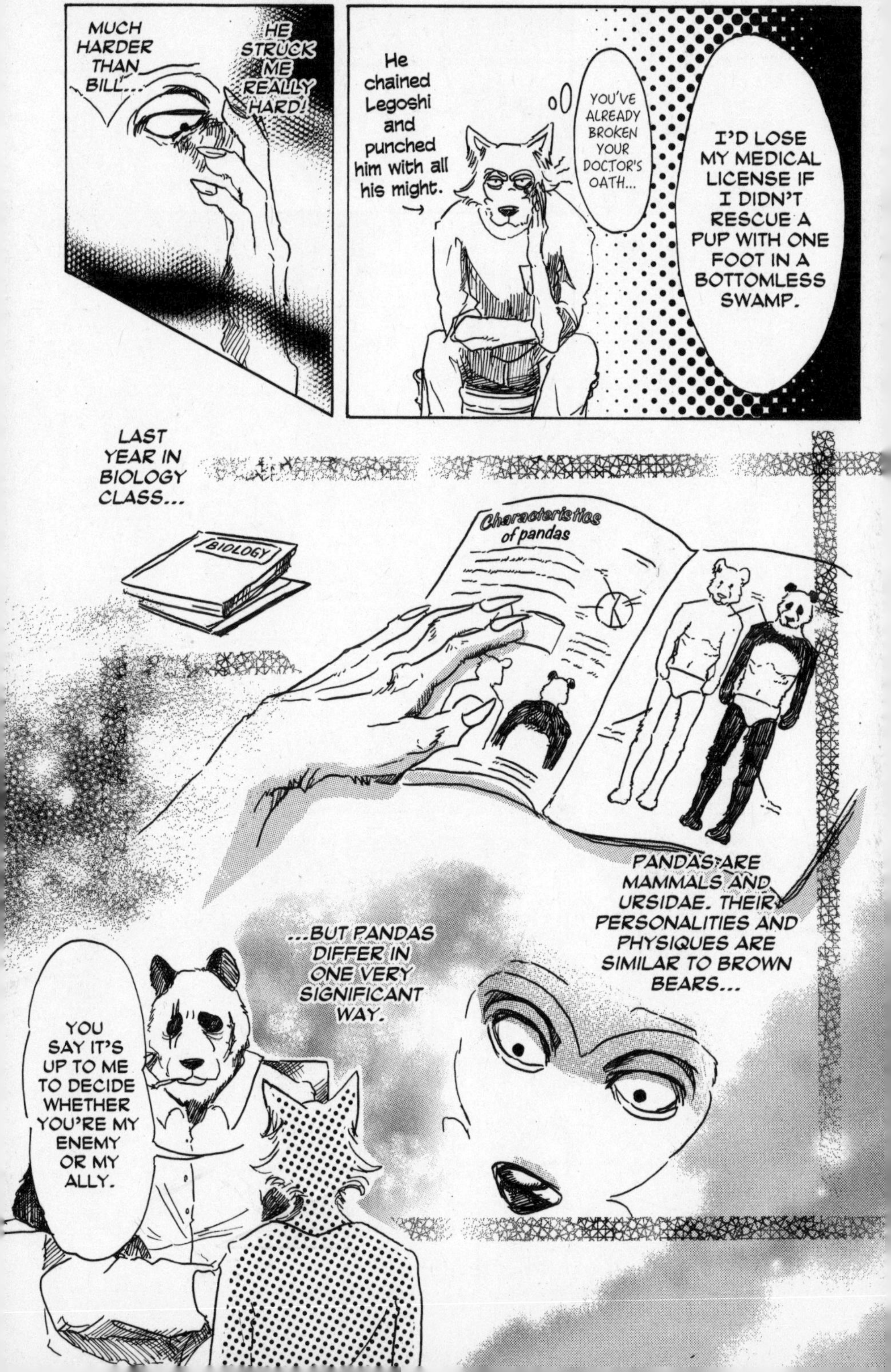
I'D LOSE MY MEDICAL LICENSE IF I DIDN'T RESCUE A PUP WITH ONE FOOT IN A BOTTOMLESS SWAMP.
YOU'VE ALREADY BROKEN YOUR DOCTOR'S OATH...
He chained Legoshi and punched him with all his might.
HE STRUCK ME REALLY HARD!
MUCH HARDER THAN BILL...
LAST YEAR IN BIOLOGY CLASS...
Characteristics of pandas
BIOLOGY
PANDAS ARE MAMMALS AND URSIDAE. THEIR PERSONALITIES AND PHYSIQUES ARE SIMILAR TO BROWN BEARS...
...BUT PANDAS DIFFER IN ONE VERY SIGNIFICANT WAY.
YOU SAY IT'S UP TO ME TO DECIDE WHETHER YOU'RE MY ENEMY OR MY ALLY.

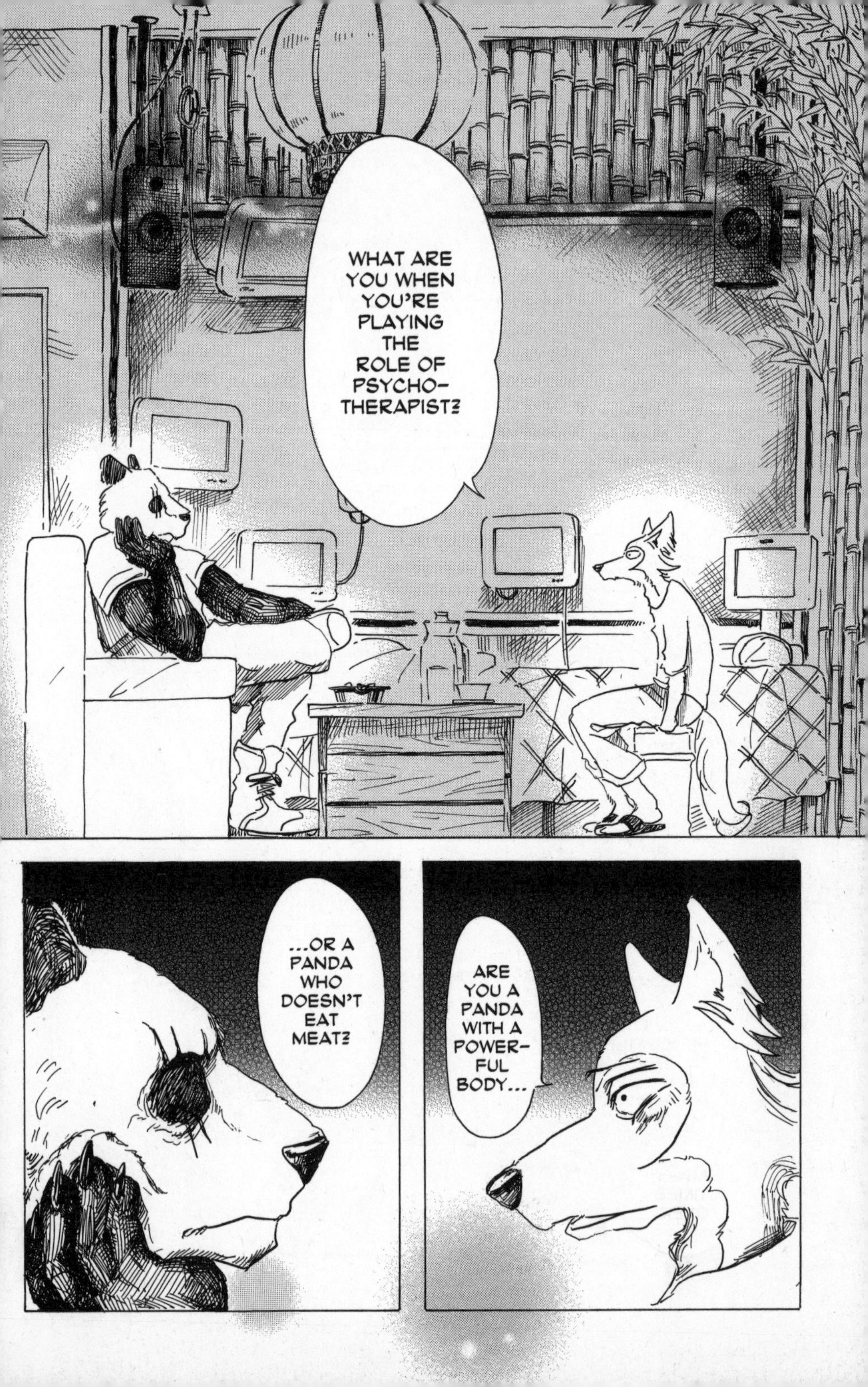
WHAT ARE YOU WHEN YOU'RE PLAYING THE ROLE OF PSYCHO-THERAPIST?
ARE YOU A PANDA WITH A POWER-FUL BODY...
...OR A PANDA WHO DOESN'T EAT MEAT?

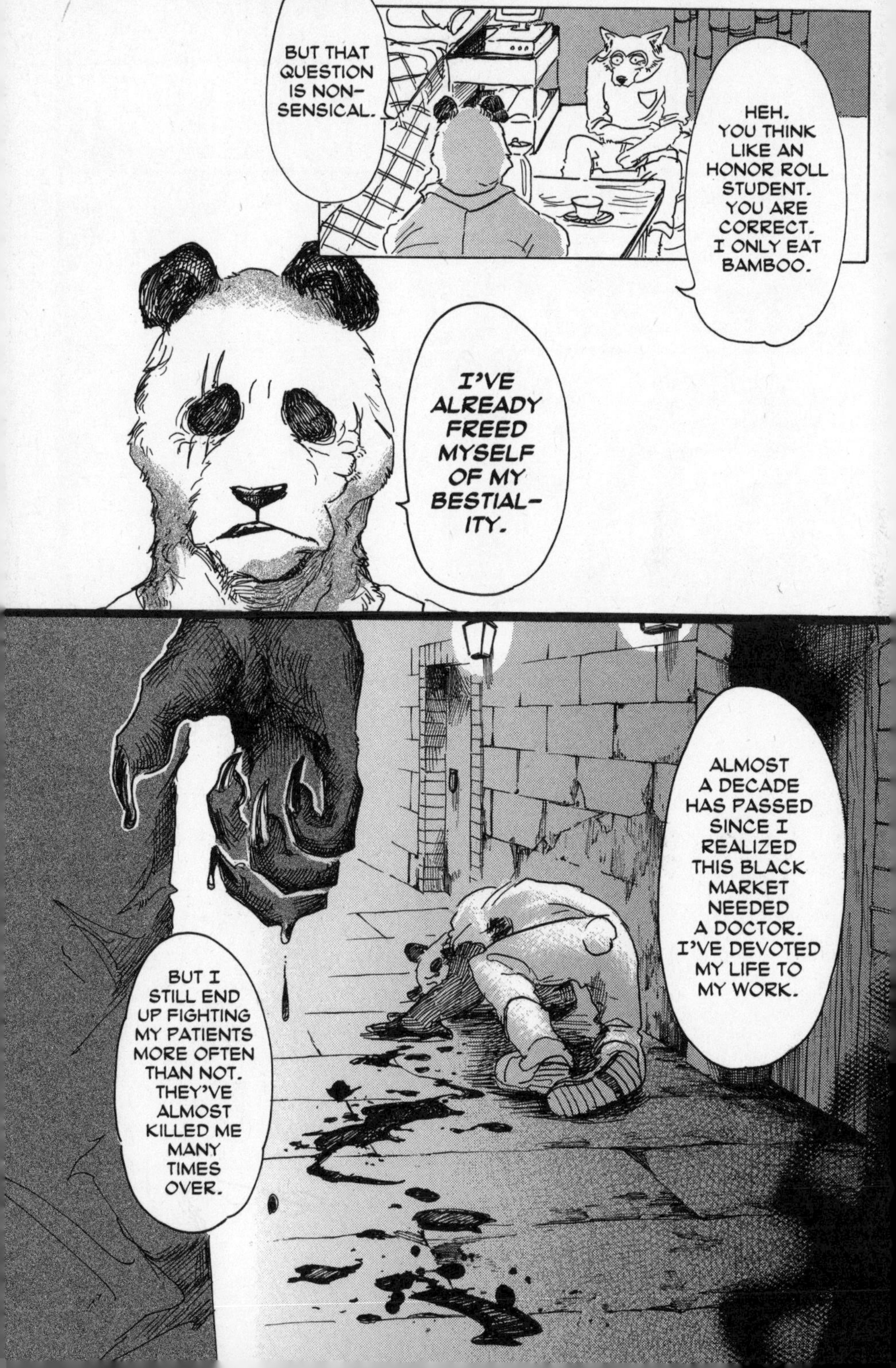
HEH. YOU THINK LIKE AN HONOR ROLL STUDENT. YOU ARE CORRECT. I ONLY EAT BAMBOO.
BUT THAT QUESTION IS NON-SENSICAL.
I'VE ALREADY FREED MYSELF OF MY BESTIAL-ITY.
ALMOST A DECADE HAS PASSED SINCE I REALIZED THIS BLACK MARKET NEEDED A DOCTOR. I'VE DEVOTED MY LIFE TO MY WORK.
BUT I STILL END UP FIGHTING MY PATIENTS MORE OFTEN THAN NOT. THEY'VE ALMOST KILLED ME MANY TIMES OVER.

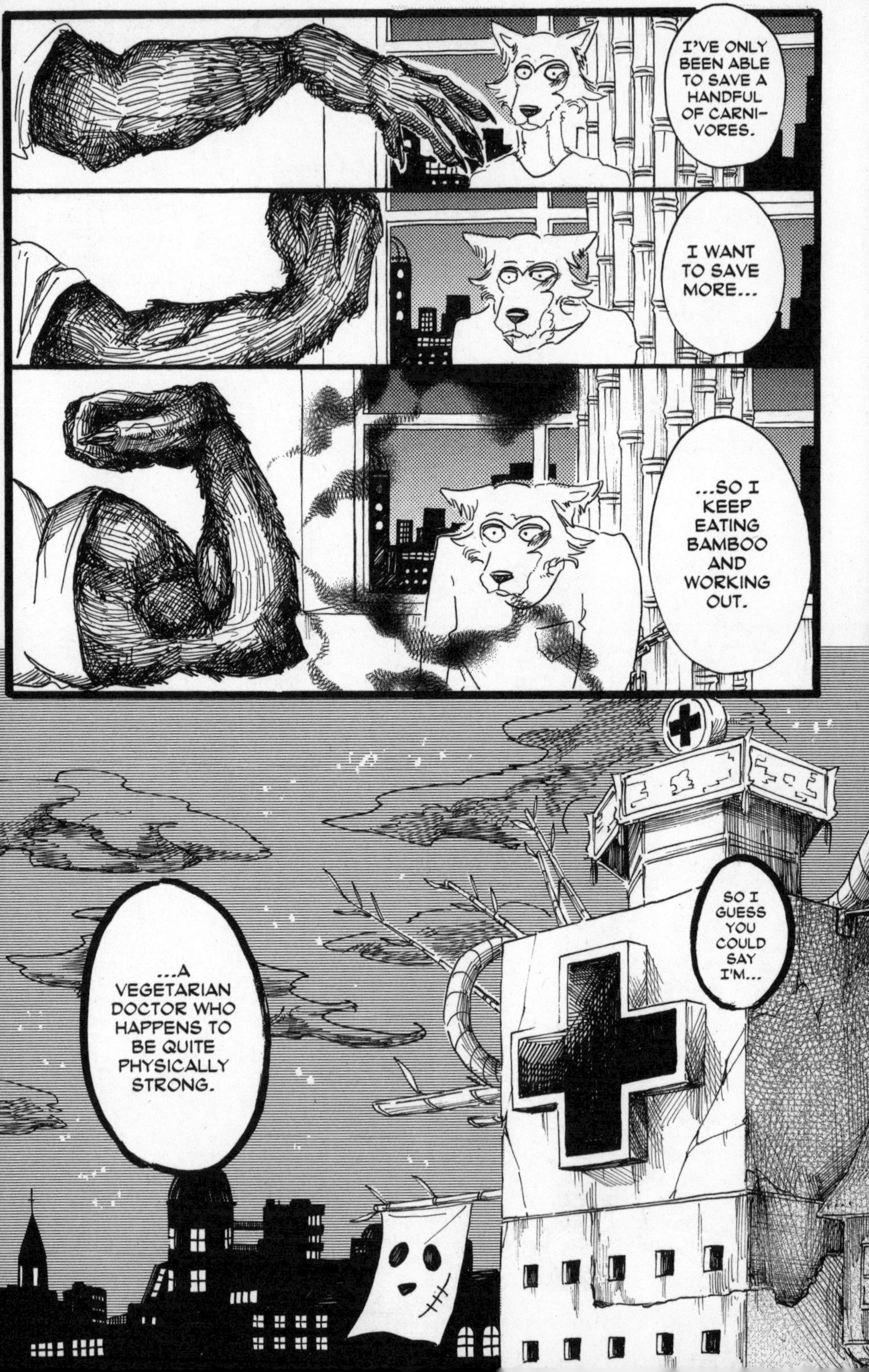
I'VE ONLY BEEN ABLE TO SAVE A HANDFUL OF CARNI-VORES.
I WANT TO SAVE MORE...
...SO I KEEP EATING BAMBOO AND WORKING OUT.
SO I GUESS YOU COULD SAY I'M...
...A VEGETARIAN DOCTOR WHO HAPPENS TO BE QUITE PHYSICALLY STRONG.

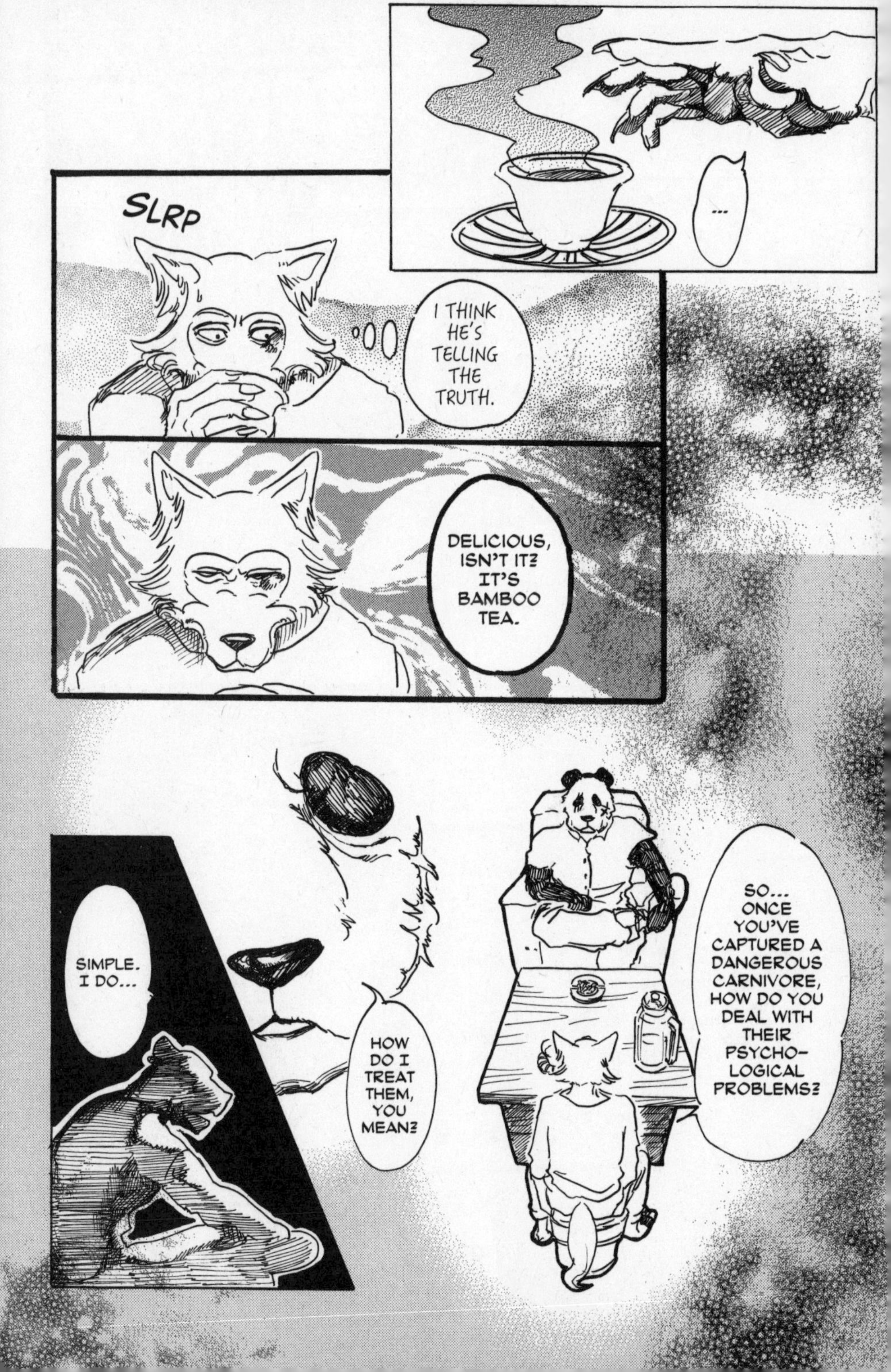
...
SLRP
I THINK HE'S TELLING THE TRUTH.
DELICIOUS, ISN'T IT? IT'S BAMBOO TEA.
SO... ONCE YOU'VE CAPTURED A DANGEROUS CARNIVORE, HOW DO YOU DEAL WITH THEIR PSYCHO-LOGICAL PROBLEMS?
HOW DO I TREAT THEM, YOU MEAN?
SIMPLE. I DO...

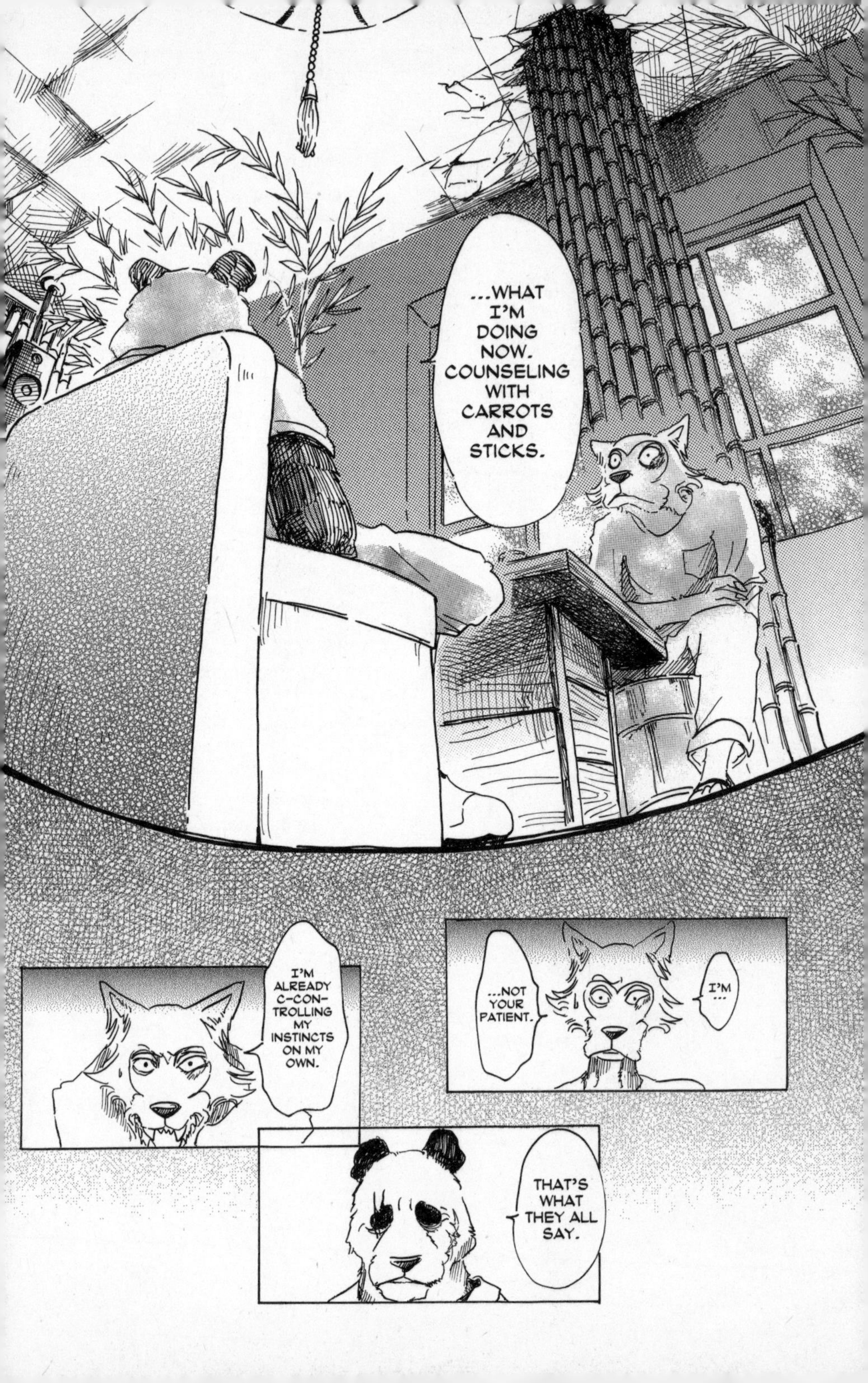
...WHAT I'M DOING NOW. COUNSELING WITH CARROTS AND STICKS.
I'M ...
...NOT YOUR PATIENT.
I'M ALREADY C-CON-TROLLING MY INSTINCTS ON MY OWN.
THAT'S WHAT THEY ALL SAY.

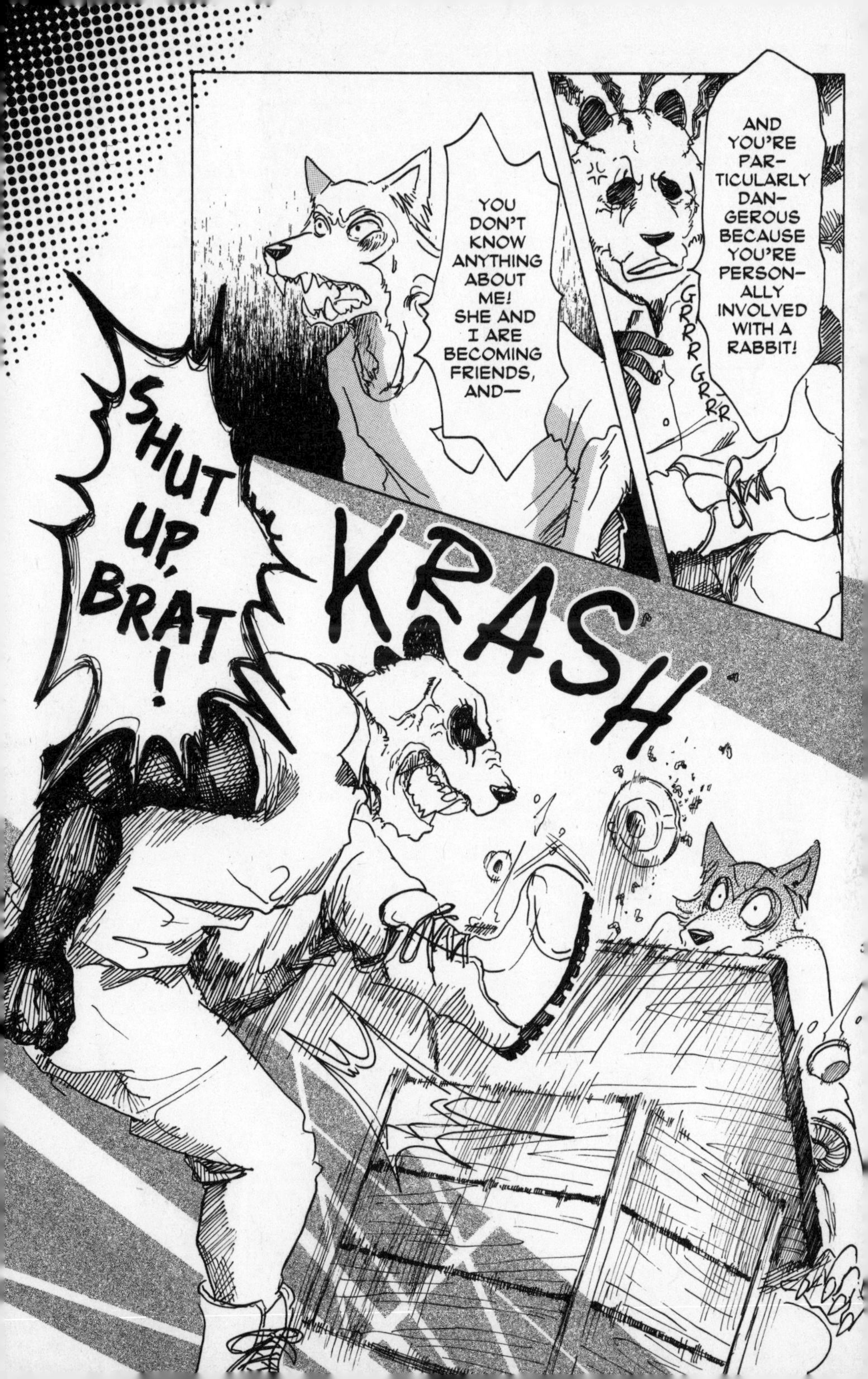
AND YOU'RE PAR-TICULARLY DAN-GEROUS BECAUSE YOU'RE PERSON-ALLY INVOLVED WITH A RABBIT!
GRRR GRRR
YOU DON'T KNOW ANYTHING ABOUT ME! SHE AND I ARE BECOMING FRIENDS, AND—
KRASH
SHUT UP, BRAT!

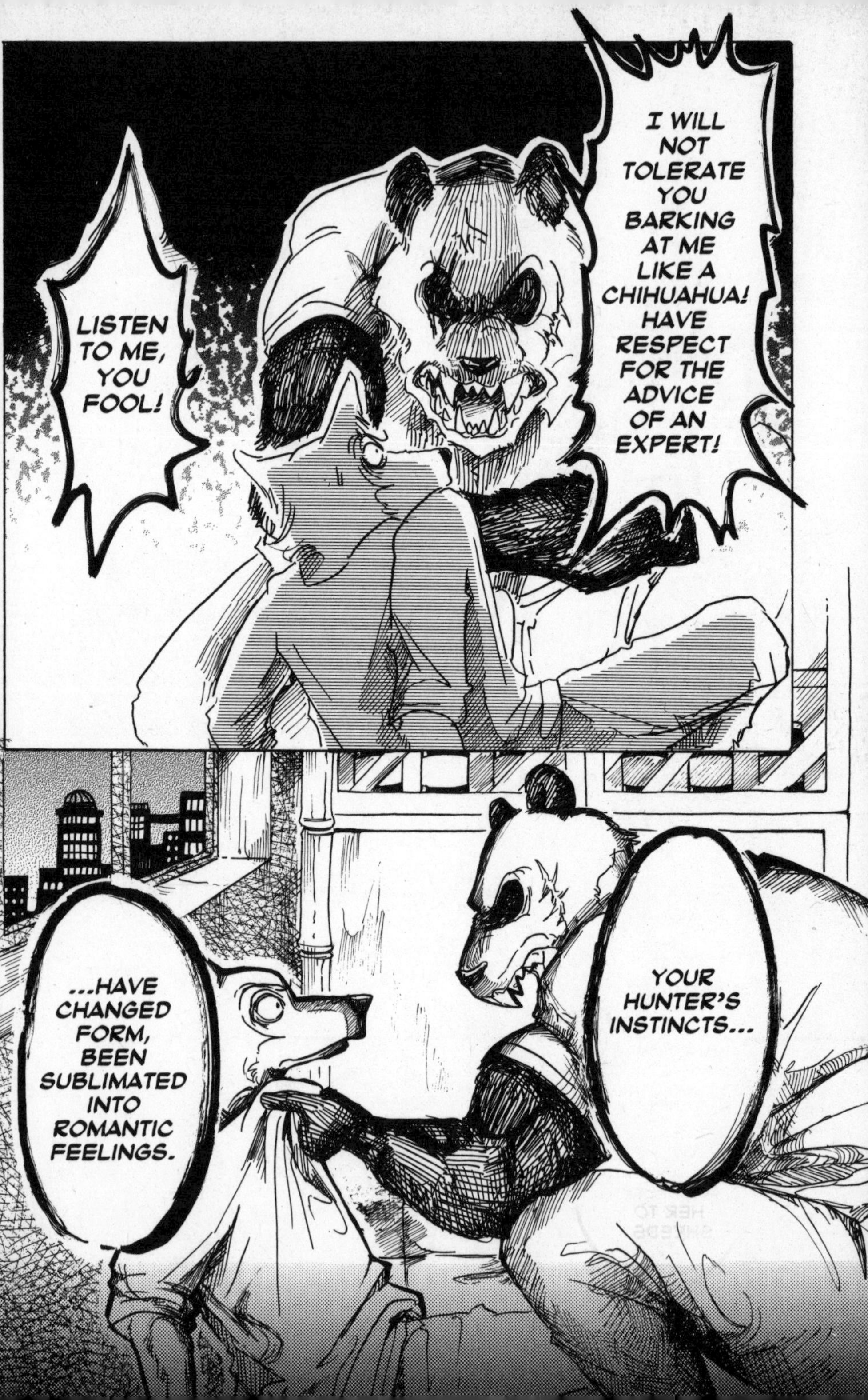
I WILL NOT TOLERATE YOU BARKING AT ME LIKE A CHIHUAHUA! HAVE RESPECT FOR THE ADVICE OF AN EXPERT!
LISTEN TO ME, YOU FOOL!
YOUR HUNTER'S INSTINCTS...
...HAVE CHANGED FORM, BEEN SUBLIMATED INTO ROMANTIC FEELINGS.

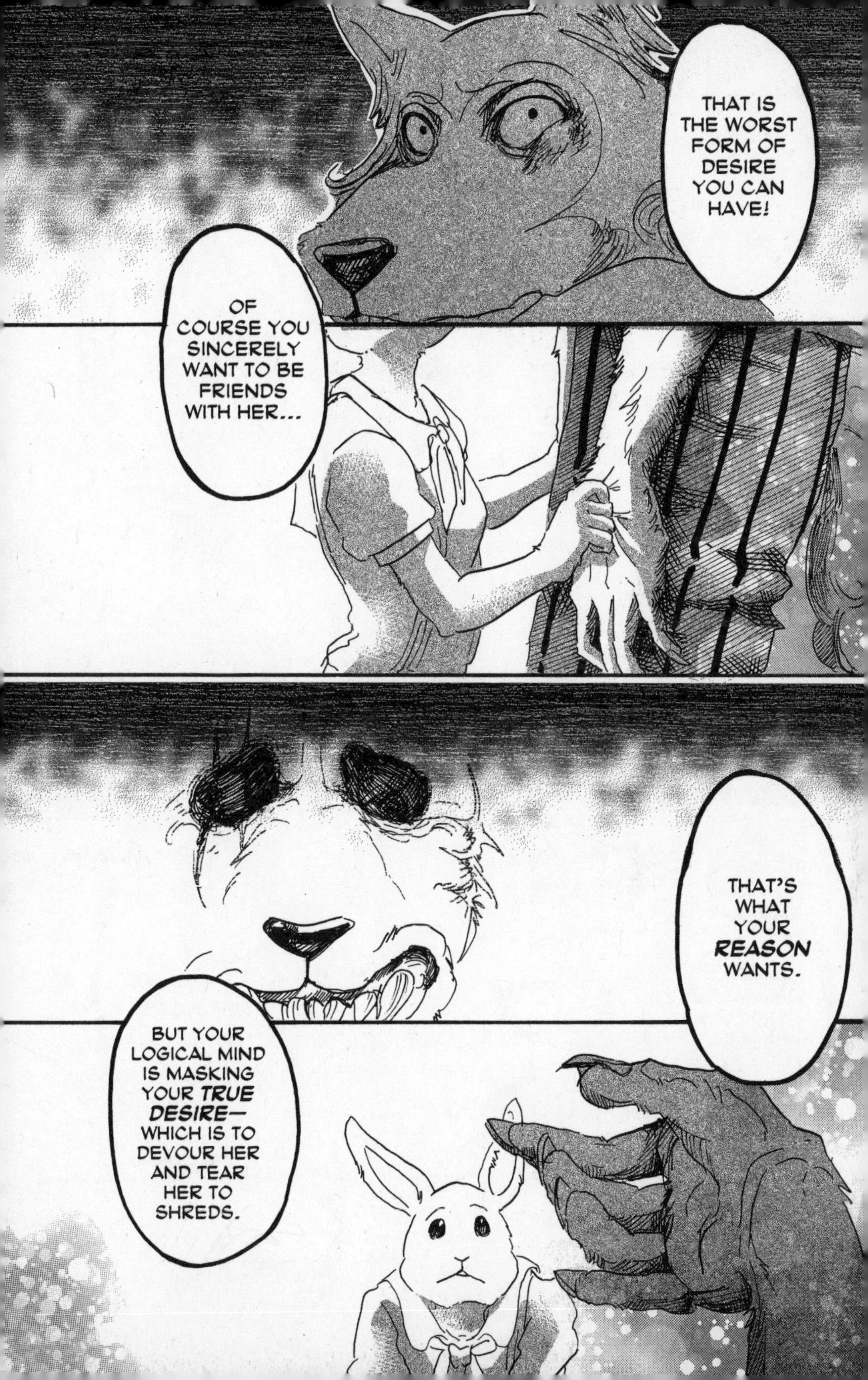
THAT IS THE WORST FORM OF DESIRE YOU CAN HAVE!
OF COURSE YOU SINCERELY WANT TO BE FRIENDS WITH HER...
THAT'S WHAT YOUR *REASON* WANTS.
BUT YOUR LOGICAL MIND IS MASKING YOUR *TRUE DESIRE*— WHICH IS TO DEVOUR HER AND TEAR HER TO SHREDS.

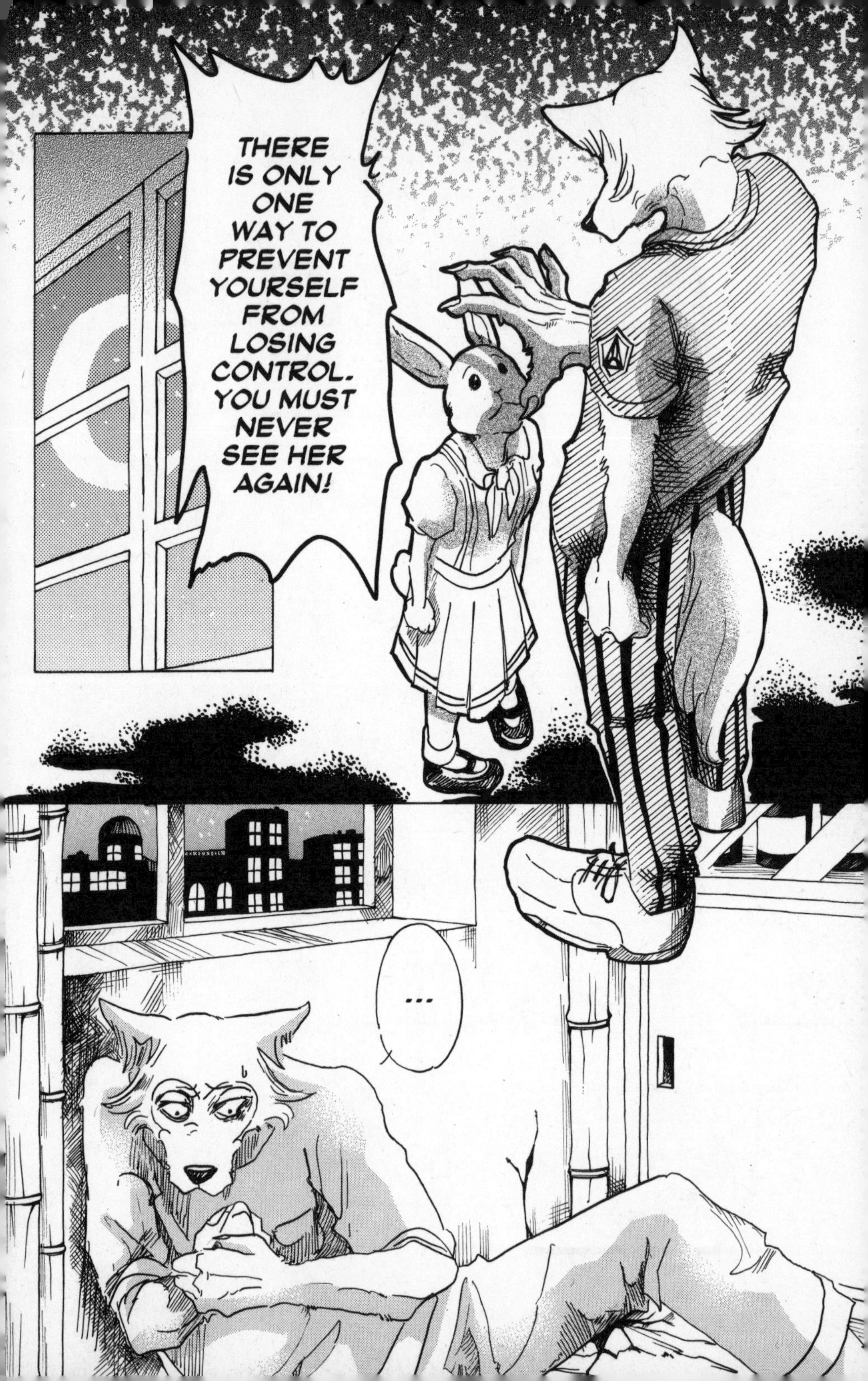
THERE IS ONLY ONE WAY TO PREVENT YOURSELF FROM LOSING CONTROL. YOU MUST NEVER SEE HER AGAIN!
...

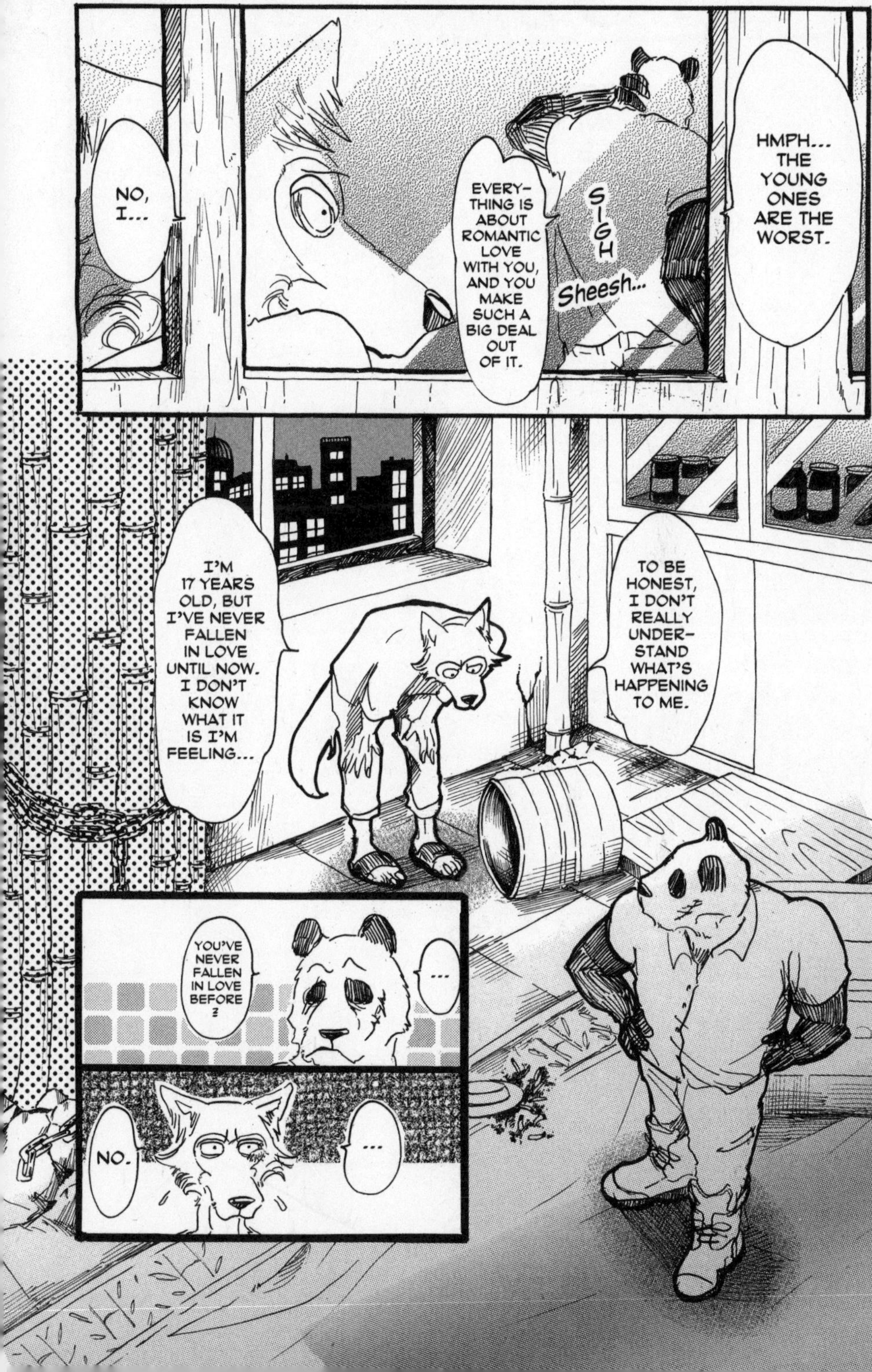
HMPH... THE YOUNG ONES ARE THE WORST.
SIGH
Sheesh...
EVERYTHING IS ABOUT ROMANTIC LOVE WITH YOU, AND YOU MAKE SUCH A BIG DEAL OUT OF IT.
NO, I...
TO BE HONEST, I DON'T REALLY UNDERSTAND WHAT'S HAPPENING TO ME.
I'M 17 YEARS OLD, BUT I'VE NEVER FALLEN IN LOVE UNTIL NOW. I DON'T KNOW WHAT IT IS I'M FEELING...
...
YOU'VE NEVER FALLEN IN LOVE BEFORE?
...
NO.

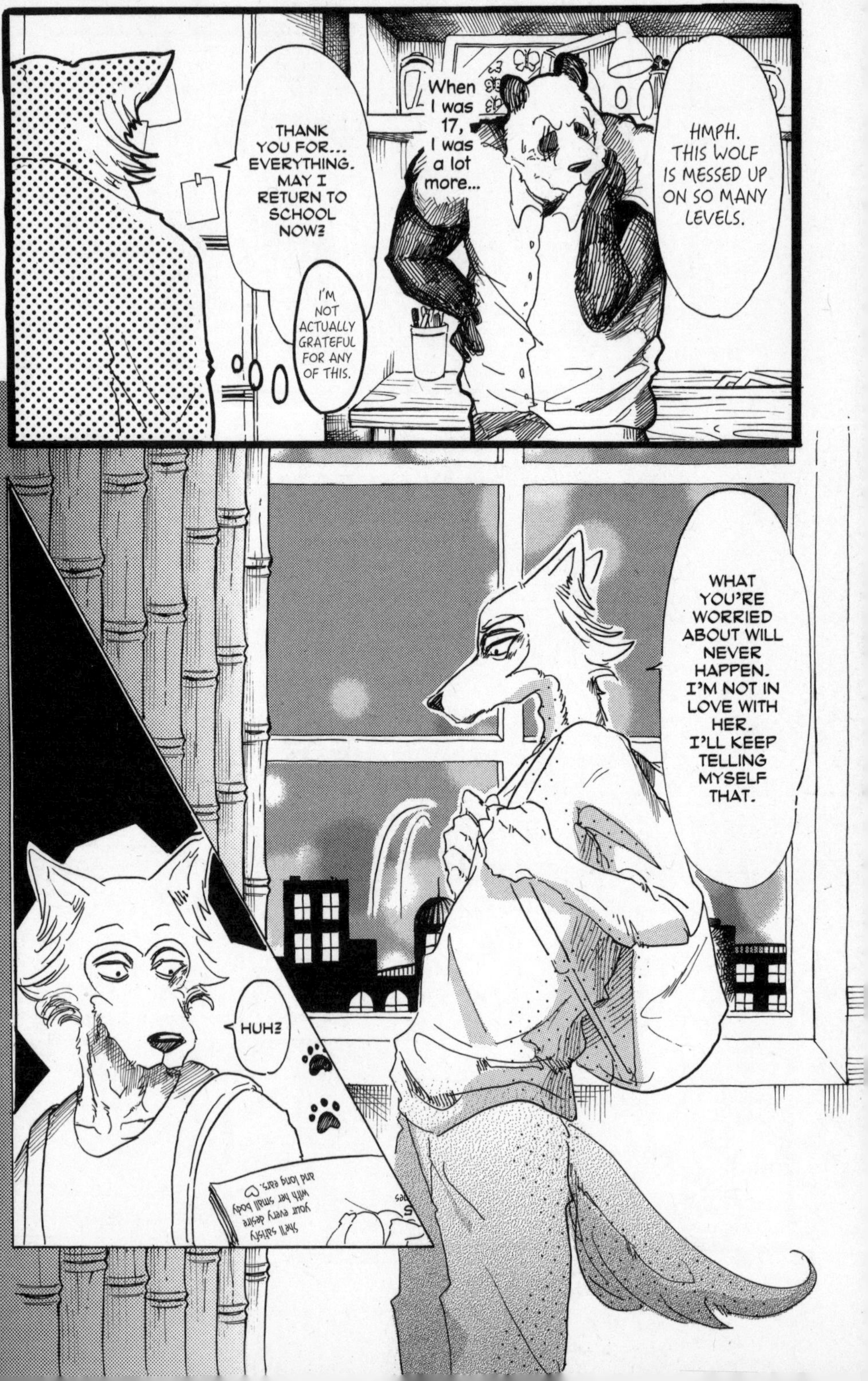
HMPH. THIS WOLF IS MESSED UP ON SO MANY LEVELS.
When I was 17, I was a lot more...
THANK YOU FOR... EVERYTHING. MAY I RETURN TO SCHOOL NOW?
I'M NOT ACTUALLY GRATEFUL FOR ANY OF THIS.
WHAT YOU'RE WORRIED ABOUT WILL NEVER HAPPEN. I'M NOT IN LOVE WITH HER. I'LL KEEP TELLING MYSELF THAT.
HUH?
She'll satisfy your every desire with her small body and long ears. ♡

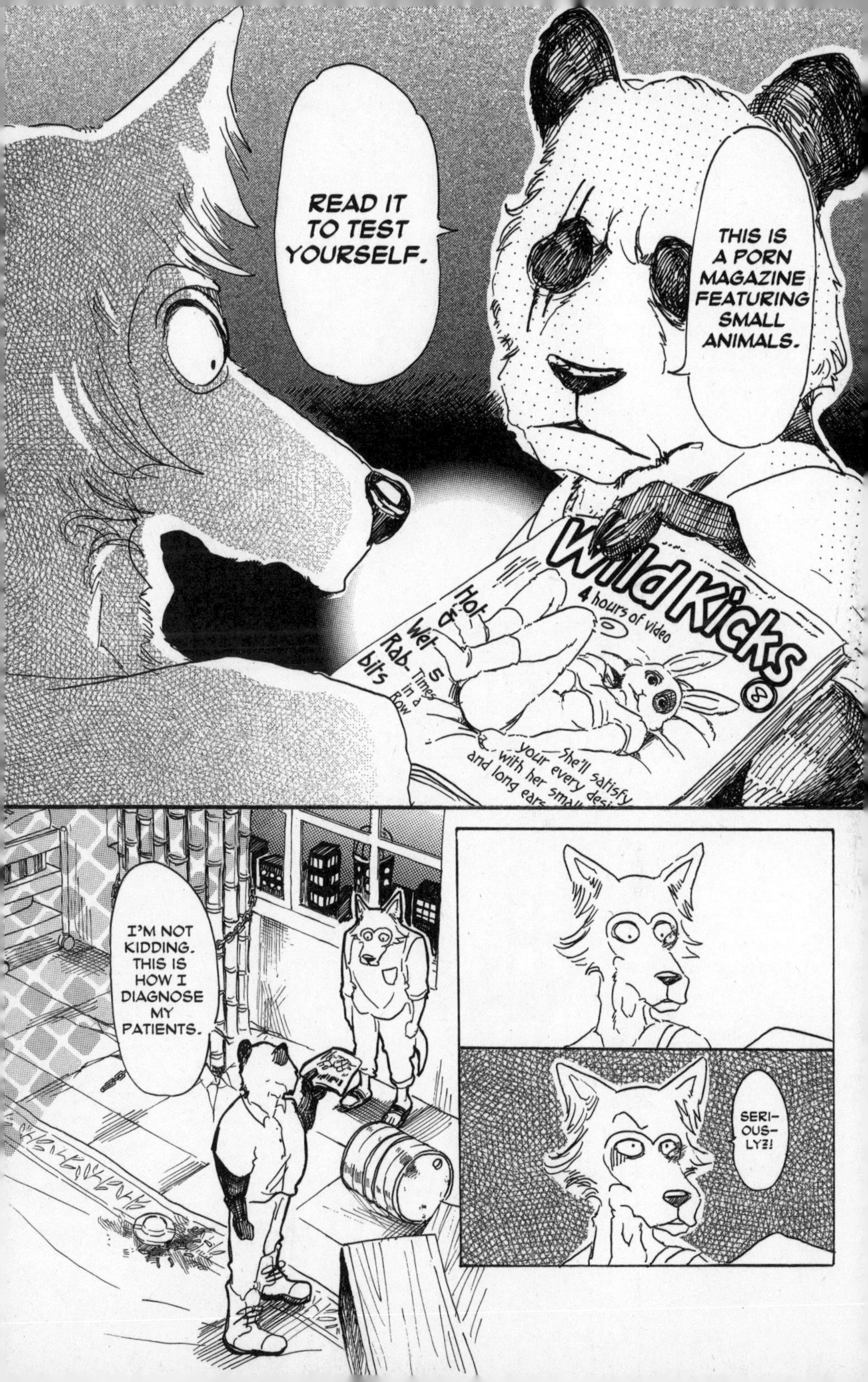
THIS IS A PORN MAGAZINE FEATURING SMALL ANIMALS.
READ IT TO TEST YOURSELF.
Wild Kicks 8
4 hours of video
Hot & Wet Rab- bit's
5 Times in a Row
She'll satisfy your every desi with her small and long ears
SERI-OUS-LY?!
I'M NOT KIDDING. THIS IS HOW I DIAGNOSE MY PATIENTS.

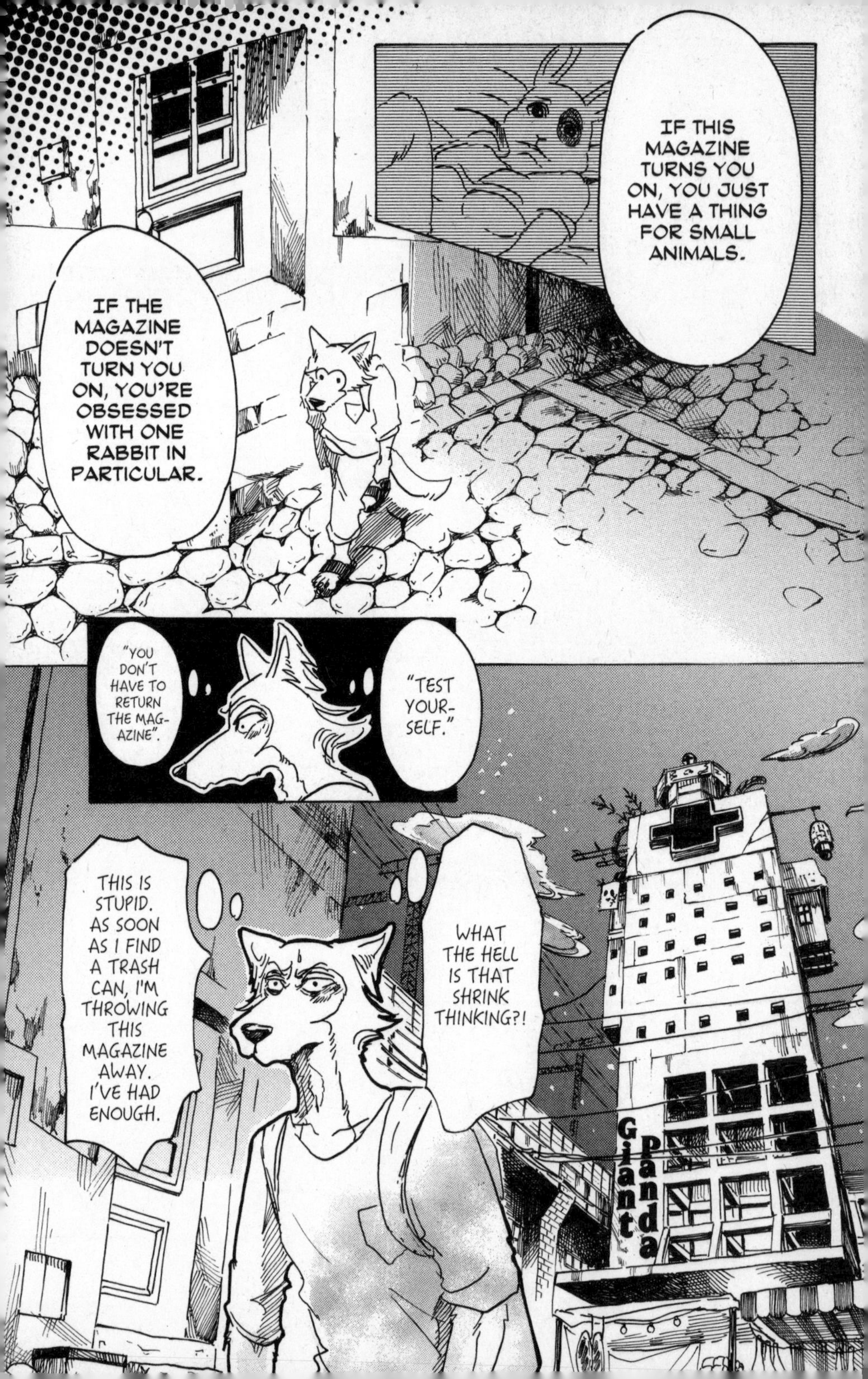
IF THIS MAGAZINE TURNS YOU ON, YOU JUST HAVE A THING FOR SMALL ANIMALS.
IF THE MAGAZINE DOESN'T TURN YOU ON, YOU'RE OBSESSED WITH ONE RABBIT IN PARTICULAR.
"TEST YOUR-SELF."
"YOU DON'T HAVE TO RETURN THE MAG-AZINE".
WHAT THE HELL IS THAT SHRINK THINKING?!
THIS IS STUPID. AS SOON AS I FIND A TRASH CAN, I'M THROWING THIS MAGAZINE AWAY. I'VE HAD ENOUGH.
Giant Panda

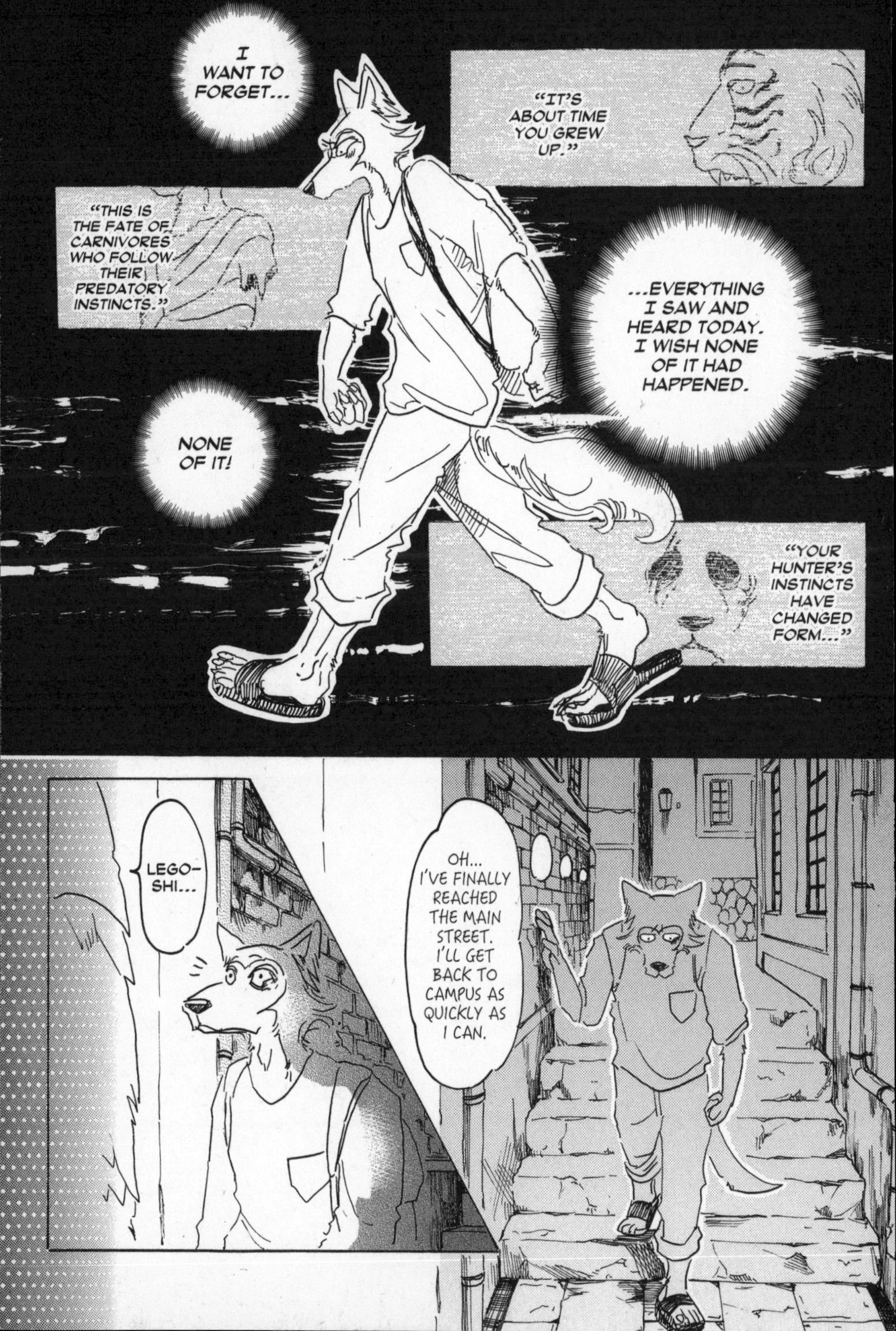
"IT'S ABOUT TIME YOU GREW UP."
I WANT TO FORGET...
"THIS IS THE FATE OF CARNIVORES WHO FOLLOW THEIR PREDATORY INSTINCTS."
...EVERYTHING I SAW AND HEARD TODAY. I WISH NONE OF IT HAD HAPPENED.
NONE OF IT!
"YOUR HUNTER'S INSTINCTS HAVE CHANGED FORM..."
OH... I'VE FINALLY REACHED THE MAIN STREET. I'LL GET BACK TO CAMPUS AS QUICKLY AS I CAN.
LEGO-SHI...

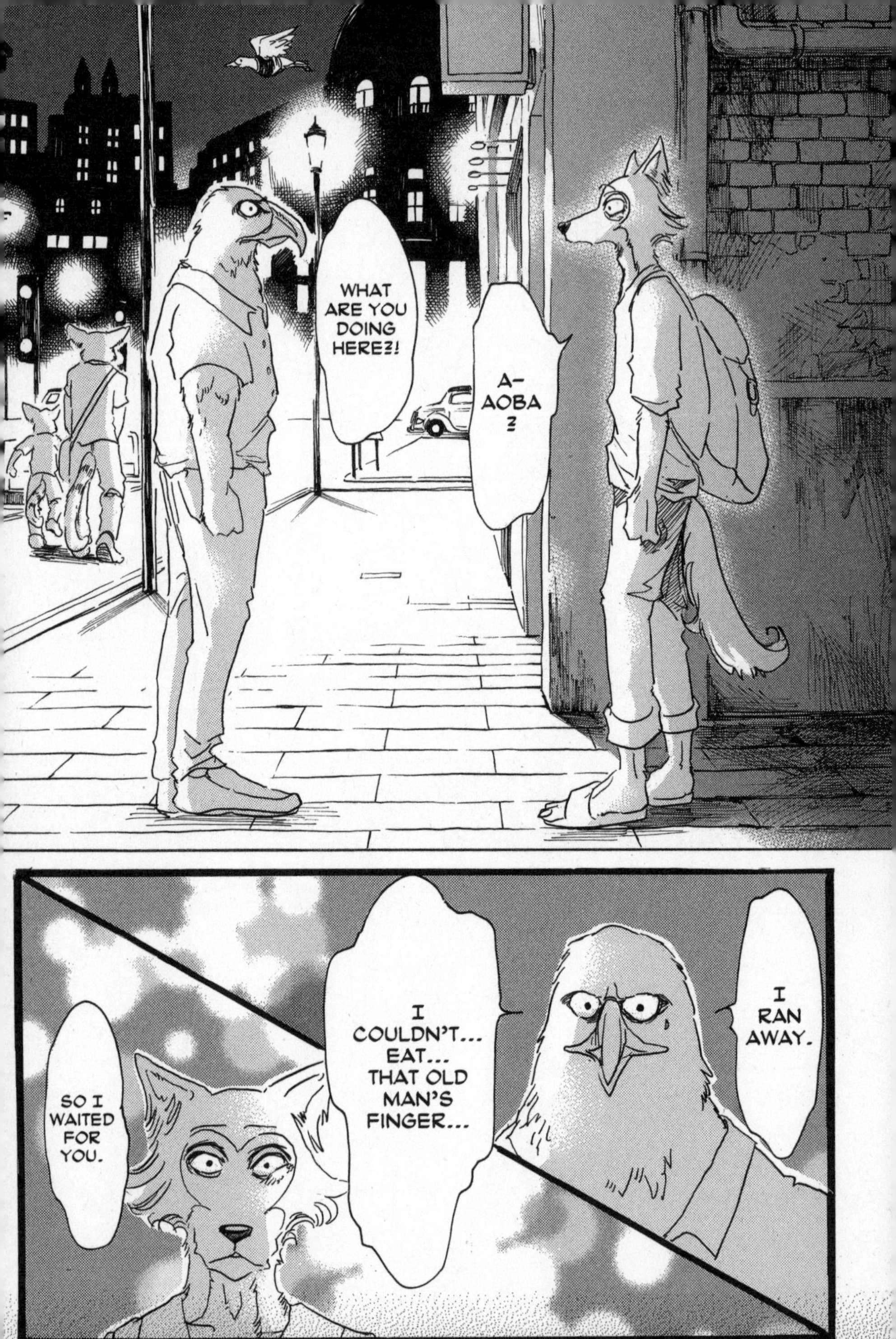
A- AOBA?
WHAT ARE YOU DOING HERE?!
I RAN AWAY.
I COULDN'T... EAT... THAT OLD MAN'S FINGER...
SO I WAITED FOR YOU.

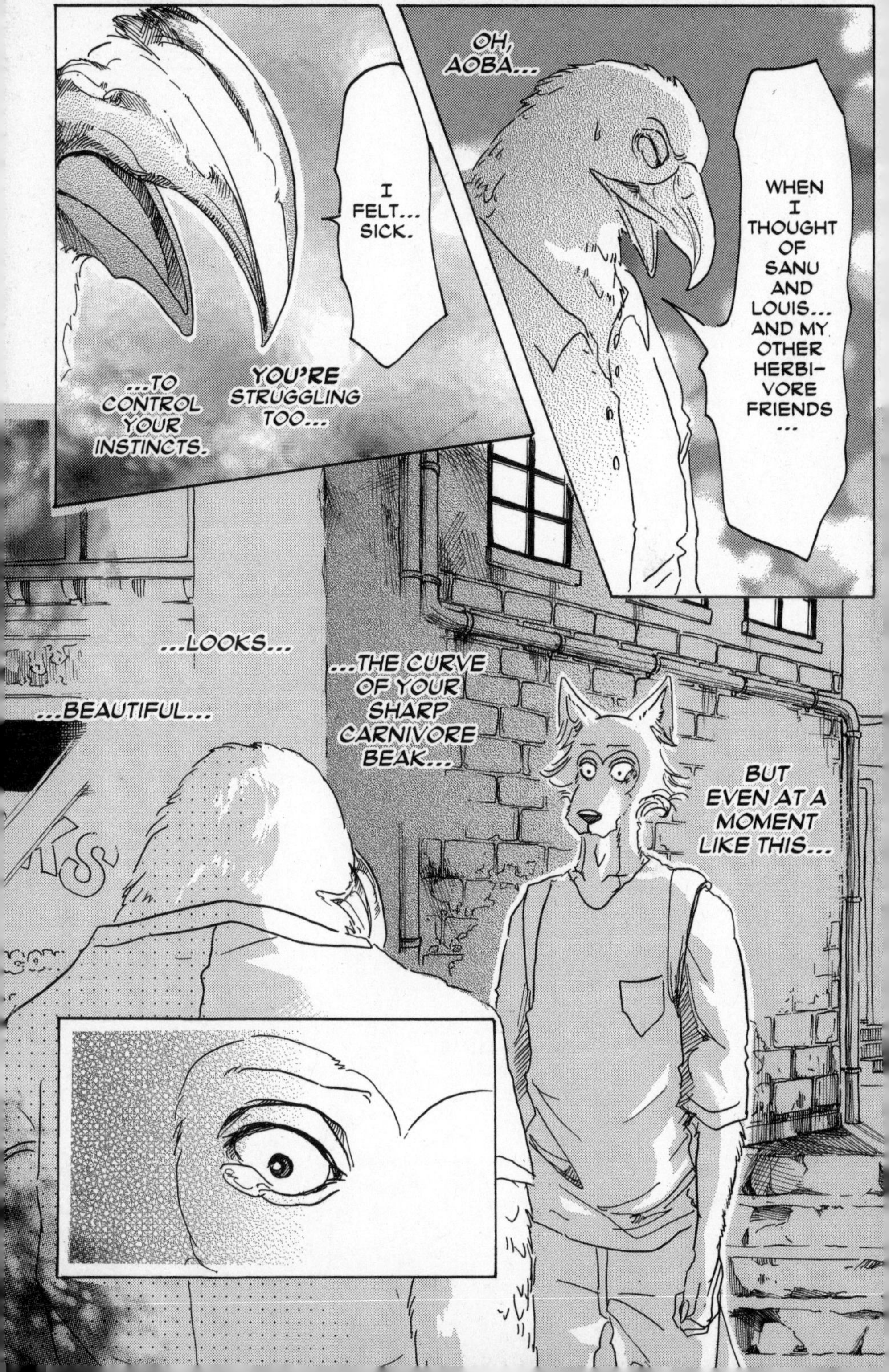
OH, AOBA...
WHEN I THOUGHT OF SANU AND LOUIS... AND MY OTHER HERBI-VORE FRIENDS...
I FELT... SICK.
YOU'RE STRUGGLING TOO...
...TO CONTROL YOUR INSTINCTS.
BUT EVEN AT A MOMENT LIKE THIS...
...THE CURVE OF YOUR SHARP CARNIVORE BEAK...
...LOOKS...
...BEAUTIFUL...

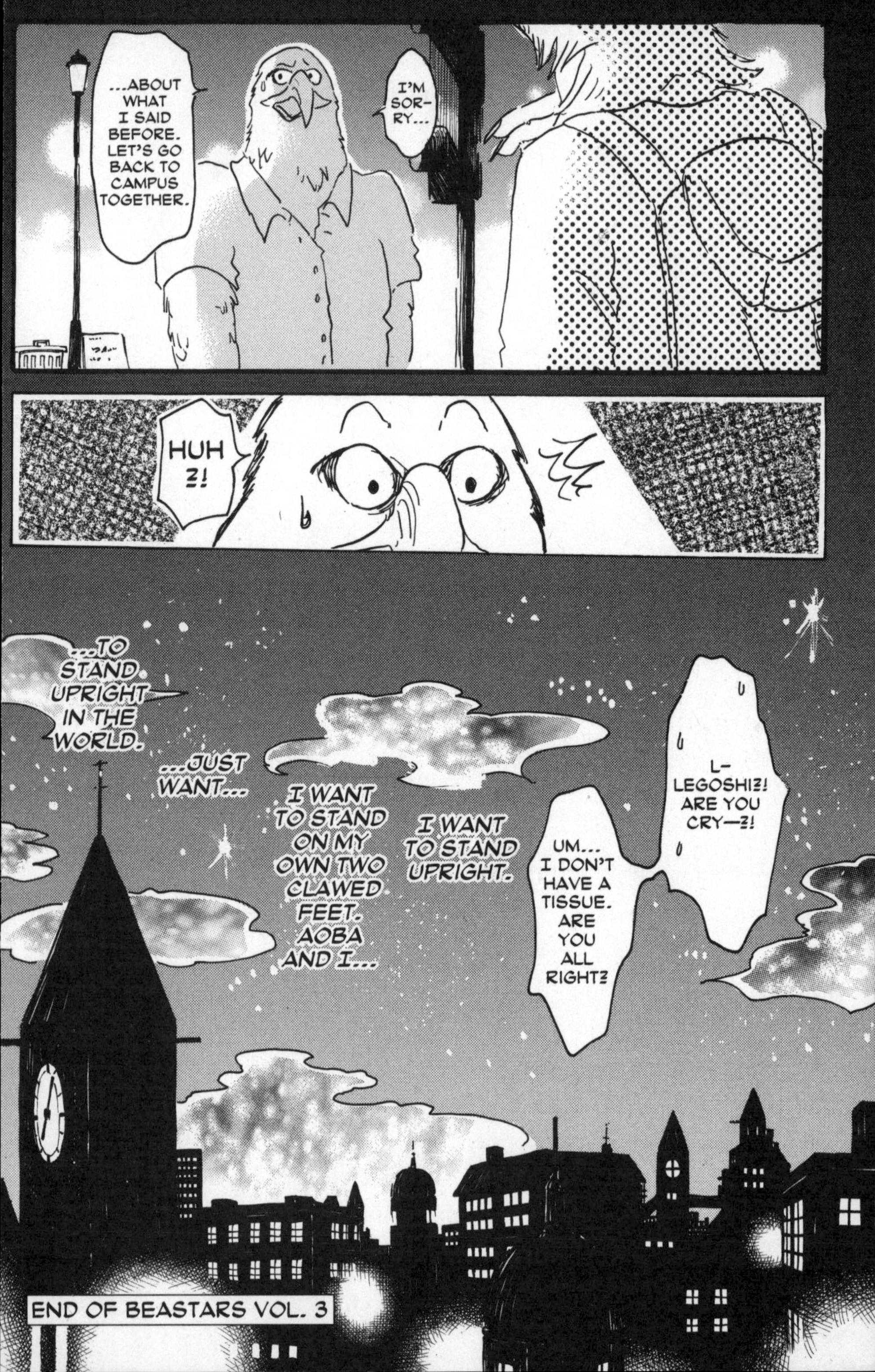
I'M SORRY...
...ABOUT WHAT I SAID BEFORE. LET'S GO BACK TO CAMPUS TOGETHER.
HUH?!
L-LEGOSHI?! ARE YOU CRY—?!
UM... I DON'T HAVE A TISSUE. ARE YOU ALL RIGHT?
I WANT TO STAND UPRIGHT.
I WANT TO STAND ON MY OWN TWO CLAWED FEET. AOBA AND I...
...JUST WANT...
...TO STAND UPRIGHT IN THE WORLD.
END OF BEASTARS VOL. 3

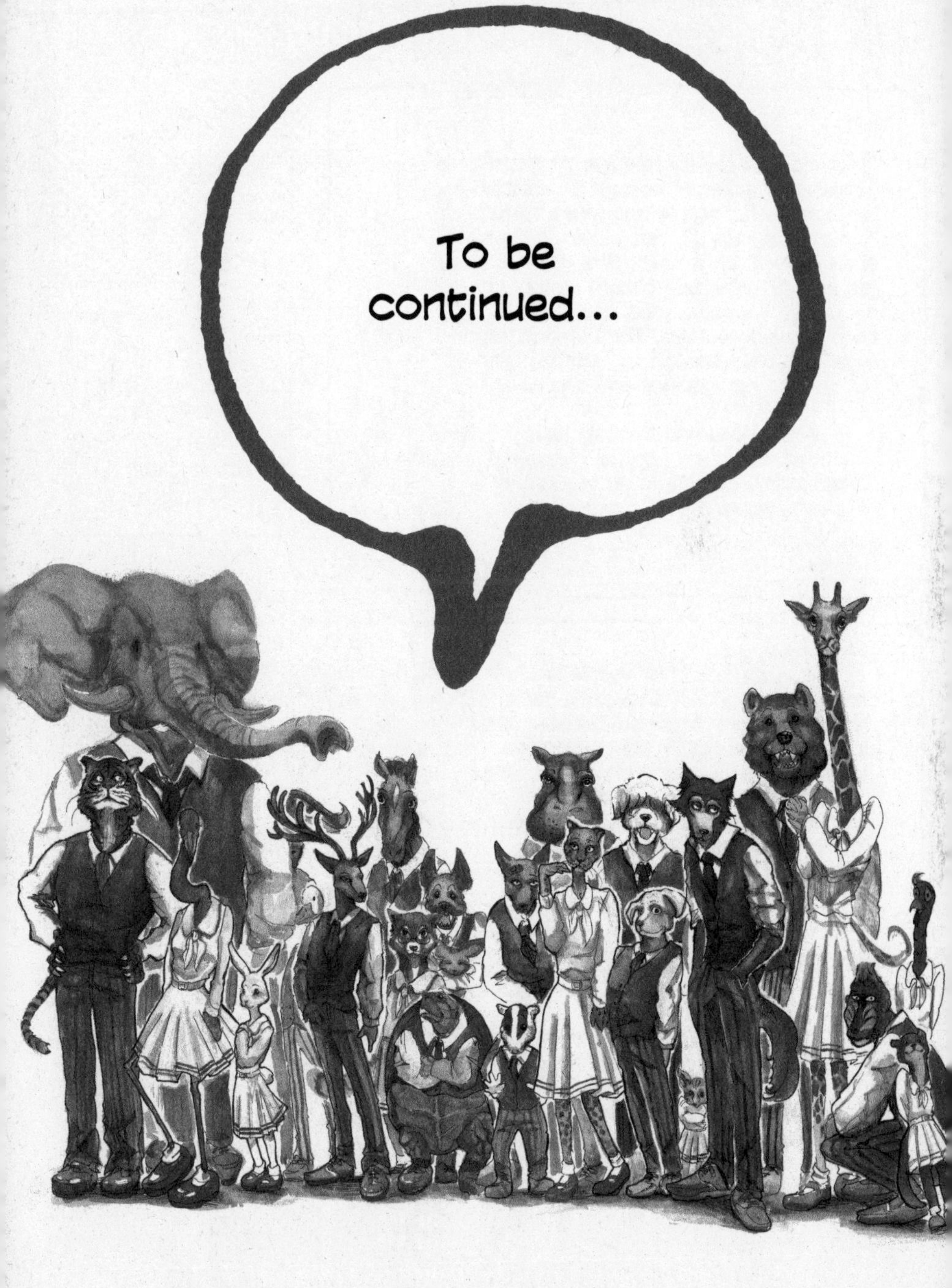
To be continued...

Haru Character Design Notes

Haru's personality

Haru's personality has many typical characteristics of women, for better or worse. But that's not where Haru's charm lies. Haru's real charm is that she's honest to a fault. She doesn't lie to herself. Whereas others usually try to keep up appearances and gloss over their flaws to survive, Haru is that rare individual bold enough to faithfully stay true to her feelings and desires.

What Haru and Legoshi have in common is a kind of childish sincerity, so this is an important characteristic of her personality.

I'M PARTICULAR ABOUT THESE DETAILS:

- SOFT CHEEKS AND ARMS
- SHE LOOKS LIKE A BABY BUT ALSO A LITTLE LIKE A MIDDLE-AGED WOMAN.

PROFILE

HARU (AGE 18)
FEMALE LEPORIDAE (NETHERLAND DWARF RABBIT)
BIRTHDAY: OCTOBER 19
ASTROLOGICAL SIGN: LIBRA
BLOOD TYPE: O
HEIGHT: 3 FT., 4 IN.
WEIGHT: 33 LB.
ENJOYS TV DRAMA SERIES

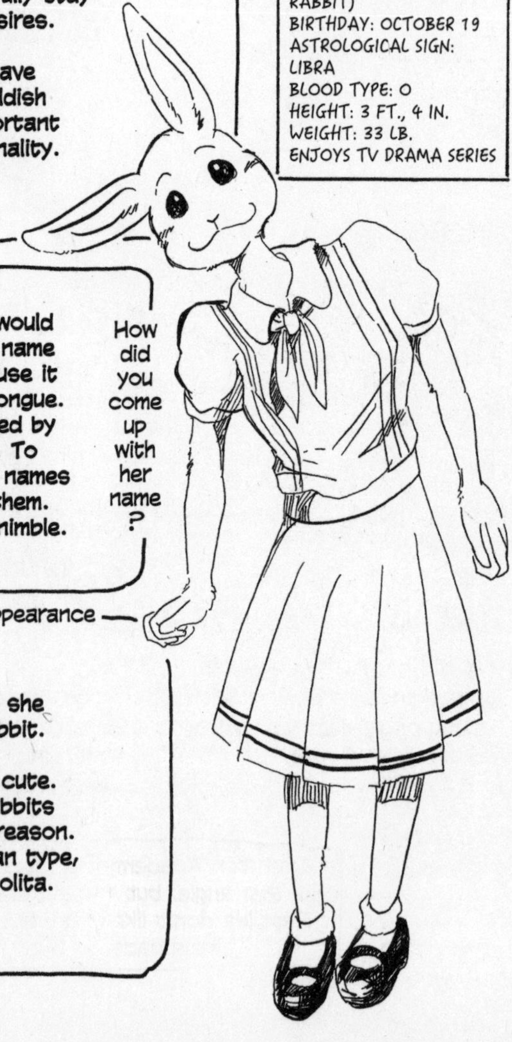

How did you come up with her name?

I wanted a name that people would enjoy saying aloud. Legoshi's name is difficult to pronounce because it doesn't roll smoothly off the tongue. Haru's name can be pronounced by a simple slide of the tongue. To Legoshi, the difference in their names symbolizes the gulf between them. Unlike him, "Haru" is light and nimble.

Haru's appearance

Haru has black eyes, so she looks a lot like a real rabbit.

Most humans find babies cute. Large carnivores think rabbits are adorable for the same reason. If I had to give Haru a human type, it would be a Japanese Lolita.

The Outside World and Cherryton Academy

The outside world appears for the first time in this volume. Cherryton Academy is on top of a hill far from the center of the city, a port surrounded by the sea.

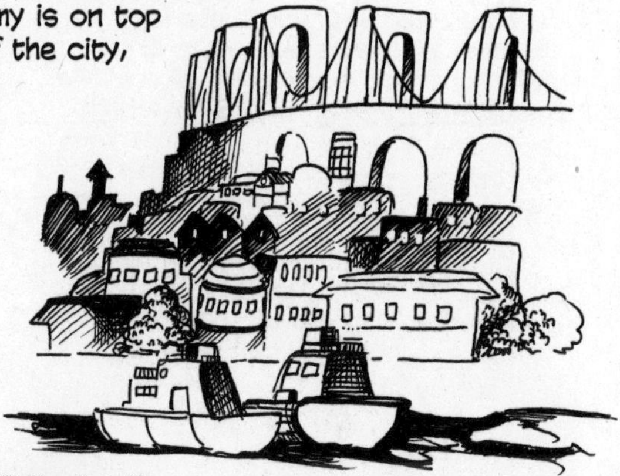

I modeled the city center after Ginza, Shibuya and New York.

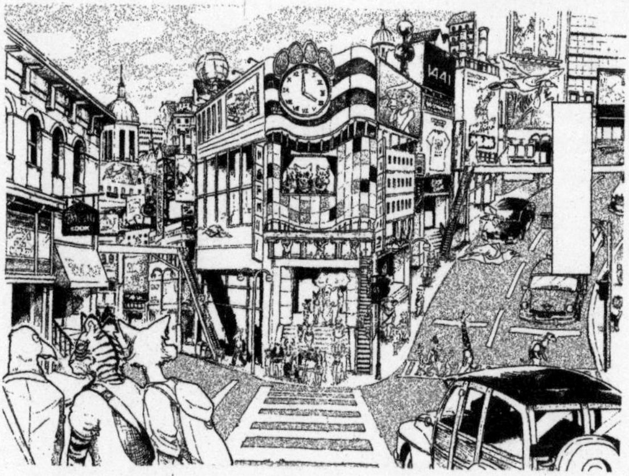

I forgot to mention that it doesn't get too hot in the summer here. Almost everyone is covered in fur, so they would suffer in hot weather. I guess the high seventies (Fahrenheit) would be considered a very hot day. Winters, however, are cold! The temperature can go down to below freezing!

Mr. Panda is familiar with Cherryton Academy, so the school must be pretty renowned. It's an elite academic institution, which means that Legoshi is smart. Jack is even smarter than Legoshi. He's a prodigy who is always at the top of his grade.

Cherryton Academy's school emblem looks like a triangle, but it's actually a footprint. Reptiles don't like it because they don't have pads on their feet.

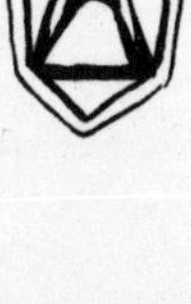

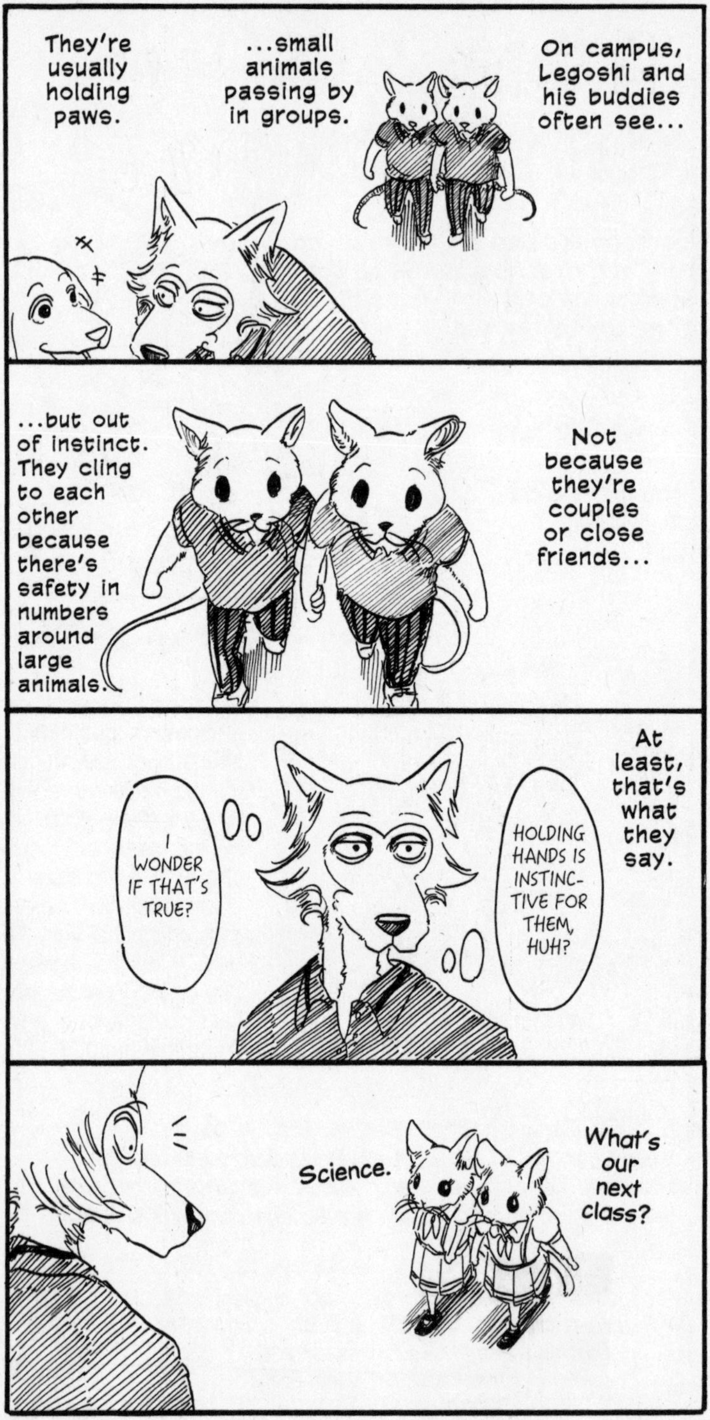
On campus, Legoshi and his buddies often see...
...small animals passing by in groups.
They're usually holding paws.
Not because they're couples or close friends...
...but out of instinct. They cling to each other because there's safety in numbers around large animals.
At least, that's what they say.
HOLDING HANDS IS INSTINCTIVE FOR THEM, HUH?
I WONDER IF THAT'S TRUE?
What's our next class?
Science.

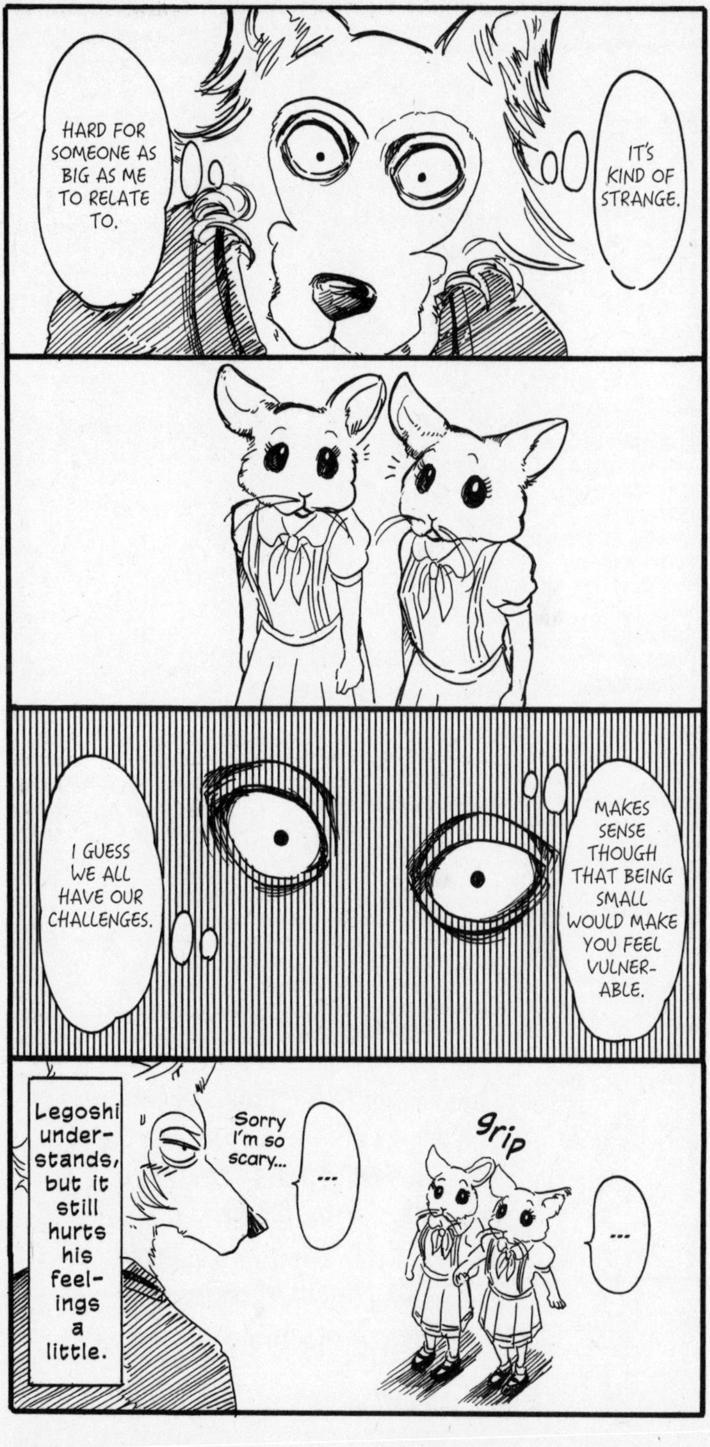
IT'S KIND OF STRANGE.
HARD FOR SOMEONE AS BIG AS ME TO RELATE TO.
MAKES SENSE THOUGH THAT BEING SMALL WOULD MAKE YOU FEEL VULNER-ABLE.
I GUESS WE ALL HAVE OUR CHALLENGES.
grip
...
...
Sorry I'm so scary...
Legoshi under-stands, but it still hurts his feel-ings a little.

AFTER I BEGAN DRAWING
THIS MANGA, I STOPPED
BUYING CLOTHES WITH
ANIMAL PRINTS...

PARU ITAGAKI

Paru Itagaki began her professional
career as a manga author in 2016 with the
short story collection **BEAST COMPLEX**.
BEASTARS is her first serialization.
BEASTARS has won multiple awards in
Japan, including the prestigious 2018
Manga Taisho Award.

BEASTARS

VOL. 3
VIZ Signature Edition

Story & Art by
Paru Itagaki

Translation/Tomoko Kimura
English Adaptation/Annette Roman
Touch-Up Art & Lettering/Susan Daigle-Leach
Cover & Interior Design/Yukiko Whitley
Editor/Annette Roman

First published in 2017 by Akita Publishing Co., Ltd., Tokyo
English translation rights arranged with AKITA PUBLISHING CO., LTD. through Tuttle-Mori Agency, Inc., Tokyo

Printed in the U.S.A.

Published by VIZ Media, LLC
P.O. Box 77010
San Francisco, CA 94107

10 9 8 7 6 5 4 3 2 1
First printing, November 2019

VIZ MEDIA
viz.com

VIZ SIGNATURE
vizsignature.com

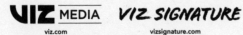

COMING IN VOLUME 4...

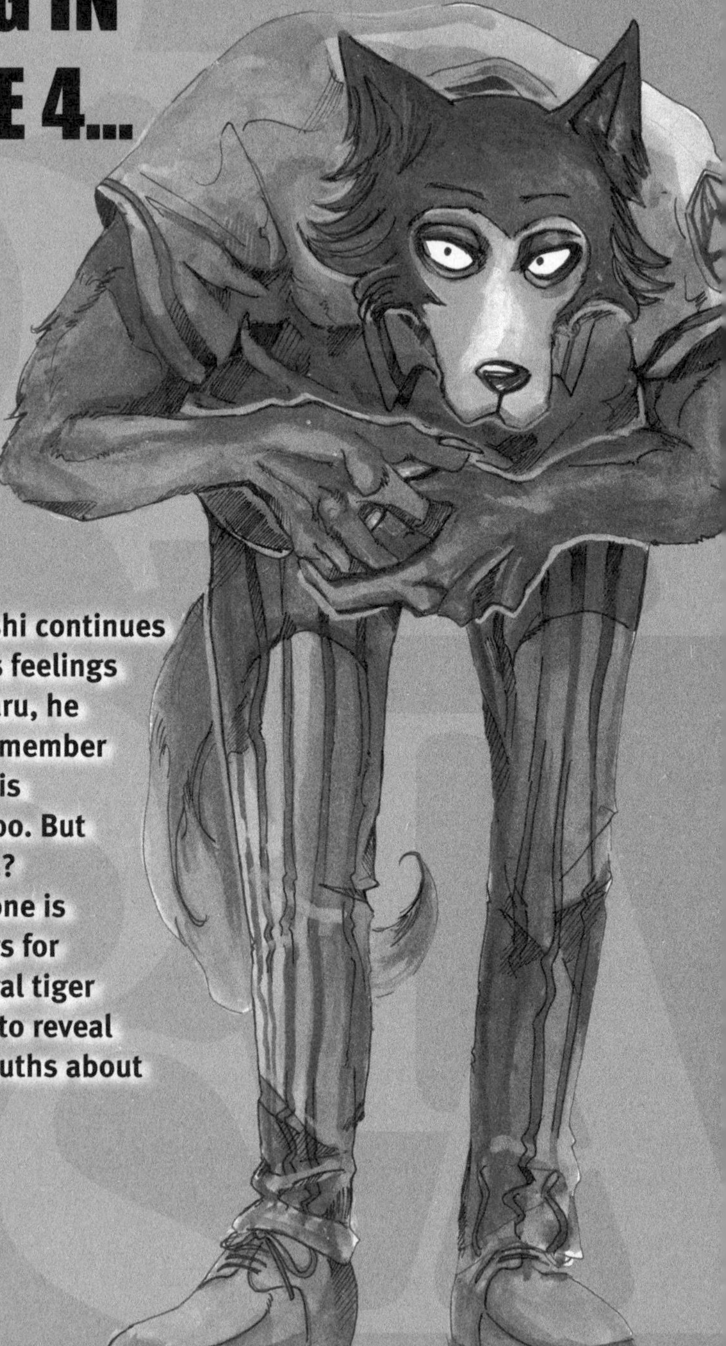

As gray wolf Legoshi continues to grapple with his feelings for dwarf rabbit Haru, he discovers another member of the Drama Club is friendly with her too. But just *how* friendly...? Meanwhile, someone is developing feelings for Legoshi. And Bengal tiger Bill is threatening to reveal some disturbing truths about someone's past...

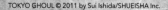

ABARA
COMPLETE DELUXE EDITION
TSUTOMU NIHEI

A visually stunning work of sci-fi horror from the creator of **BIOMEGA** and **BLAME**!

ABARA
COMPLETE DELUXE EDITION
TSUTOMU NIHEI

A vast city lies under the shadow of colossal, ancient tombs, the identity of their builders lost to time. In the streets of the city something is preying on the inhabitants, something that moves faster than the human eye can see and leaves unimaginable horror in its wake.

Tsutomu Nihei's dazzling, harrowing dystopian thriller is presented here in a single-volume hardcover edition featuring full-color pages and foldout illustrations. This volume also includes the early short story "Digimortal."

This is the last page.

BEASTARS reads from right to left to preserve the orientation of the original Japanese artwork.